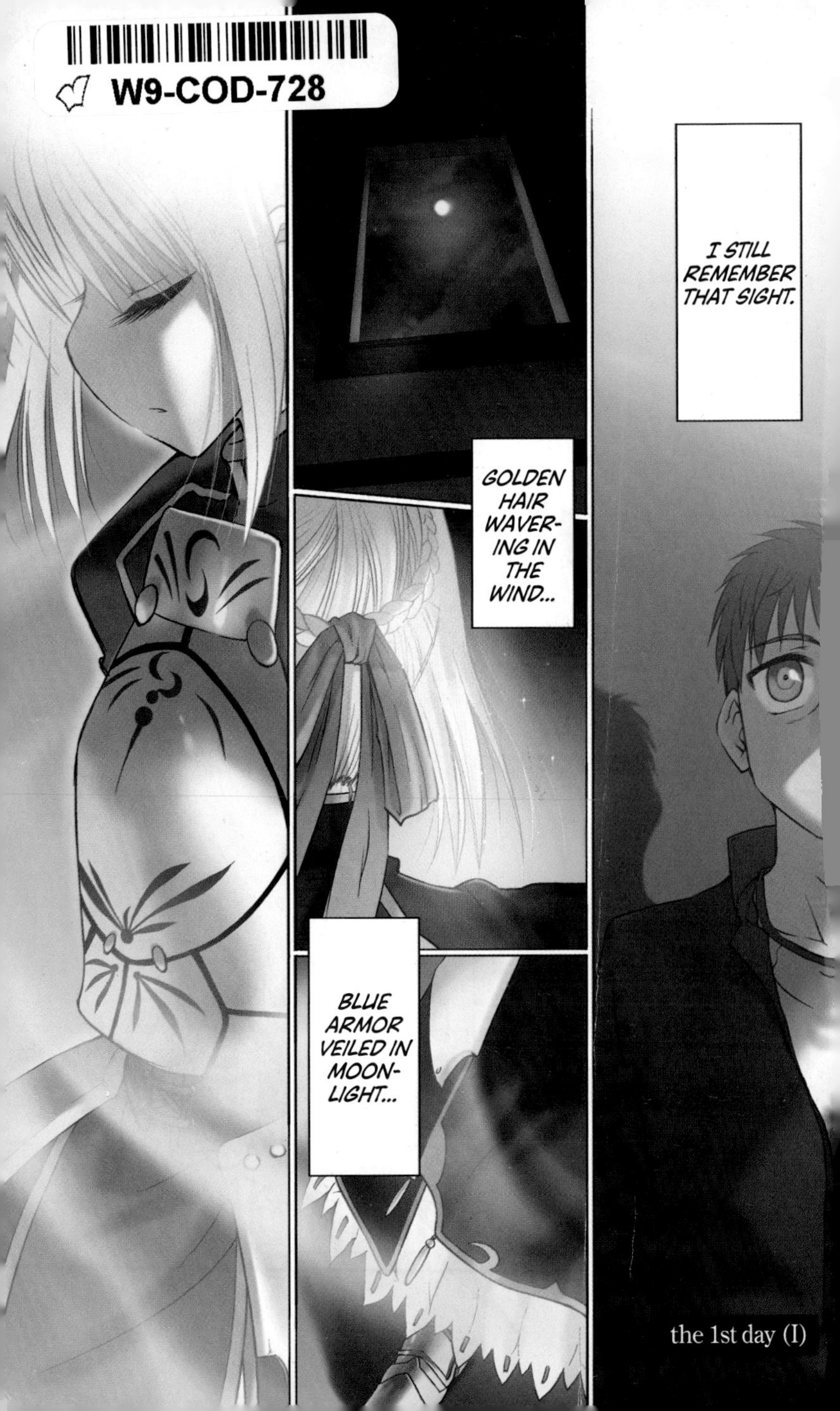
I STILL REMEMBER THAT SIGHT.
the 1st day (I)
GOLDEN HAIR WAVERING IN THE WIND...
BLUE ARMOR VEILED IN MOONLIGHT...

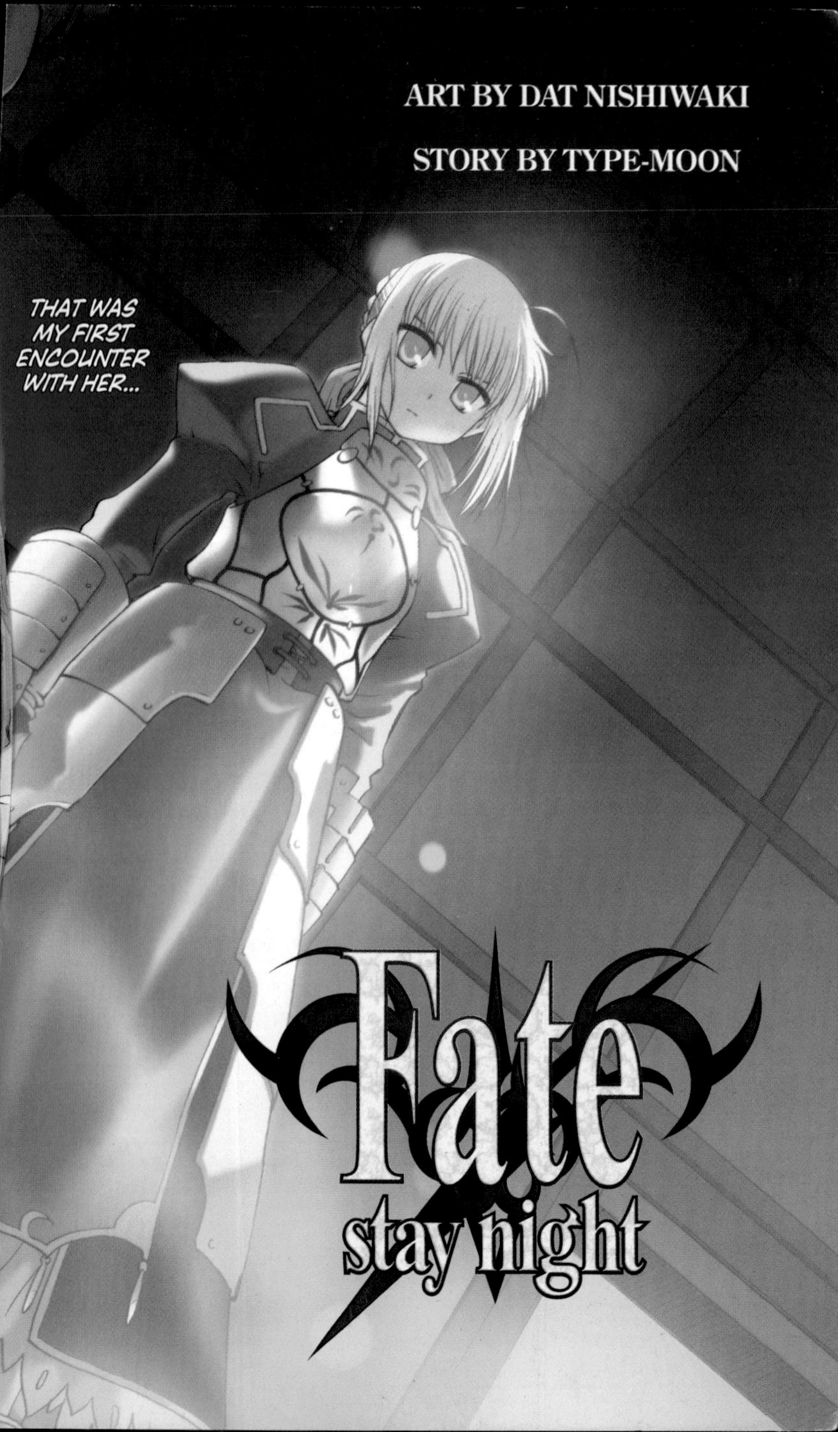
ART BY DAT NISHIWAKI
STORY BY TYPE-MOON
THAT WAS MY FIRST ENCOUNTER WITH HER...
Fate
stay night

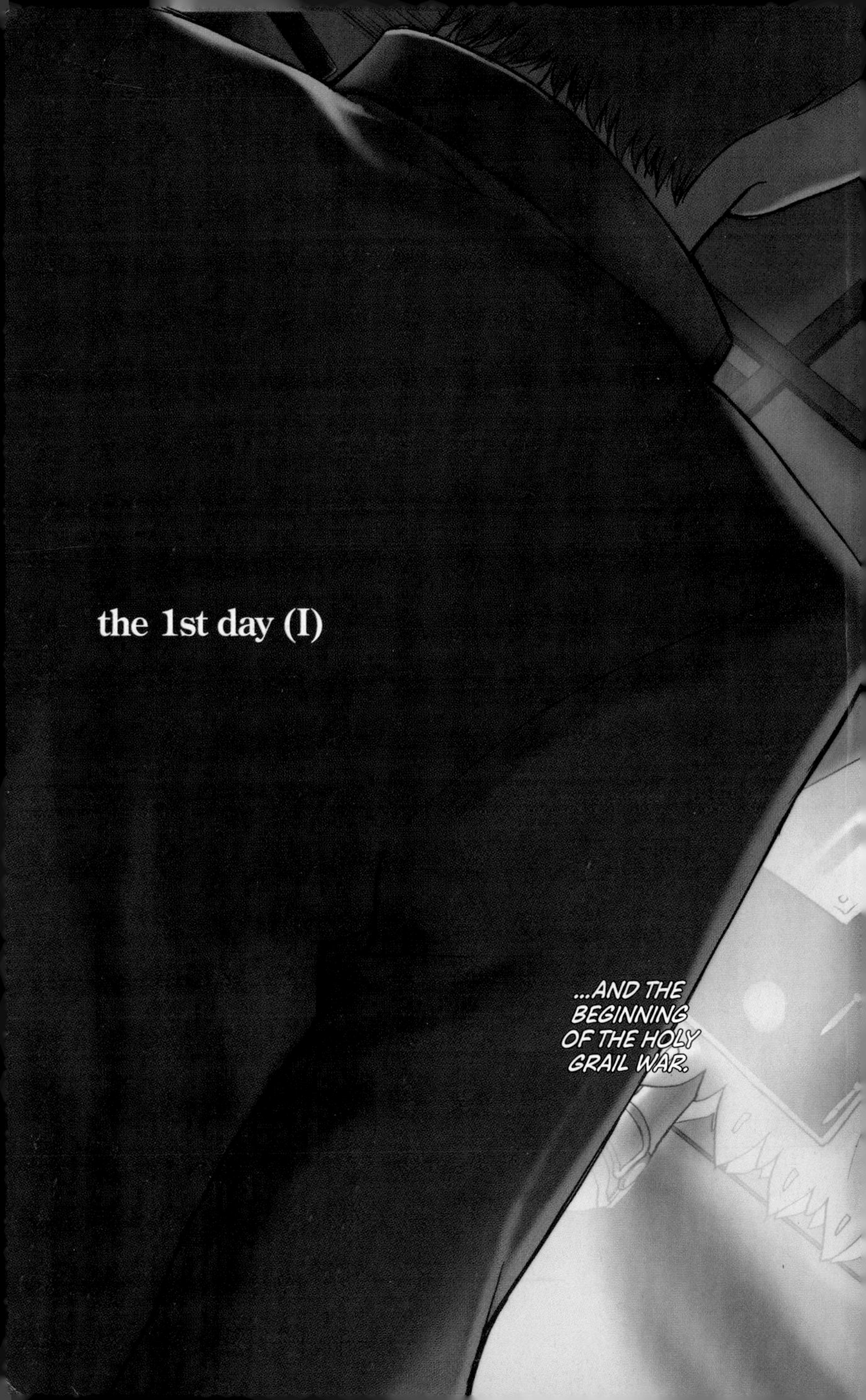
the 1st day (I)
...AND THE BEGINNING OF THE HOLY GRAIL WAR.

Fate
stay night

Fate/stay night

VOLUME 1

ART BY DAT NISHIWAKI
STORY BY TYPE-MOON

HAMBURG // LONDON // LOS ANGELES // TOKYO

Fate/Stay Night Vol. 1
Art By: Dat Nishiwaki
Story By: TYPE-MOON

Translation - Lori Riser
English Adaptation - Jake Forbes
Retouch and Lettering - Star Print Brokers
Production Artist - Michael Paolilli
Graphic Designer - Monalisa De Asis

Editor - Hyun Joo Kim
Pre-Production Supervisor - Vicente Rivera, Jr.
Pre-Production Specialist - Lucas Rivera
Managing Editor - Vy Nguyen
Senior Designer - Louis Csontos
Senior Designer - James Lee
Senior Editor - Bryce P. Coleman
Senior Editor - Jenna Winterberg
Associate Publisher - Marco F. Pavia
President and C.O.O. - John Parker
C.E.O. and Chief Creative Officer - Stu Levy

A  Manga

TOKYOPOP and 🔴 are trademarks or registered trademarks of TOKYOPOP Inc.

TOKYOPOP Inc.
5900 Wilshire Blvd. Suite 2000
Los Angeles, CA 90036

E-mail: info@TOKYOPOP.com
Come visit us online at www.TOKYOPOP.com

Fate/Stay Night Volume 1 © 2006 Dat NISHIWAKI © TYPE-MOON First published in Japan in 2006 by KADOKAWA SHOTEN PUBLISHING CO., LTD., Tokyo. English translation rights arranged with KADOKAWA SHOTEN PUBLISHING CO., LTD., Tokyo

ISBN: 978-1-4278-1037-3

First TOKYOPOP printing: October 2008
10 9 8 7 6 5 4 3 2 1
Printed in the USA

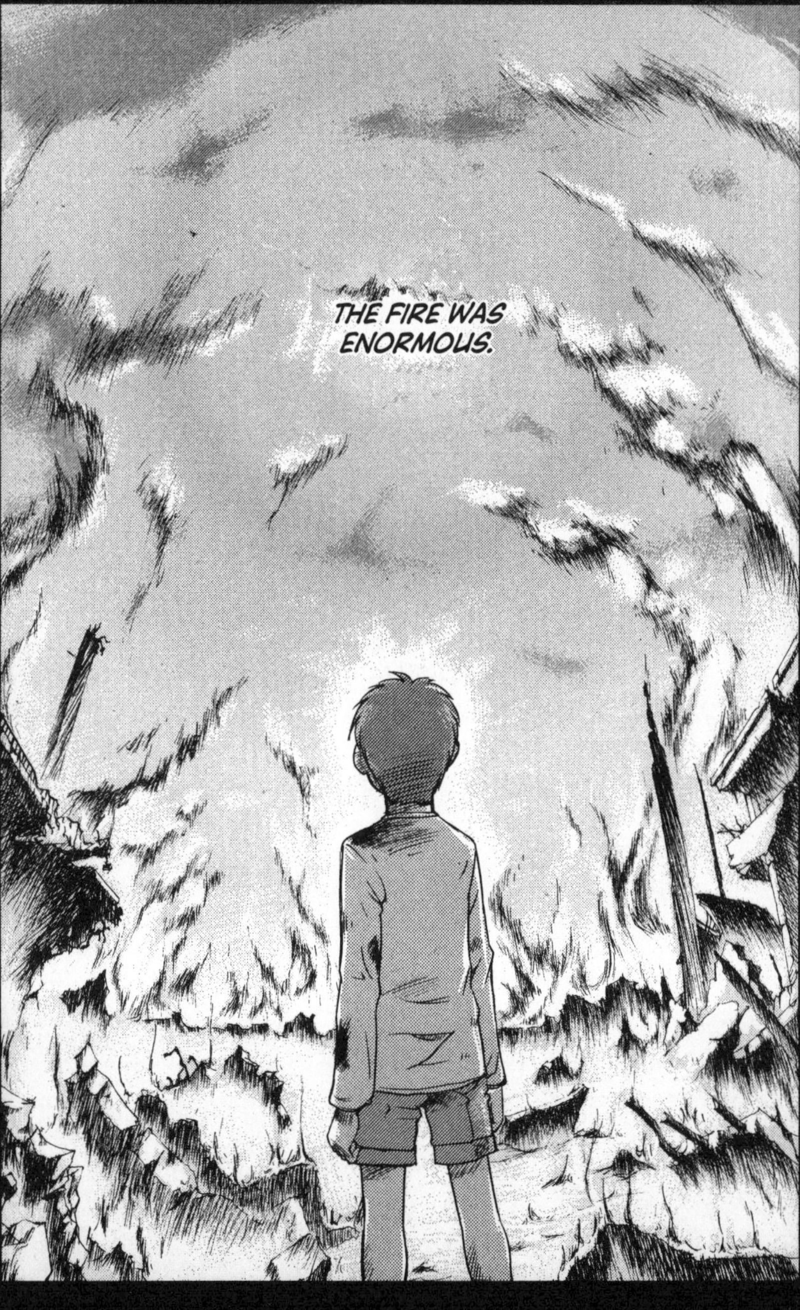
THE FIRE WAS ENORMOUS.

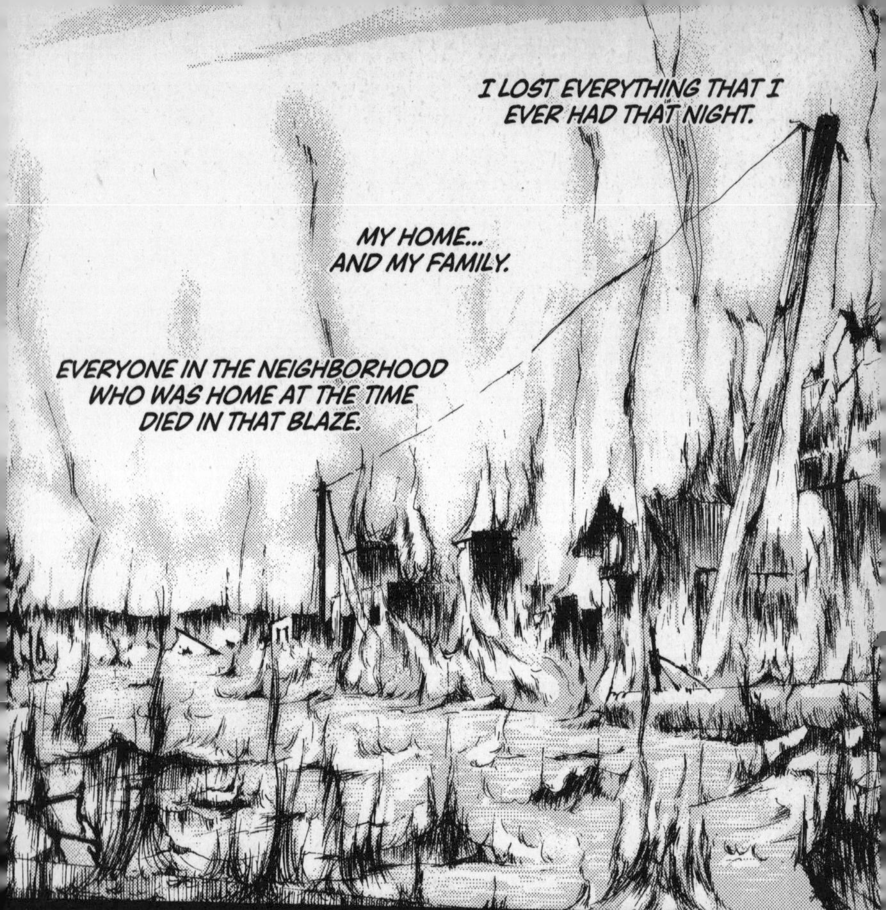
I LOST EVERYTHING THAT I EVER HAD THAT NIGHT.
MY HOME... AND MY FAMILY.
EVERYONE IN THE NEIGHBORHOOD WHO WAS HOME AT THE TIME DIED IN THAT BLAZE.
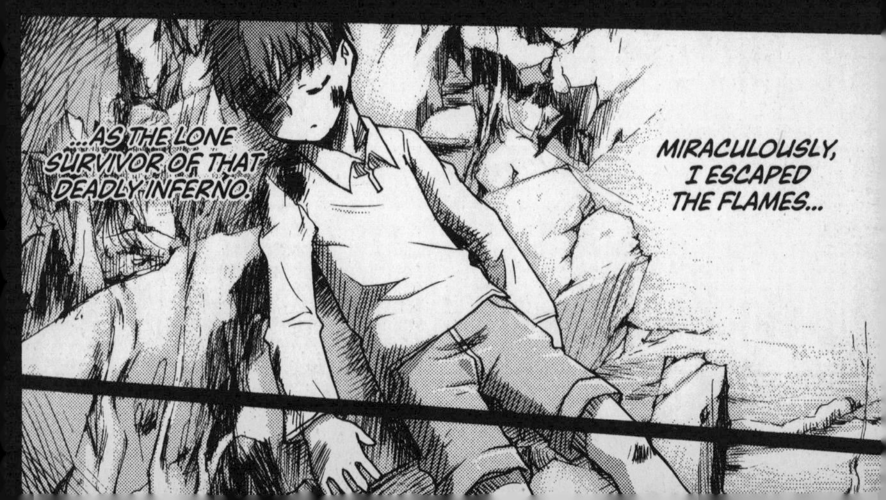
MIRACULOUSLY, I ESCAPED THE FLAMES...
...AS THE LONE SURVIVOR OF THAT DEADLY INFERNO.

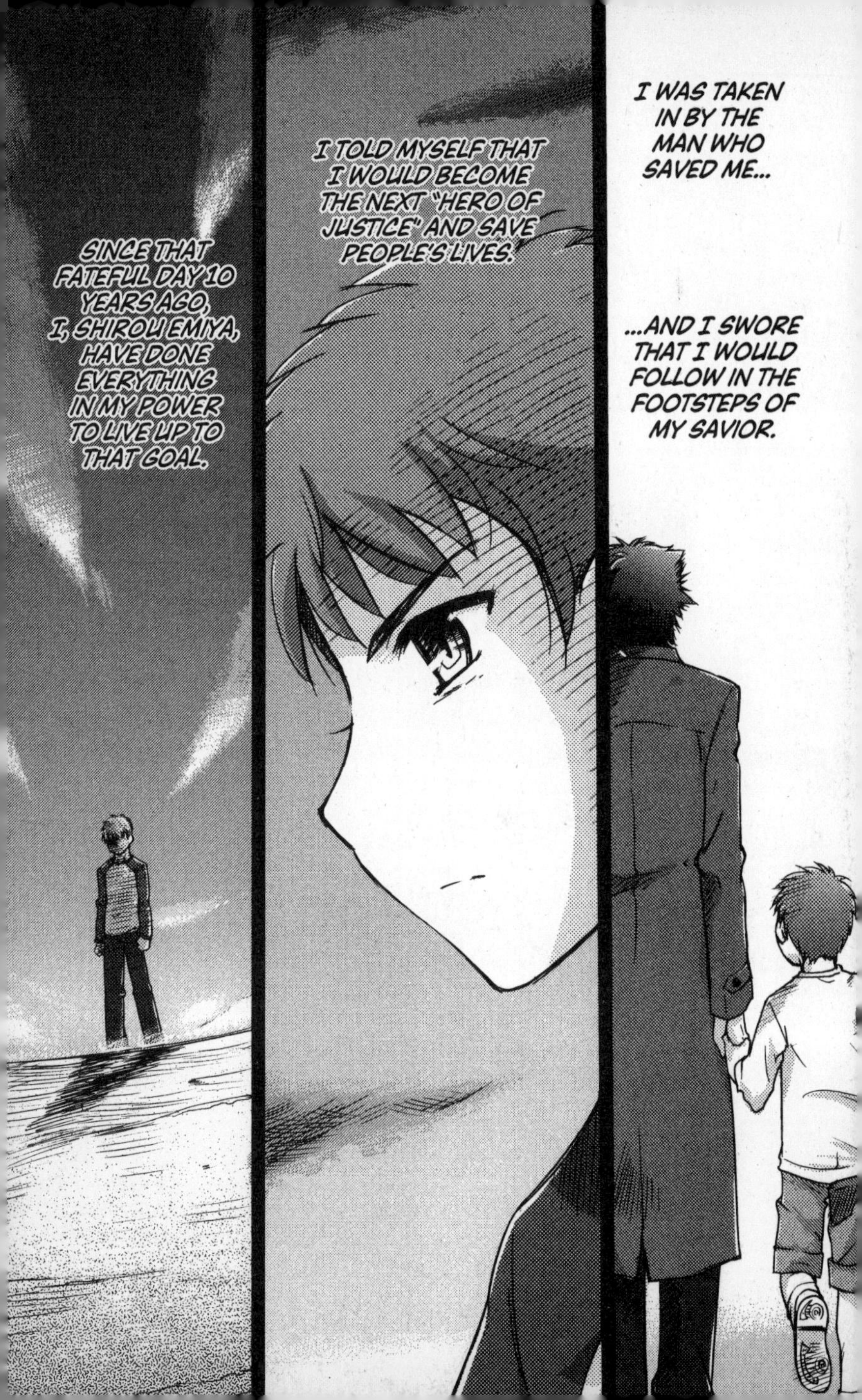
I WAS TAKEN IN BY THE MAN WHO SAVED ME...
...AND I SWORE THAT I WOULD FOLLOW IN THE FOOTSTEPS OF MY SAVIOR.
I TOLD MYSELF THAT I WOULD BECOME THE NEXT "HERO OF JUSTICE" AND SAVE PEOPLE'S LIVES.
SINCE THAT FATEFUL DAY 10 YEARS AGO, I, SHIROU EMIYA, HAVE DONE EVERYTHING IN MY POWER TO LIVE UP TO THAT GOAL.

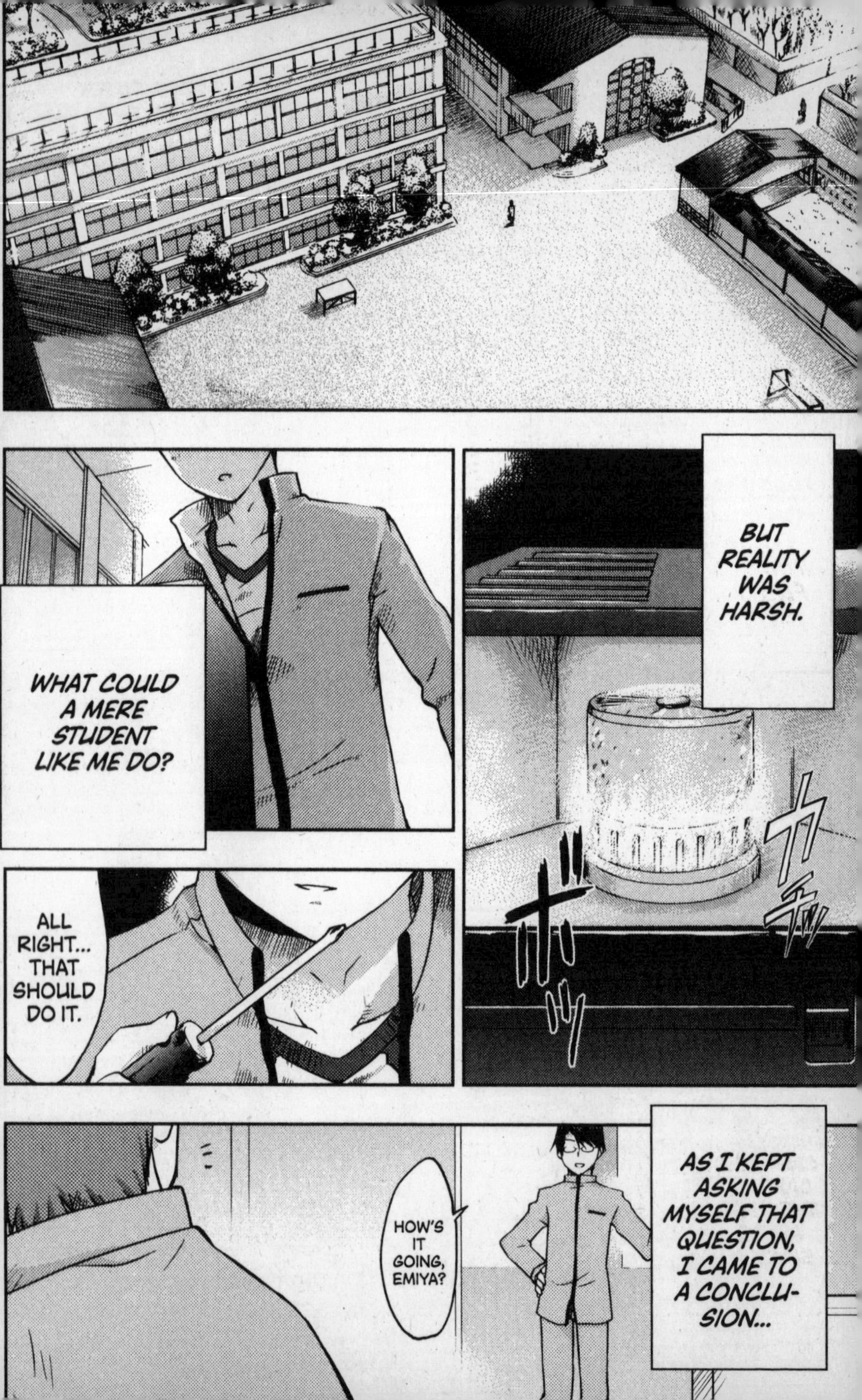
BUT REALITY WAS HARSH.
WHAT COULD A MERE STUDENT LIKE ME DO?
ALL RIGHT... THAT SHOULD DO IT.
AS I KEPT ASKING MYSELF THAT QUESTION, I CAME TO A CONCLUSION...
HOW'S IT GOING, EMIYA?

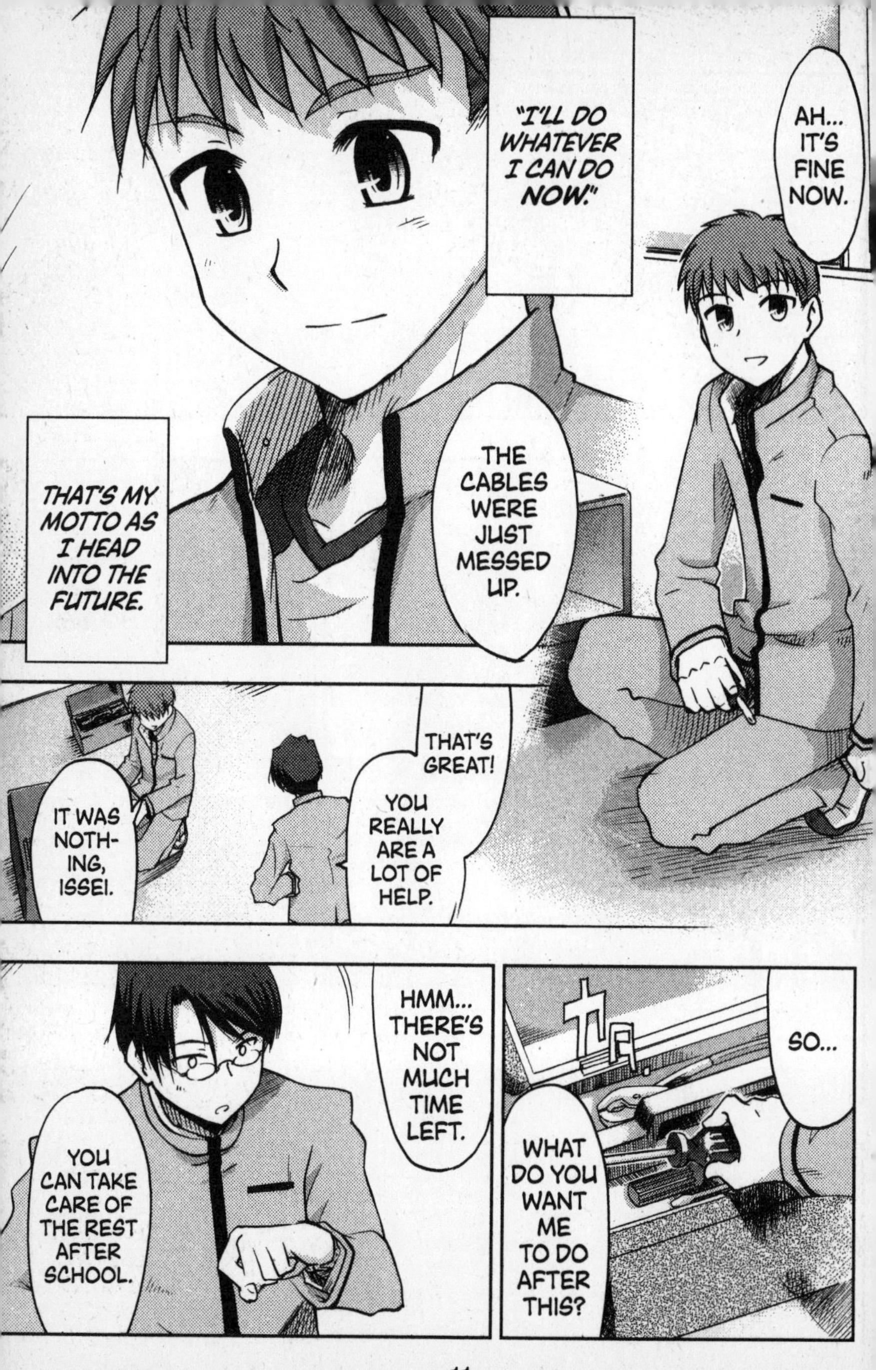
AH... IT'S FINE NOW.
THE CABLES WERE JUST MESSED UP.
"I'LL DO WHATEVER I CAN DO NOW."
THAT'S MY MOTTO AS I HEAD INTO THE FUTURE.
THAT'S GREAT!
YOU REALLY ARE A LOT OF HELP.
IT WAS NOTHING, ISSEI.
SO...
WHAT DO YOU WANT ME TO DO AFTER THIS?
HMM... THERE'S NOT MUCH TIME LEFT.
YOU CAN TAKE CARE OF THE REST AFTER SCHOOL.

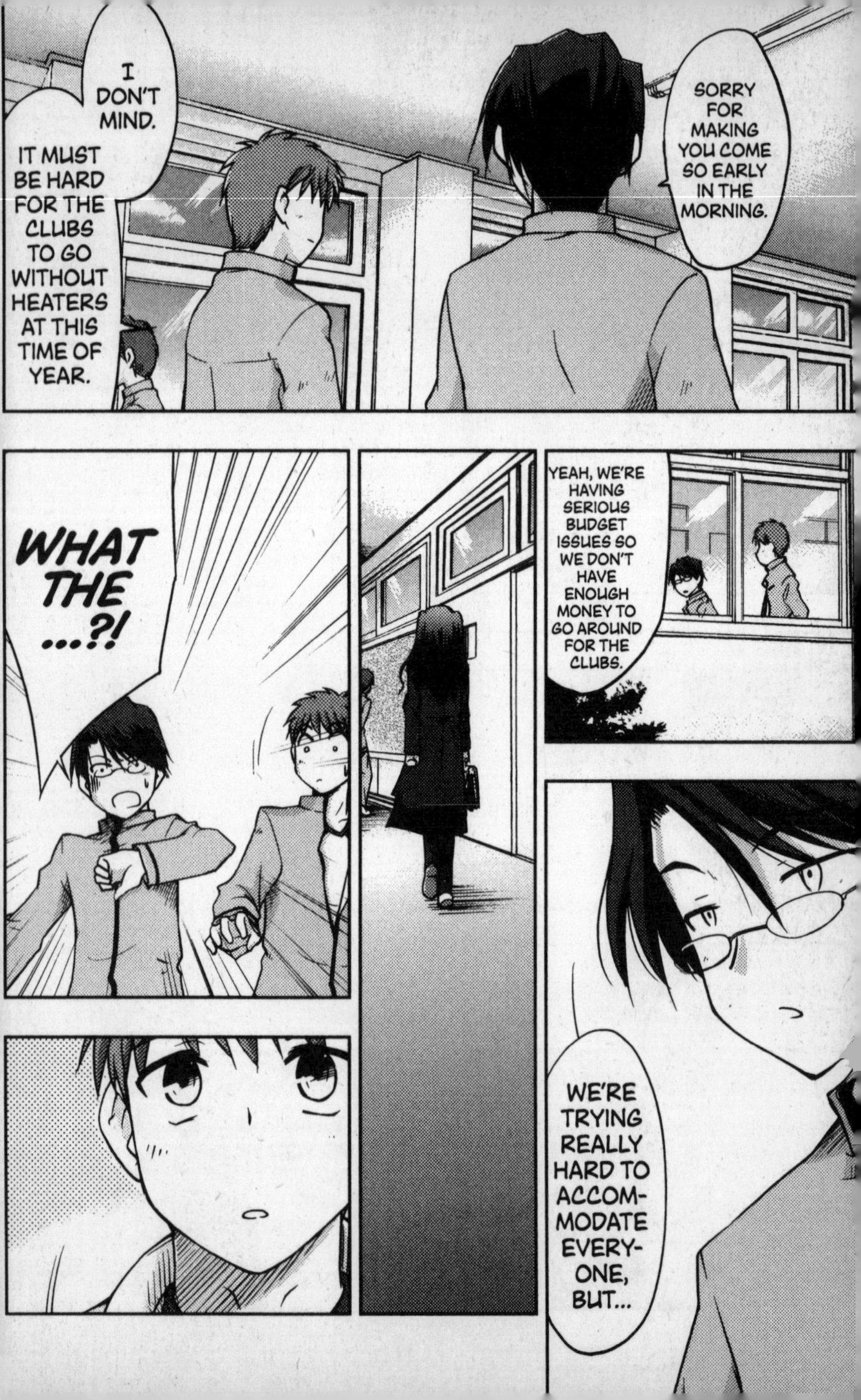
SORRY FOR MAKING YOU COME SO EARLY IN THE MORNING.
I DON'T MIND.
IT MUST BE HARD FOR THE CLUBS TO GO WITHOUT HEATERS AT THIS TIME OF YEAR.
YEAH, WE'RE HAVING SERIOUS BUDGET ISSUES SO WE DON'T HAVE ENOUGH MONEY TO GO AROUND FOR THE CLUBS.
WE'RE TRYING REALLY HARD TO ACCOM-MODATE EVERY-ONE, BUT...
WHAT THE...?!

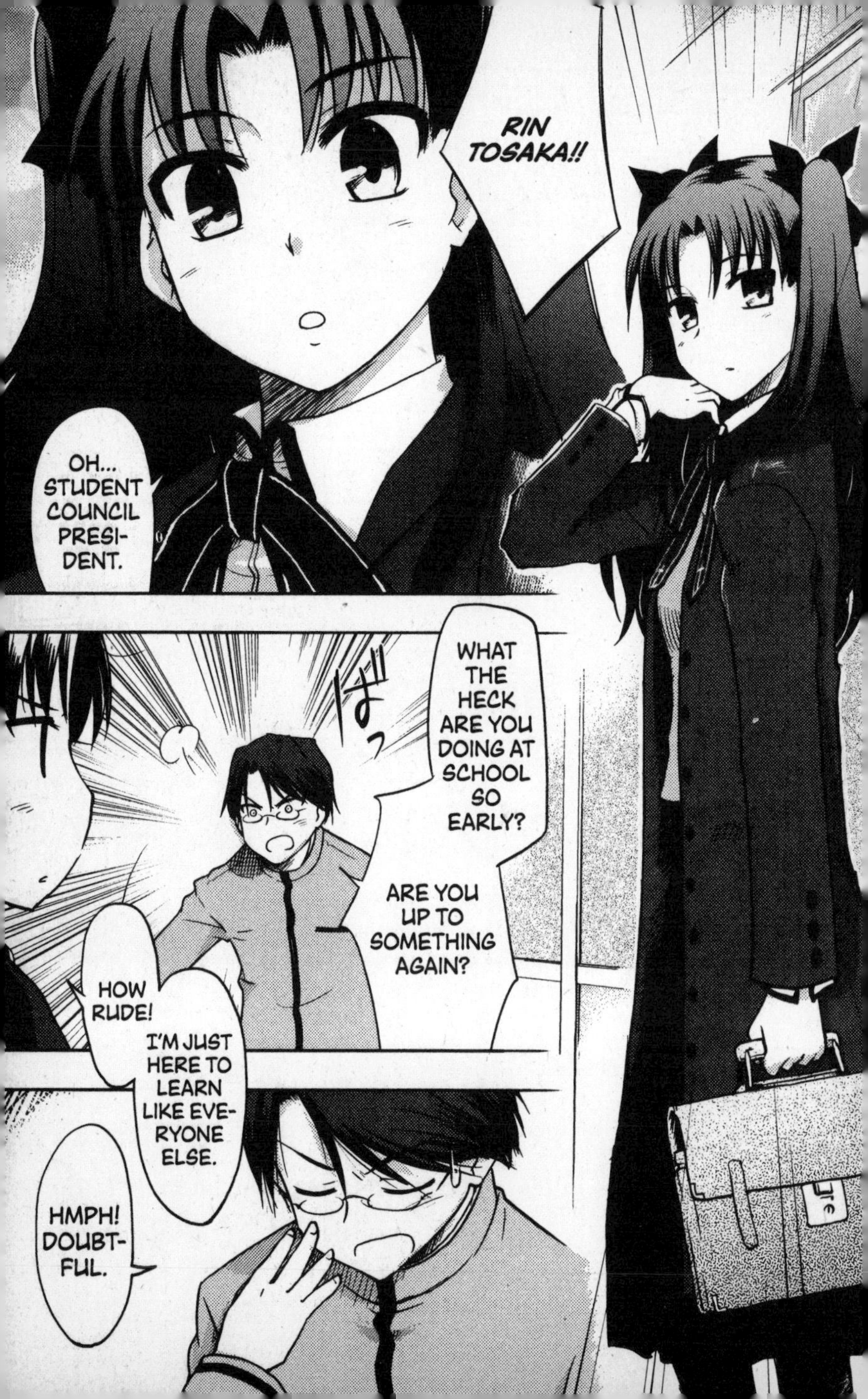
RIN TOSAKA!!
OH... STUDENT COUNCIL PRESI-DENT.
ばっ
WHAT THE HECK ARE YOU DOING AT SCHOOL SO EARLY?
ARE YOU UP TO SOMETHING AGAIN?
HOW RUDE!
I'M JUST HERE TO LEARN LIKE EVE-RYONE ELSE.
HMPH! DOUBT-FUL.

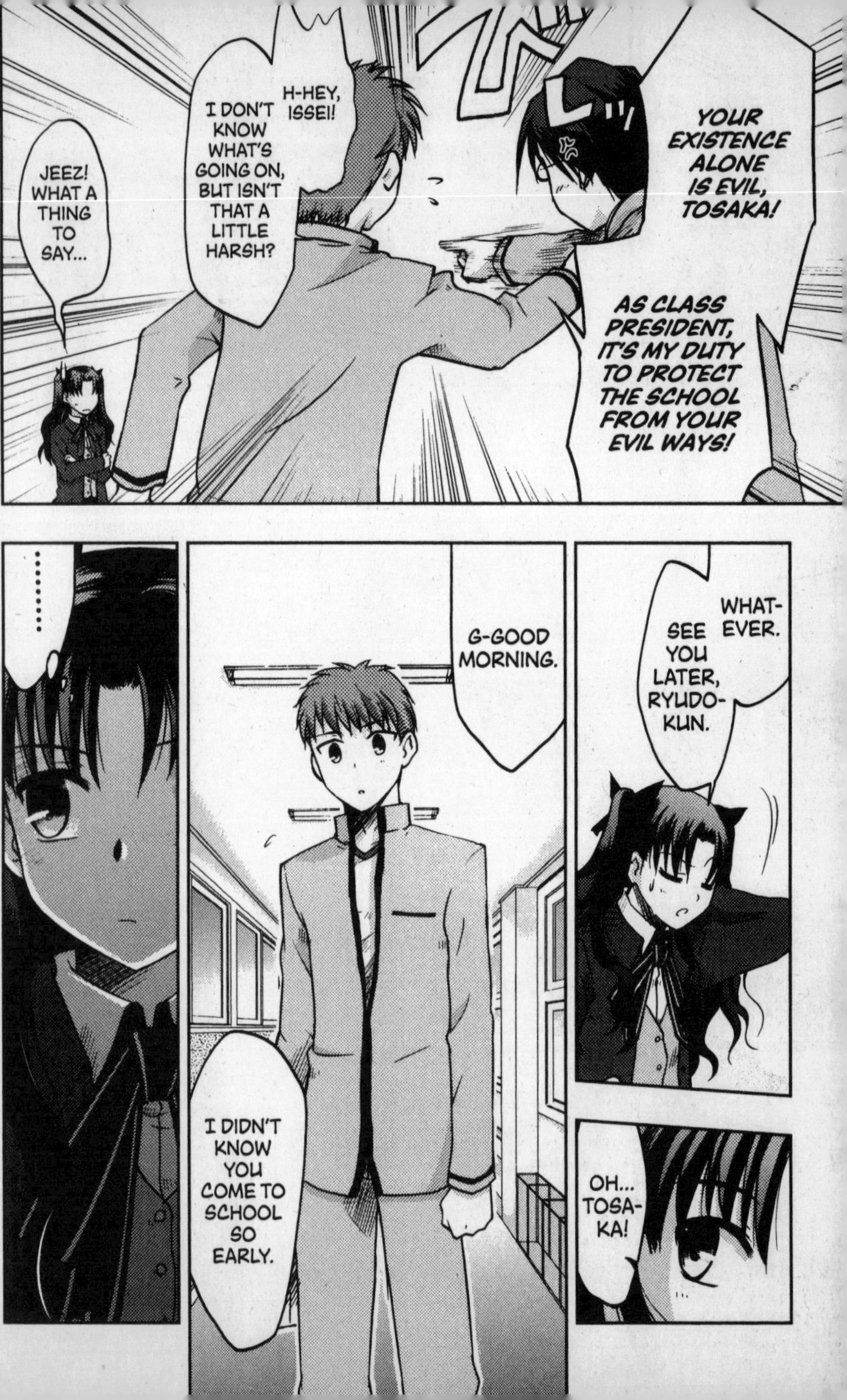
YOUR EXISTENCE ALONE IS EVIL, TOSAKA!
AS CLASS PRESIDENT, IT'S MY DUTY TO PROTECT THE SCHOOL FROM YOUR EVIL WAYS!
H-HEY, ISSEI!
I DON'T KNOW WHAT'S GOING ON, BUT ISN'T THAT A LITTLE HARSH?
JEEZ! WHAT A THING TO SAY...
WHAT-EVER.
SEE YOU LATER, RYUDO-KUN.
OH... TOSA-KA!
G-GOOD MORNING.
I DIDN'T KNOW YOU COME TO SCHOOL SO EARLY.
....

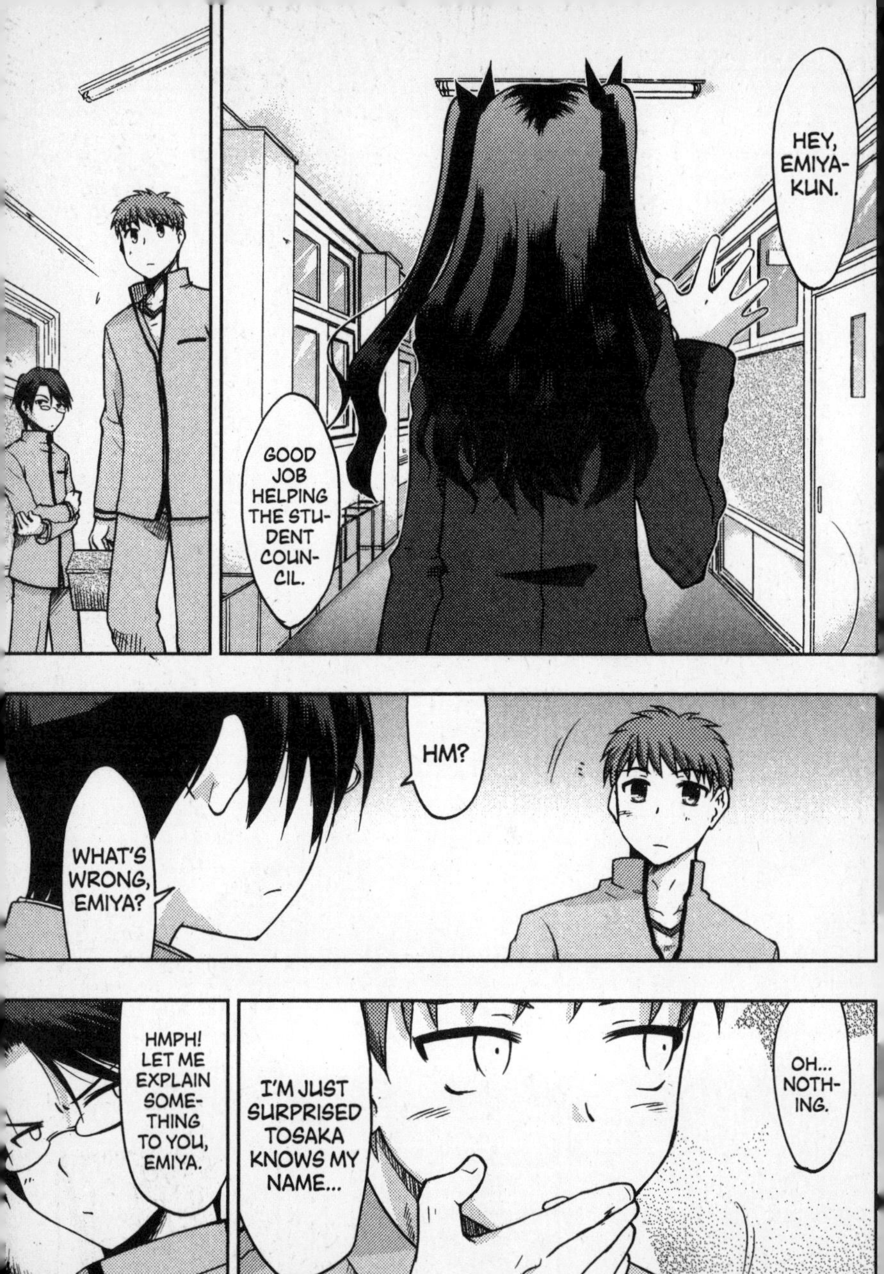
HEY, EMIYA-KUN.
GOOD JOB HELPING THE STUDENT COUNCIL.
HM?
WHAT'S WRONG, EMIYA?
OH... NOTHING.
I'M JUST SURPRISED TOSAKA KNOWS MY NAME...
HMPH! LET ME EXPLAIN SOMETHING TO YOU, EMIYA.

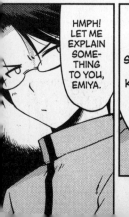

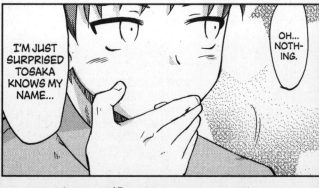

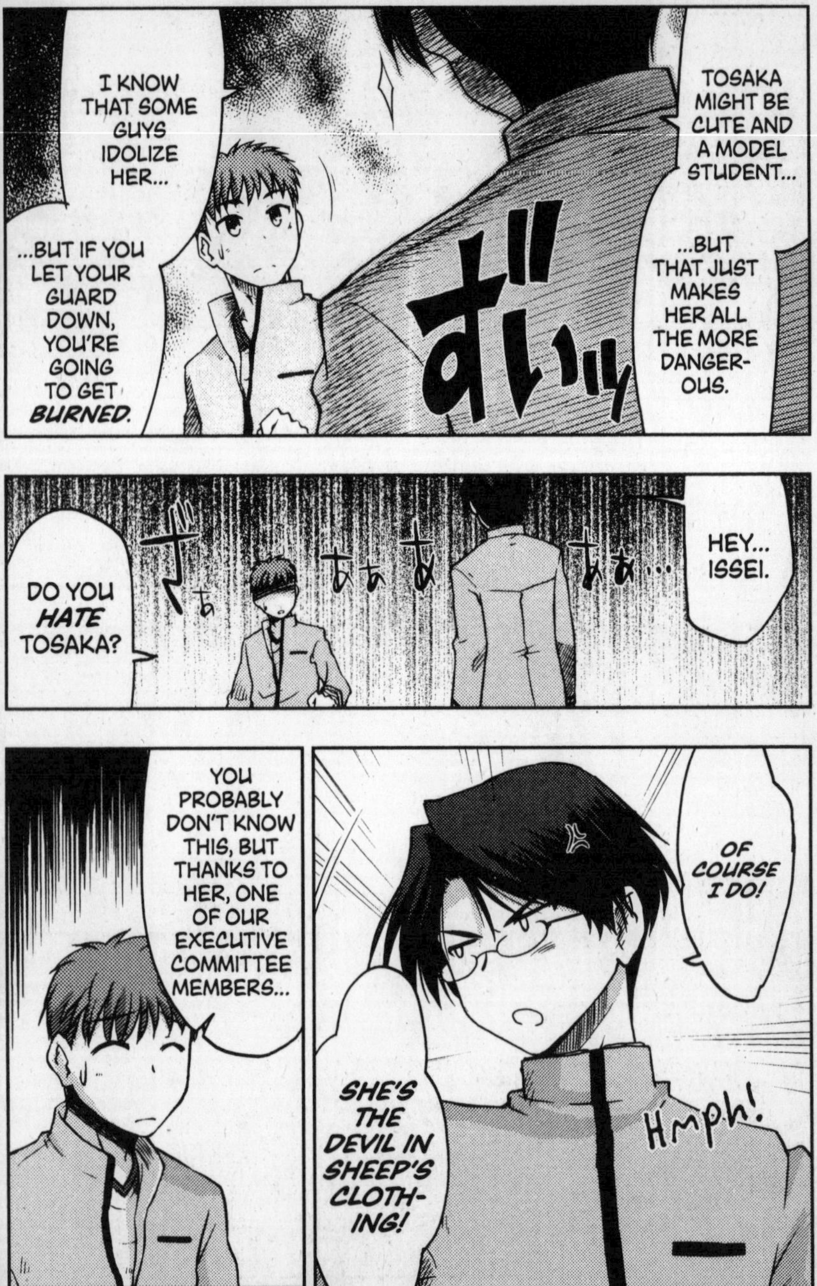
TOSAKA MIGHT BE CUTE AND A MODEL STUDENT...
...BUT THAT JUST MAKES HER ALL THE MORE DANGER-OUS.
I KNOW THAT SOME GUYS IDOLIZE HER...
...BUT IF YOU LET YOUR GUARD DOWN, YOU'RE GOING TO GET *BURNED*.
HEY... ISSEI.
DO YOU *HATE* TOSAKA?
OF COURSE I DO!
Hmph!
SHE'S THE DEVIL IN SHEEP'S CLOTH-ING!
YOU PROBABLY DON'T KNOW THIS, BUT THANKS TO HER, ONE OF OUR EXECUTIVE COMMITTEE MEMBERS...

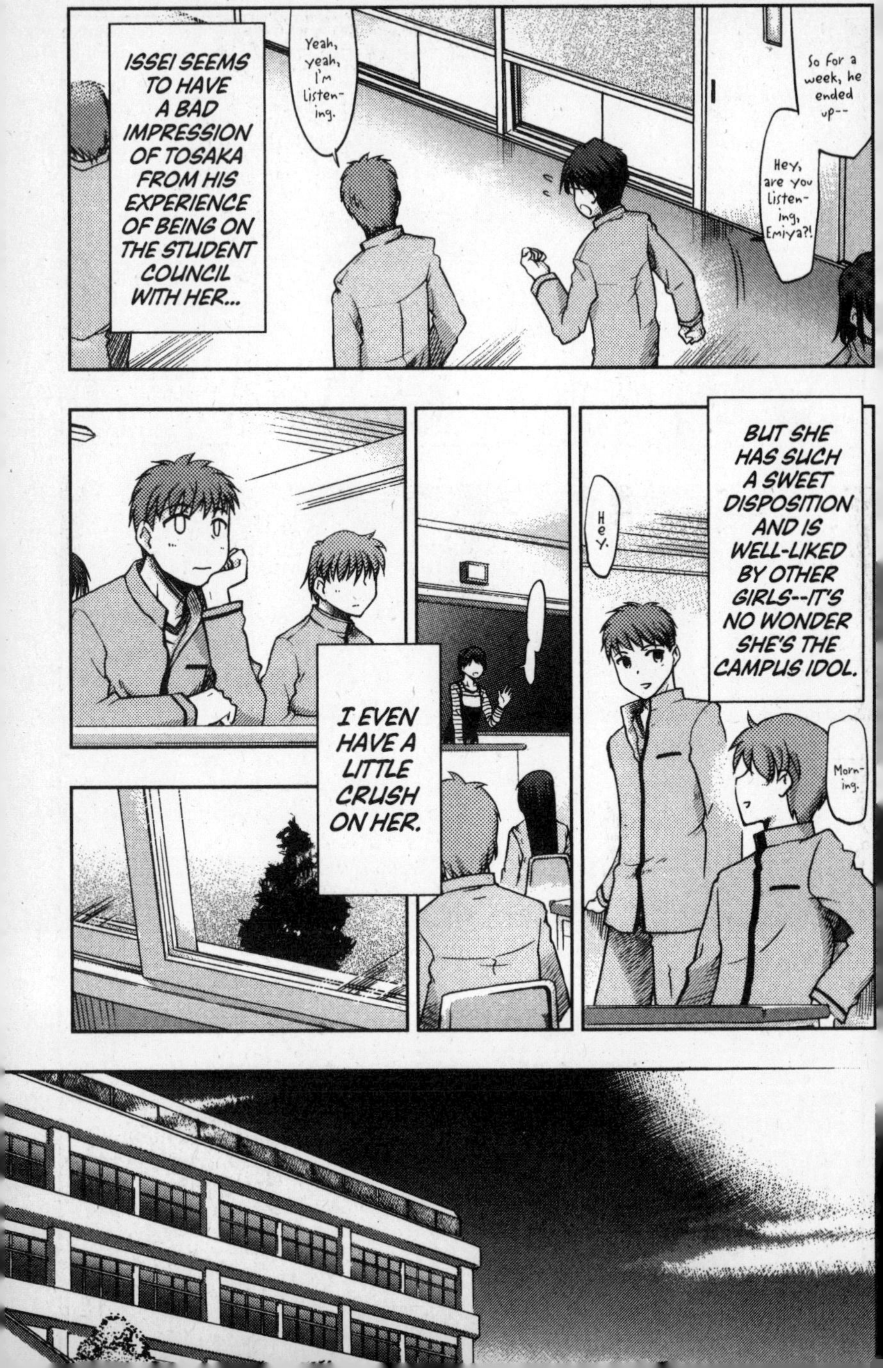
So for a week, he ended up--
Hey, are you listen-ing, Emiya?!
Yeah, yeah, I'm listen-ing.
ISSEI SEEMS TO HAVE A BAD IMPRESSION OF TOSAKA FROM HIS EXPERIENCE OF BEING ON THE STUDENT COUNCIL WITH HER...
BUT SHE HAS SUCH A SWEET DISPOSITION AND IS WELL-LIKED BY OTHER GIRLS--IT'S NO WONDER SHE'S THE CAMPUS IDOL.
Hey.
Morn-ing.
I EVEN HAVE A LITTLE CRUSH ON HER.

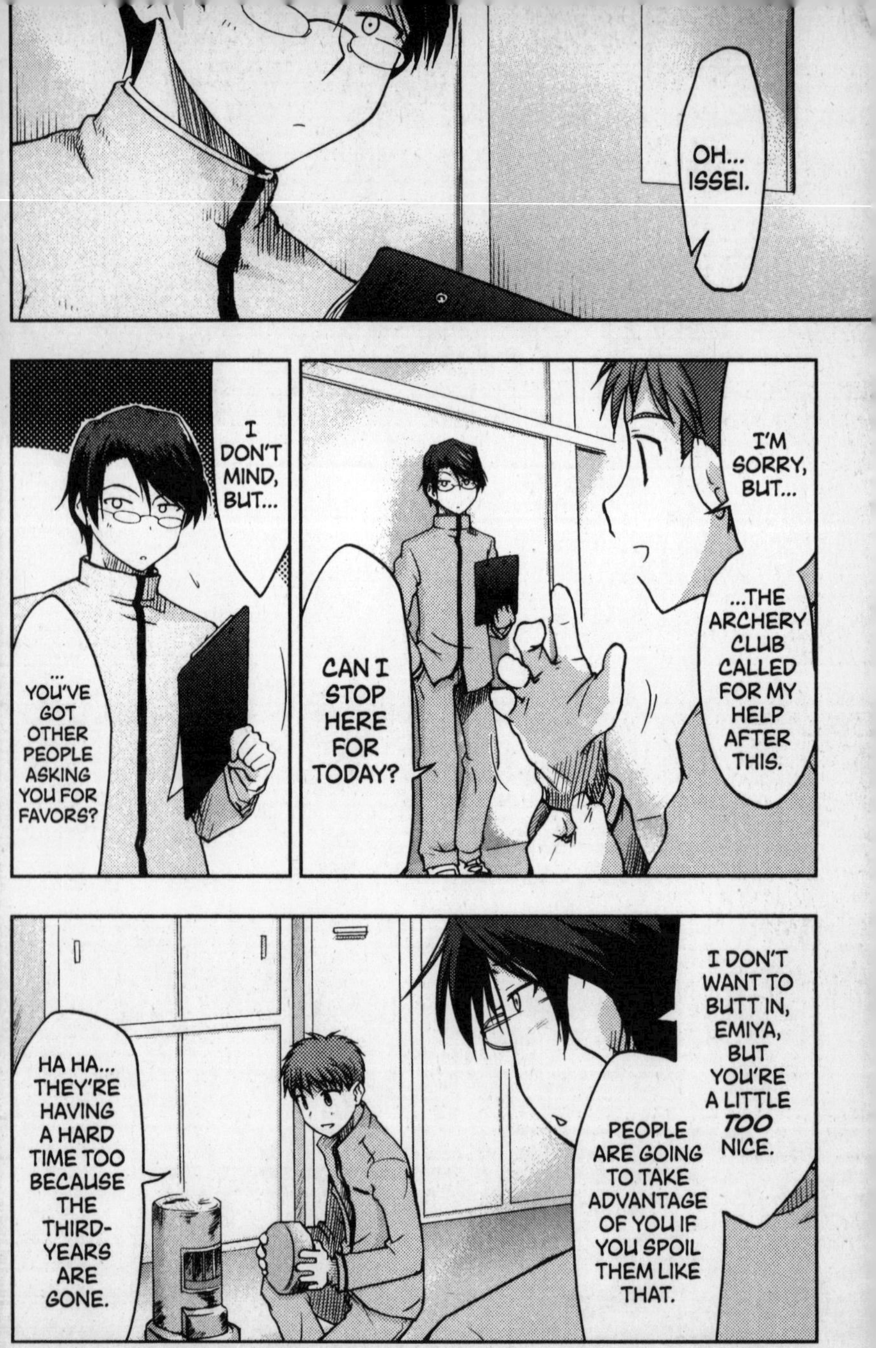
OH... ISSEI.
I'M SORRY, BUT...
...THE ARCHERY CLUB CALLED FOR MY HELP AFTER THIS.
CAN I STOP HERE FOR TODAY?
I DON'T MIND, BUT...
...YOU'VE GOT OTHER PEOPLE ASKING YOU FOR FAVORS?
I DON'T WANT TO BUTT IN, EMIYA, BUT YOU'RE A LITTLE *TOO* NICE.
PEOPLE ARE GOING TO TAKE ADVANTAGE OF YOU IF YOU SPOIL THEM LIKE THAT.
HA HA... THEY'RE HAVING A HARD TIME TOO BECAUSE THE THIRD-YEARS ARE GONE.

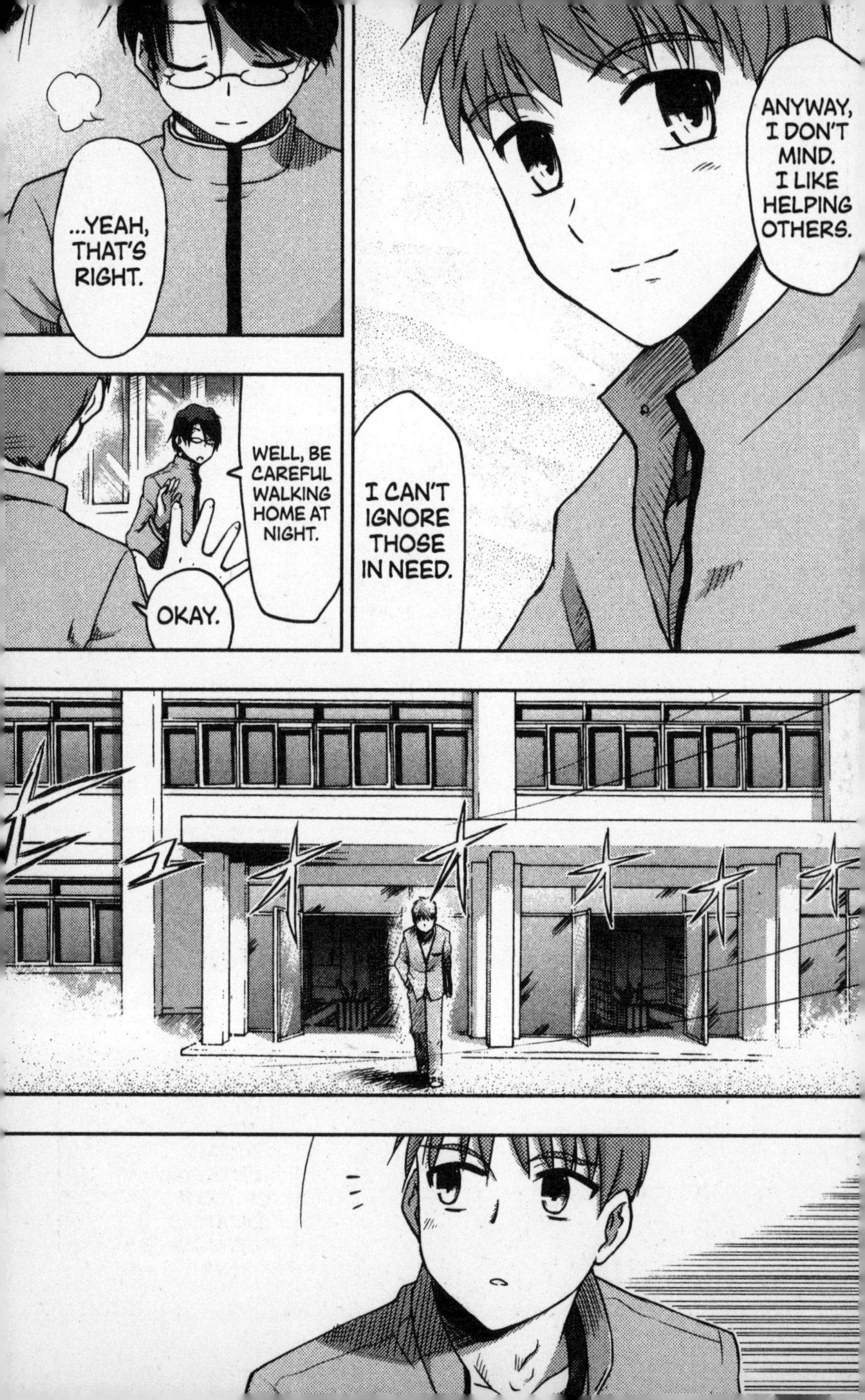
ANYWAY, I DON'T MIND. I LIKE HELPING OTHERS.
I CAN'T IGNORE THOSE IN NEED.
...YEAH, THAT'S RIGHT.
WELL, BE CAREFUL WALKING HOME AT NIGHT.
OKAY.

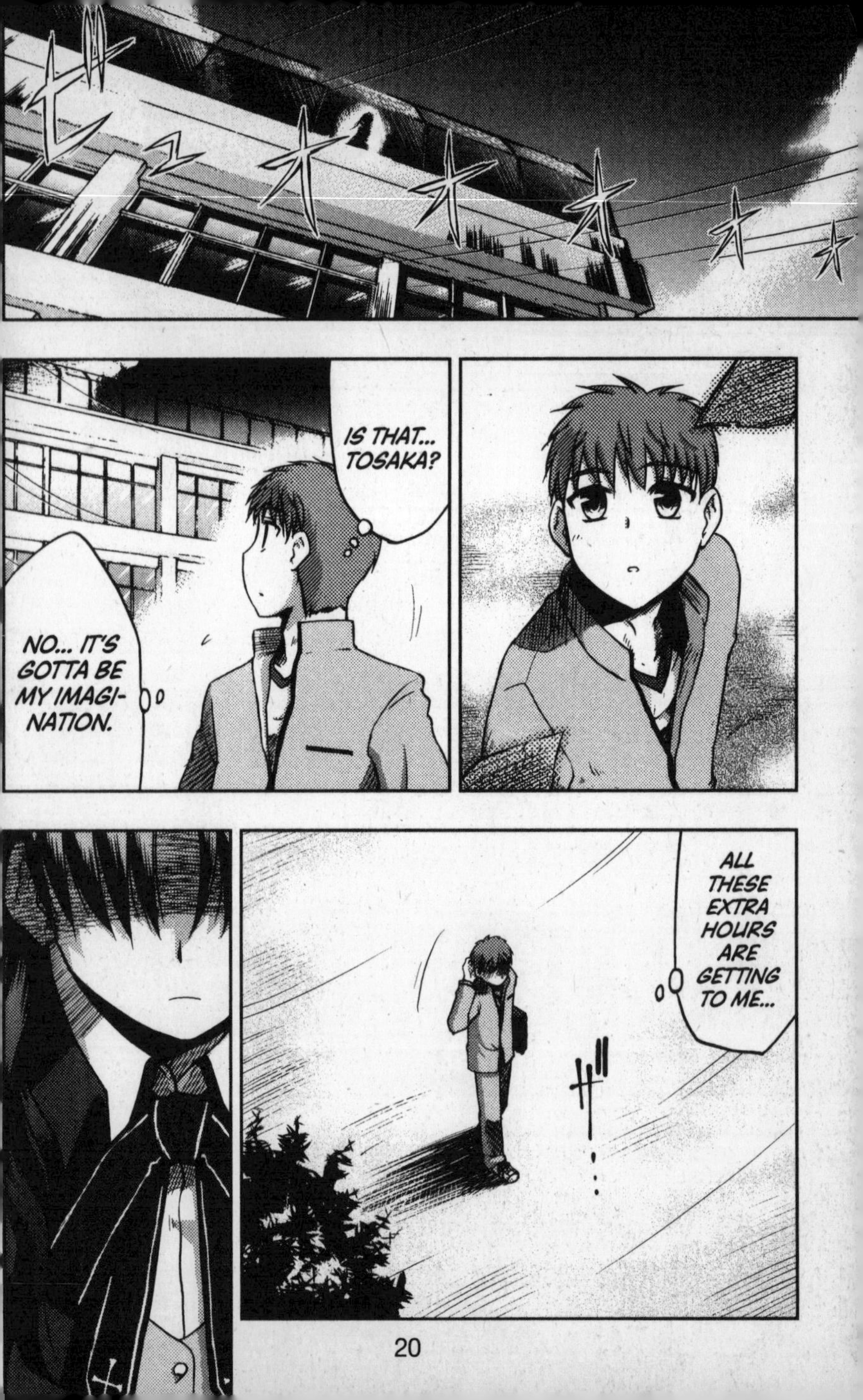
IS THAT... TOSAKA?
NO... IT'S GOTTA BE MY IMAGI-NATION.
ALL THESE EXTRA HOURS ARE GETTING TO ME...

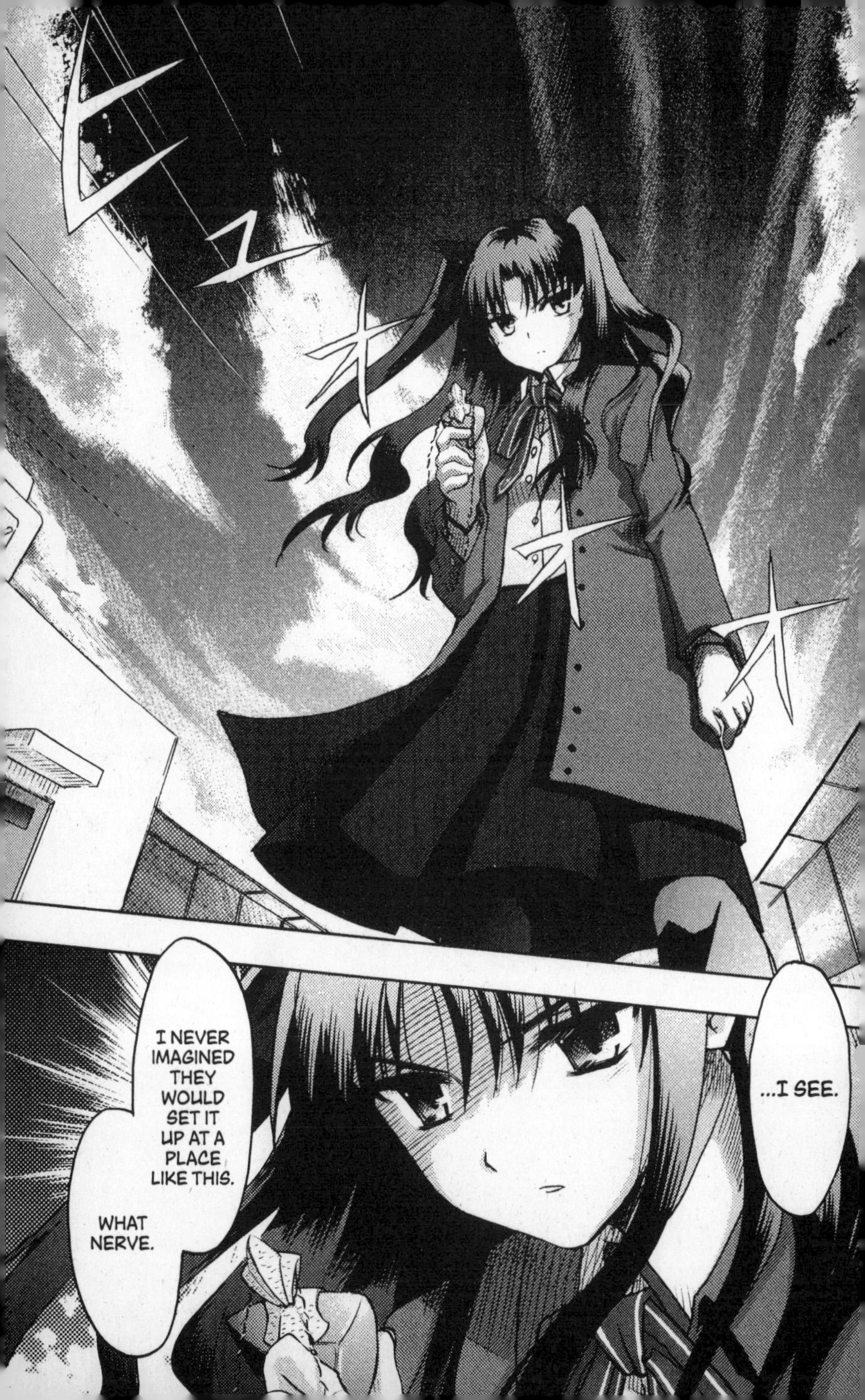
ヒュオオオ
...I SEE.
I NEVER IMAGINED THEY WOULD SET IT UP AT A PLACE LIKE THIS.
WHAT NERVE.

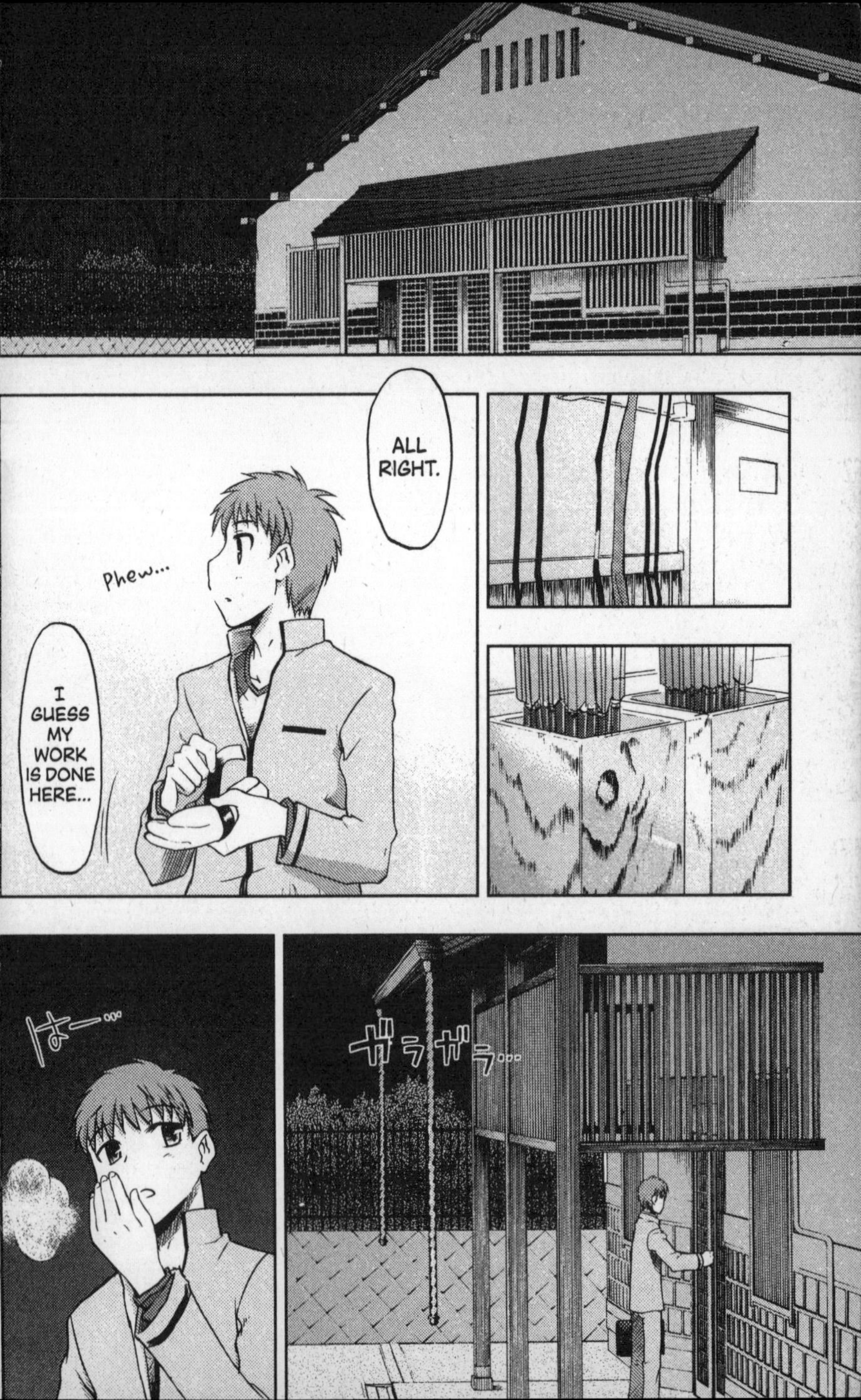
ALL RIGHT.
Phew...
I GUESS MY WORK IS DONE HERE...
ガラガラ…
はー…

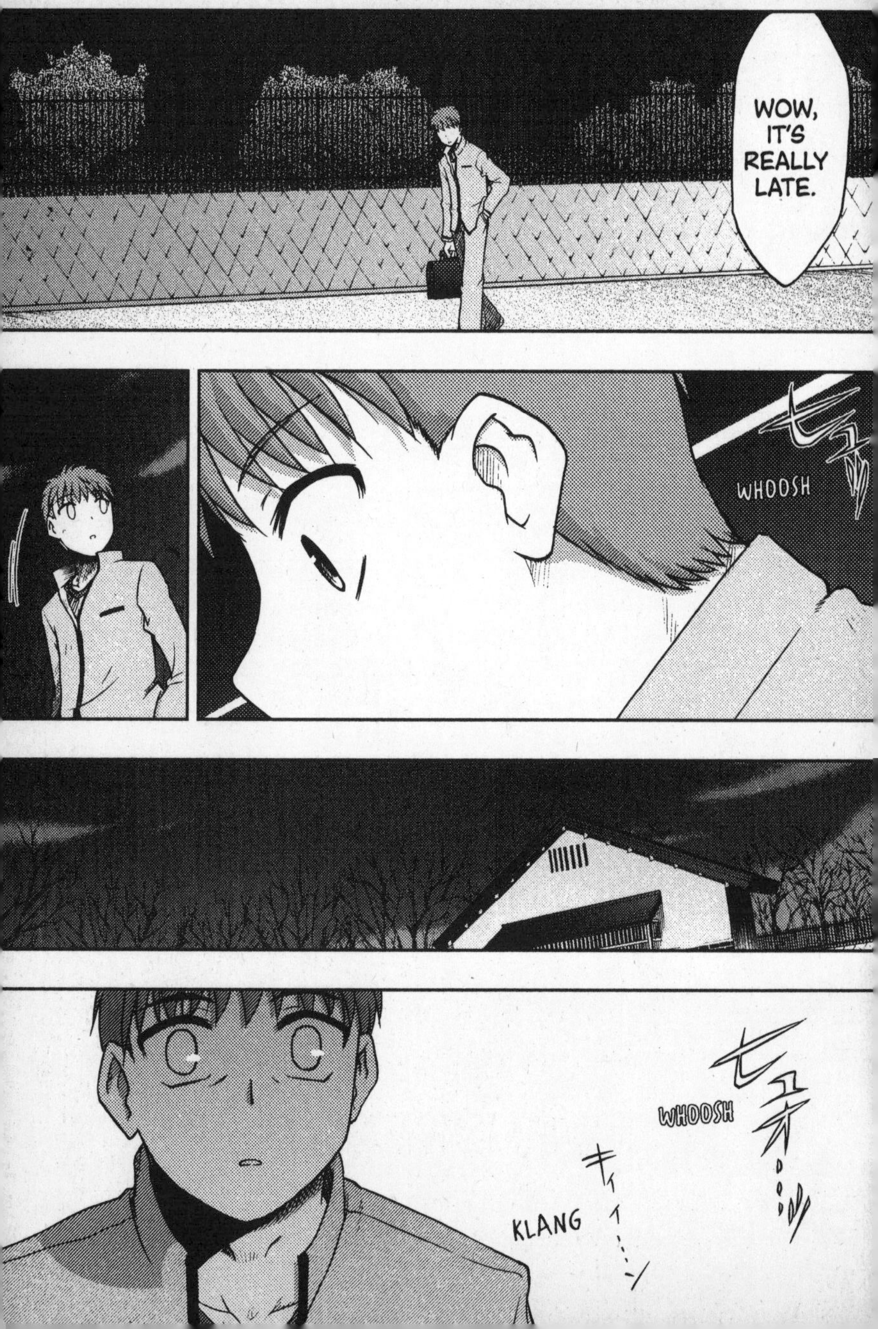
WOW, IT'S REALLY LATE.
WHOOSH
WHOOSH
KLANG

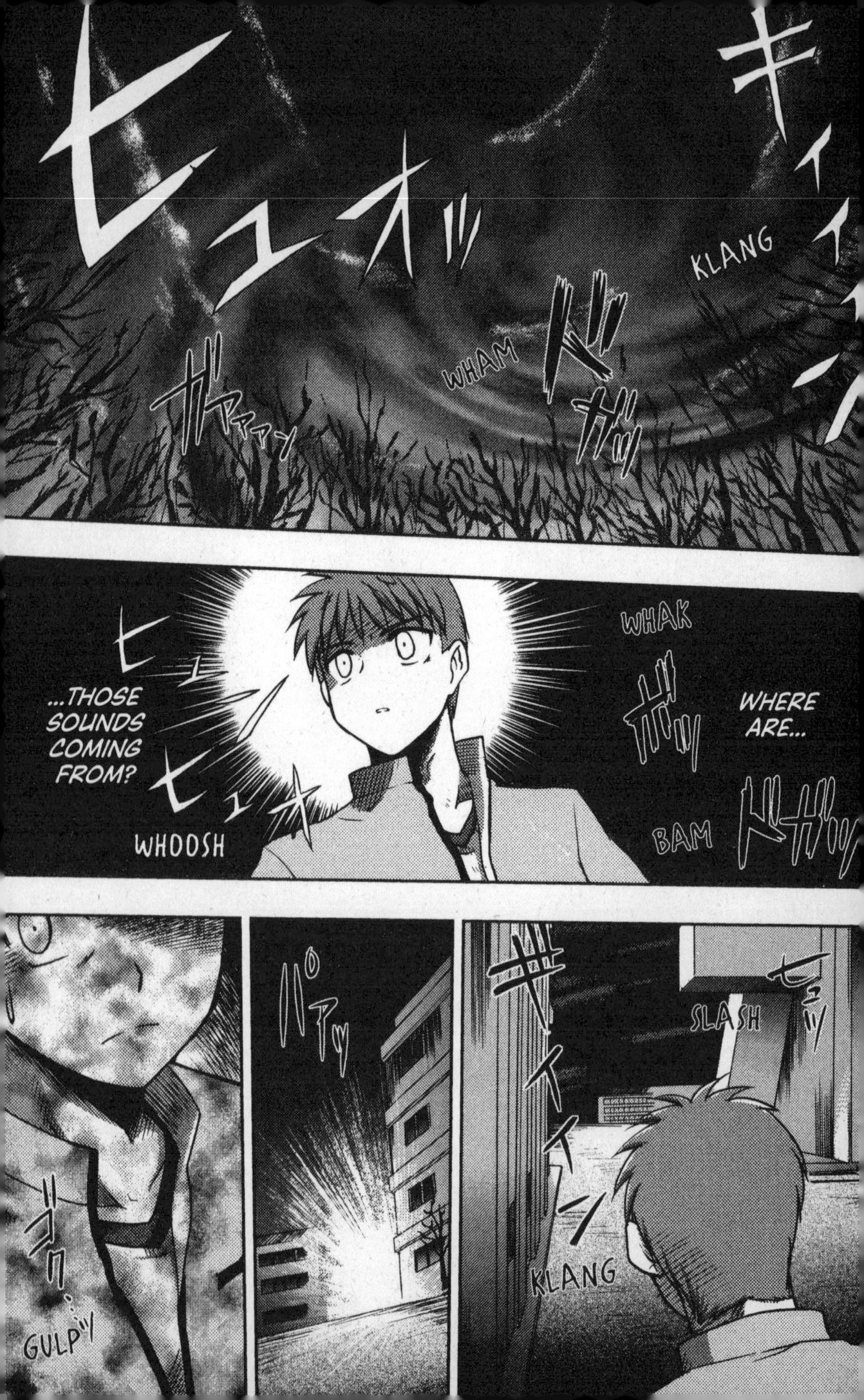
KLANG
WHAM
WHERE ARE...
WHAK
BAM
...THOSE SOUNDS COMING FROM?
WHOOSH
SLASH
KLANG
GULP

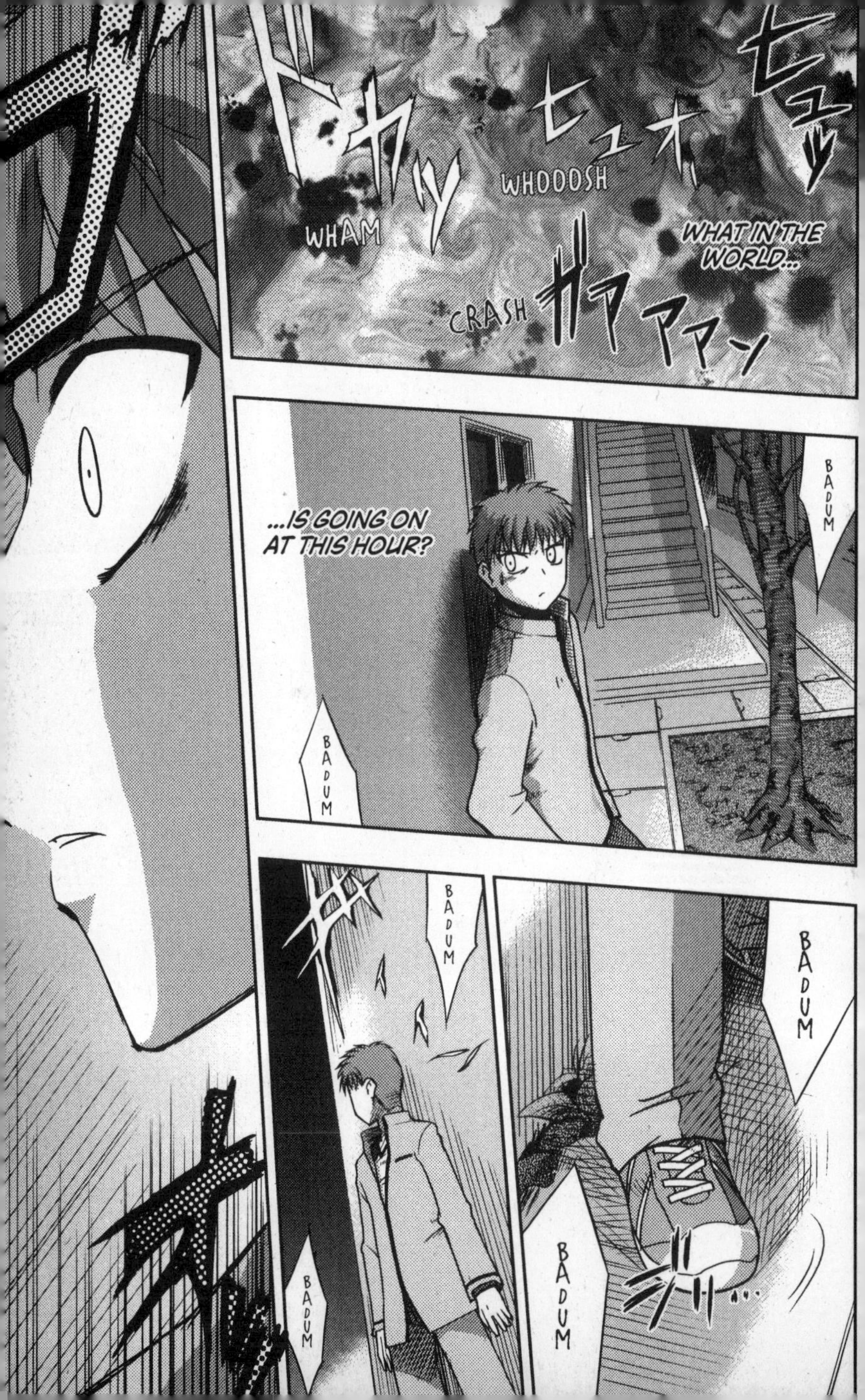
WHOOOSH
WHAT IN THE WORLD...
WHAM
CRASH
BADUM
...IS GOING ON AT THIS HOUR?
BADUM
BADUM
BADUM
BADUM
BADUM

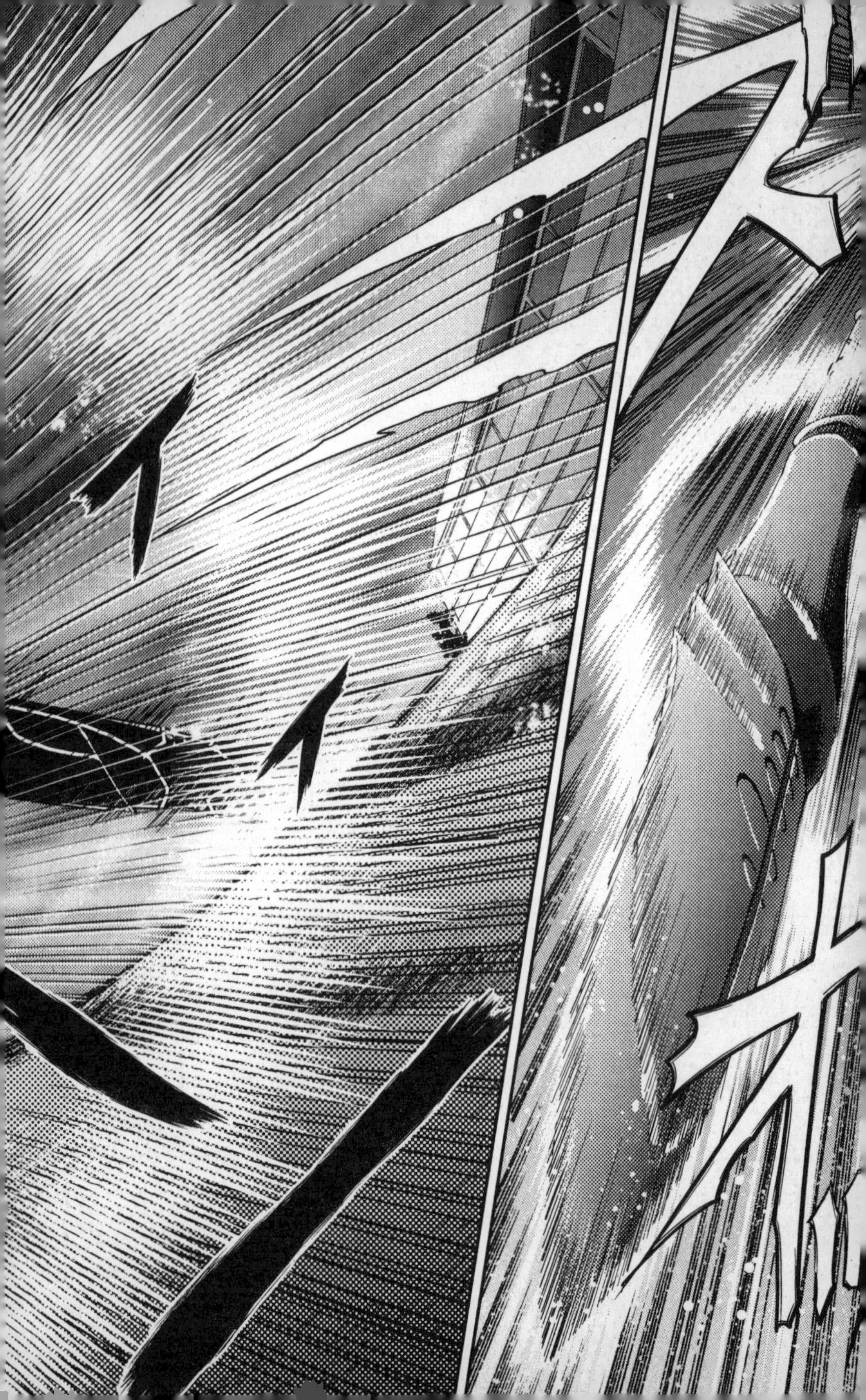

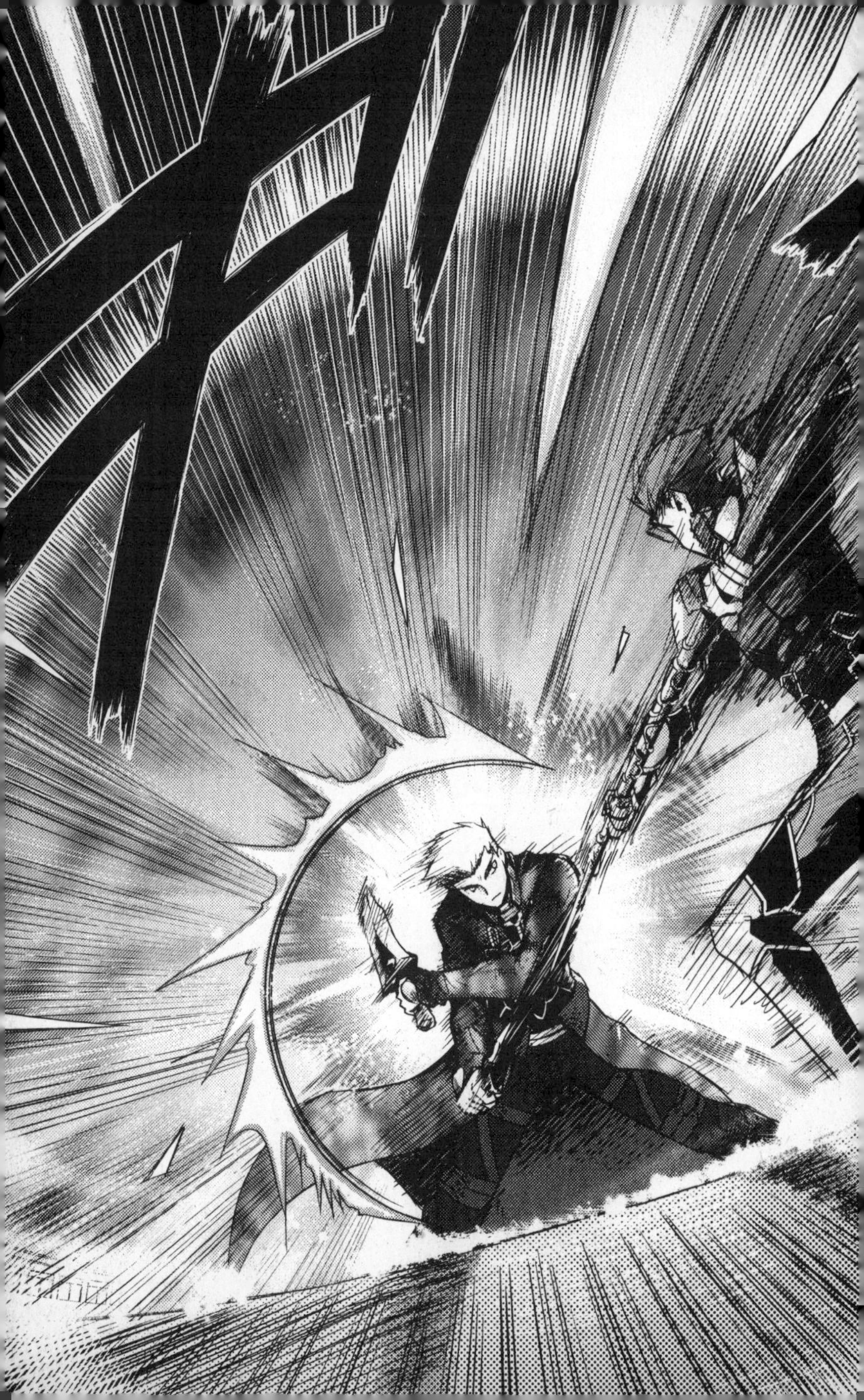

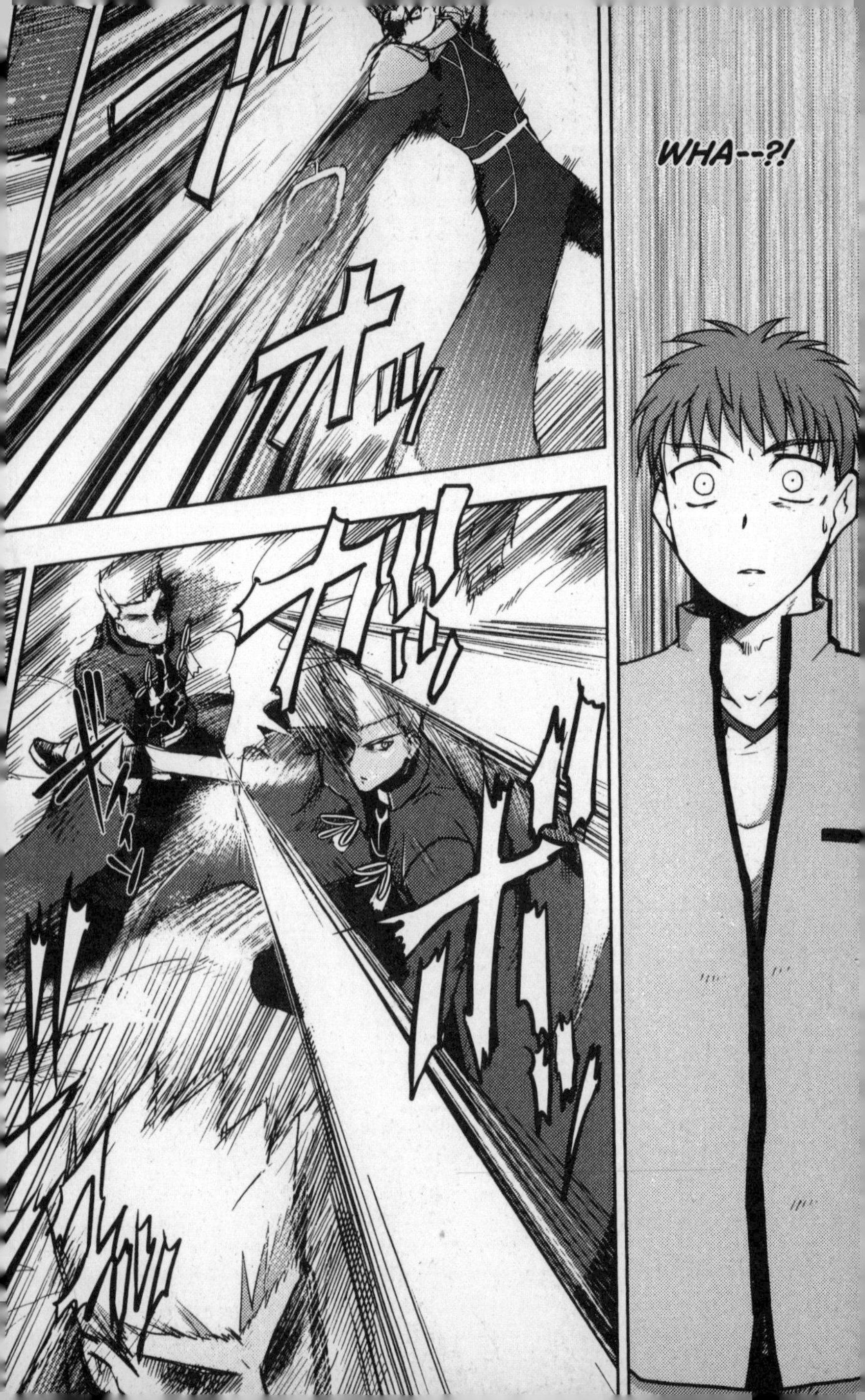
WHA--?!

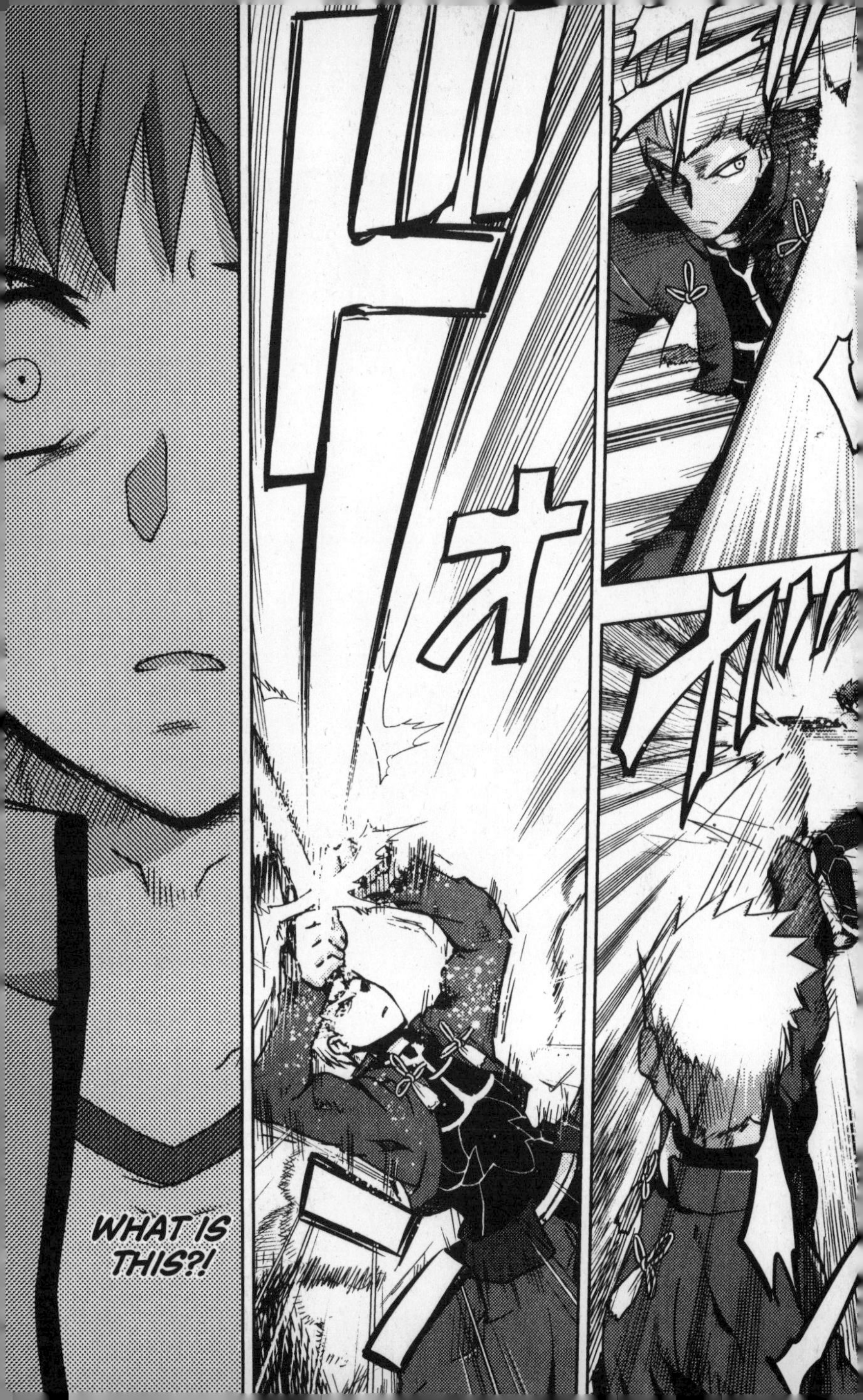
WHAT IS THIS?!

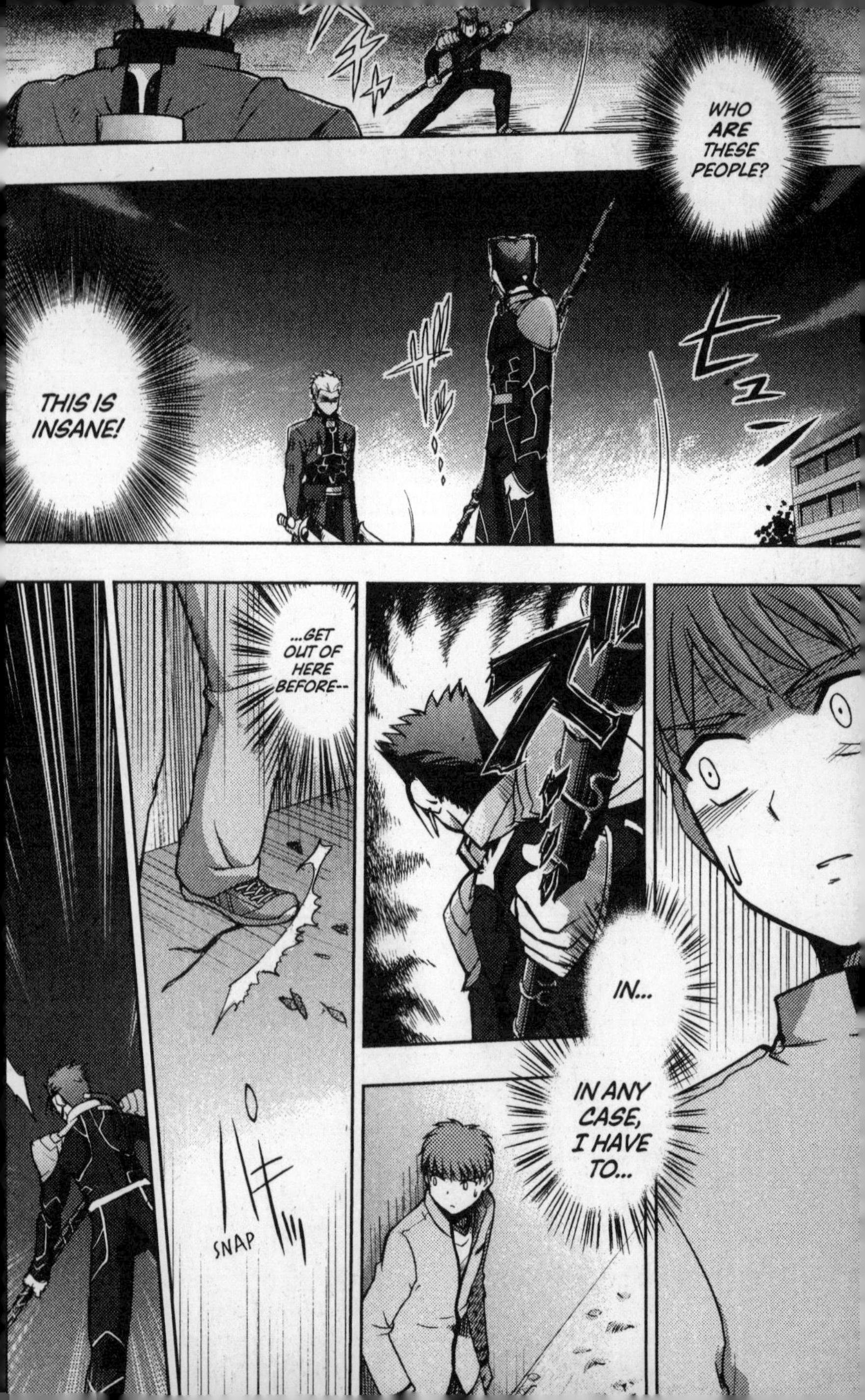
WHO ARE THESE PEOPLE?
THIS IS INSANE!
IN...
IN ANY CASE, I HAVE TO...
...GET OUT OF HERE BEFORE--
SNAP

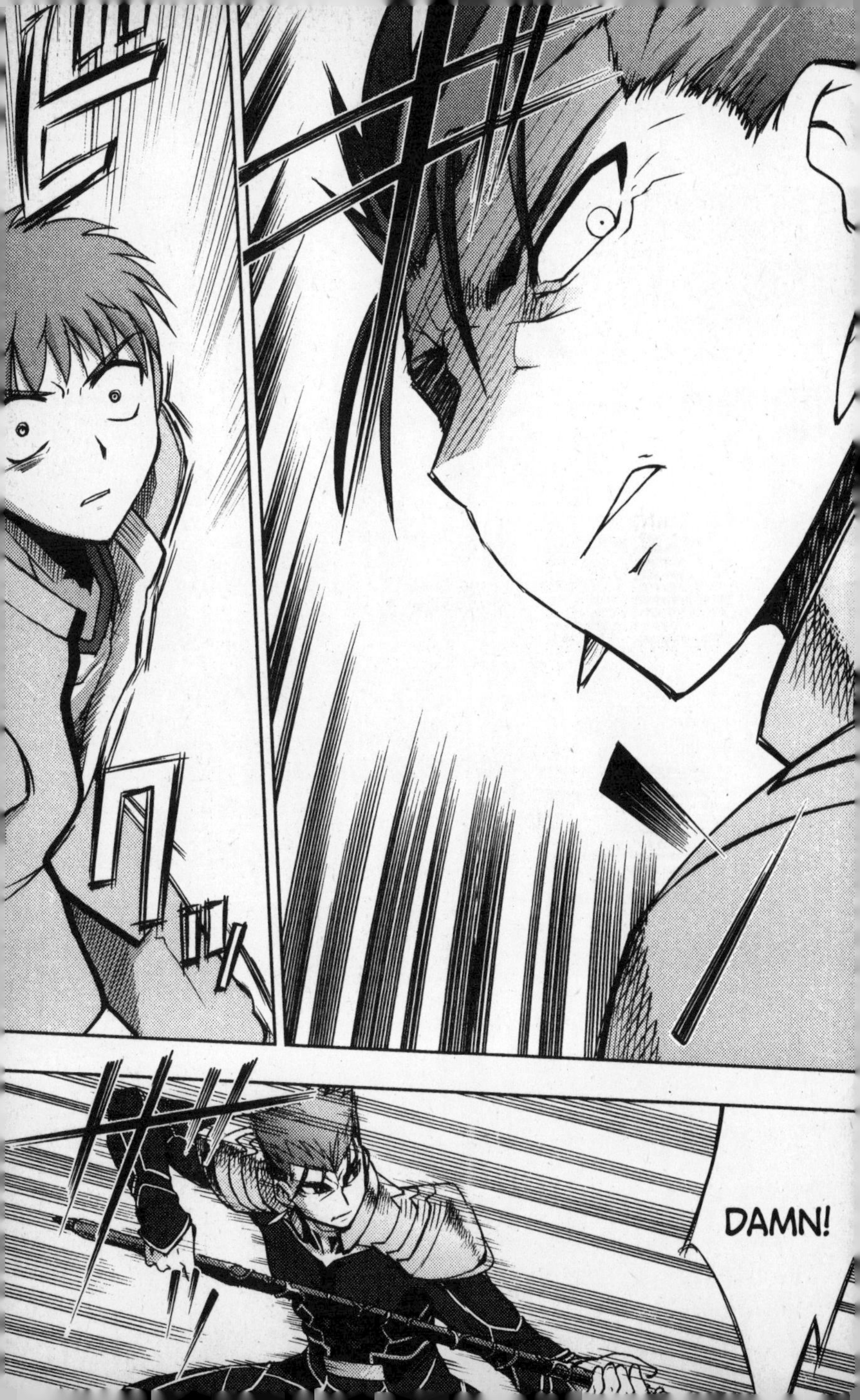
DAMN!

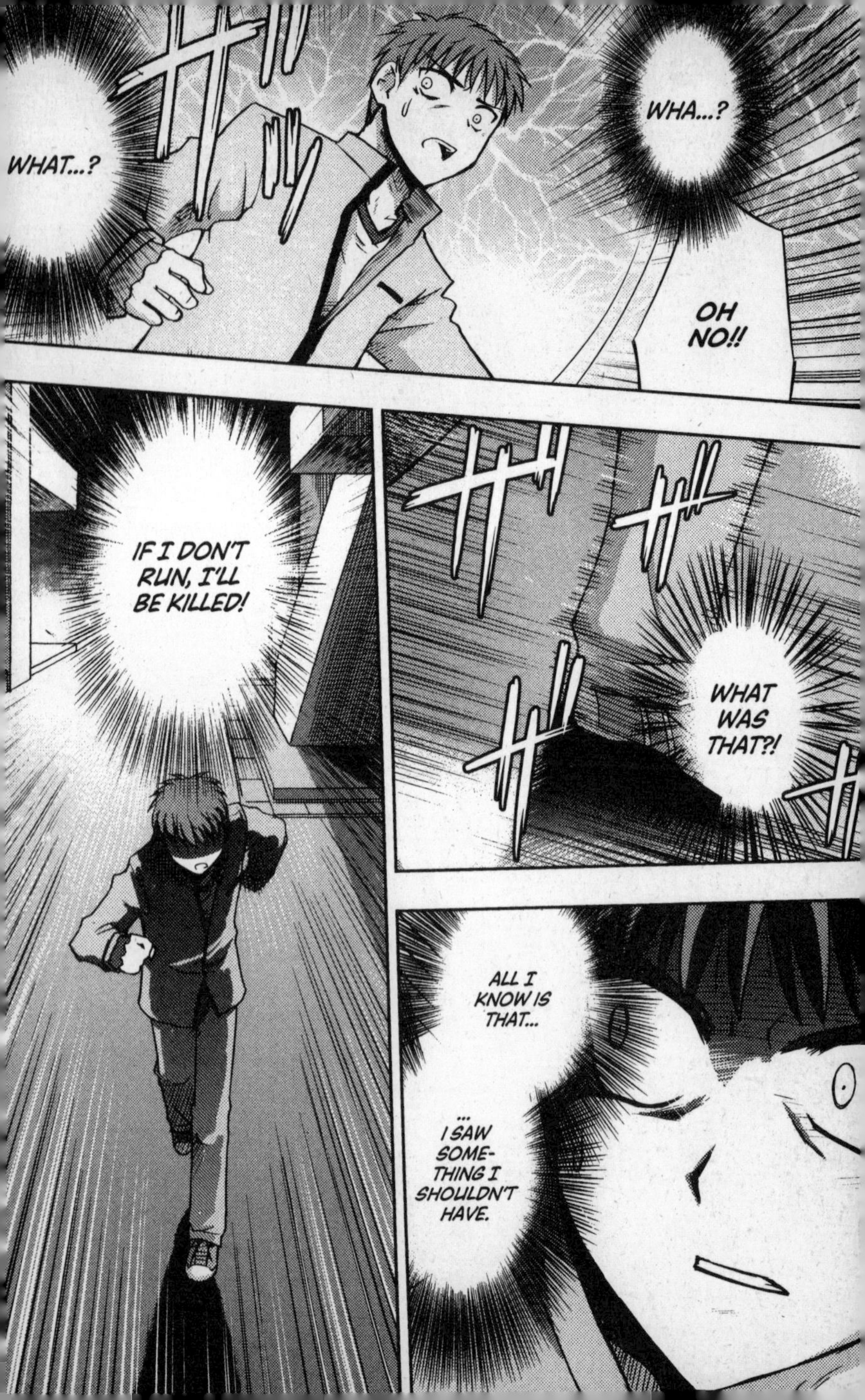
WHA...?
WHAT...?
OH NO!!
WHAT WAS THAT?!
ALL I KNOW IS THAT...
... I SAW SOMETHING I SHOULDN'T HAVE.
IF I DON'T RUN, I'LL BE KILLED!

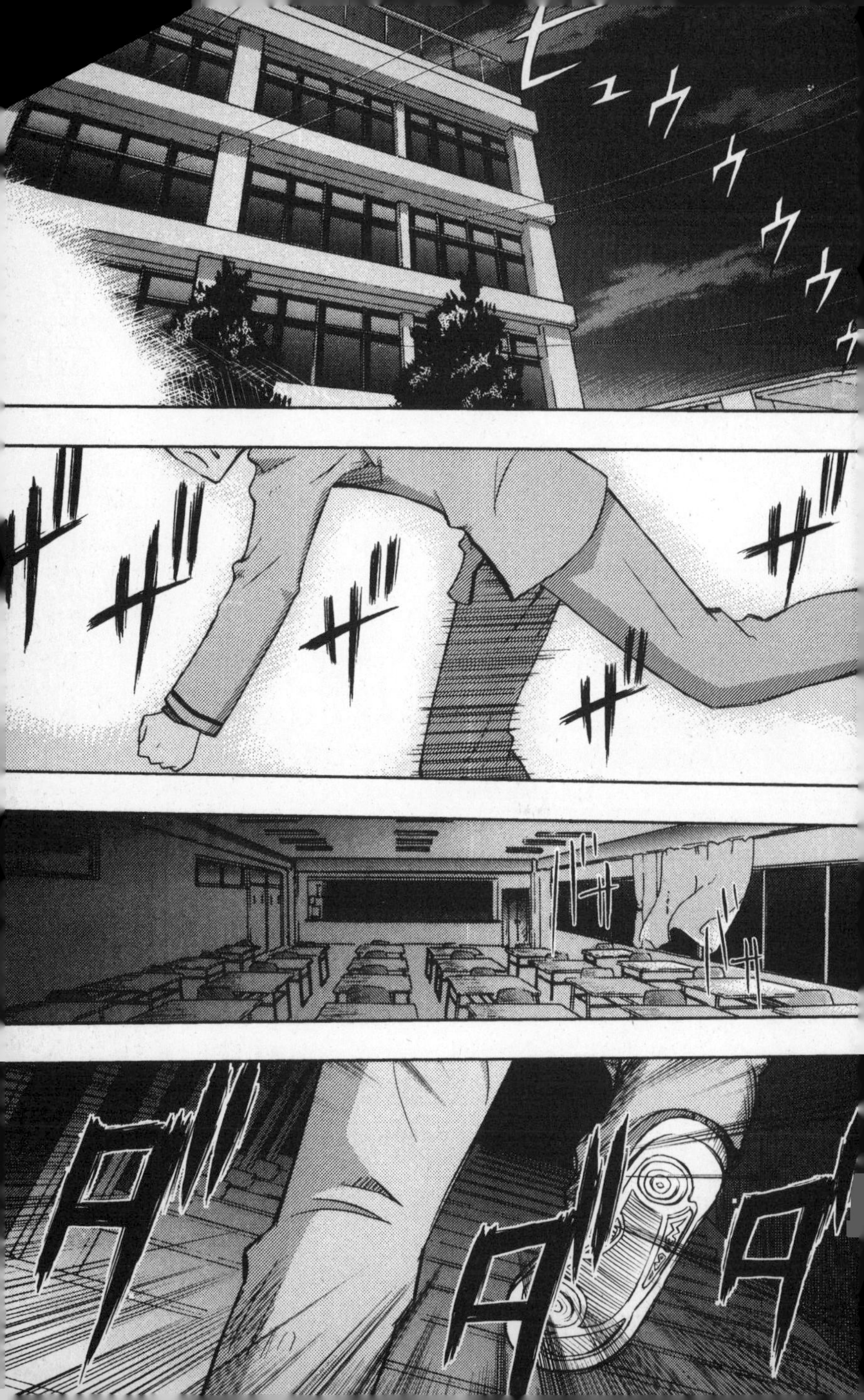

ヒュウウウウウ
ザ
ザ
ザ
ザ
ザ
ザザ
ザザ
タッ
タッ
タッ

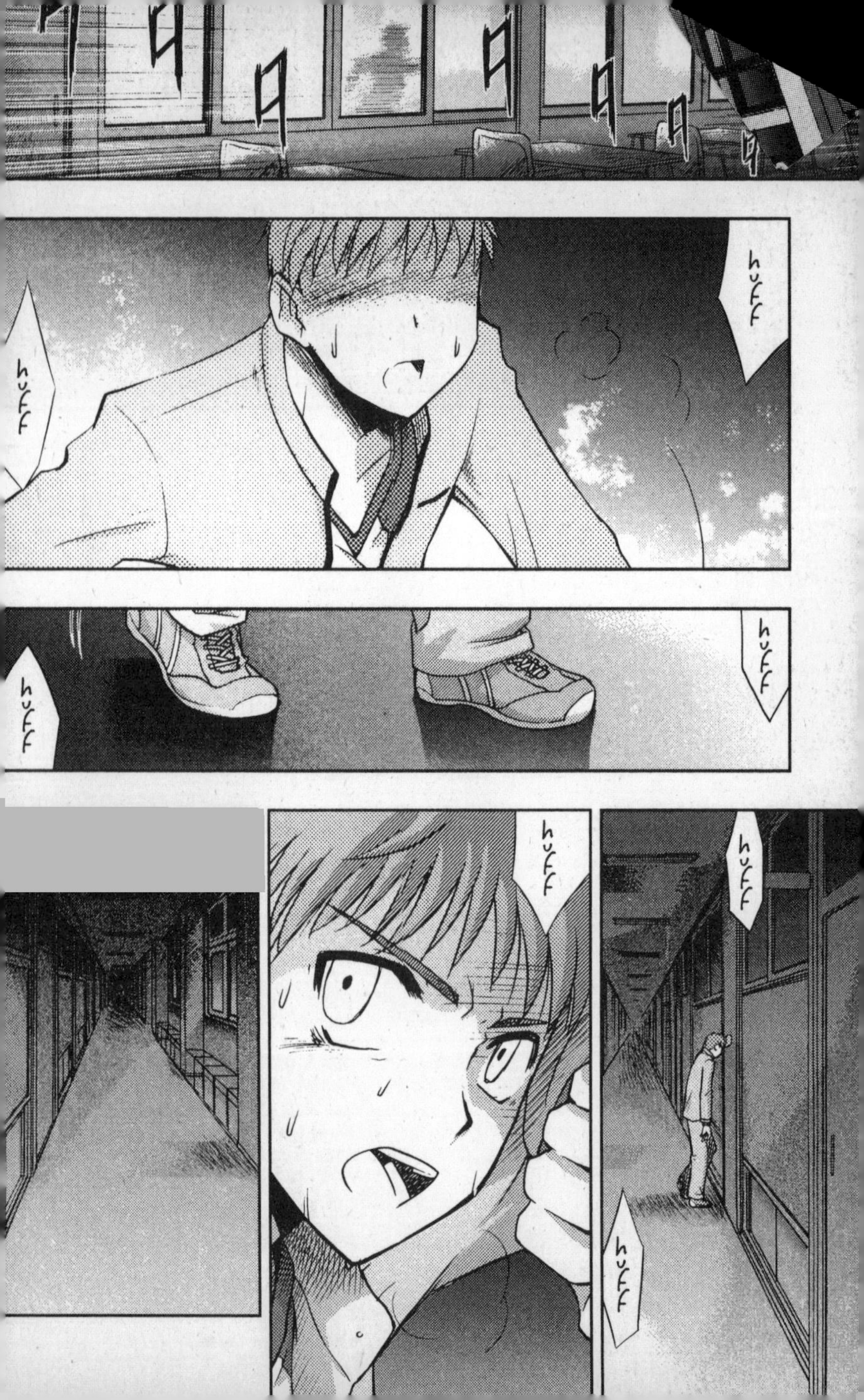
huff
huff
huff
huff
huff
huff
huff

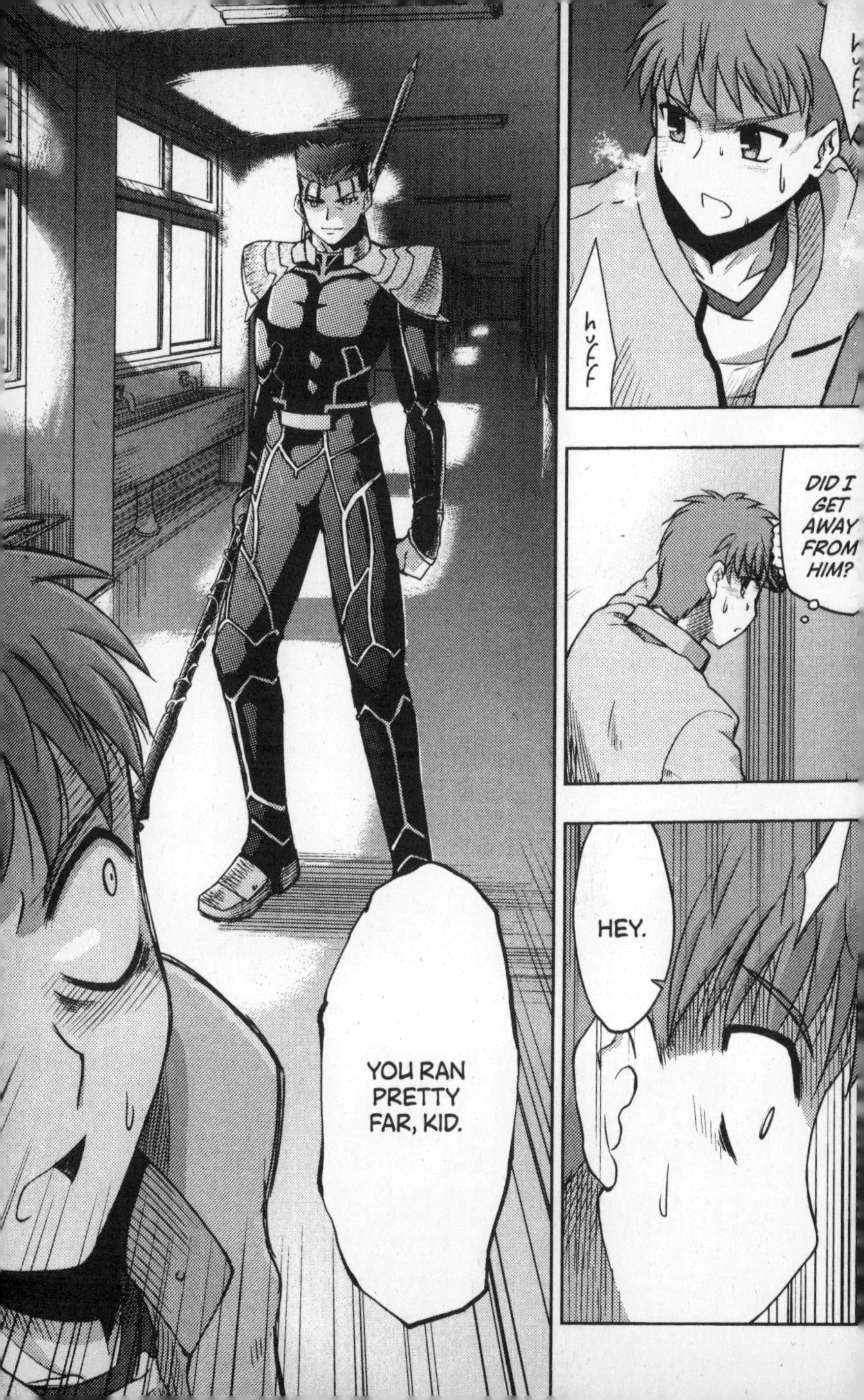
huff
huff
DID I GET AWAY FROM HIM?
HEY.
YOU RAN PRETTY FAR, KID.

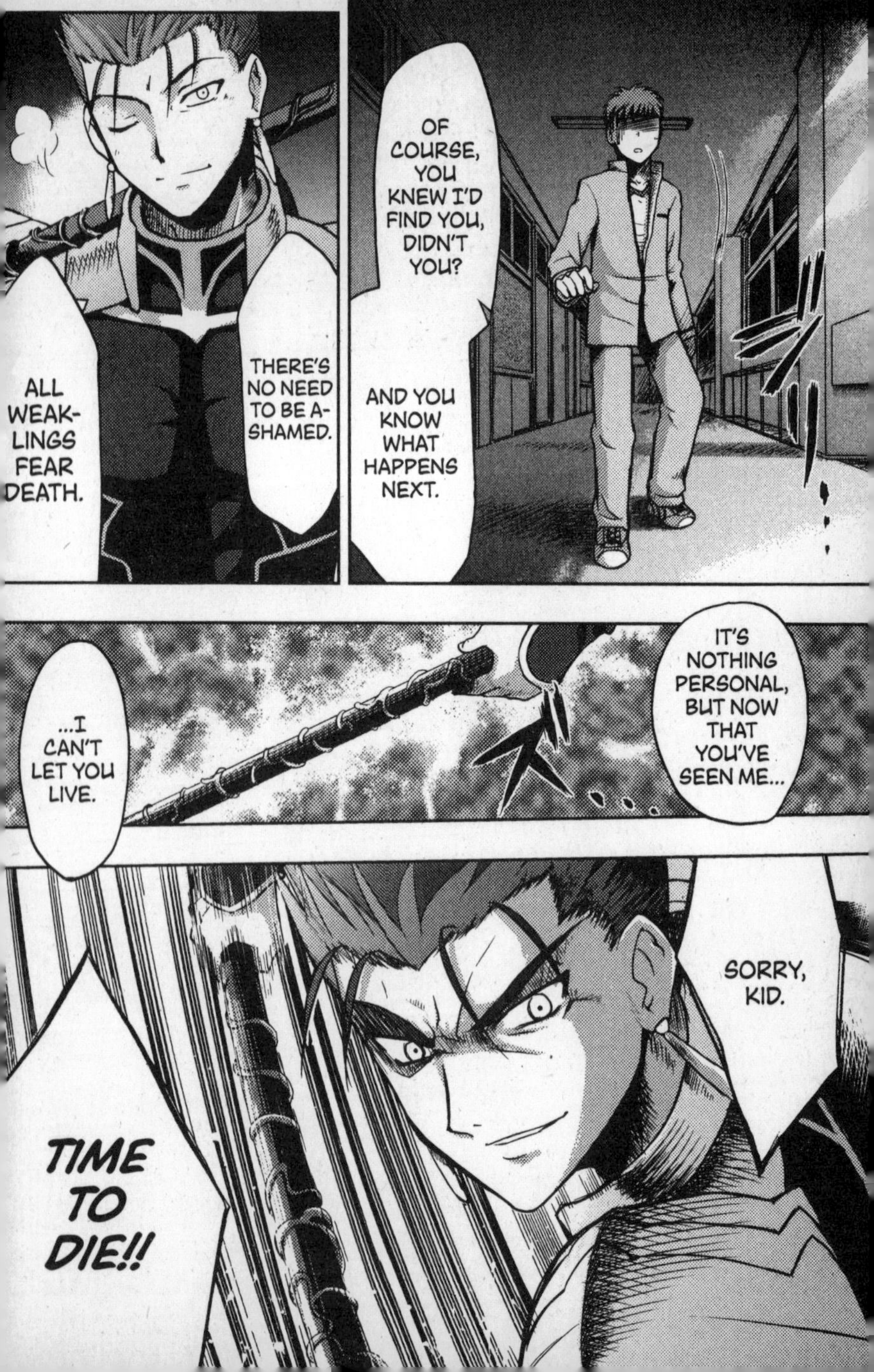
OF COURSE, YOU KNEW I'D FIND YOU, DIDN'T YOU?
AND YOU KNOW WHAT HAPPENS NEXT.
THERE'S NO NEED TO BE A-SHAMED.
ALL WEAK-LINGS FEAR DEATH.
IT'S NOTHING PERSONAL, BUT NOW THAT YOU'VE SEEN ME...
...I CAN'T LET YOU LIVE.
SORRY, KID.
TIME TO DIE!!

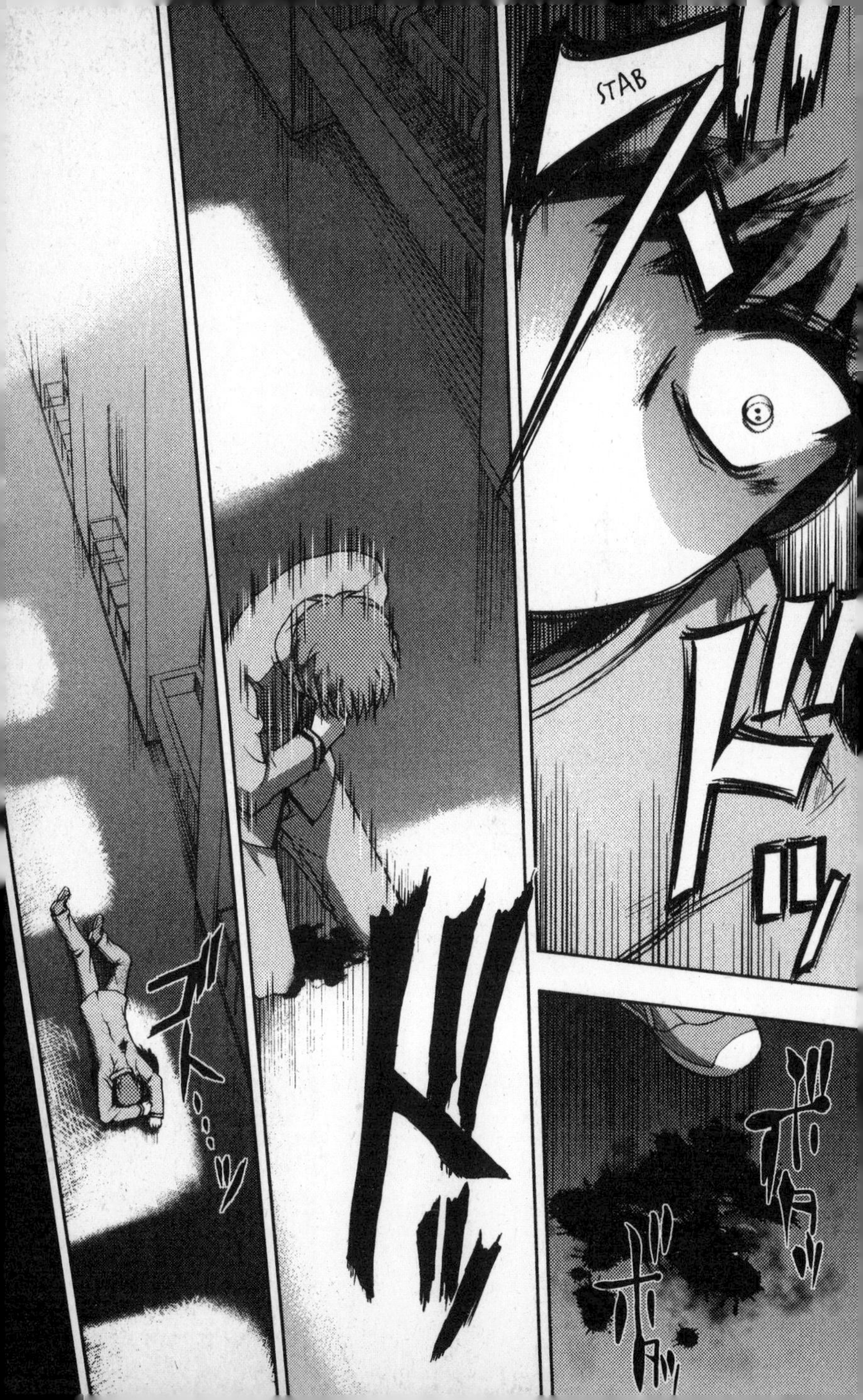
STAB

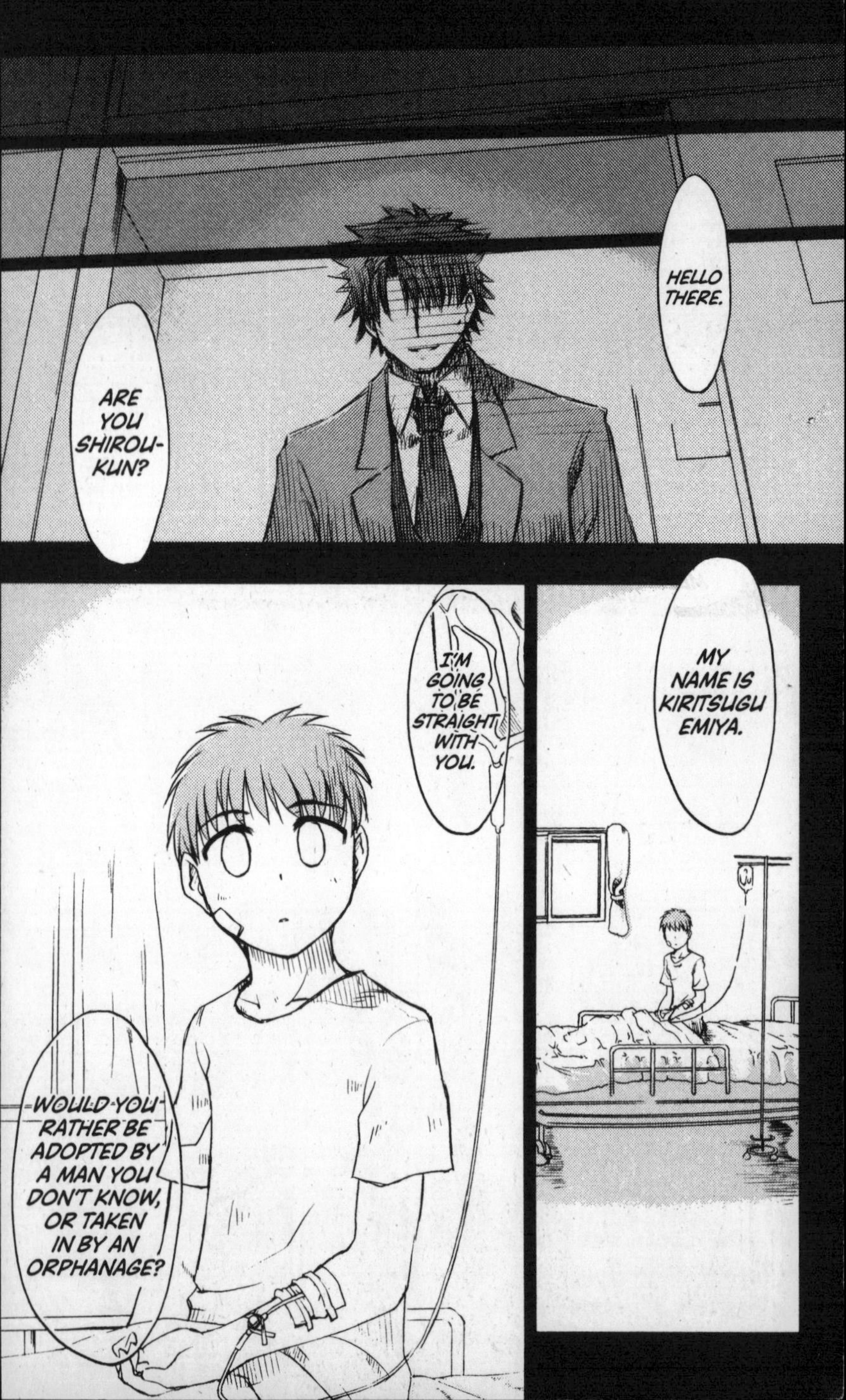
HELLO THERE.
ARE YOU SHIROU-KUN?
MY NAME IS KIRITSUGU EMIYA.
I'M GOING TO BE STRAIGHT WITH YOU.
WOULD YOU RATHER BE ADOPTED BY A MAN YOU DON'T KNOW, OR TAKEN IN BY AN ORPHANAGE?

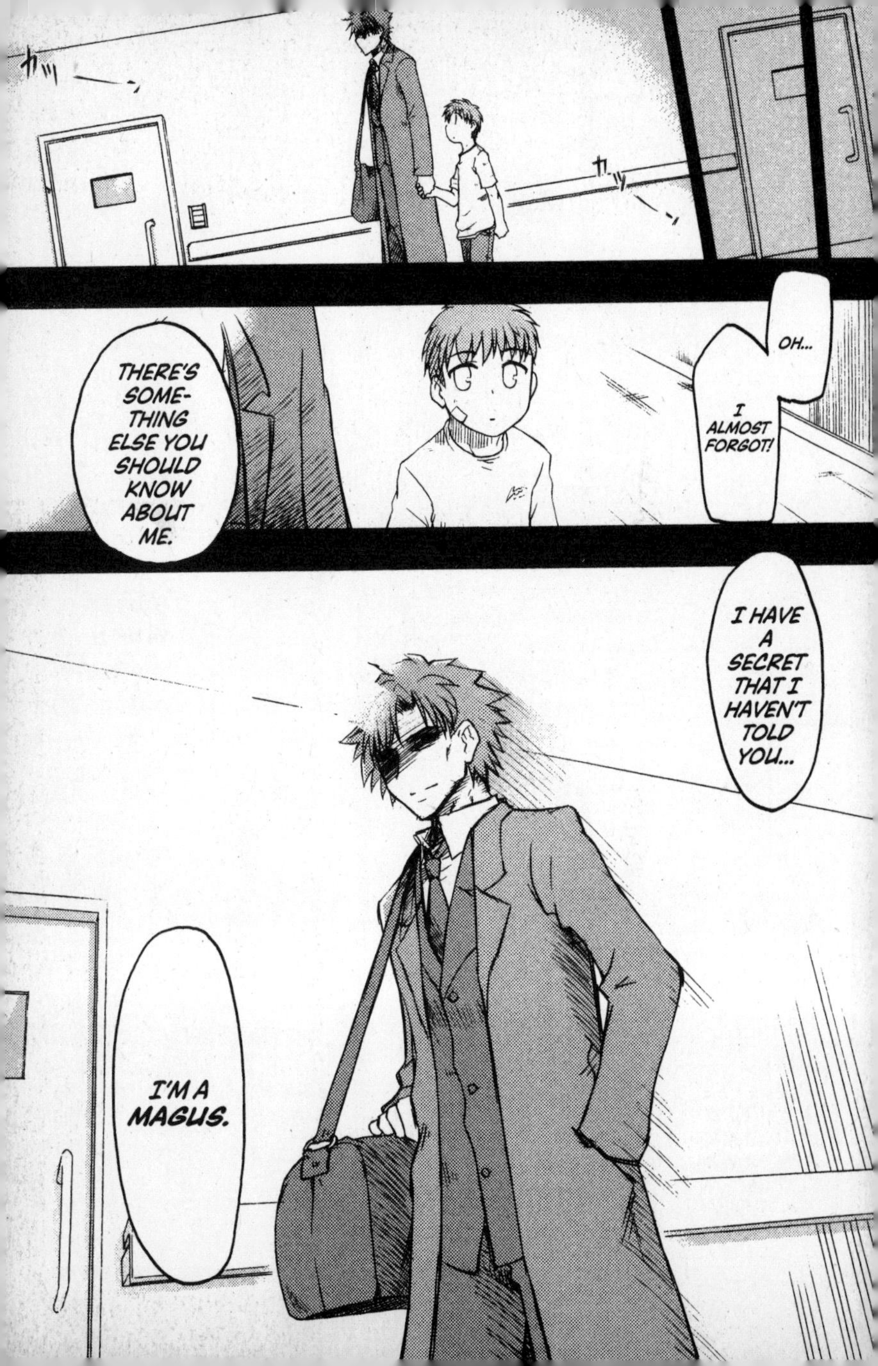
OH... I ALMOST FORGOT!
THERE'S SOME-THING ELSE YOU SHOULD KNOW ABOUT ME.
I HAVE A SECRET THAT I HAVEN'T TOLD YOU...
I'M A MAGUS.

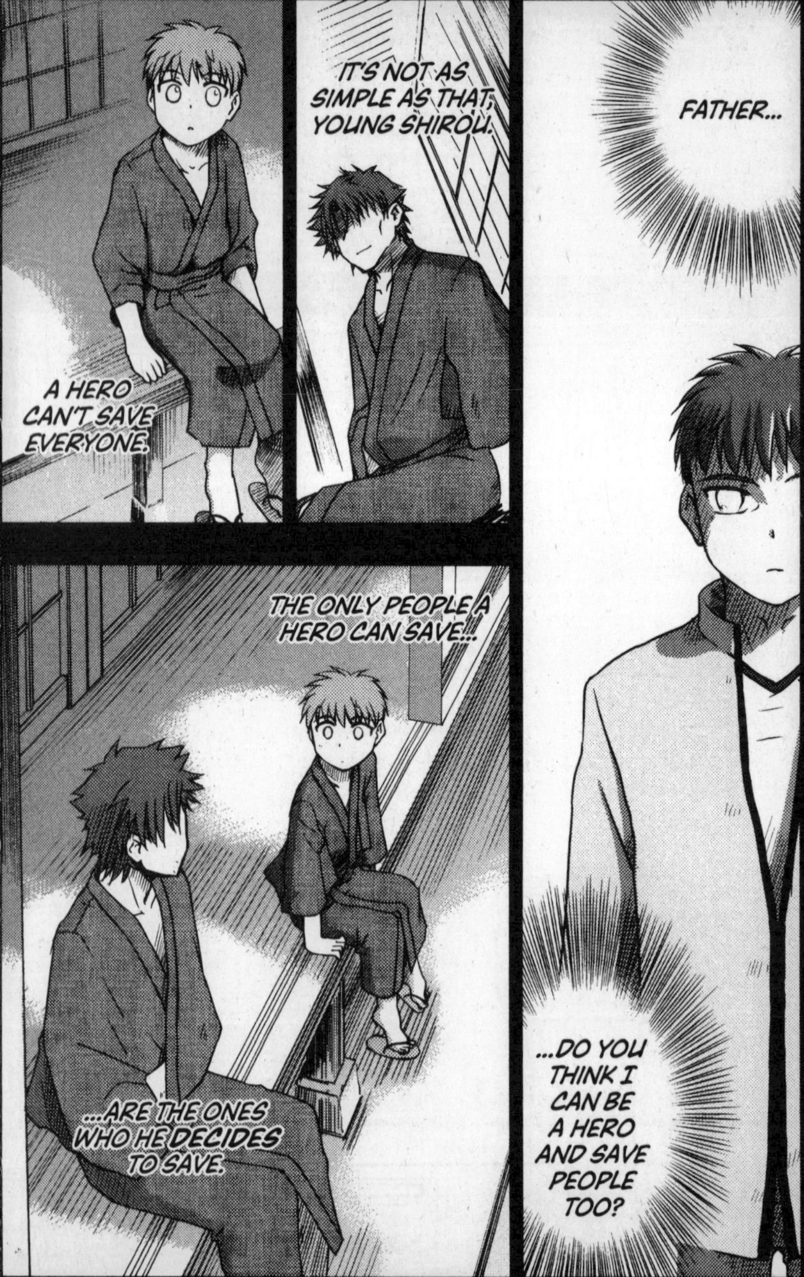
FATHER...
...DO YOU THINK I CAN BE A HERO AND SAVE PEOPLE TOO?
IT'S NOT AS SIMPLE AS THAT, YOUNG SHIROU.
A HERO CAN'T SAVE EVERYONE.
THE ONLY PEOPLE A HERO CAN SAVE...
...ARE THE ONES WHO HE DECIDES TO SAVE.

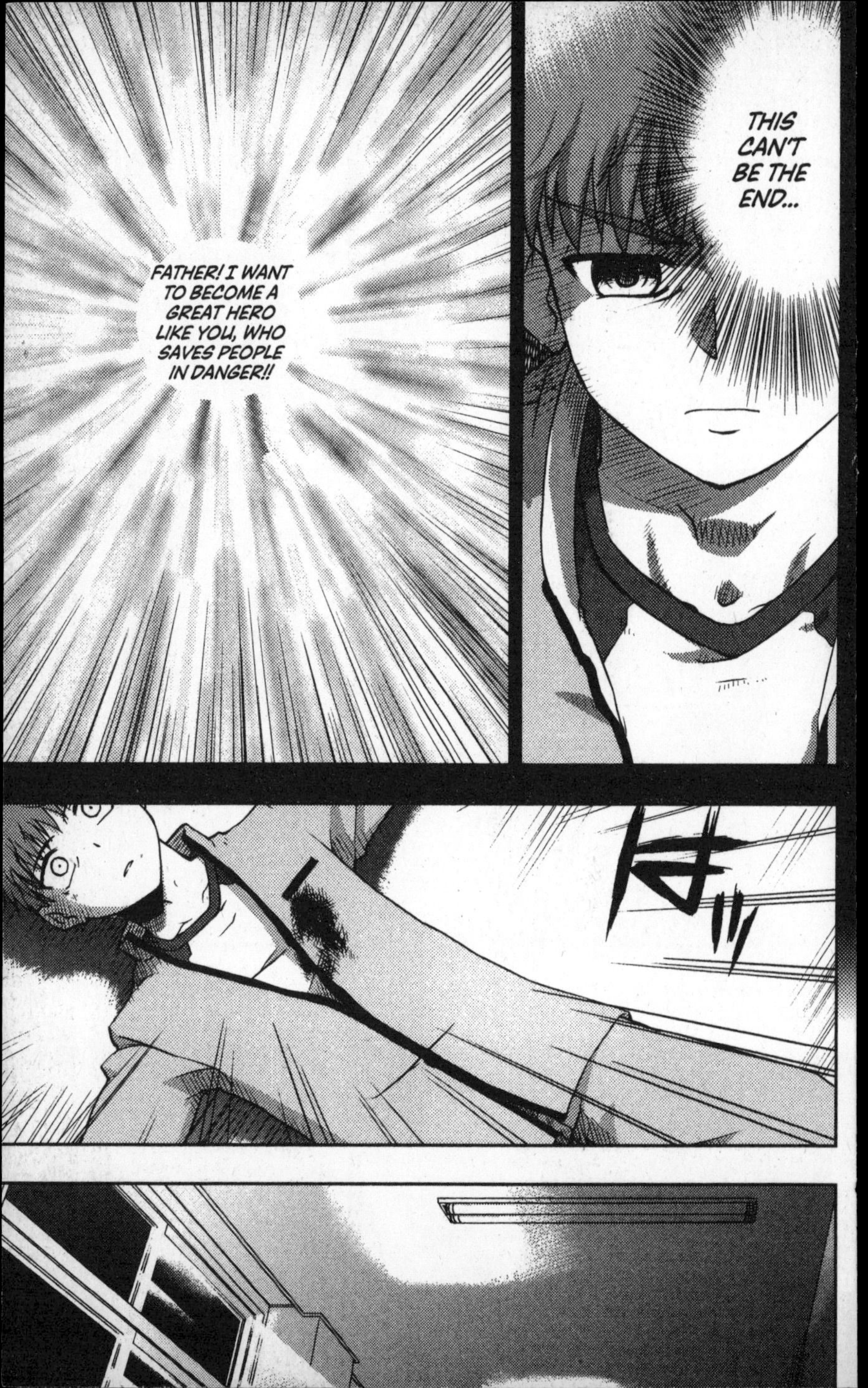
THIS CAN'T BE THE END...
FATHER! I WANT TO BECOME A GREAT HERO LIKE YOU, WHO SAVES PEOPLE IN DANGER!!
はッ

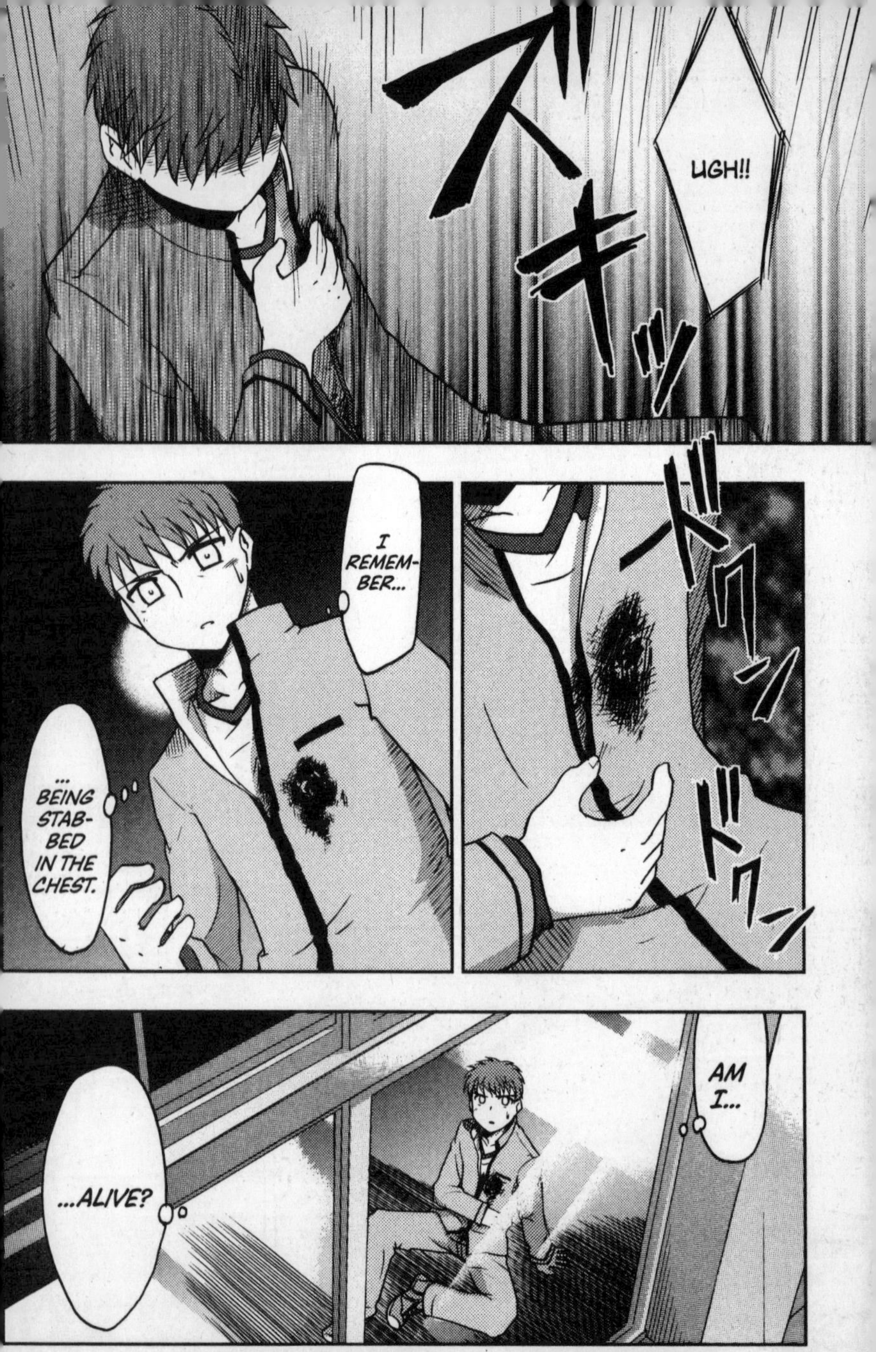
ズキッ
UGH!!
ドクン
ドクン
I REMEMBER...
...BEING STABBED IN THE CHEST.
AM I...
...ALIVE?

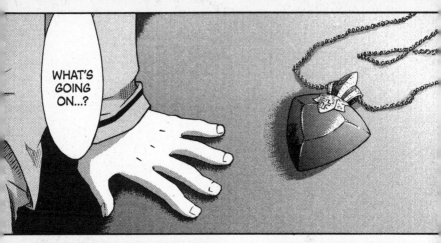

WHAT'S GOING ON...?

I'VE GOT TO GO HOME.

EVERY- THING WILL FALL INTO PLACE AFTER THAT...

HOME ...

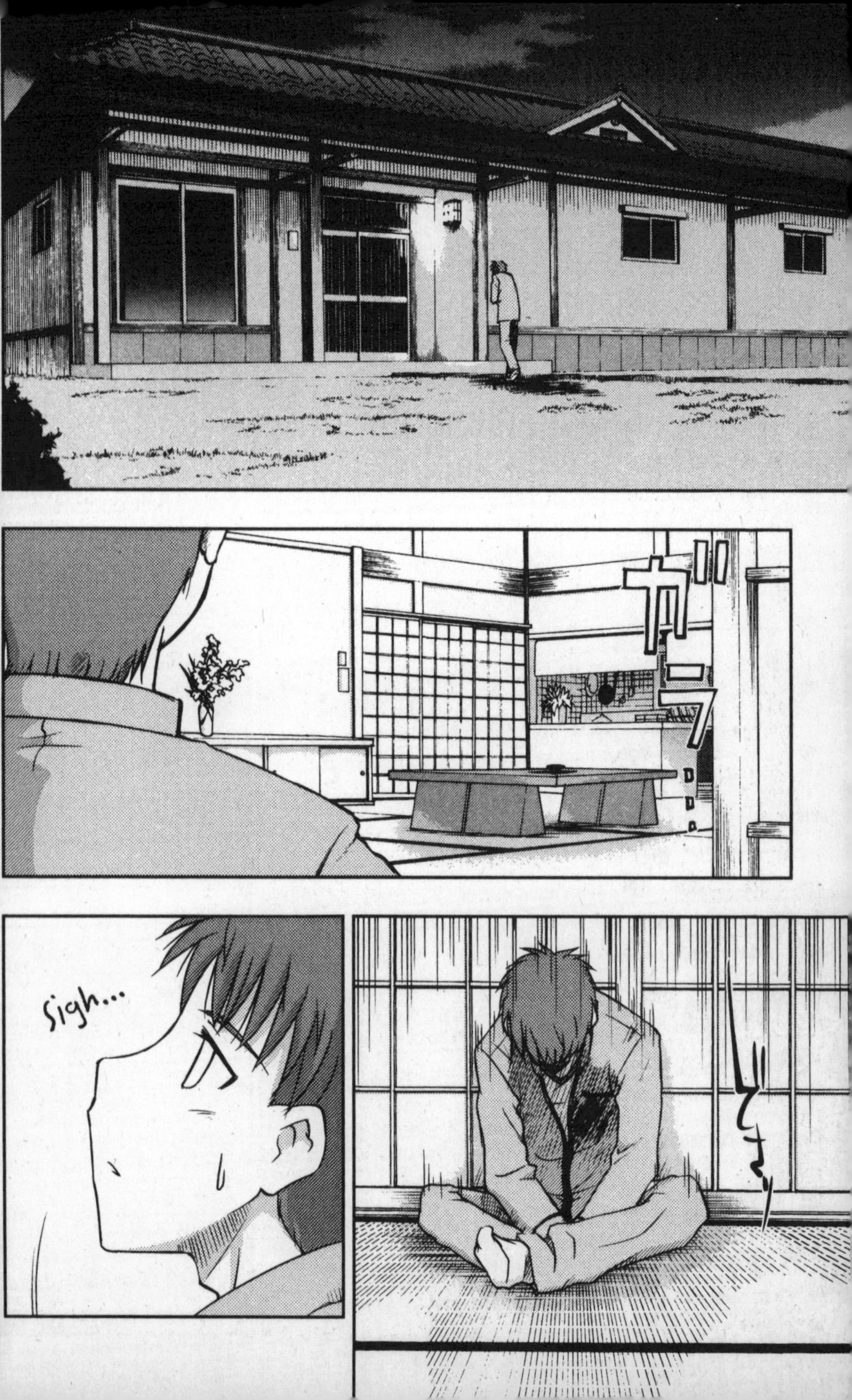
Sigh...

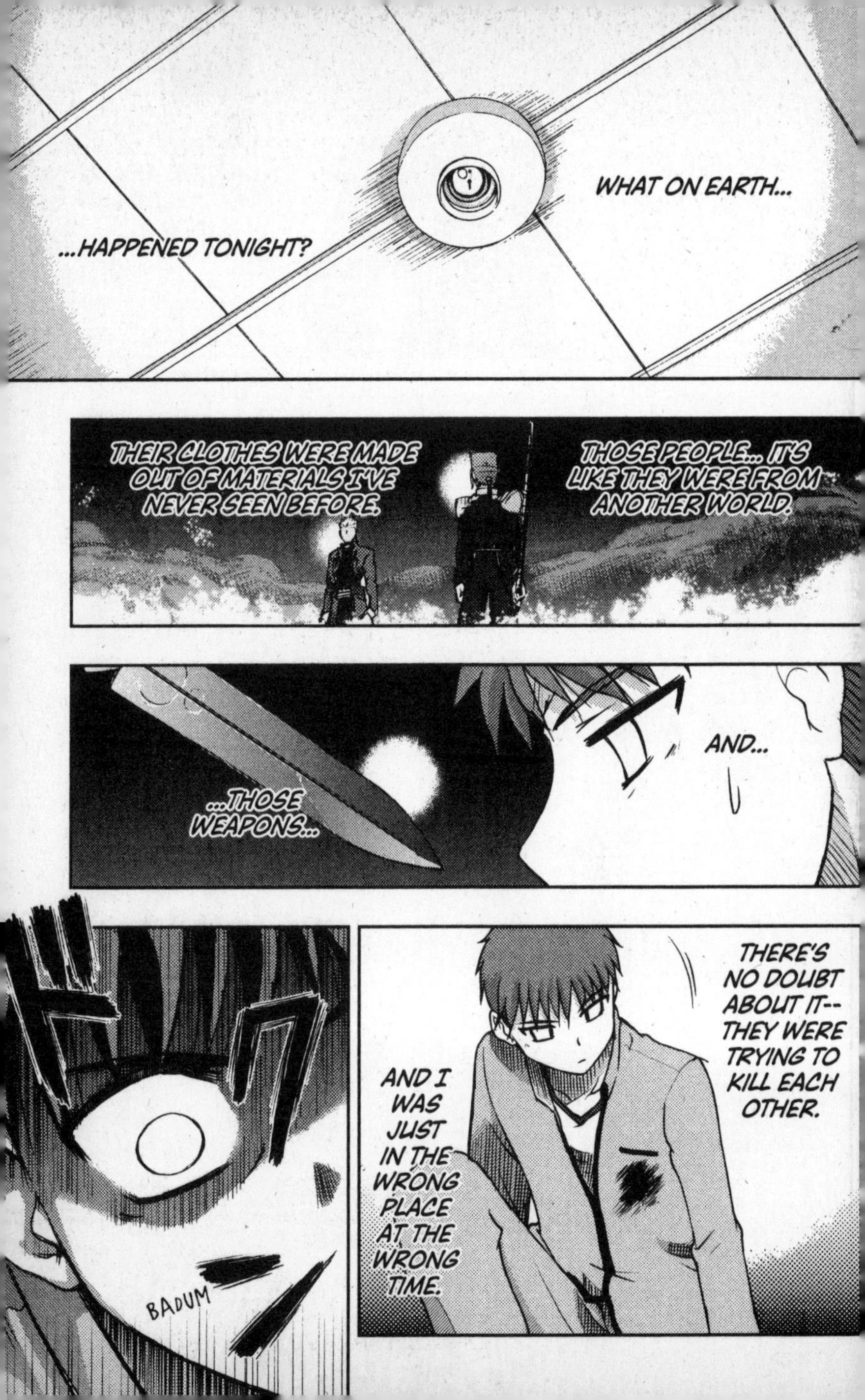
WHAT ON EARTH...
...HAPPENED TONIGHT?
THOSE PEOPLE... IT'S LIKE THEY WERE FROM ANOTHER WORLD.
THEIR CLOTHES WERE MADE OUT OF MATERIALS I'VE NEVER SEEN BEFORE.
AND...
...THOSE WEAPONS...
THERE'S NO DOUBT ABOUT IT-- THEY WERE TRYING TO KILL EACH OTHER.
AND I WAS JUST IN THE WRONG PLACE AT THE WRONG TIME.
BADUM

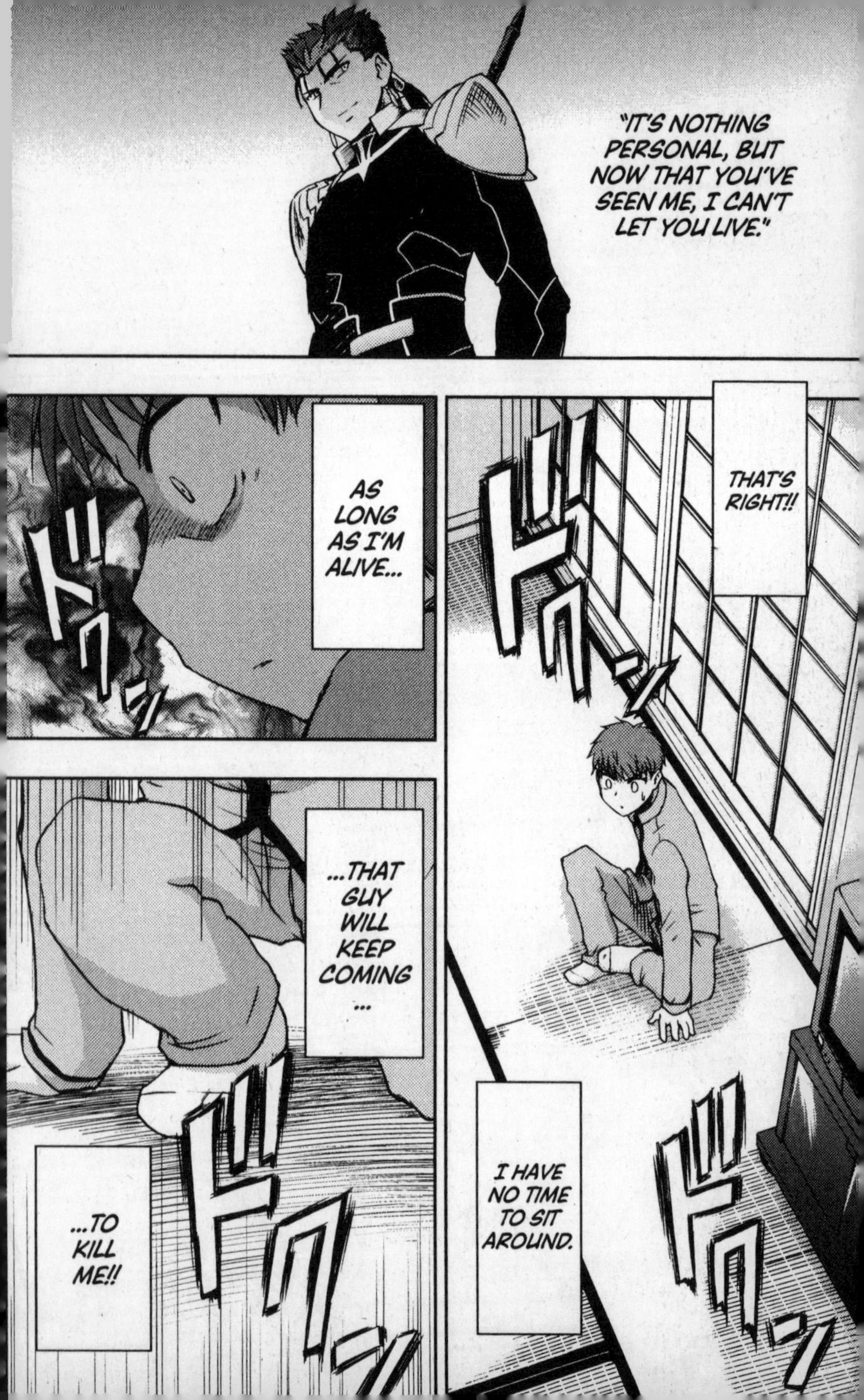
"IT'S NOTHING PERSONAL, BUT NOW THAT YOU'VE SEEN ME, I CAN'T LET YOU LIVE."
THAT'S RIGHT!!
I HAVE NO TIME TO SIT AROUND.
AS LONG AS I'M ALIVE...
...THAT GUY WILL KEEP COMING...
...TO KILL ME!!

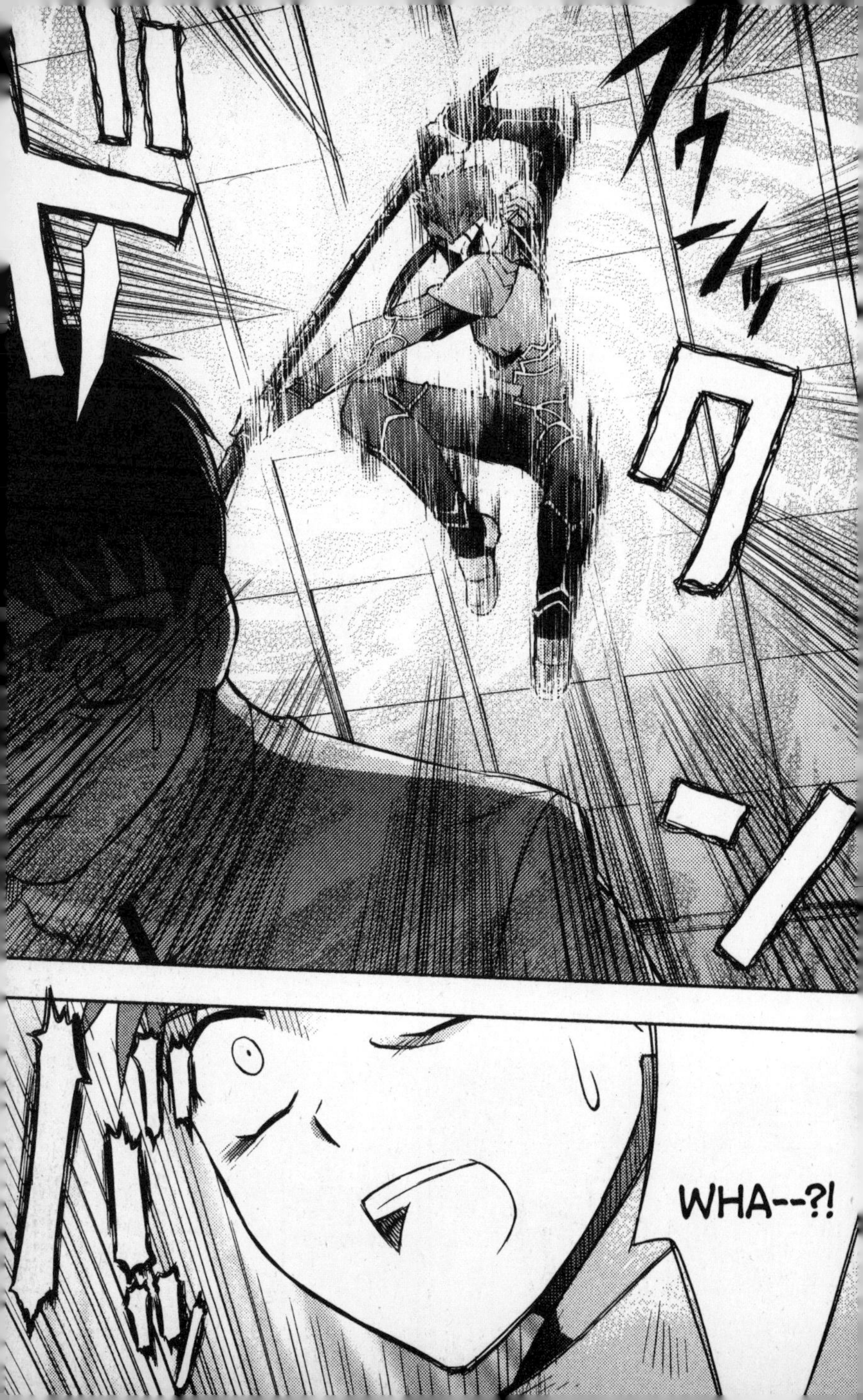
WHA--?!

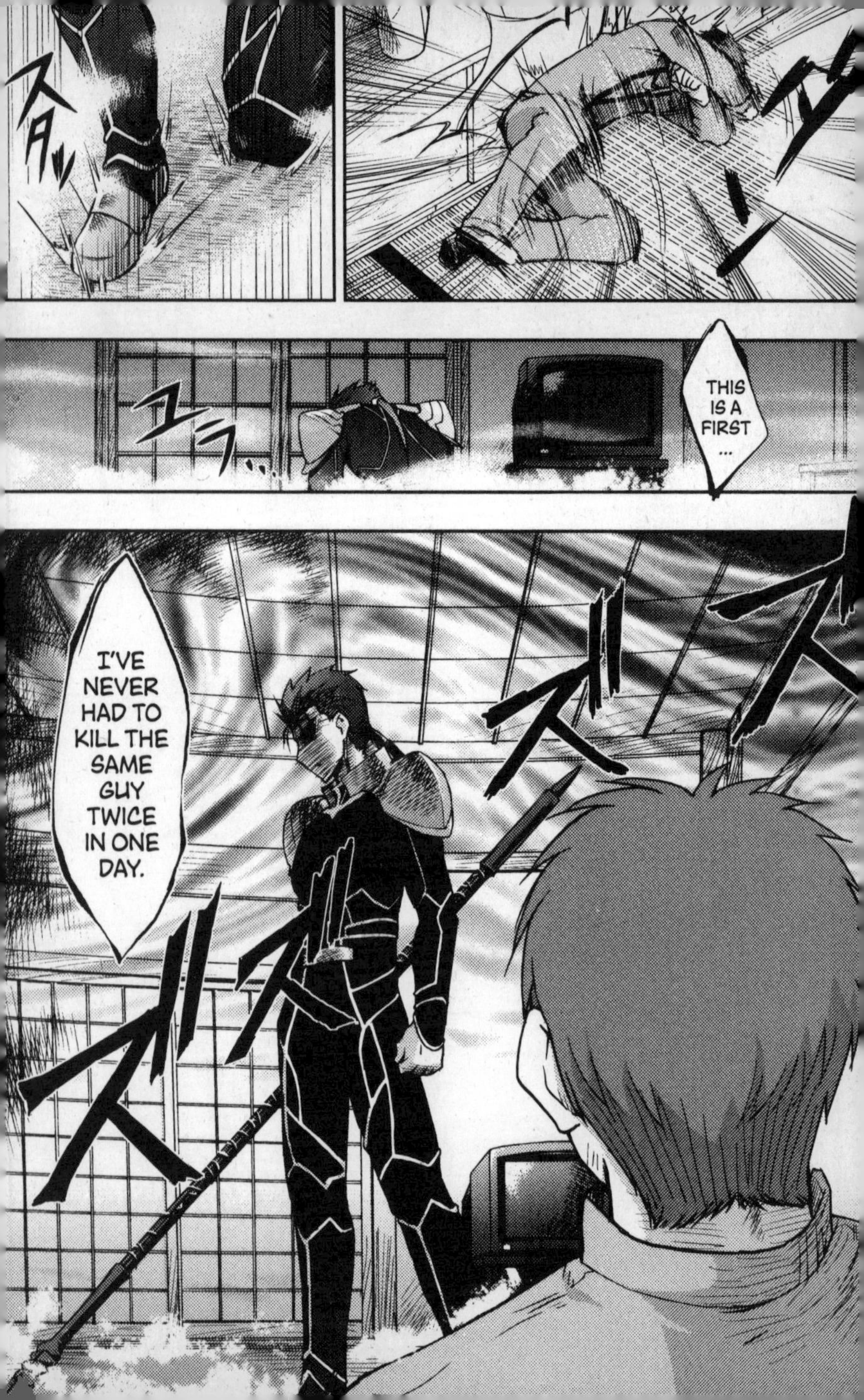
スタッ
ユラ
THIS IS A FIRST ...
I'VE NEVER HAD TO KILL THE SAME GUY TWICE IN ONE DAY.

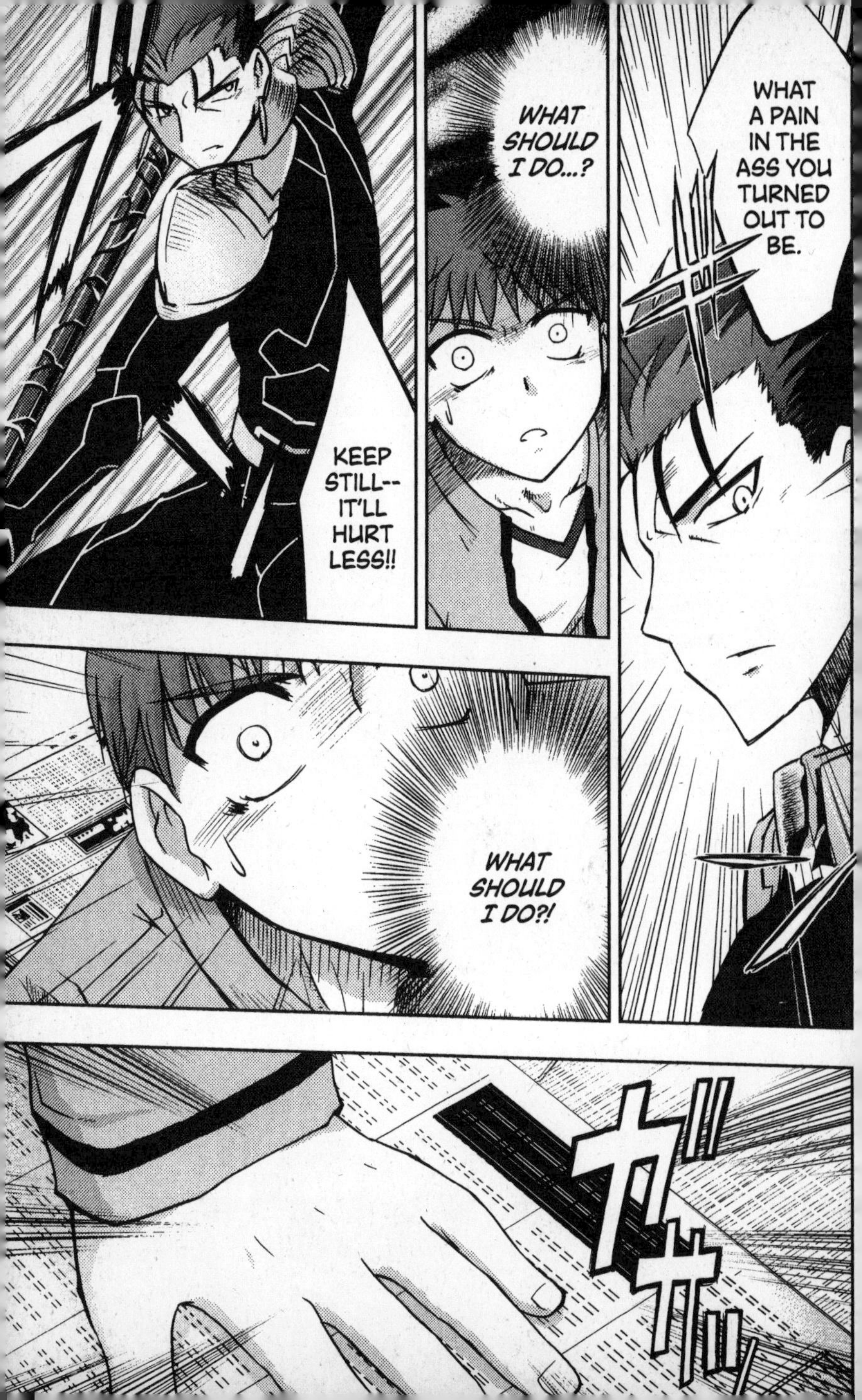
WHAT A PAIN IN THE ASS YOU TURNED OUT TO BE.
WHAT SHOULD I DO...?
KEEP STILL-- IT'LL HURT LESS!!
WHAT SHOULD I DO?!

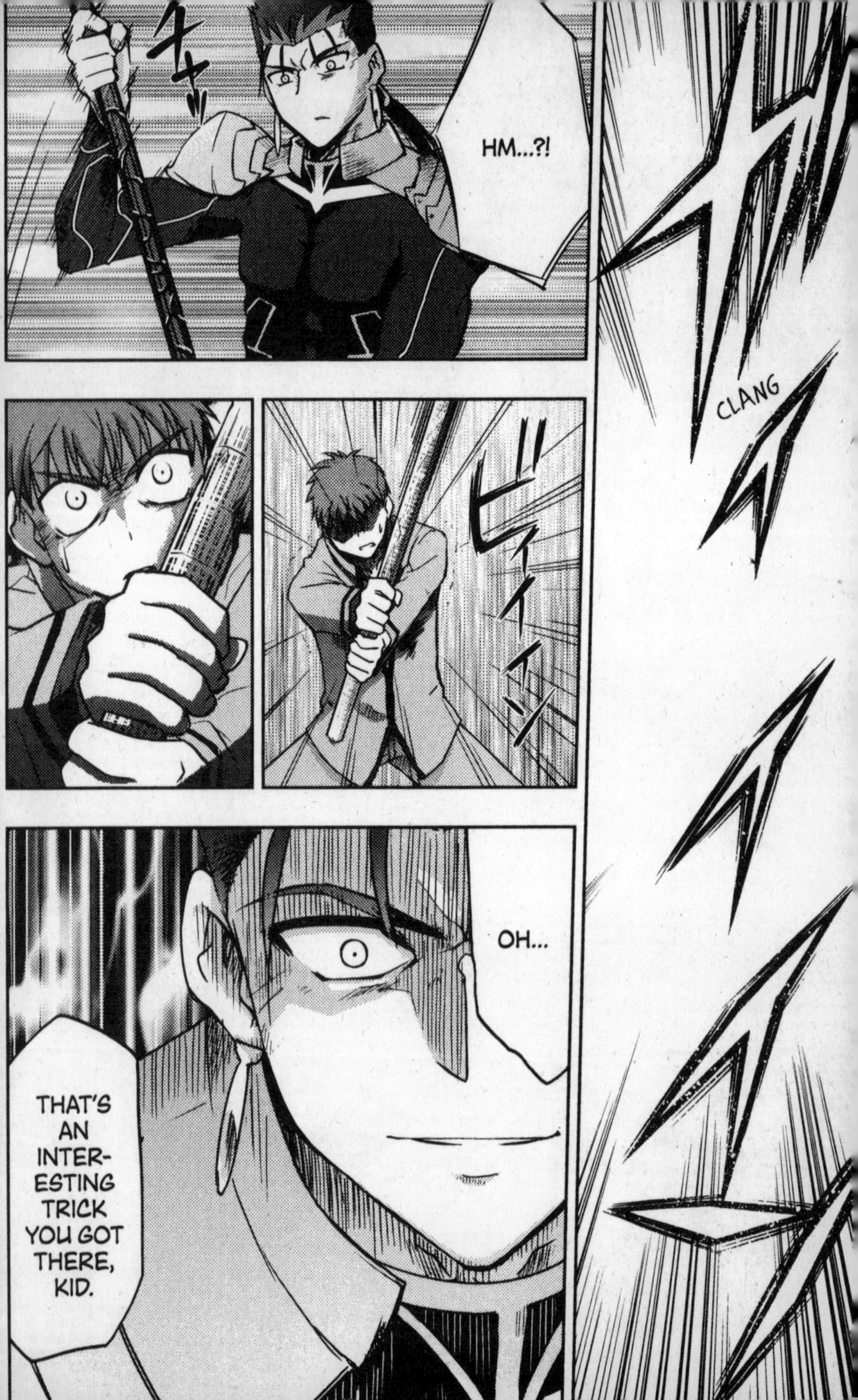
CLANG
HM...?!
OH...
THAT'S AN INTER-ESTING TRICK YOU GOT THERE, KID.

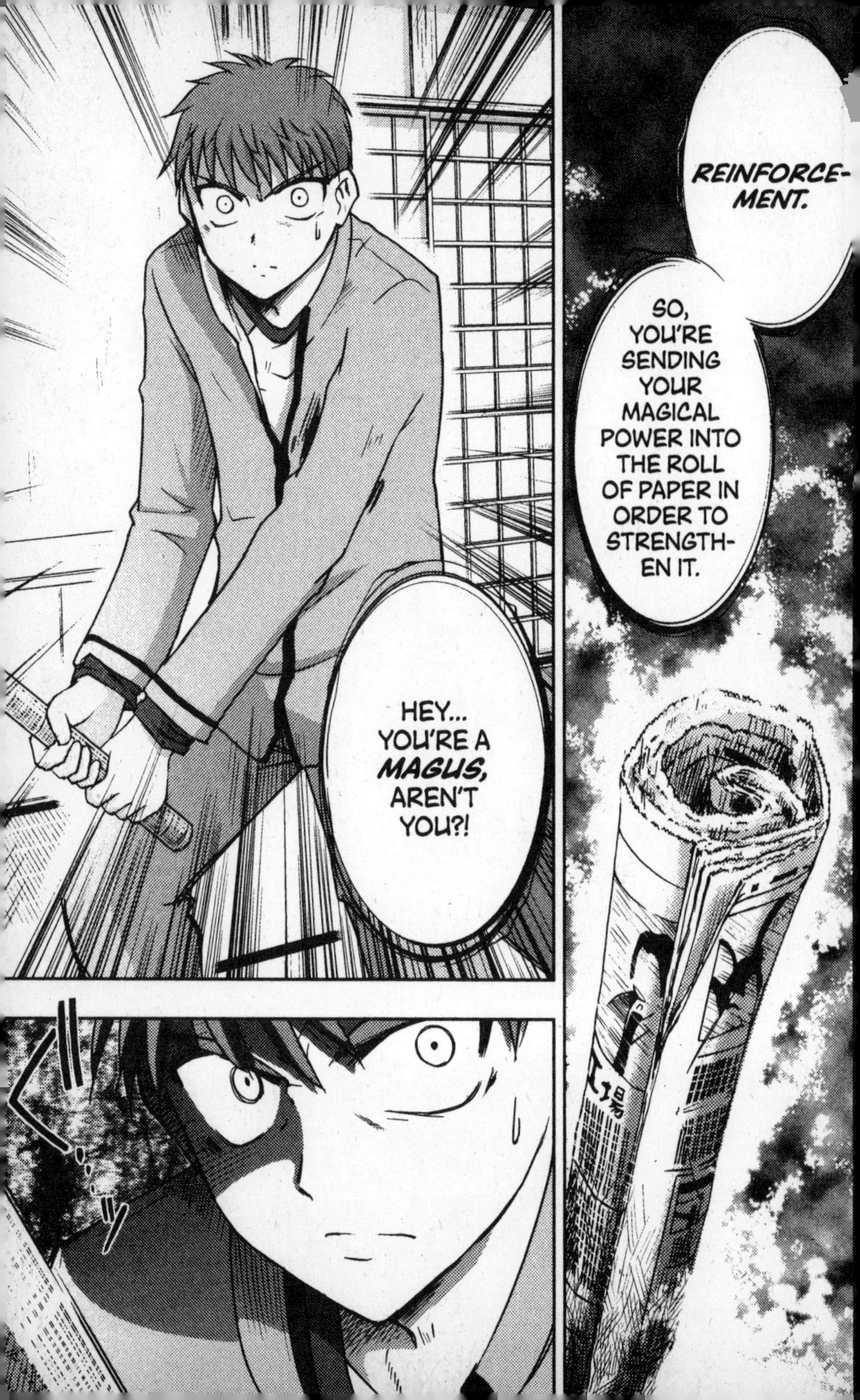
REINFORCE-MENT.
SO, YOU'RE SENDING YOUR MAGICAL POWER INTO THE ROLL OF PAPER IN ORDER TO STRENGTH-EN IT.
HEY... YOU'RE A MAGUS, AREN'T YOU?!

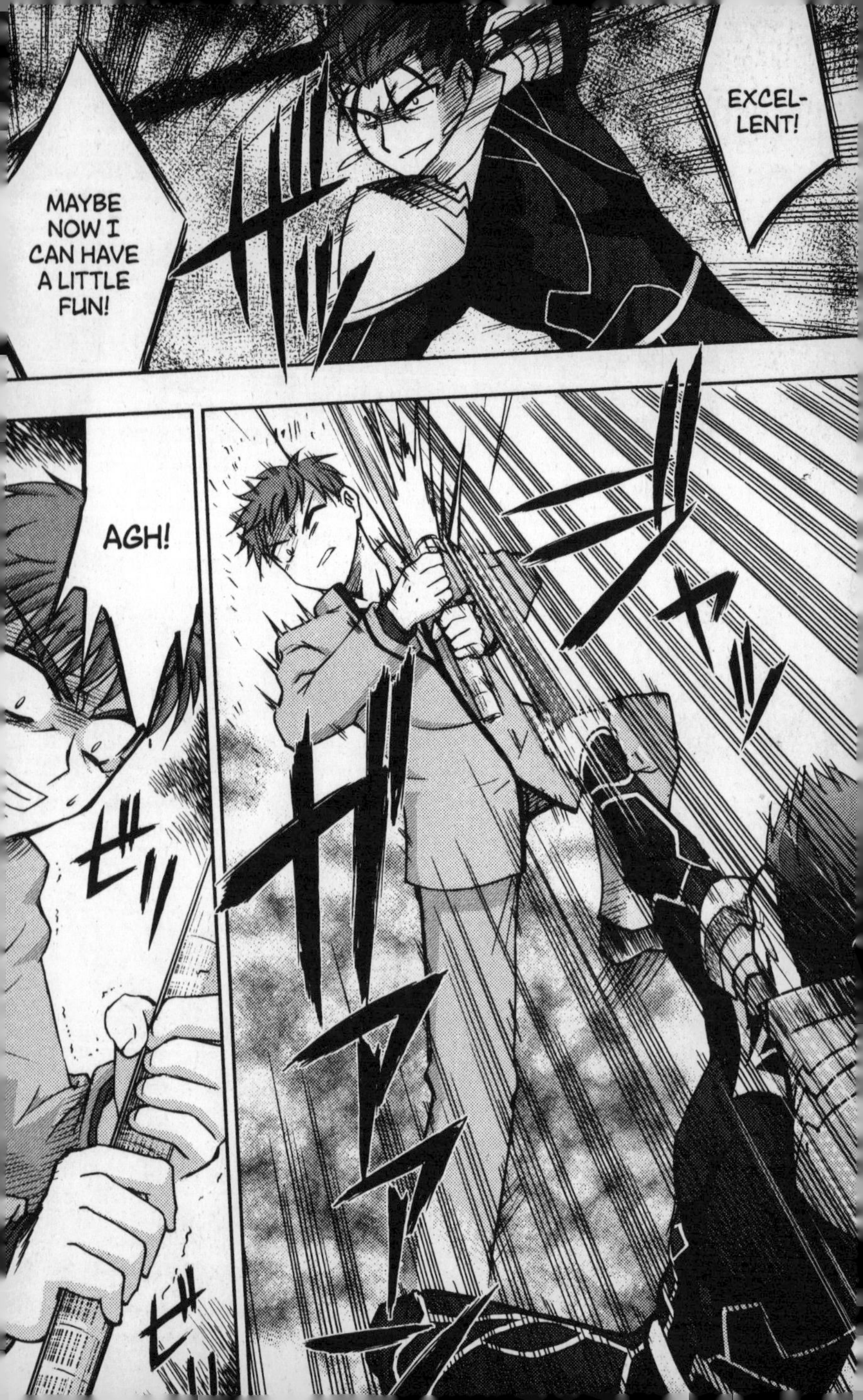
EXCEL-LENT!
MAYBE NOW I CAN HAVE A LITTLE FUN!
AGH!

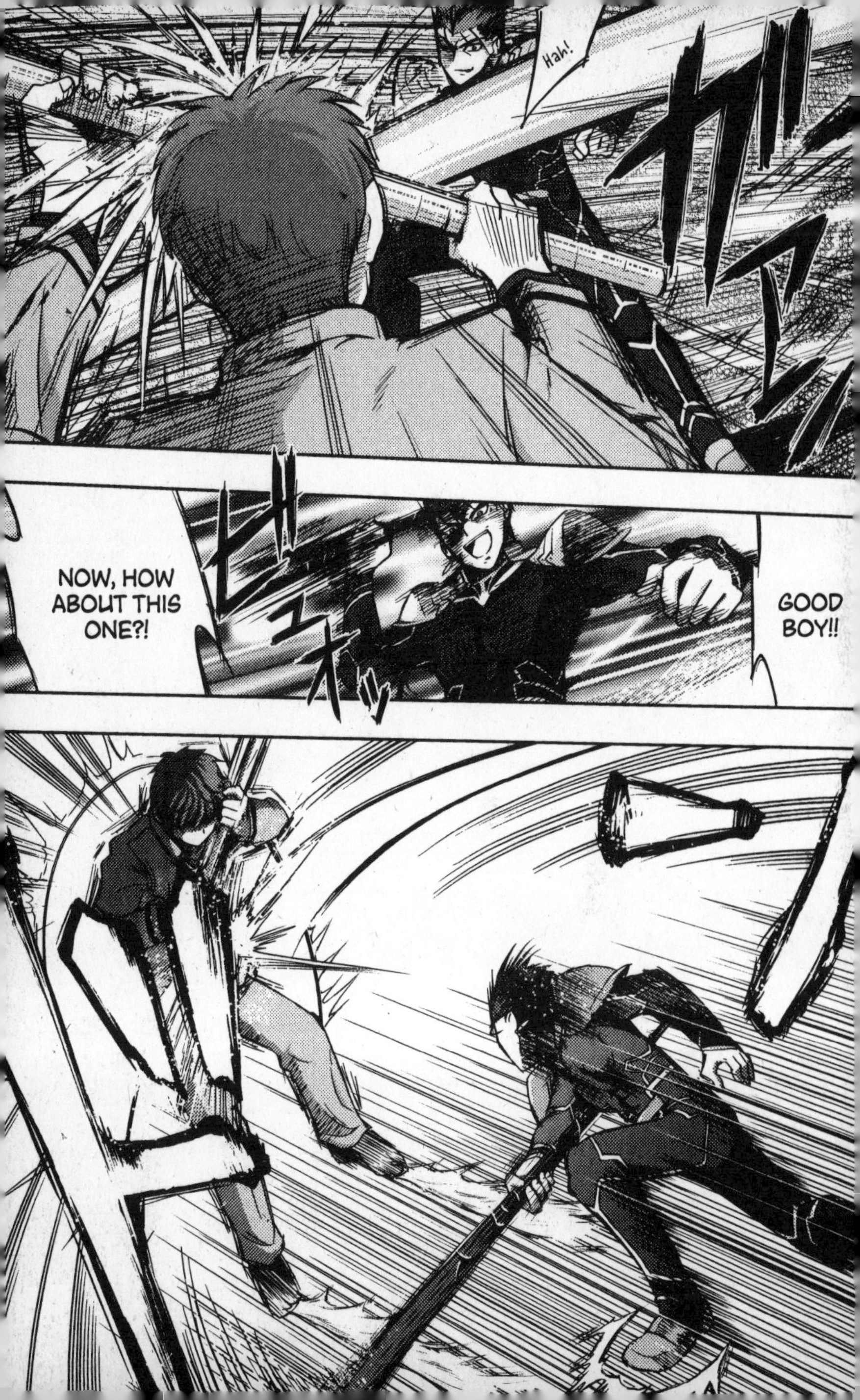
Hah!
GOOD BOY!!
NOW, HOW ABOUT THIS ONE?!

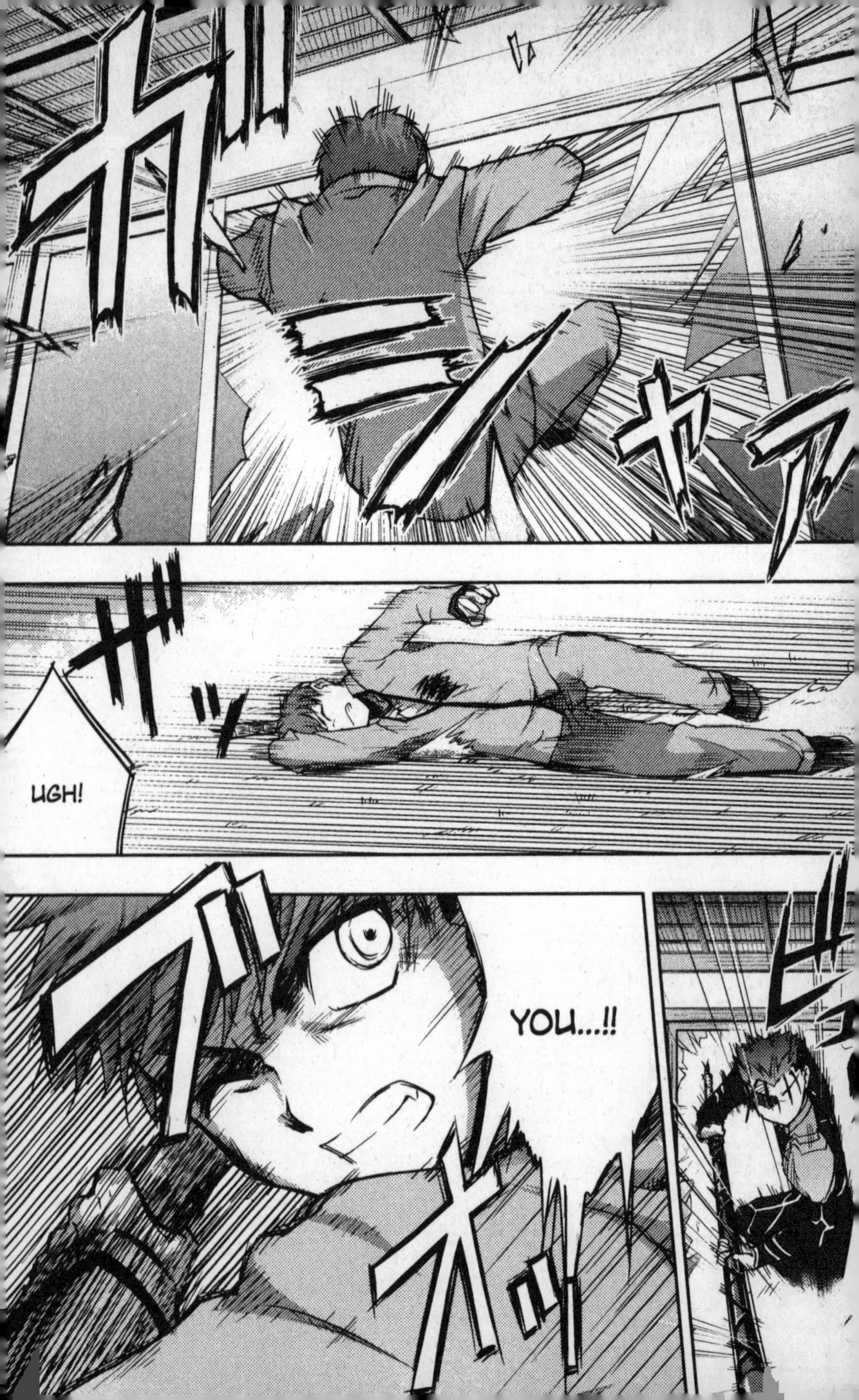
UGH!
YOU...!!

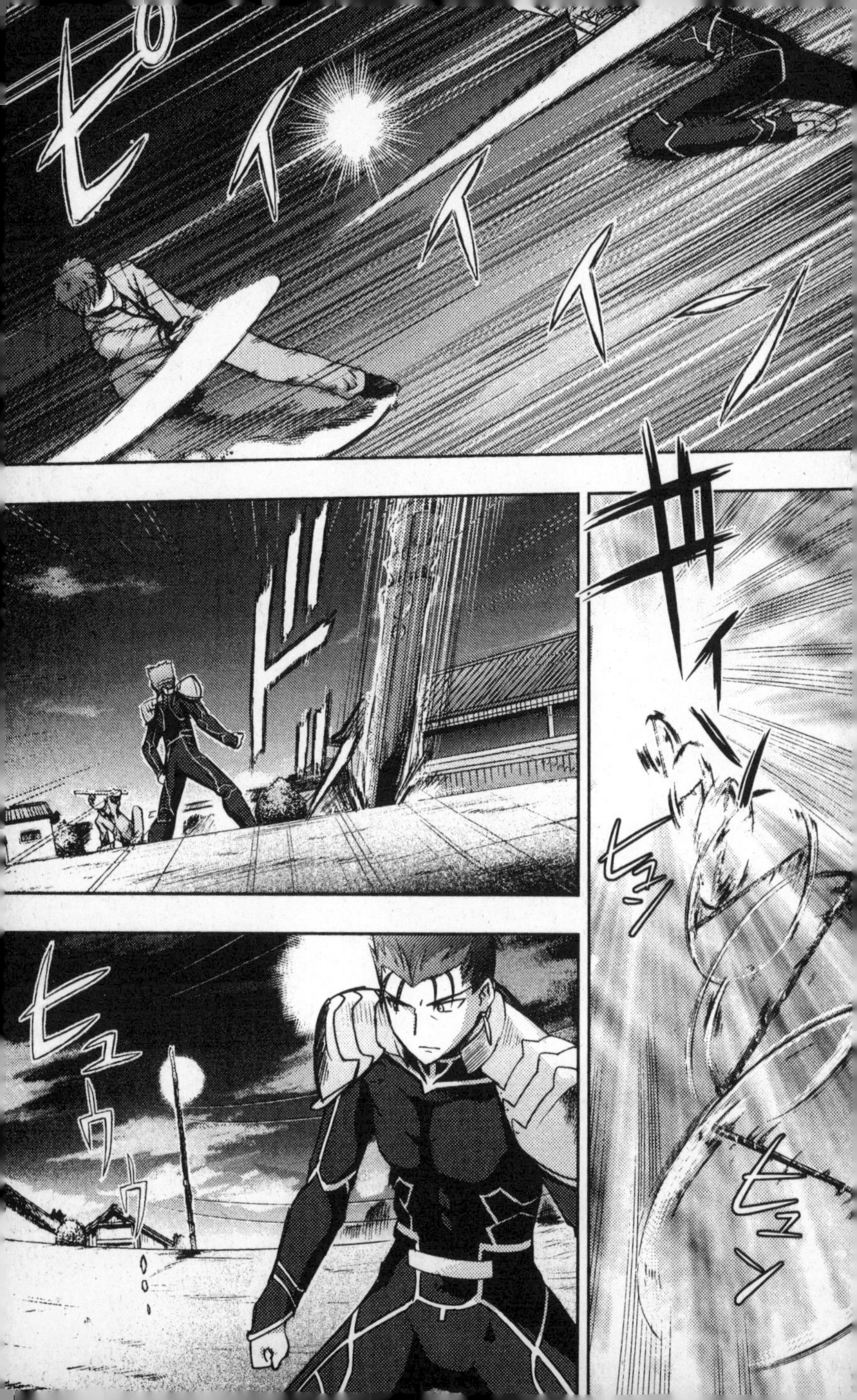
ピイイイーン
ギイーン
ヒュッ
ヒュン
ド
ヒュウウ…

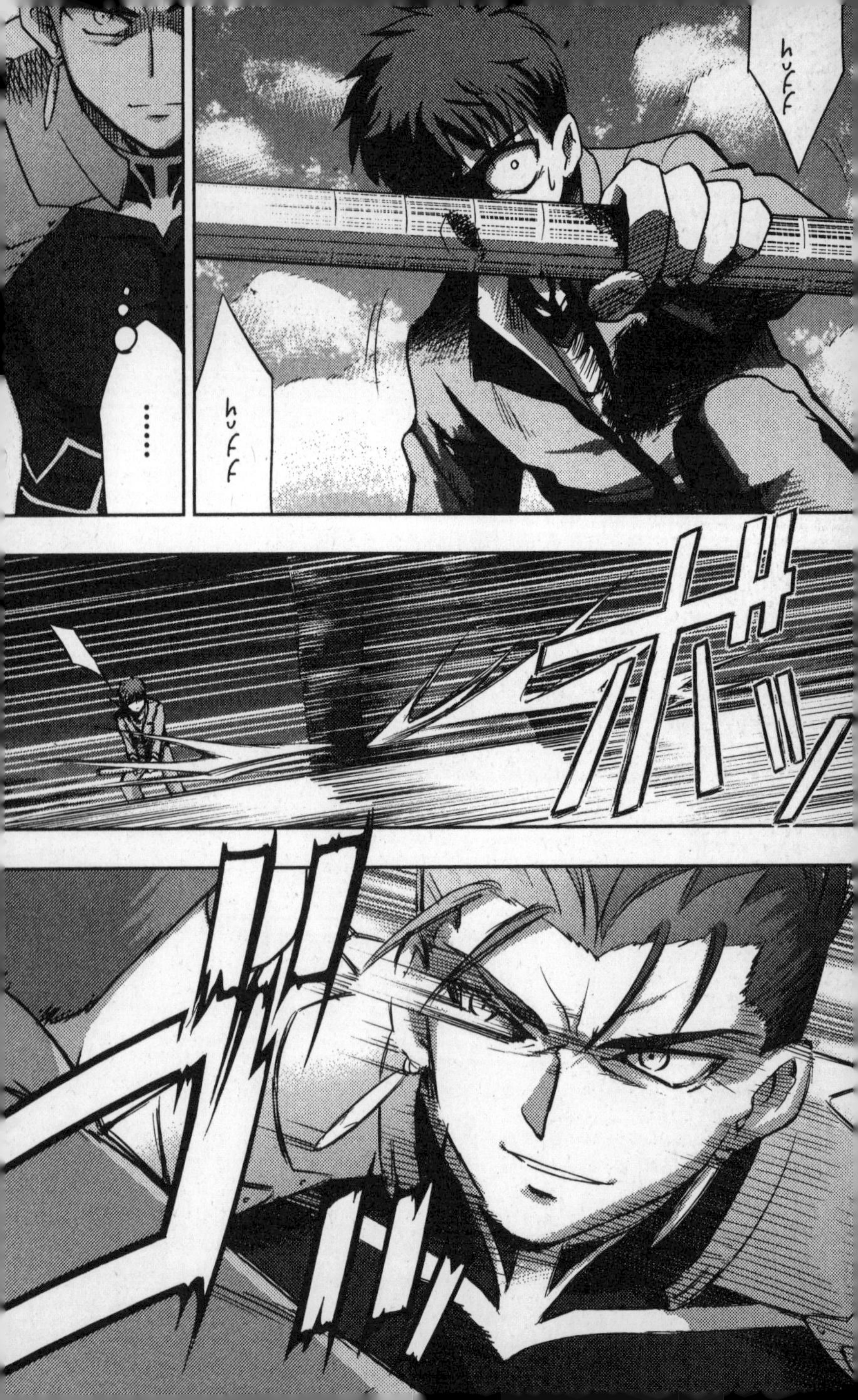
huff huff
huff huff
......

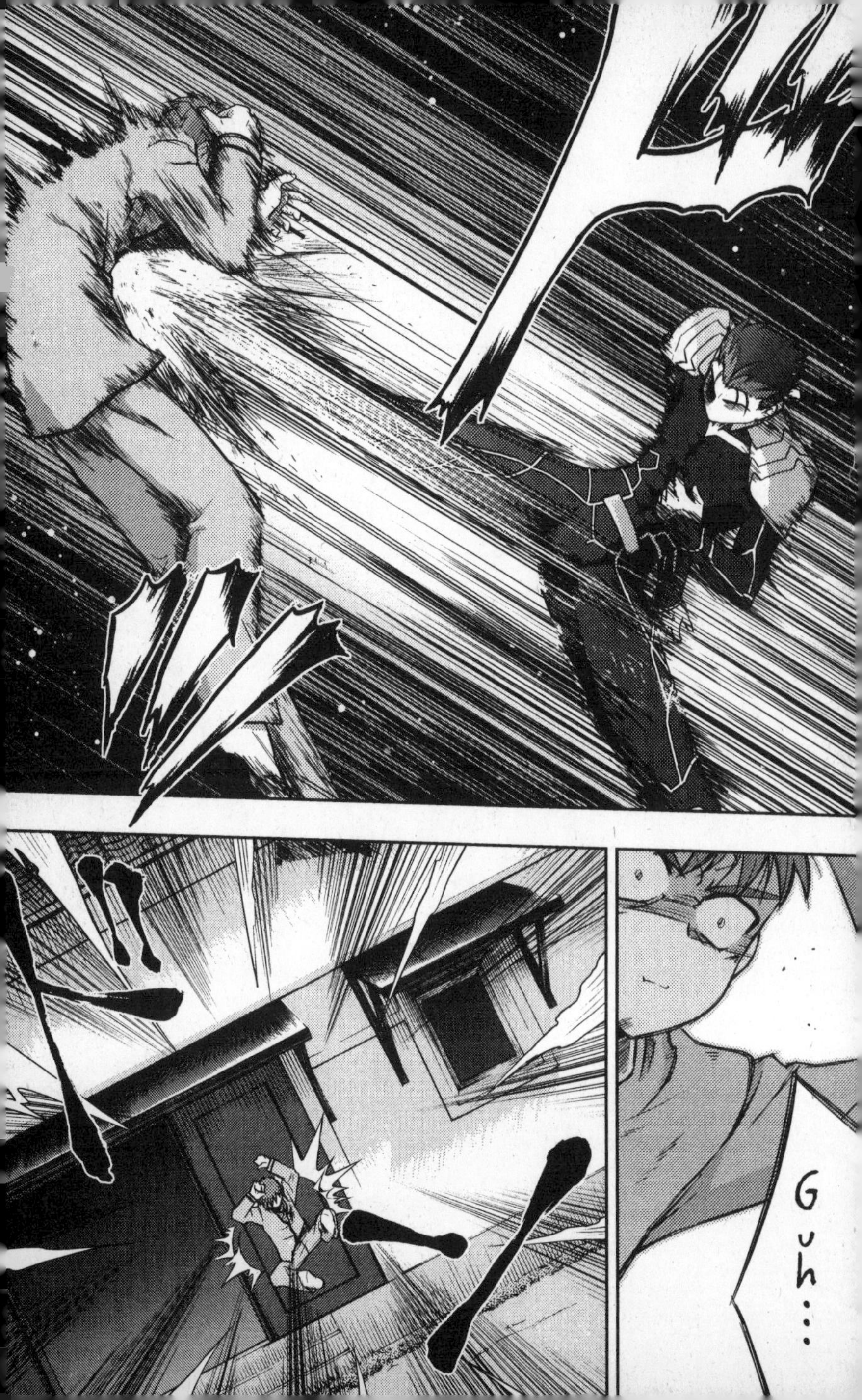
Guh...

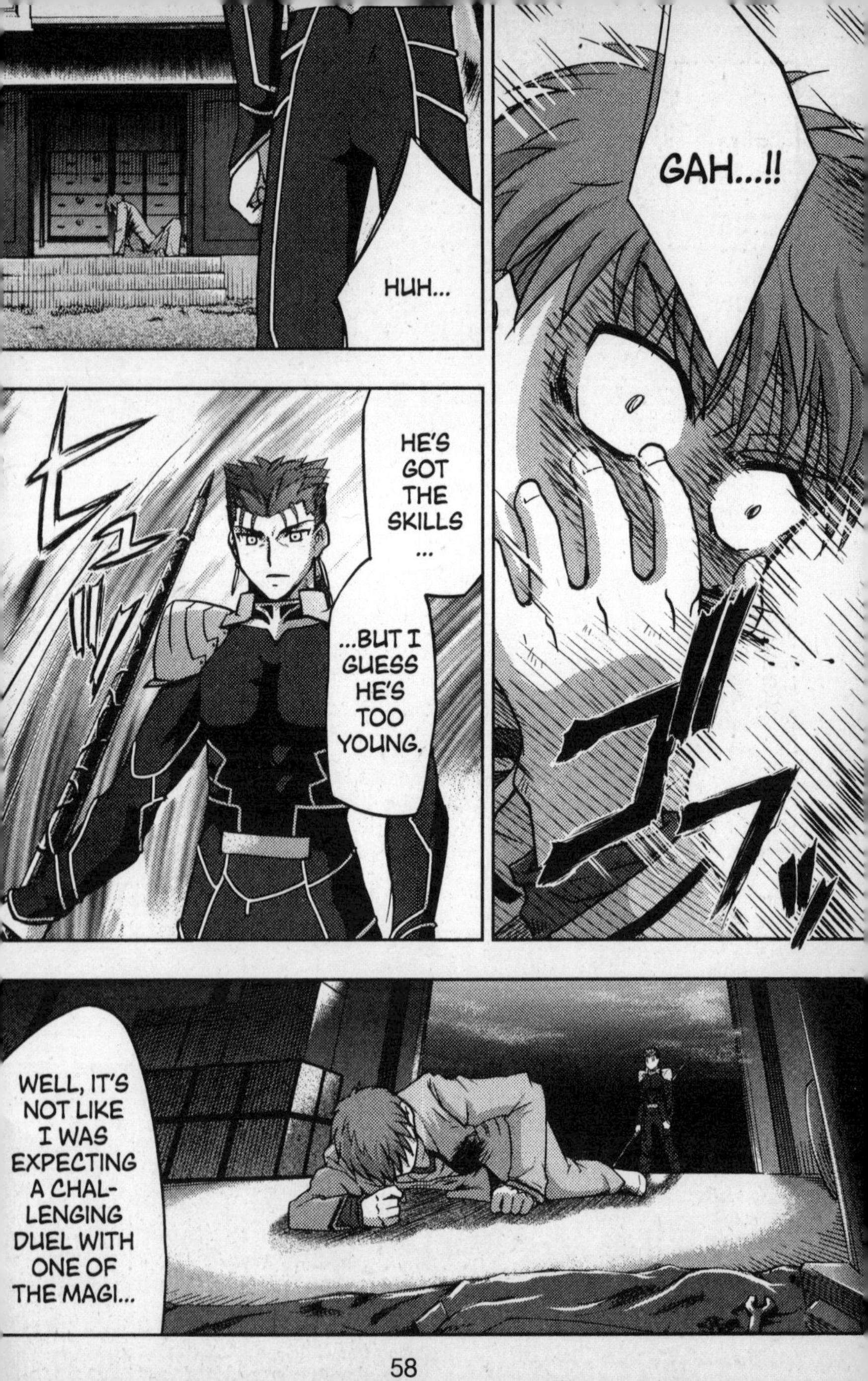
GAH...!!
HUH...
HE'S GOT THE SKILLS ...
...BUT I GUESS HE'S TOO YOUNG.
WELL, IT'S NOT LIKE I WAS EXPECTING A CHAL-LENGING DUEL WITH ONE OF THE MAGI...

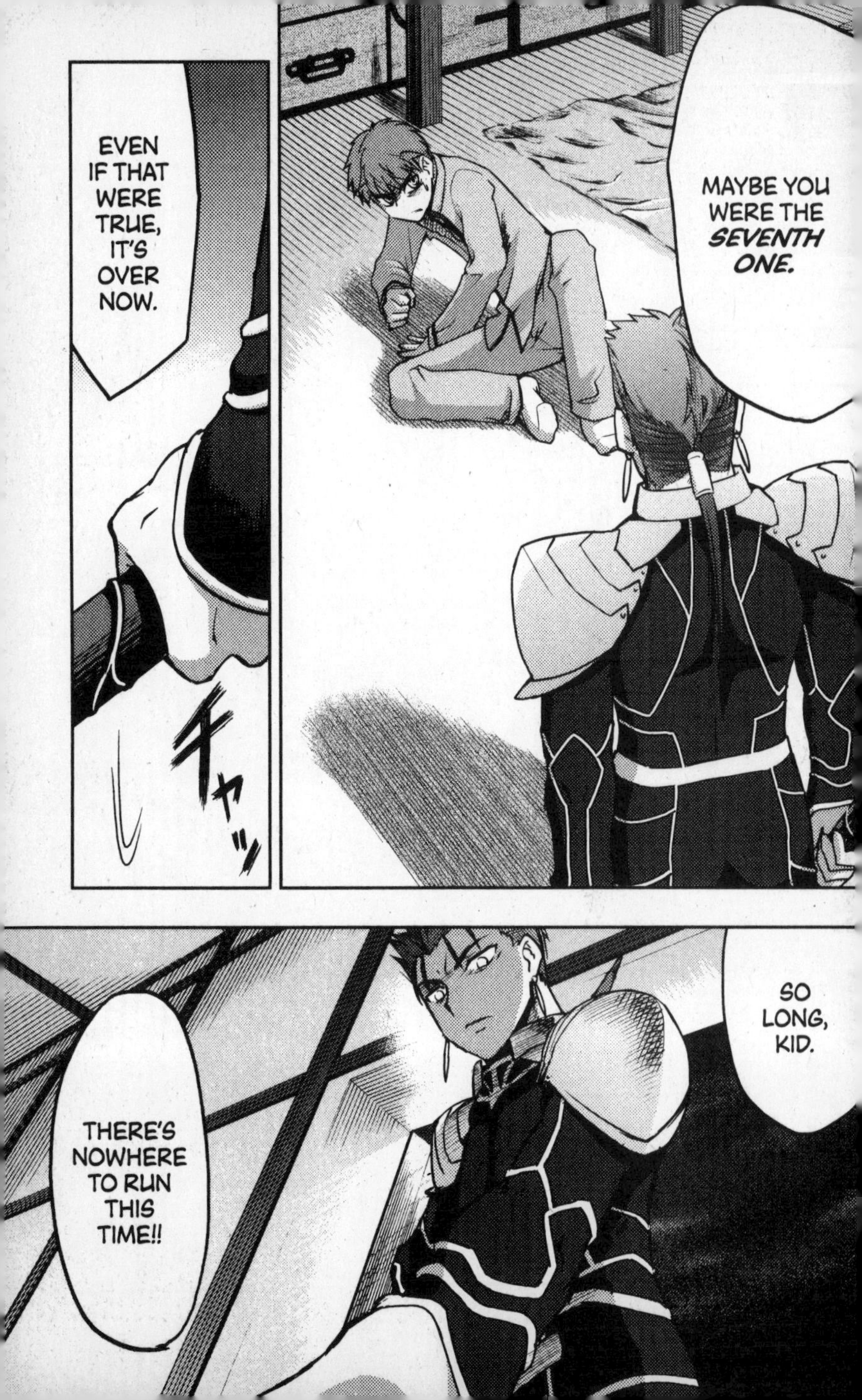
MAYBE YOU WERE THE *SEVENTH ONE.*
EVEN IF THAT WERE TRUE, IT'S OVER NOW.
チャッ
SO LONG, KID.
THERE'S NOWHERE TO RUN THIS TIME!!

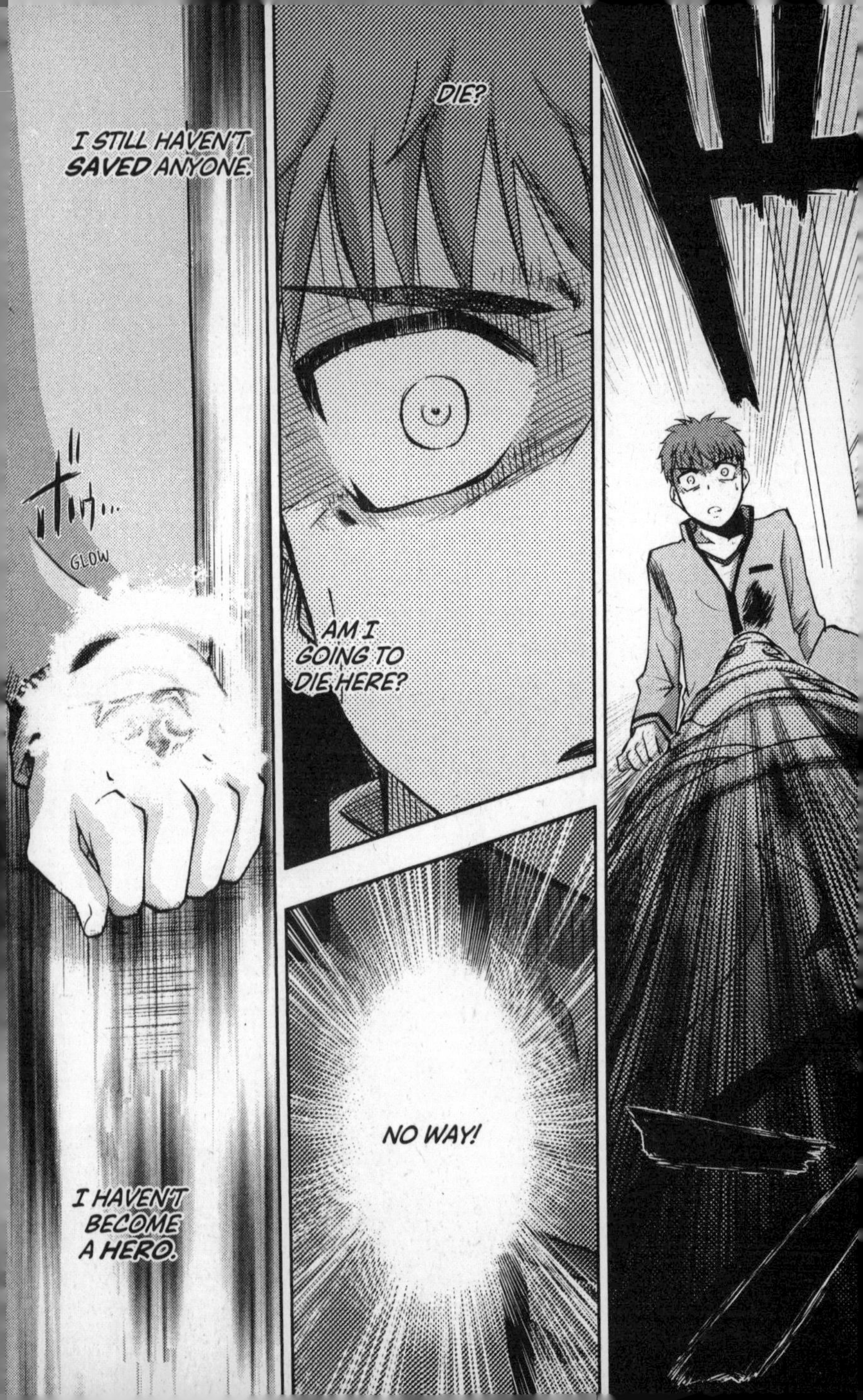
DIE?
AM I GOING TO DIE HERE?
NO WAY!
I STILL HAVEN'T SAVED ANYONE.
GLOW
I HAVEN'T BECOME A HERO.

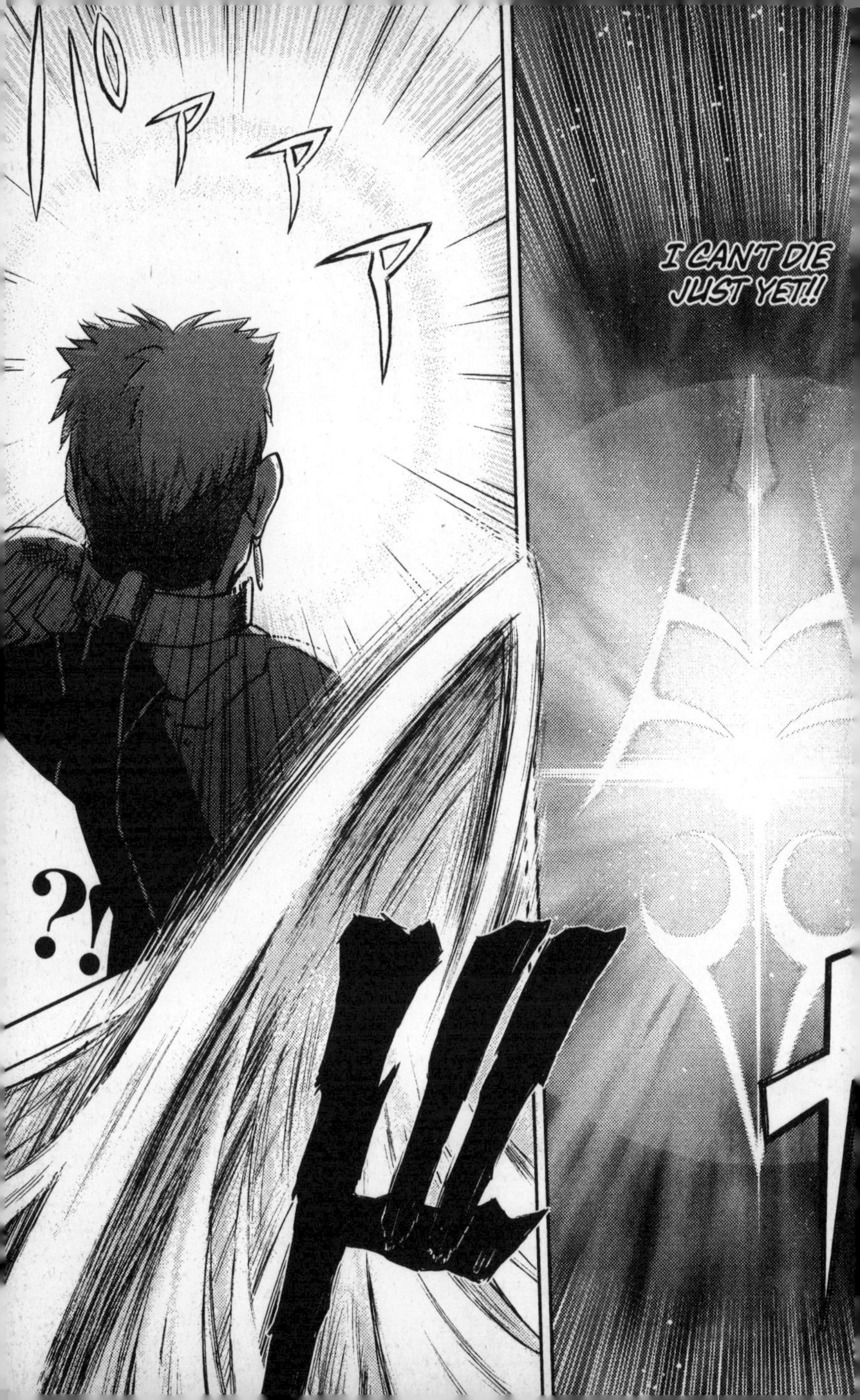
I CAN'T DIE JUST YET!!
?!

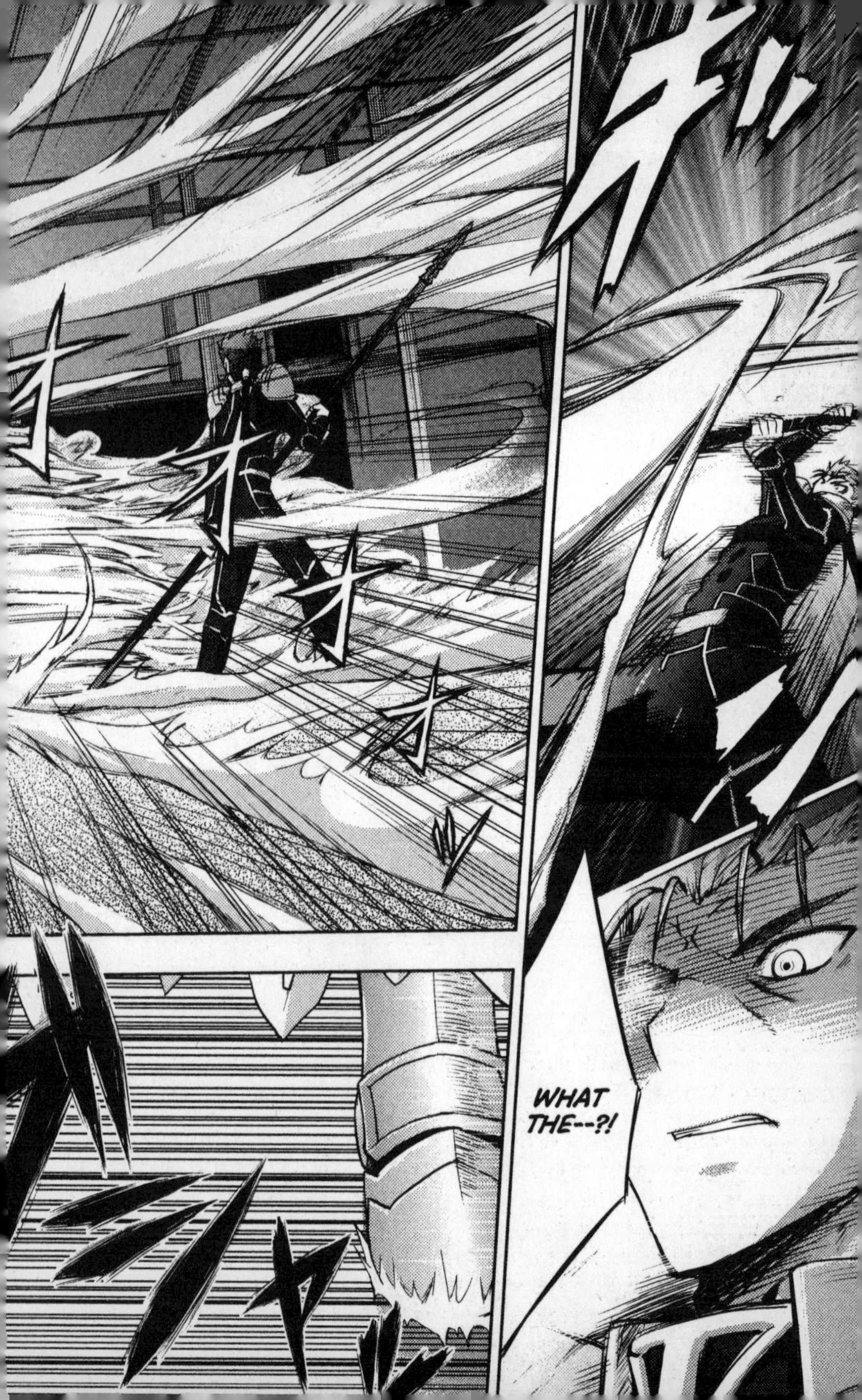
WHAT THE--?!

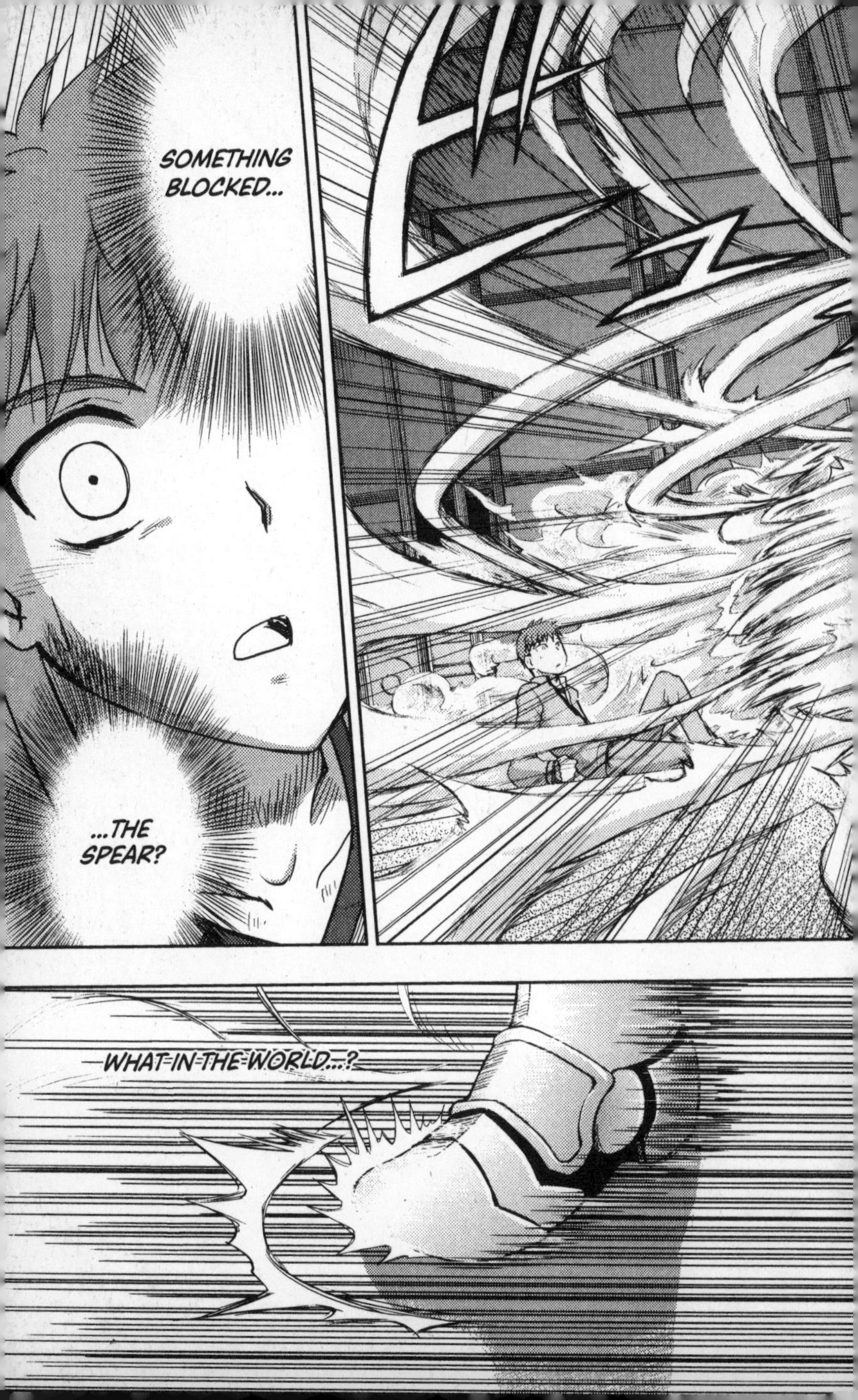
SOMETHING BLOCKED...
...THE SPEAR?
WHAT IN THE WORLD...?

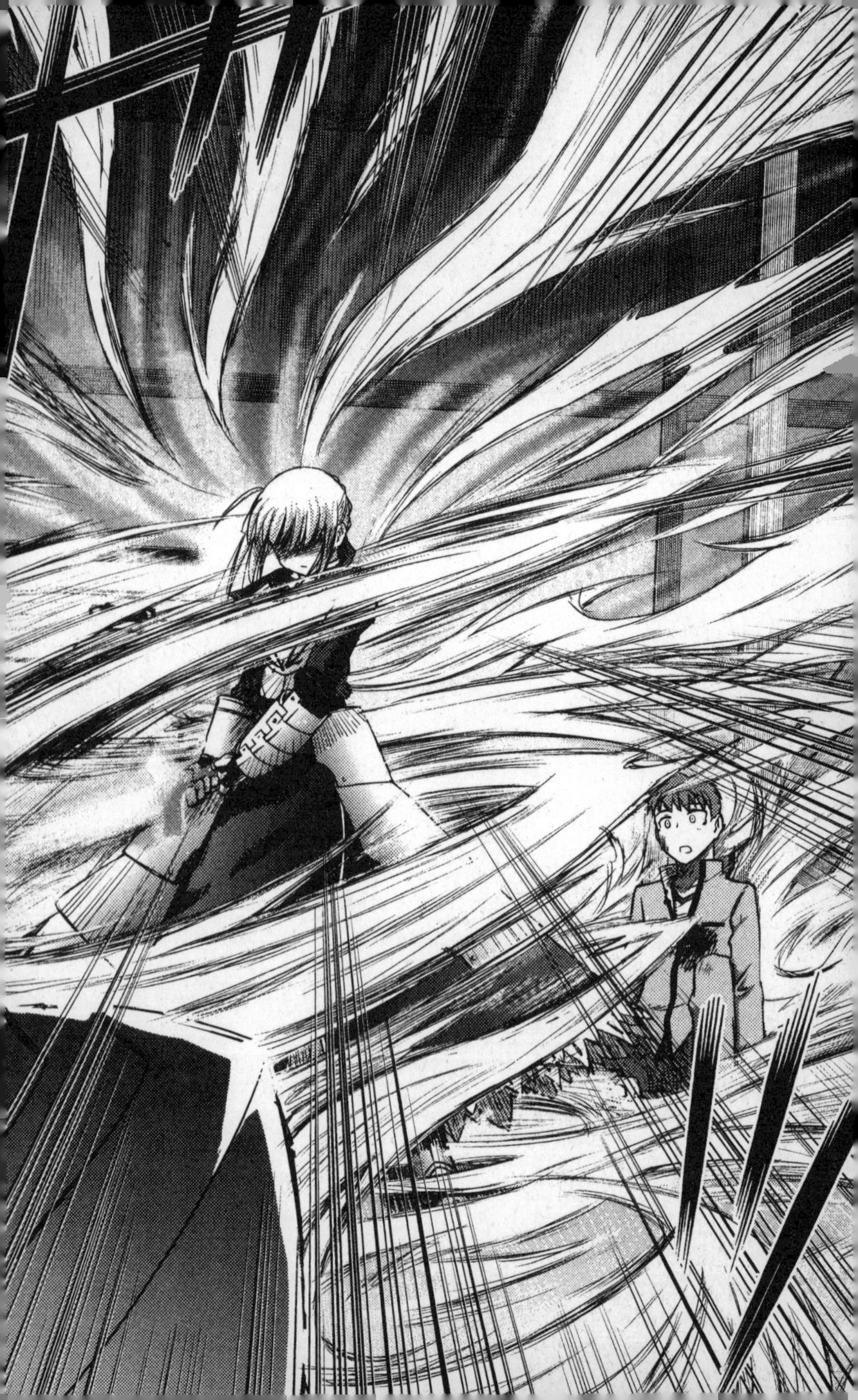

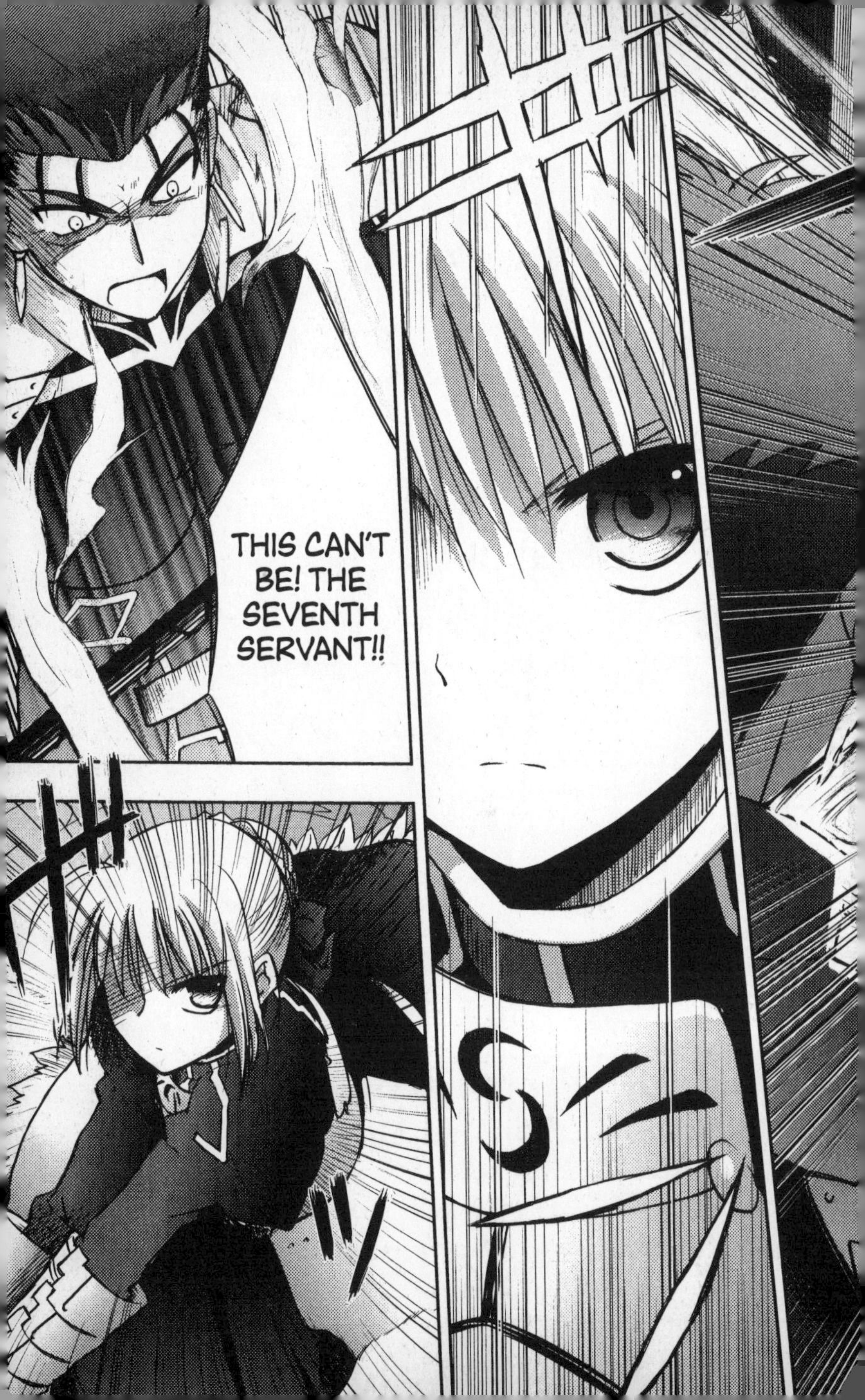
THIS CAN'T BE! THE SEVENTH SERVANT!!

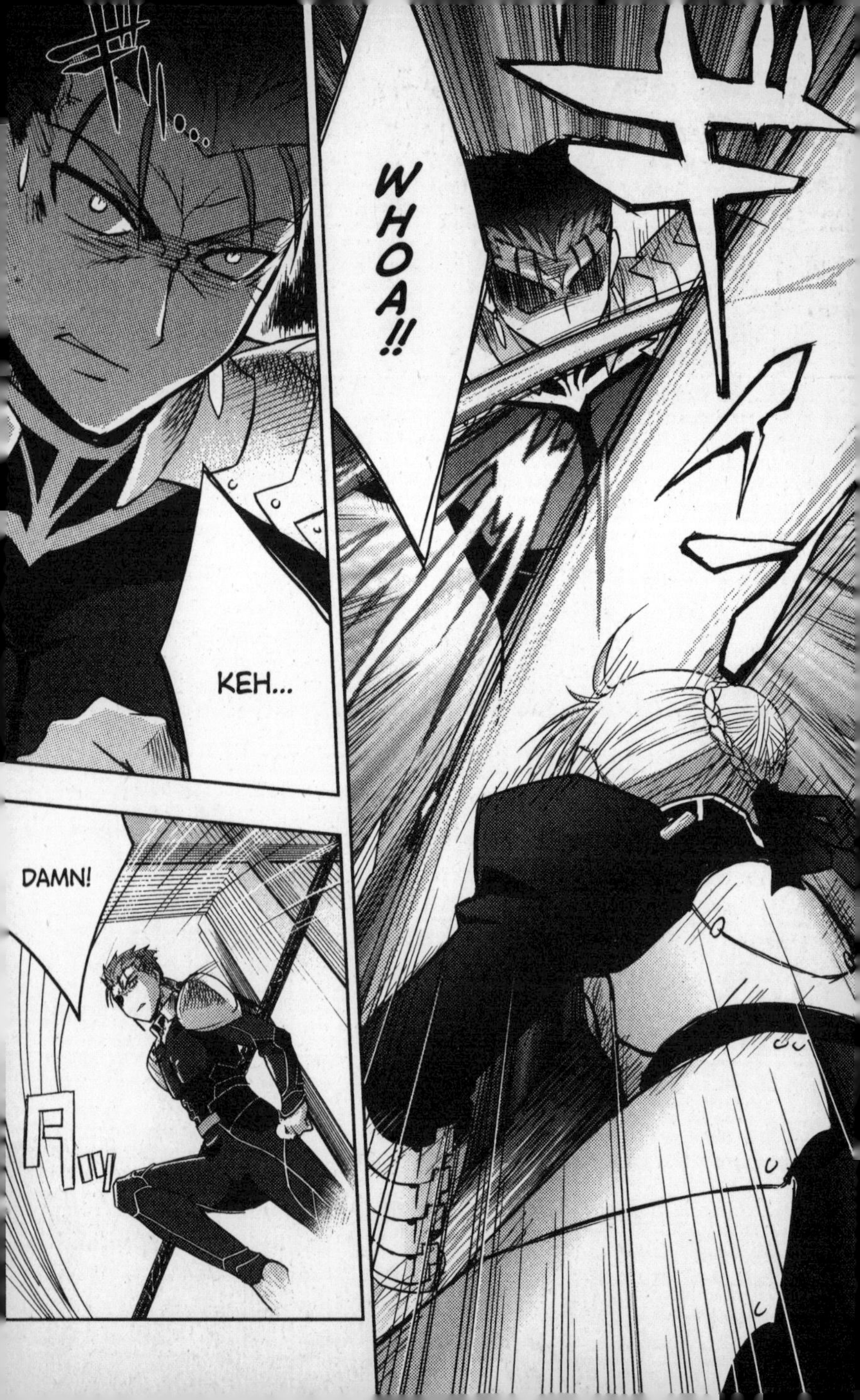
WHOA!!
KEH...
DAMN!

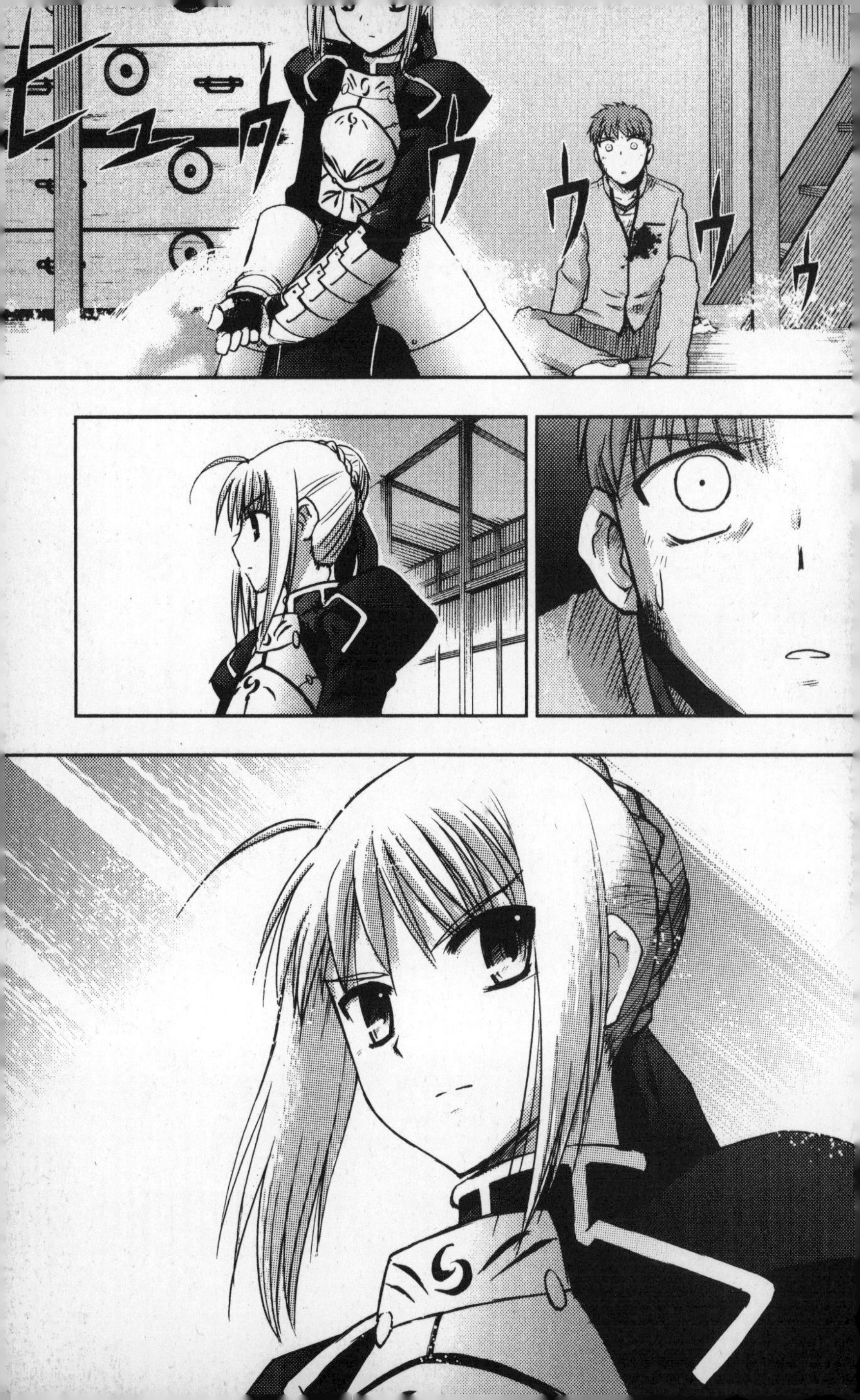
ヒュゥゥ
ゥゥゥ

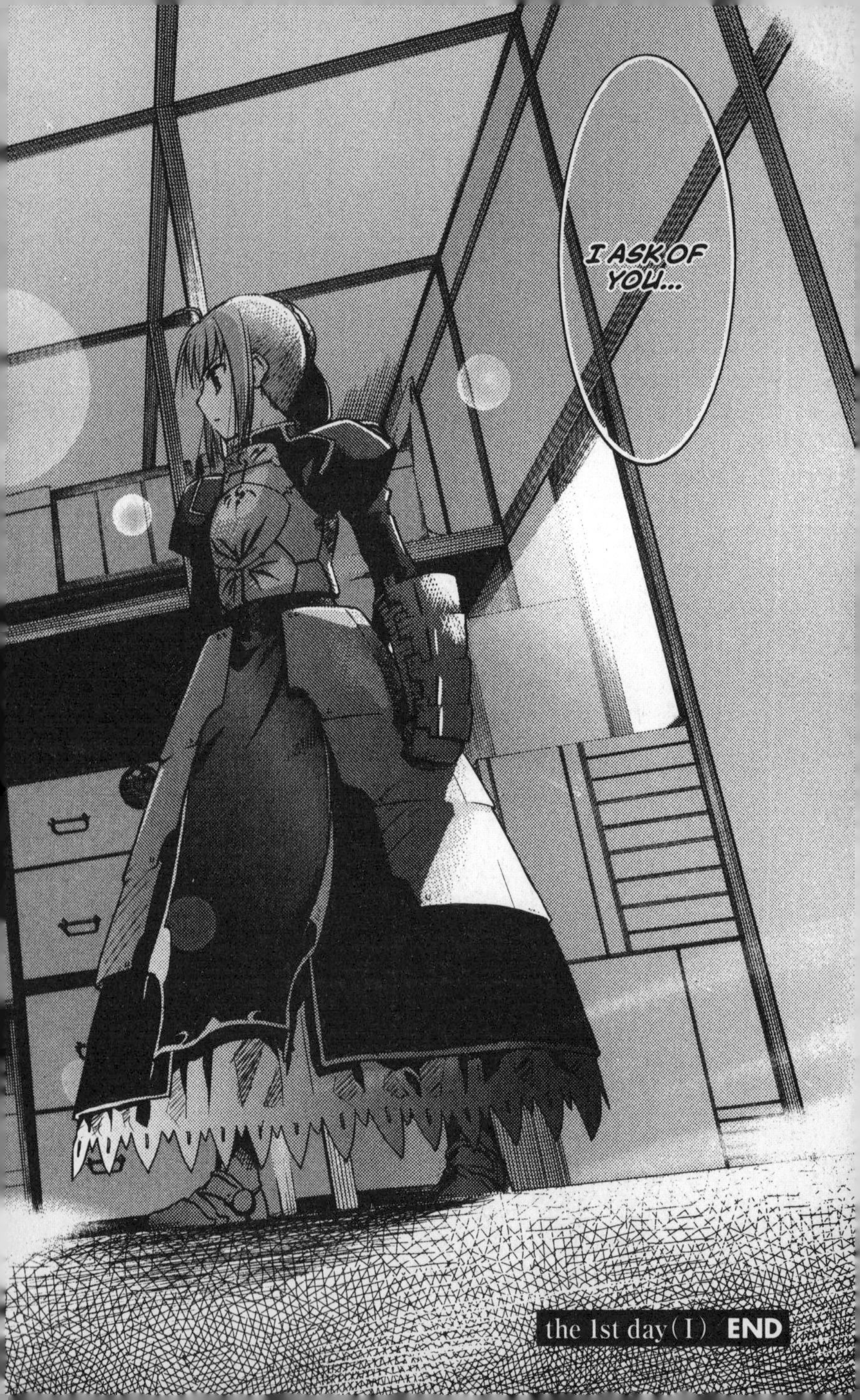
I ASK OF YOU...
the 1st day (I) END

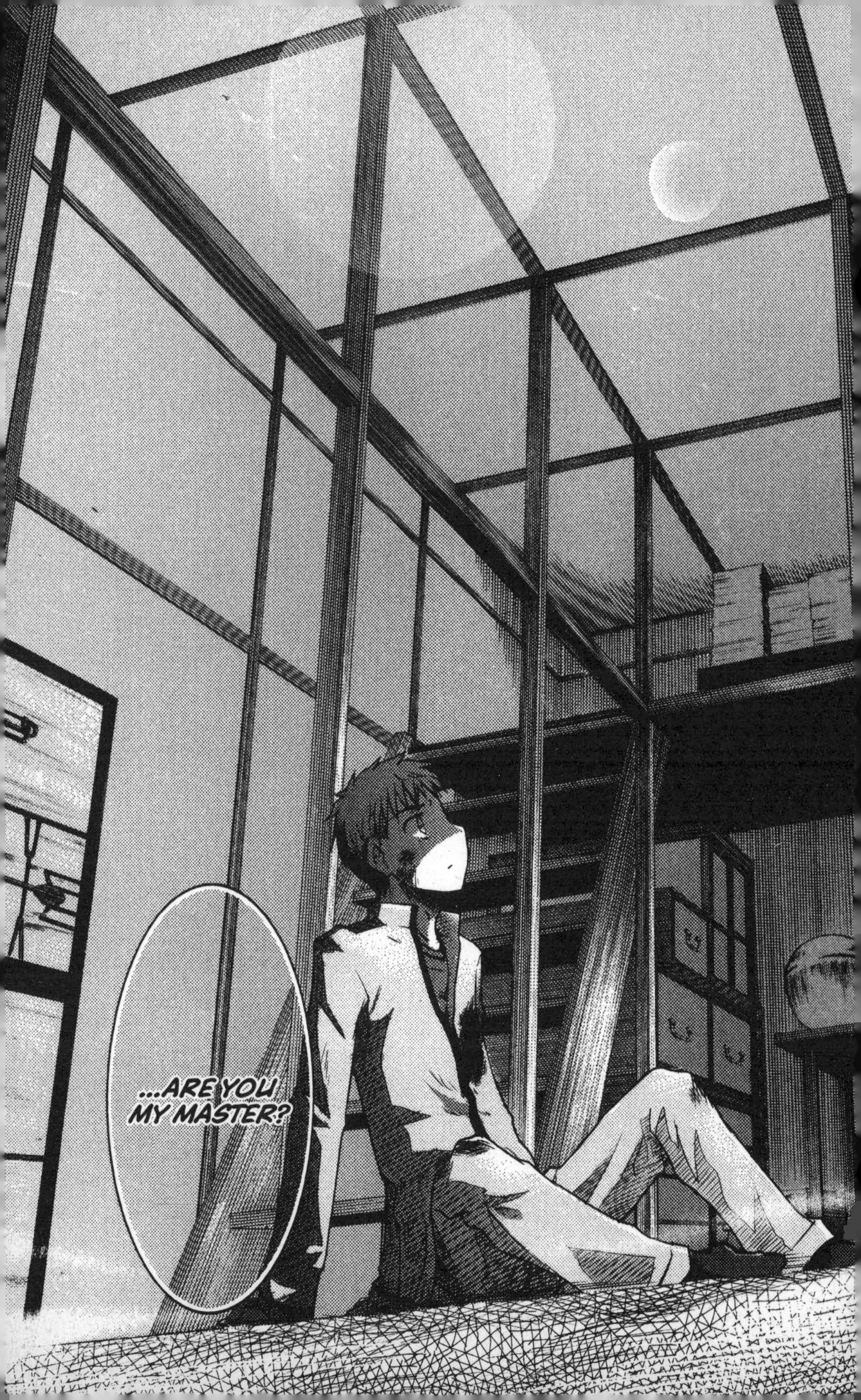
...ARE YOU MY MASTER?

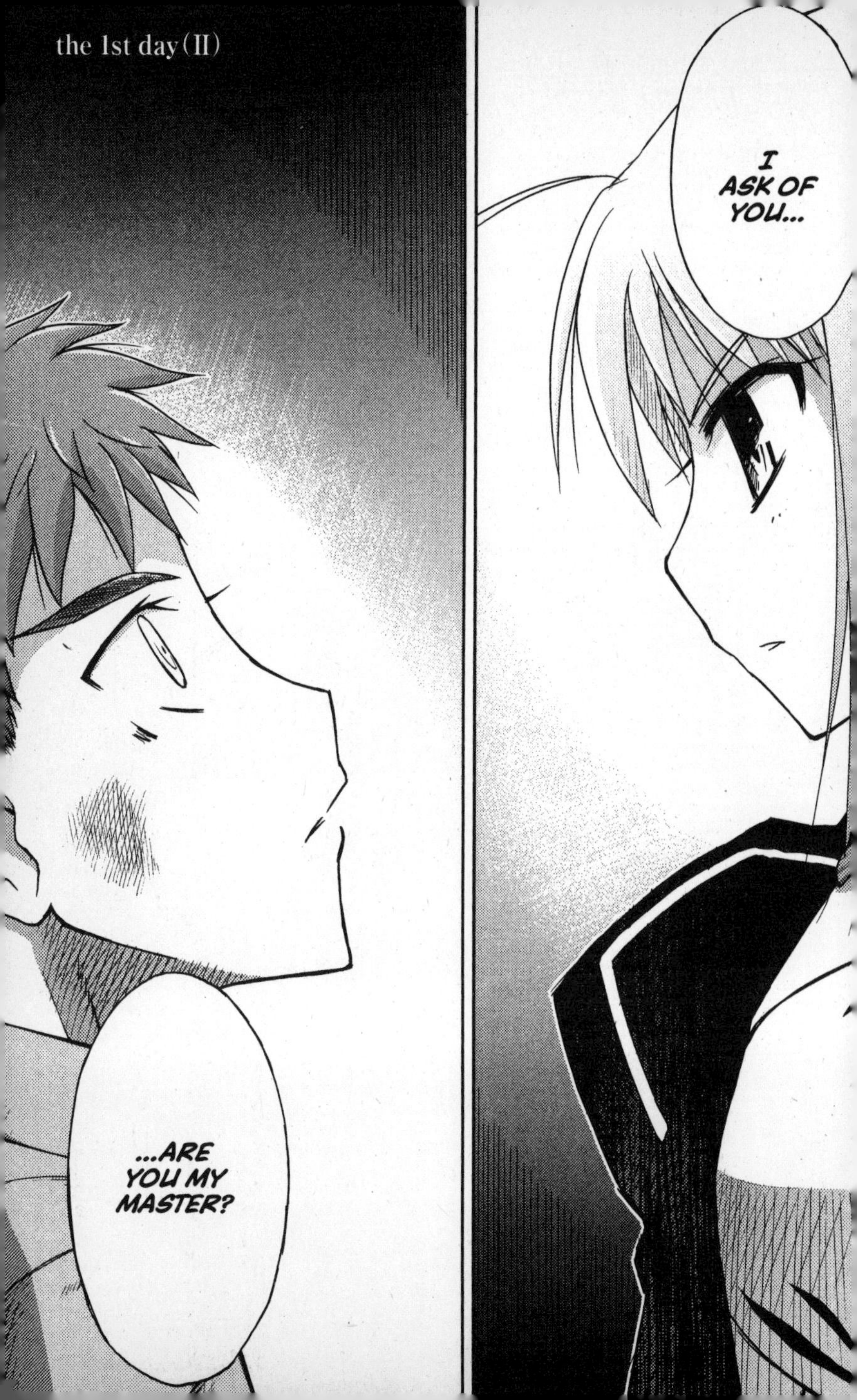
I ASK OF YOU...
...ARE YOU MY MASTER?

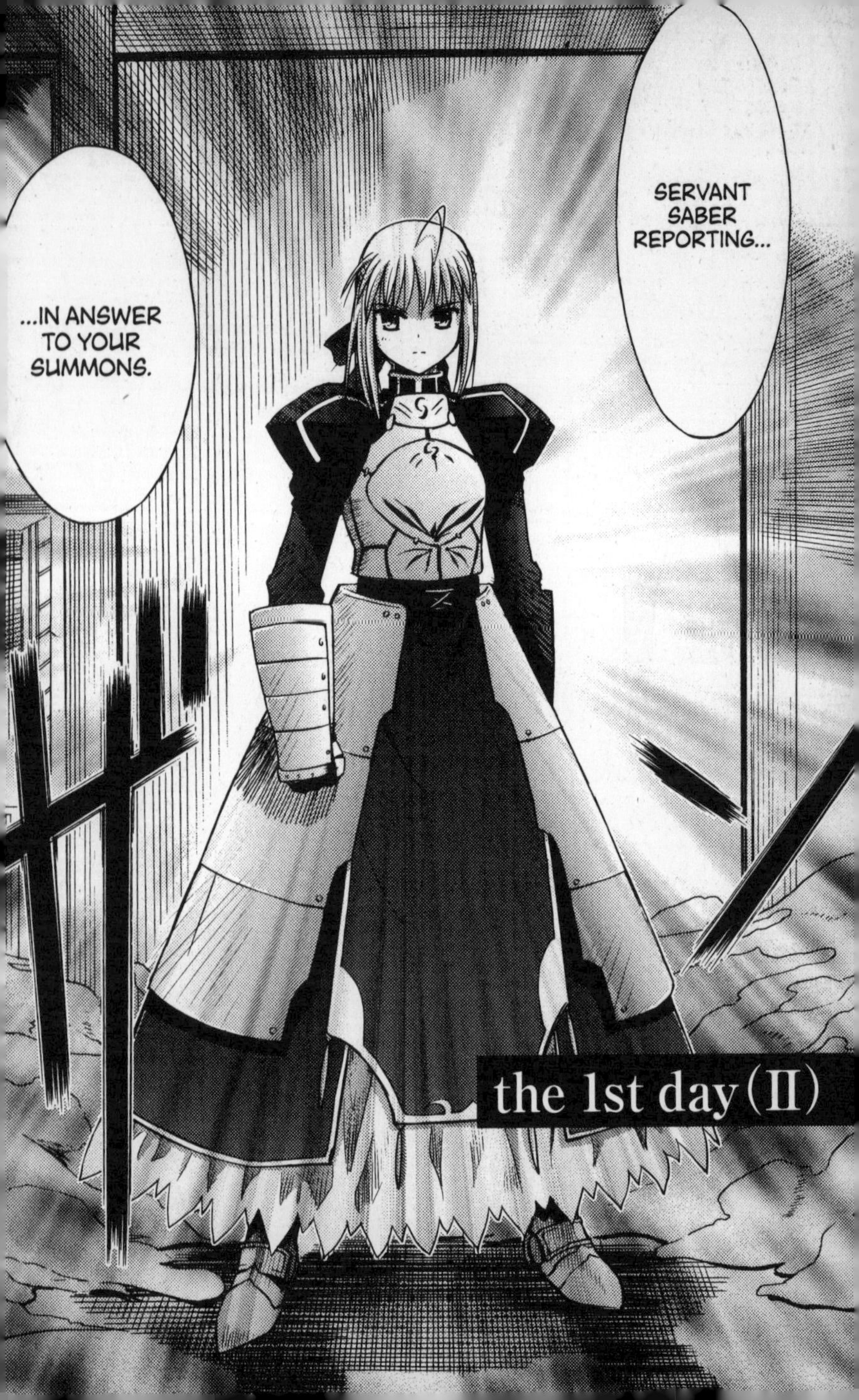
SERVANT SABER REPORTING...
...IN ANSWER TO YOUR SUMMONS.
the 1st day (II)

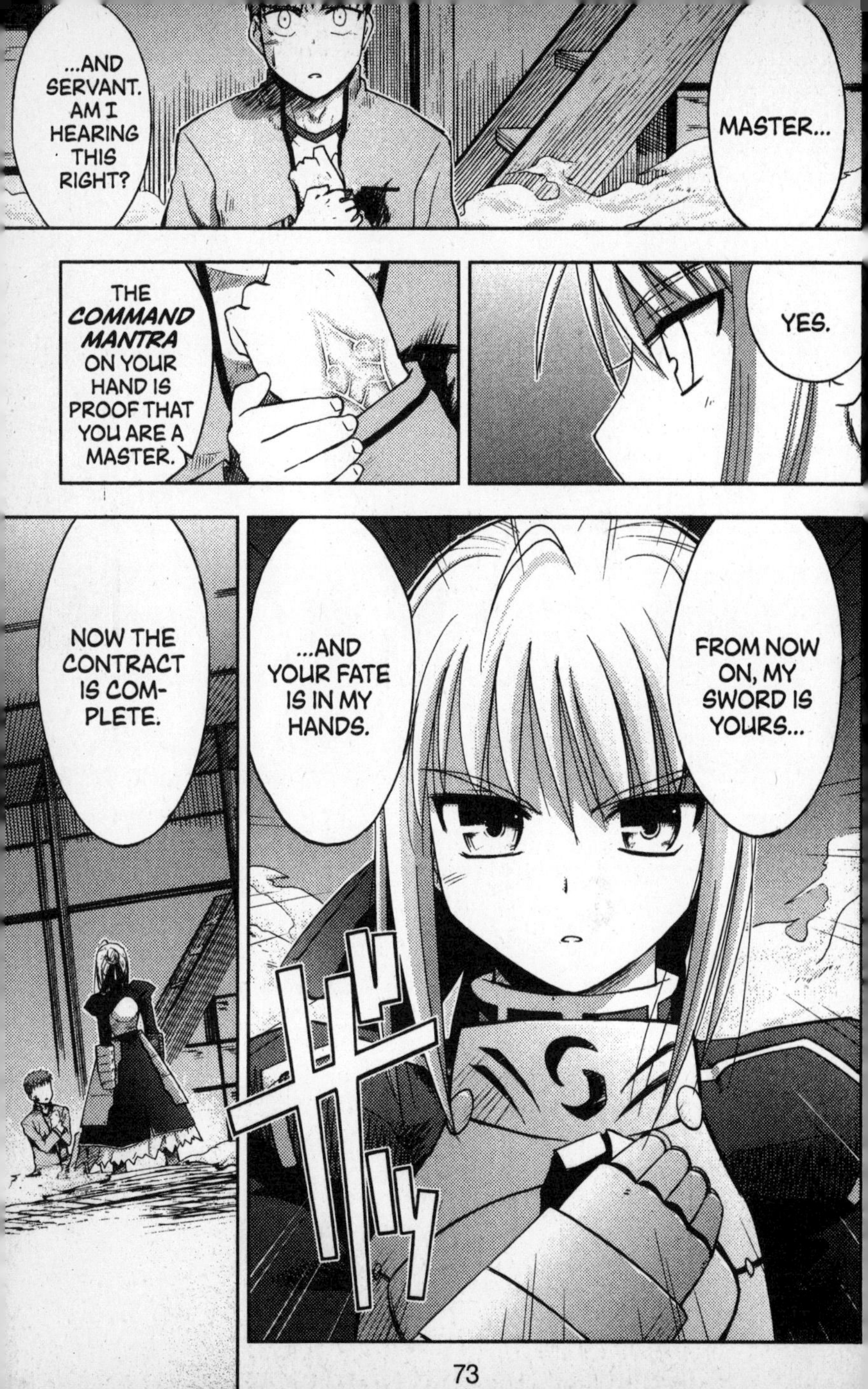
MASTER...
...AND SERVANT. AM I HEARING THIS RIGHT?
YES.
THE *COMMAND MANTRA* ON YOUR HAND IS PROOF THAT YOU ARE A MASTER.
FROM NOW ON, MY SWORD IS YOURS...
...AND YOUR FATE IS IN MY HANDS.
NOW THE CONTRACT IS COM- PLETE.

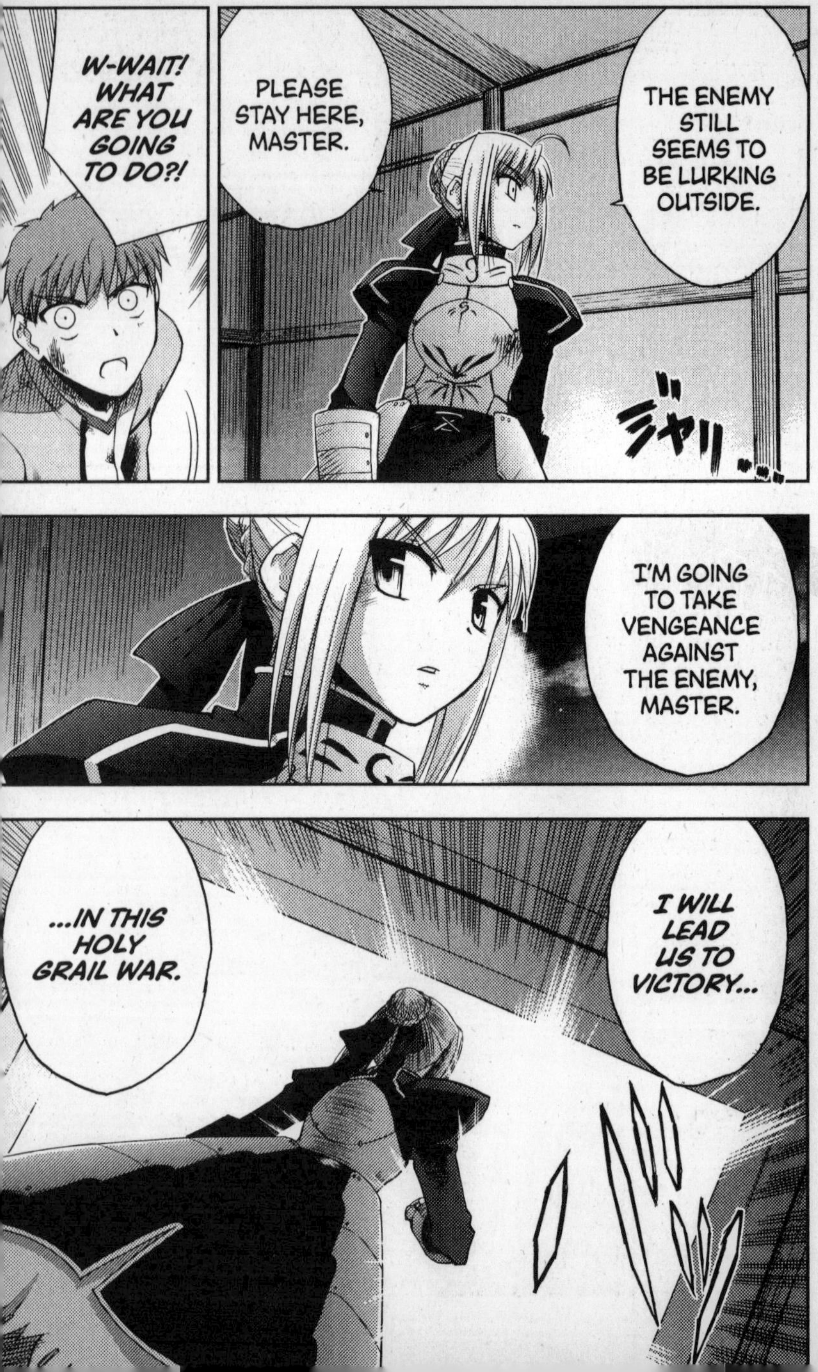
THE ENEMY STILL SEEMS TO BE LURKING OUTSIDE.
PLEASE STAY HERE, MASTER.
ジャリ…
W-WAIT! WHAT ARE YOU GOING TO DO?!
I'M GOING TO TAKE VENGEANCE AGAINST THE ENEMY, MASTER.
I WILL LEAD US TO VICTORY...
...IN THIS HOLY GRAIL WAR.

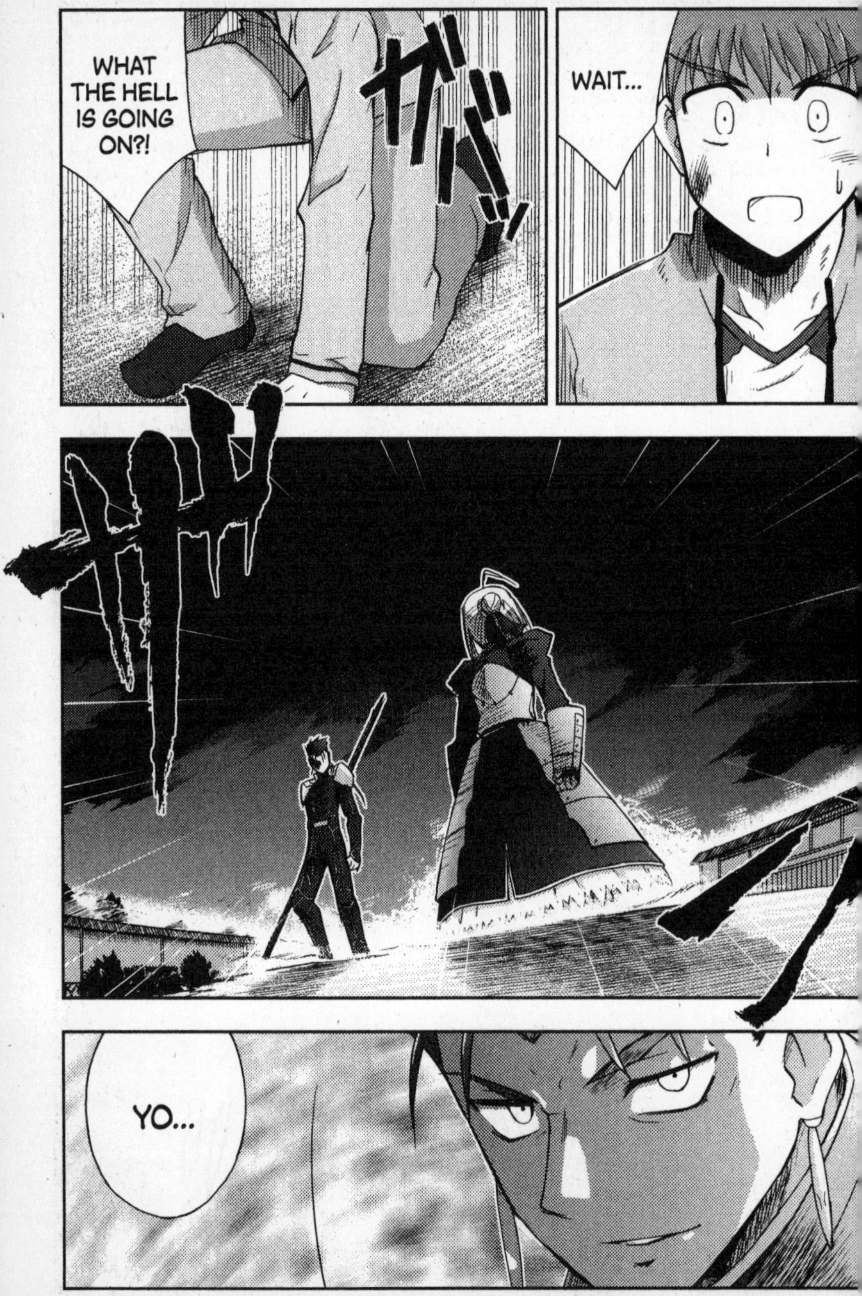
WAIT...
WHAT THE HELL IS GOING ON?!
YO...

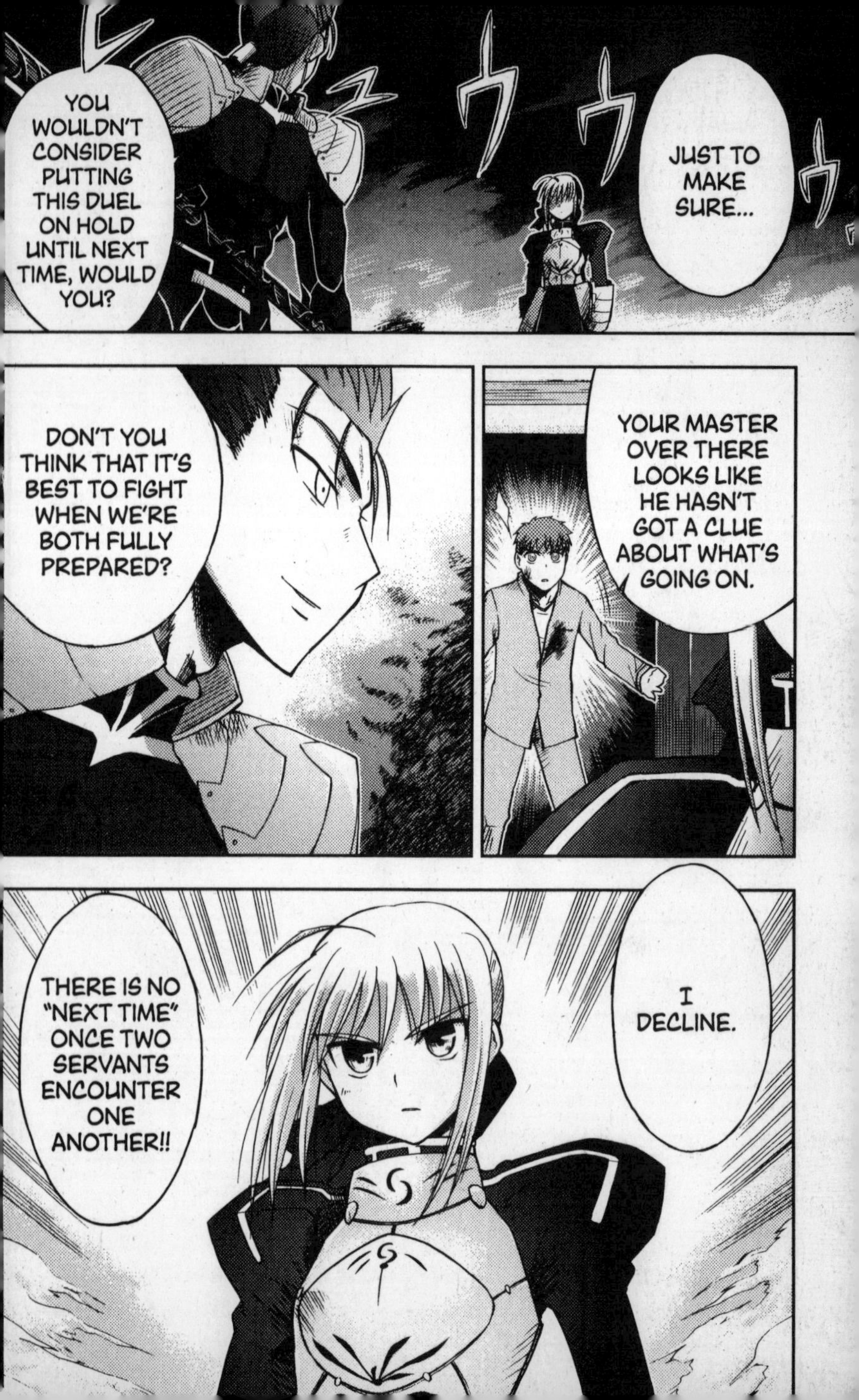
JUST TO MAKE SURE...
YOU WOULDN'T CONSIDER PUTTING THIS DUEL ON HOLD UNTIL NEXT TIME, WOULD YOU?
YOUR MASTER OVER THERE LOOKS LIKE HE HASN'T GOT A CLUE ABOUT WHAT'S GOING ON.
DON'T YOU THINK THAT IT'S BEST TO FIGHT WHEN WE'RE BOTH FULLY PREPARED?
I DECLINE.
THERE IS NO "NEXT TIME" ONCE TWO SERVANTS ENCOUNTER ONE ANOTHER!!

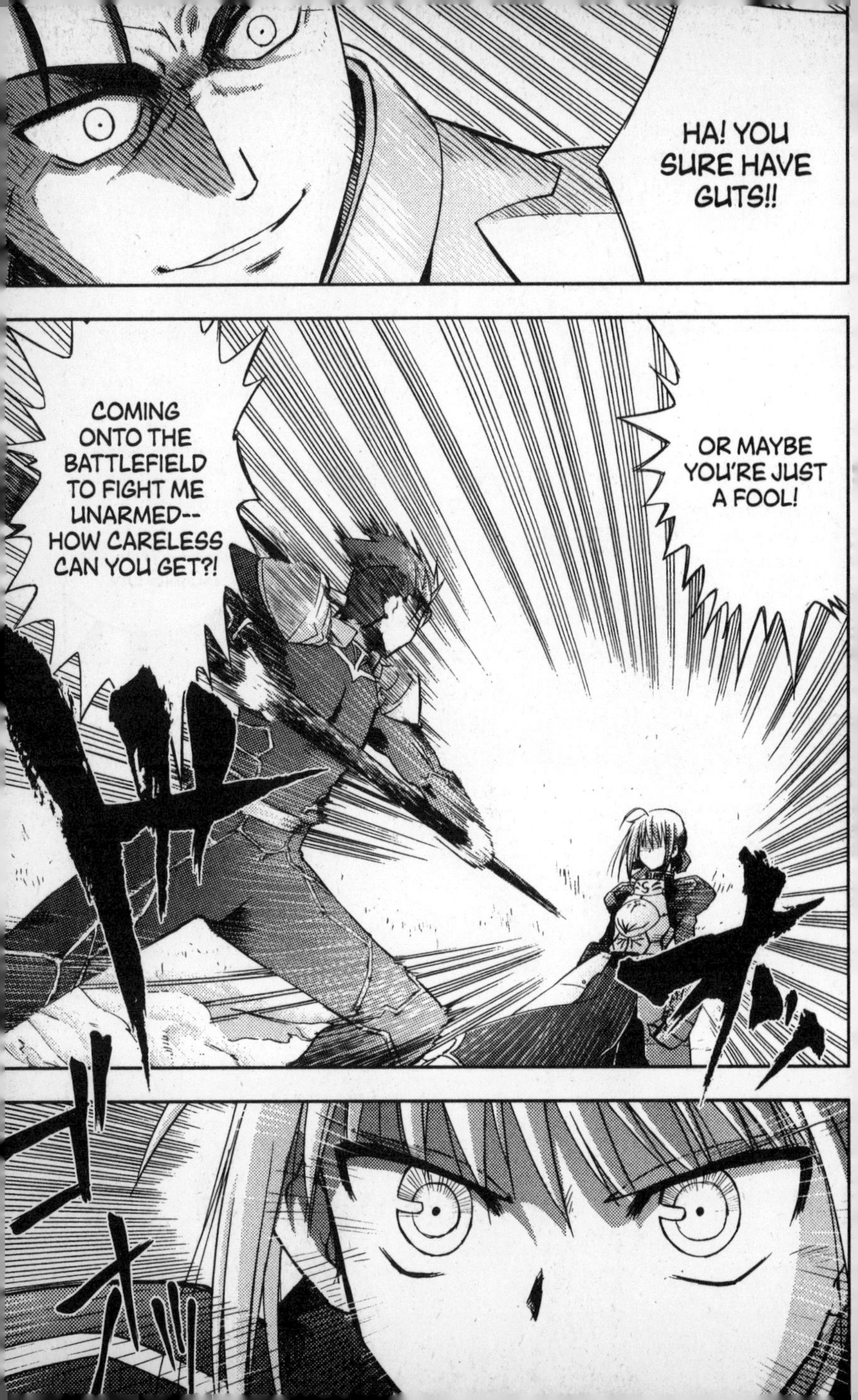
HA! YOU SURE HAVE GUTS!!
OR MAYBE YOU'RE JUST A FOOL!
COMING ONTO THE BATTLEFIELD TO FIGHT ME UNARMED-- HOW CARELESS CAN YOU GET?!

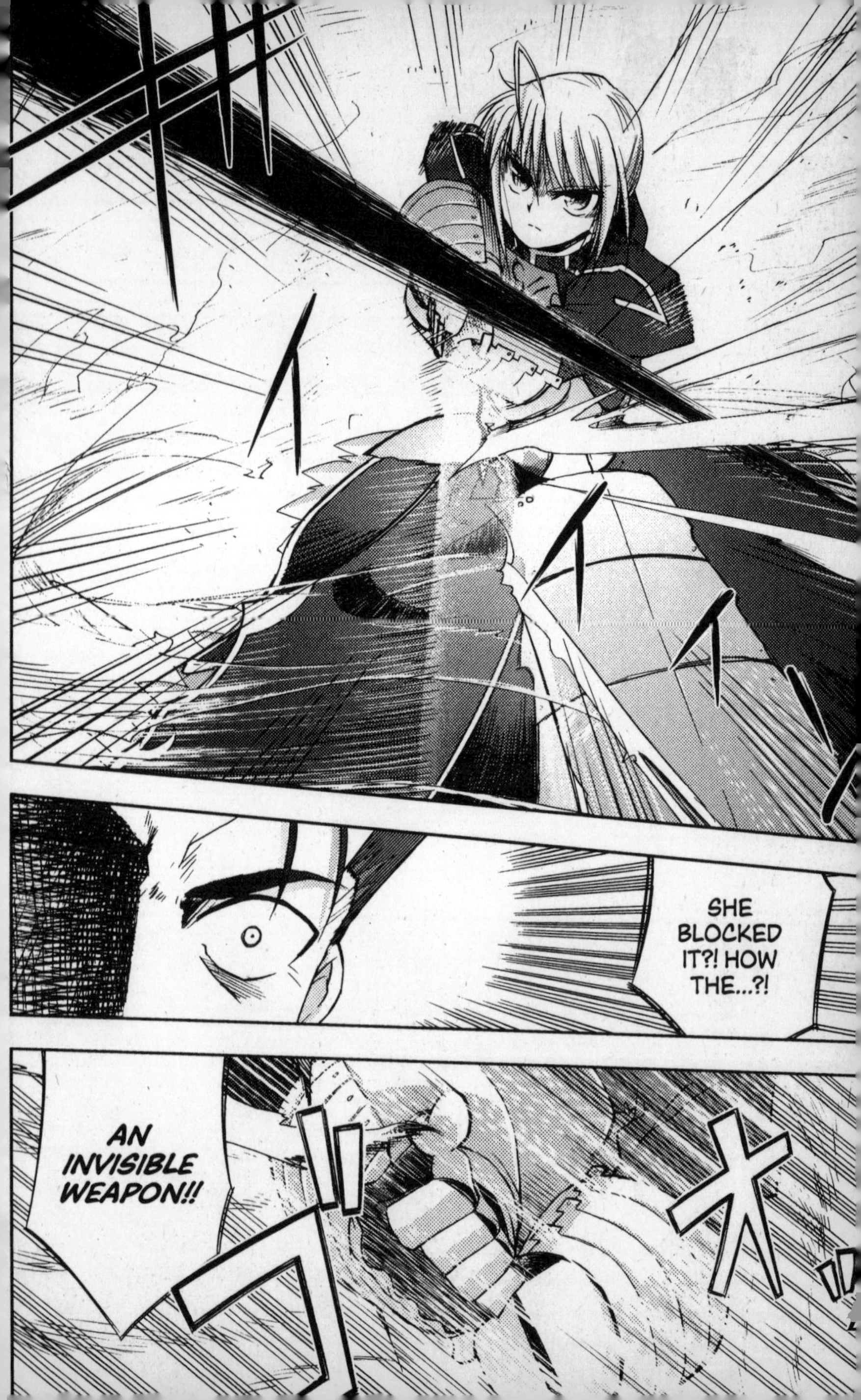
SHE BLOCKED IT?! HOW THE...?!
AN INVISIBLE WEAPON!!

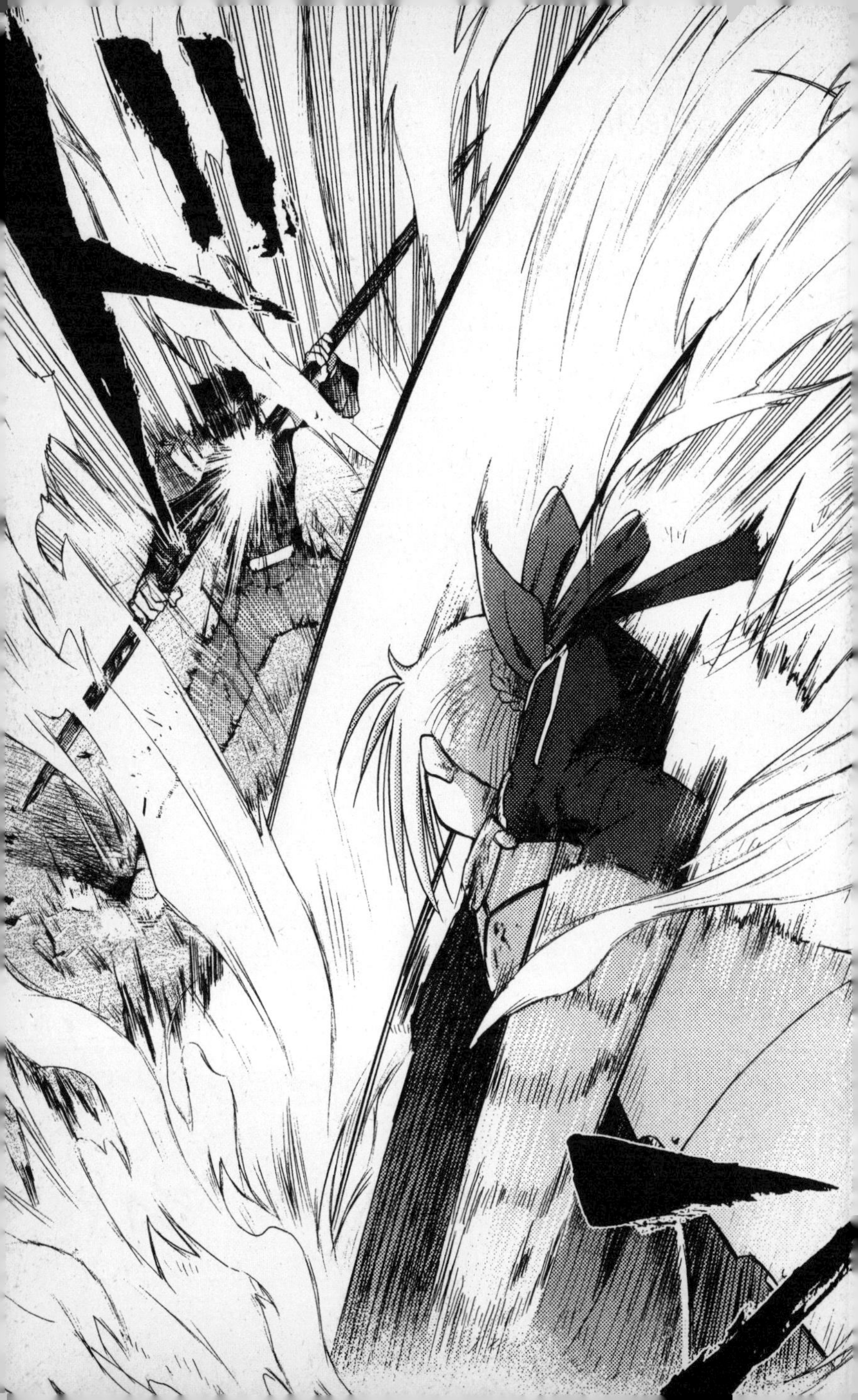

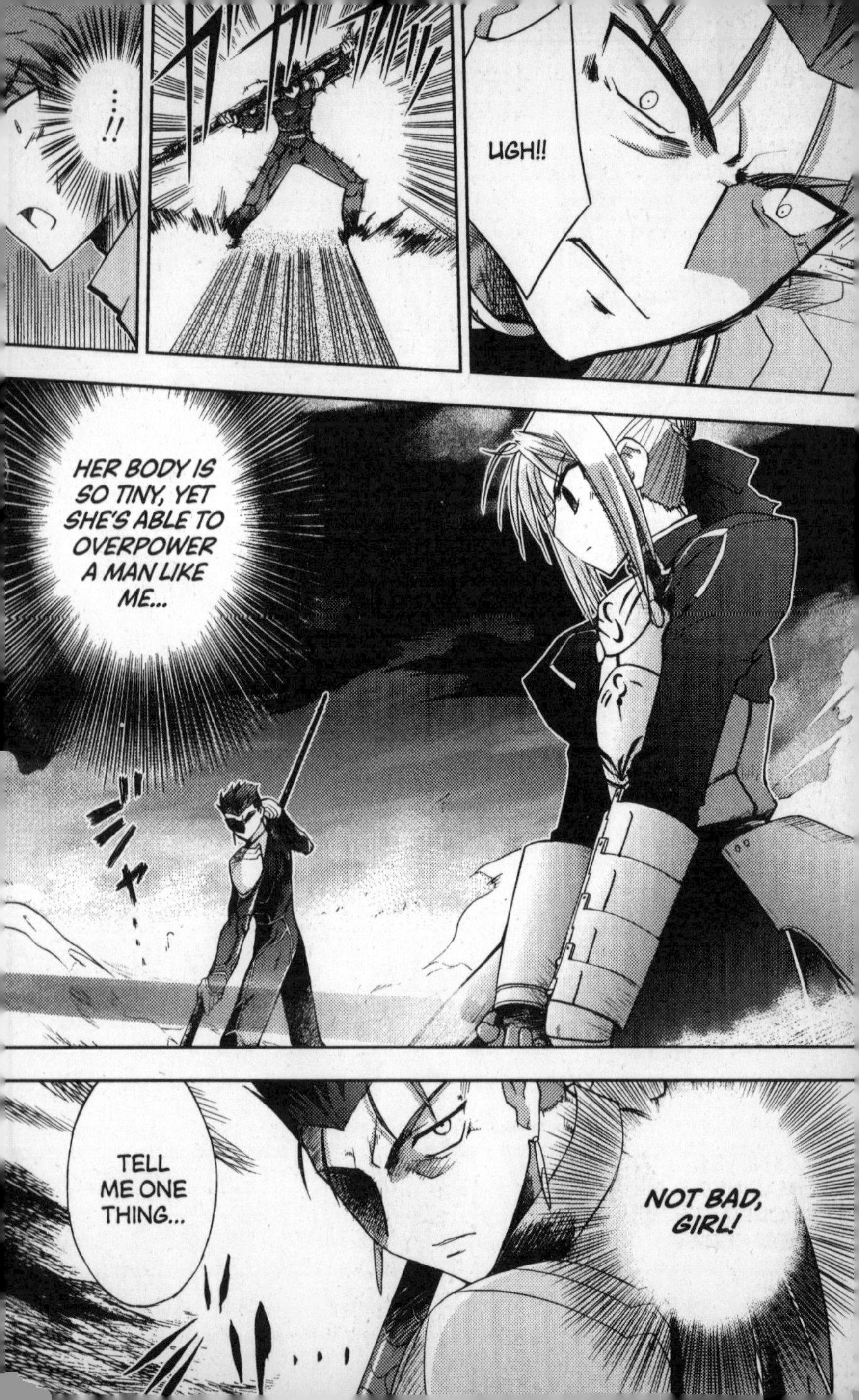
UGH!!
...!!
HER BODY IS SO TINY, YET SHE'S ABLE TO OVERPOWER A MAN LIKE ME...
NOT BAD, GIRL!
TELL ME ONE THING...
...

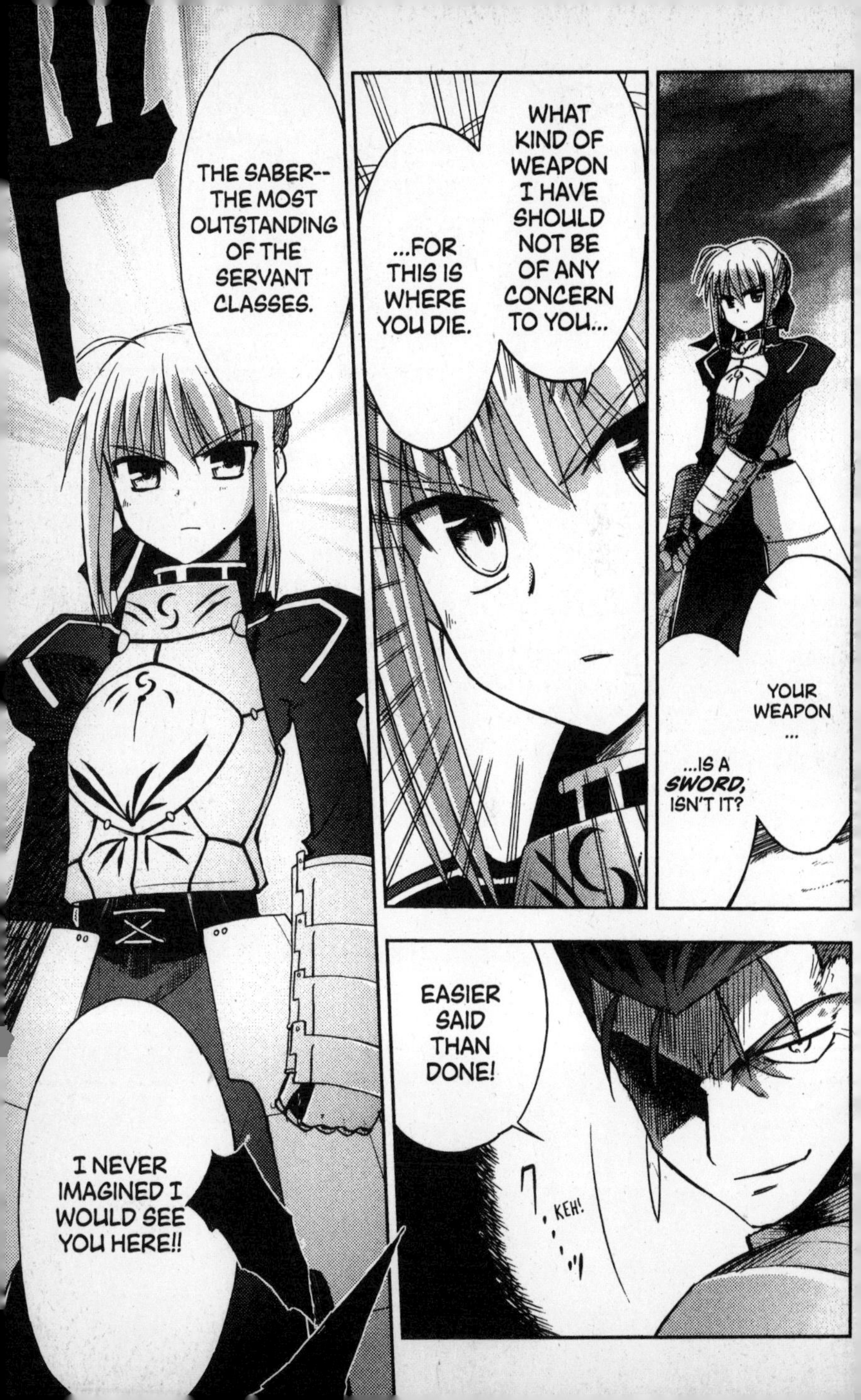
YOUR WEAPON ...
...IS A *SWORD,* ISN'T IT?
WHAT KIND OF WEAPON I HAVE SHOULD NOT BE OF ANY CONCERN TO YOU...
...FOR THIS IS WHERE YOU DIE.
EASIER SAID THAN DONE!
KEH!
THE SABER-- THE MOST OUTSTANDING OF THE SERVANT CLASSES.
I NEVER IMAGINED I WOULD SEE YOU HERE!!

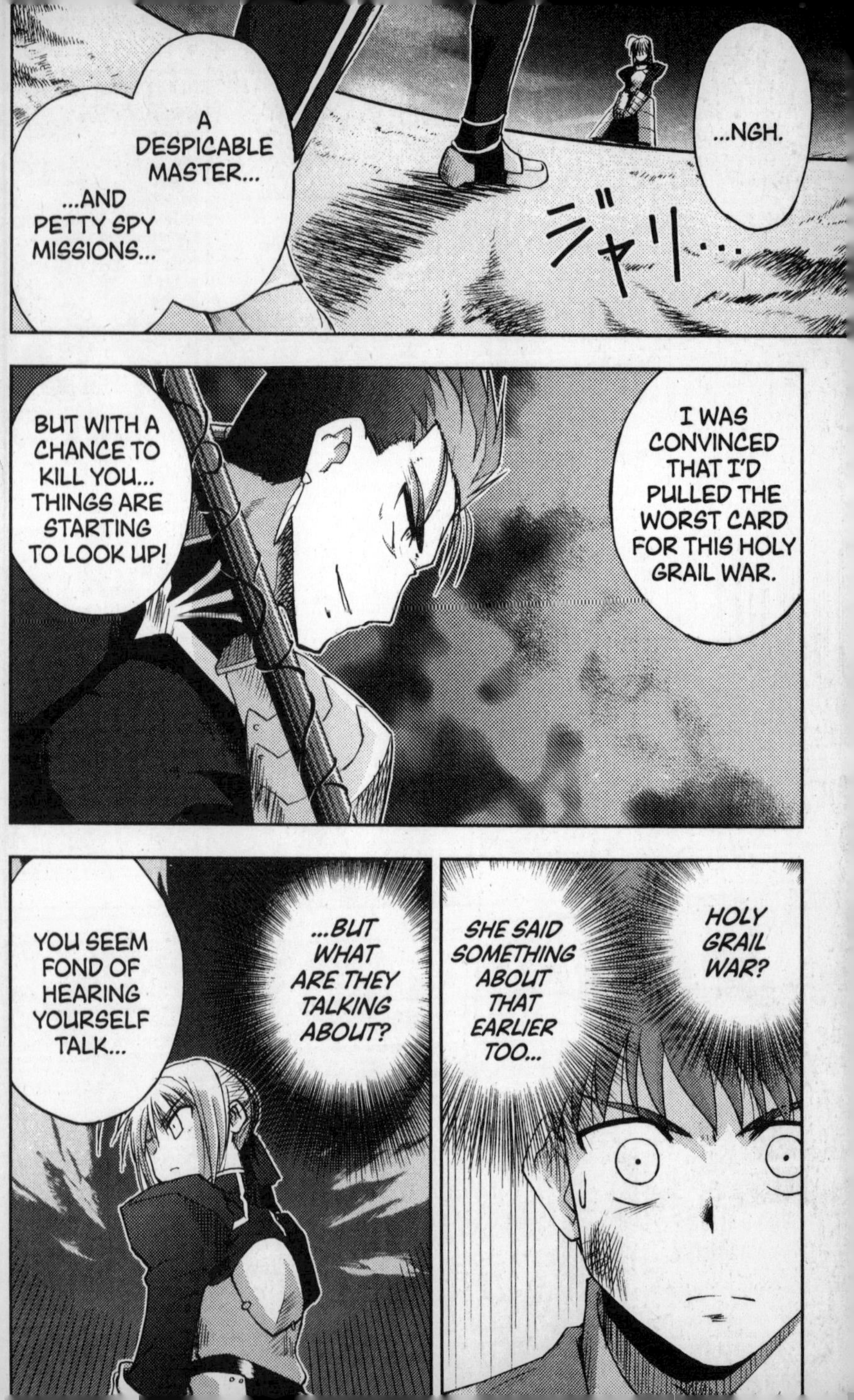
...NGH.
ジャリ...
A DESPICABLE MASTER...
...AND PETTY SPY MISSIONS...
I WAS CONVINCED THAT I'D PULLED THE WORST CARD FOR THIS HOLY GRAIL WAR.
BUT WITH A CHANCE TO KILL YOU... THINGS ARE STARTING TO LOOK UP!
HOLY GRAIL WAR?
SHE SAID SOMETHING ABOUT THAT EARLIER TOO...
...BUT WHAT ARE THEY TALKING ABOUT?
YOU SEEM FOND OF HEARING YOURSELF TALK...

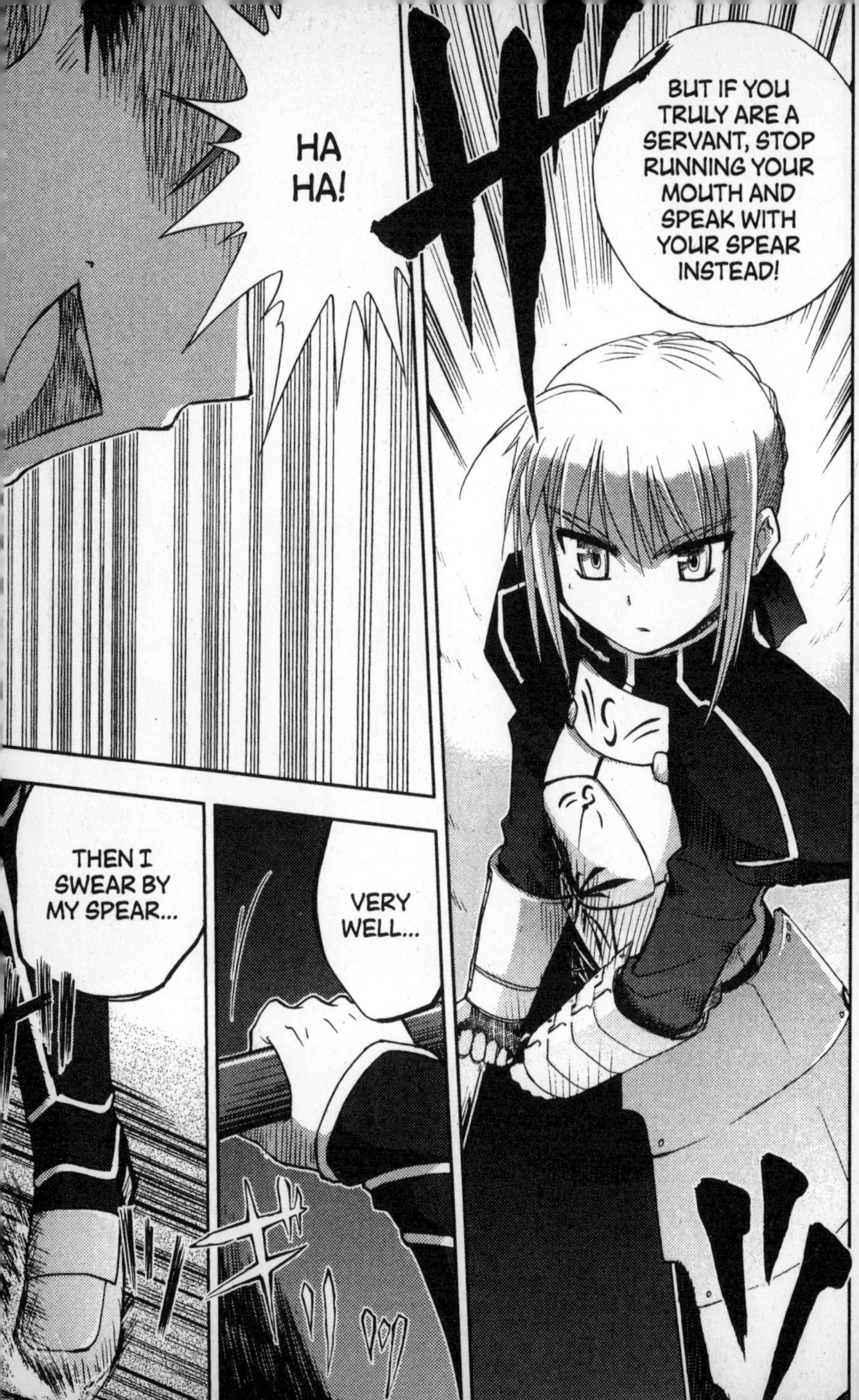

BUT IF YOU TRULY ARE A SERVANT, STOP RUNNING YOUR MOUTH AND SPEAK WITH YOUR SPEAR INSTEAD!
HA HA!
VERY WELL...
THEN I SWEAR BY MY SPEAR...

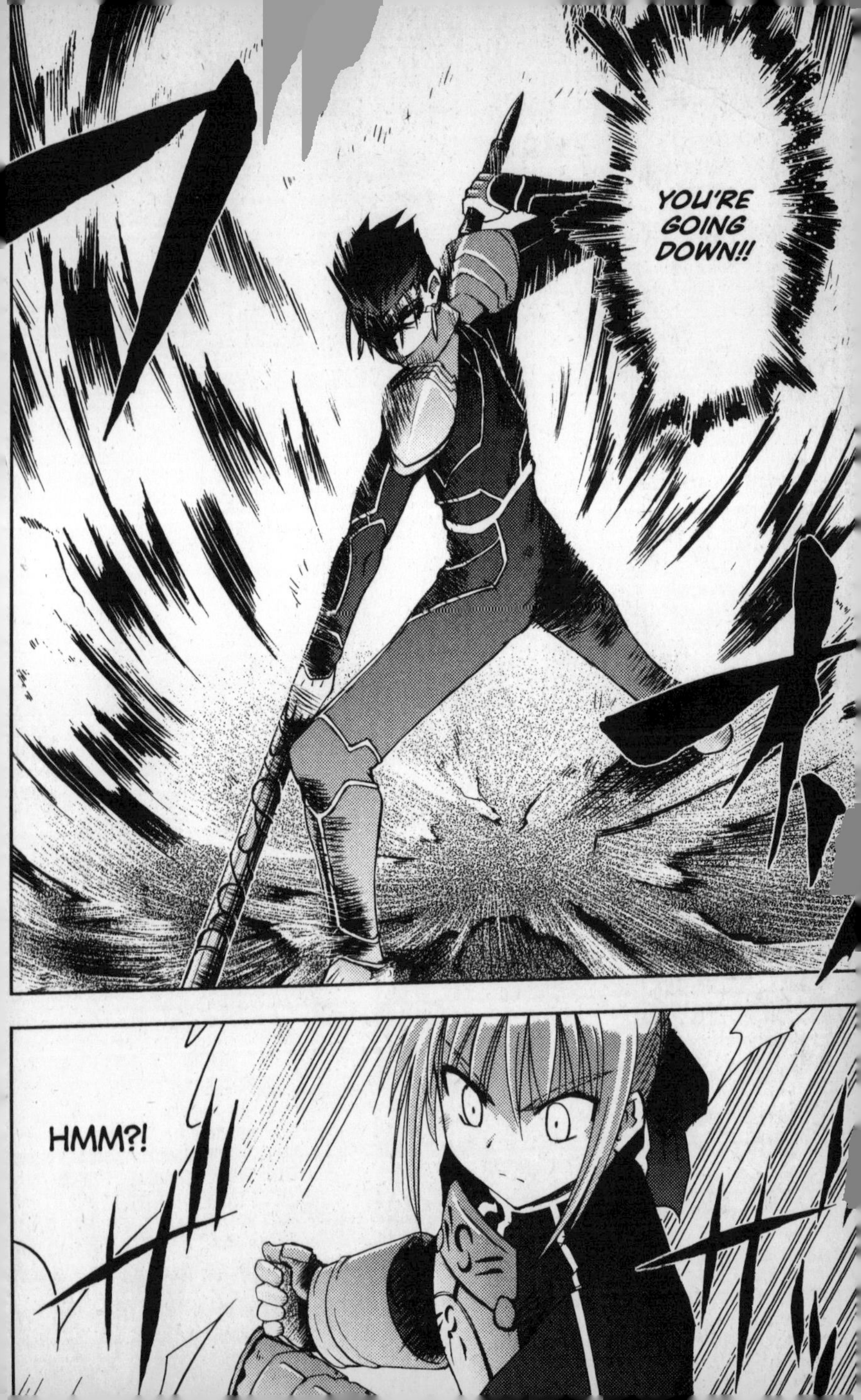
YOU'RE GOING DOWN!!
HMM?!

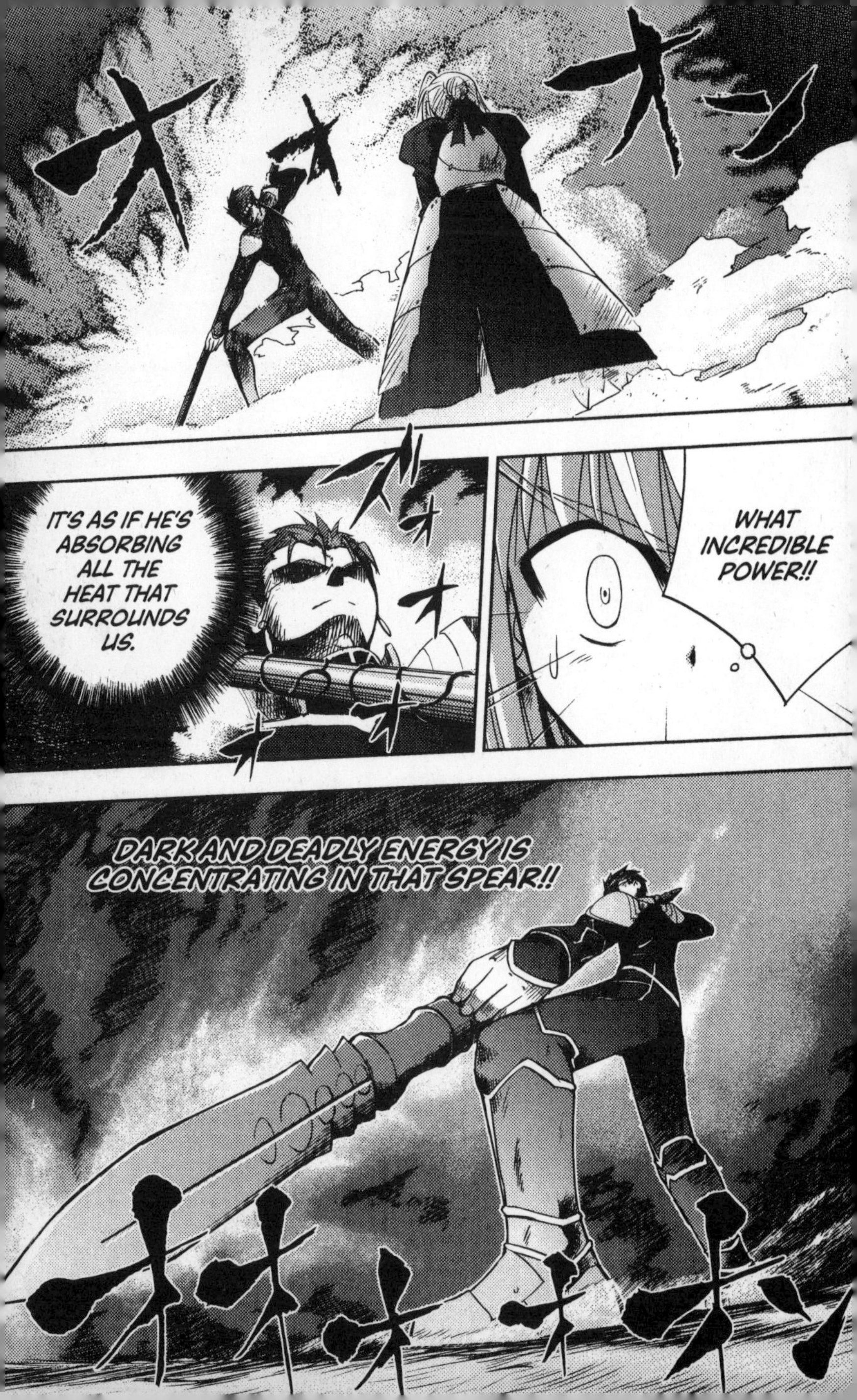
オオオーン
WHAT INCREDIBLE POWER!!
IT'S AS IF HE'S ABSORBING ALL THE HEAT THAT SURROUNDS US.
DARK AND DEADLY ENERGY IS CONCENTRATING IN THAT SPEAR!!
オオオオオン

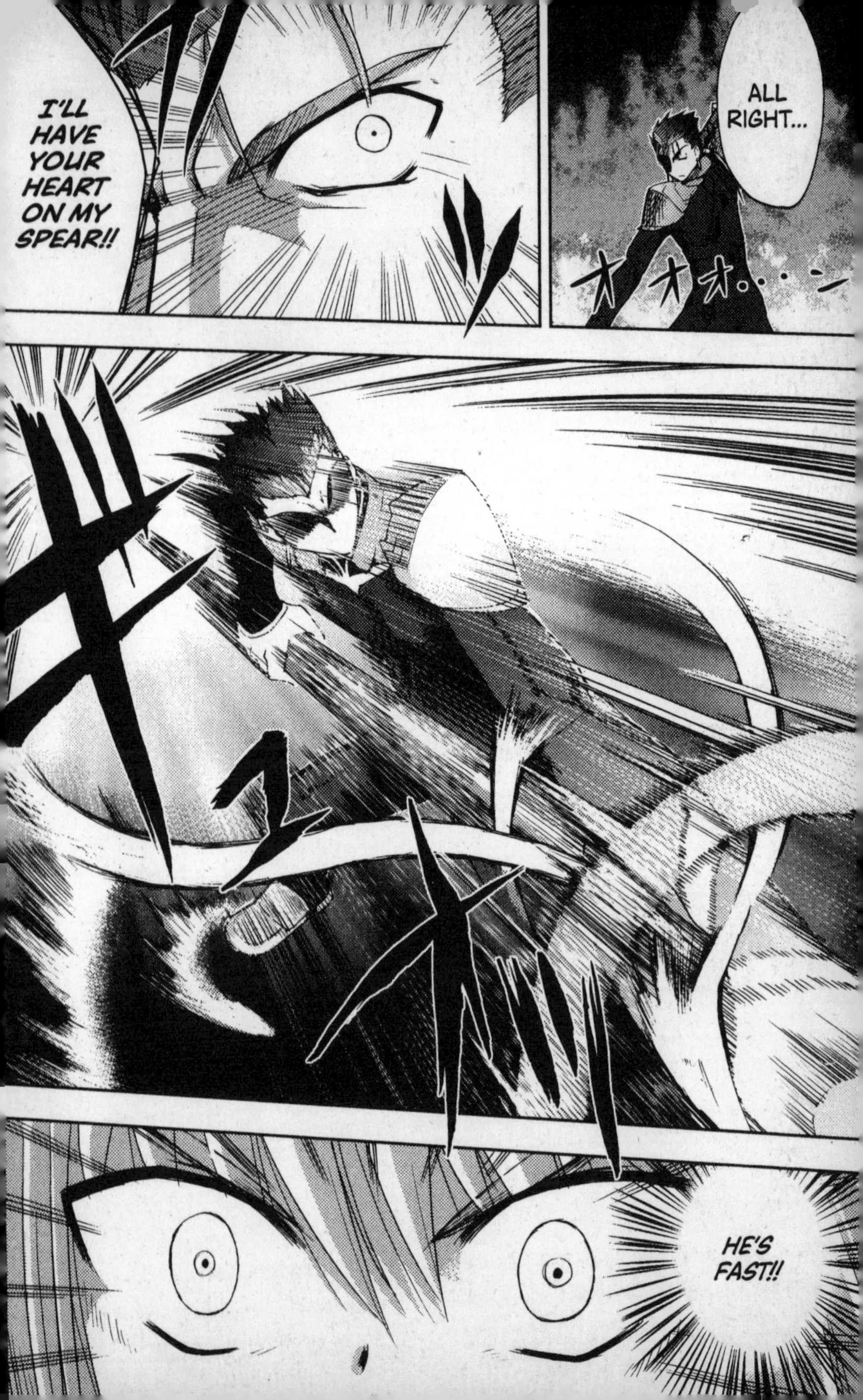
ALL RIGHT...
オオオ...
I'LL HAVE YOUR HEART ON MY SPEAR!!
HE'S FAST!!

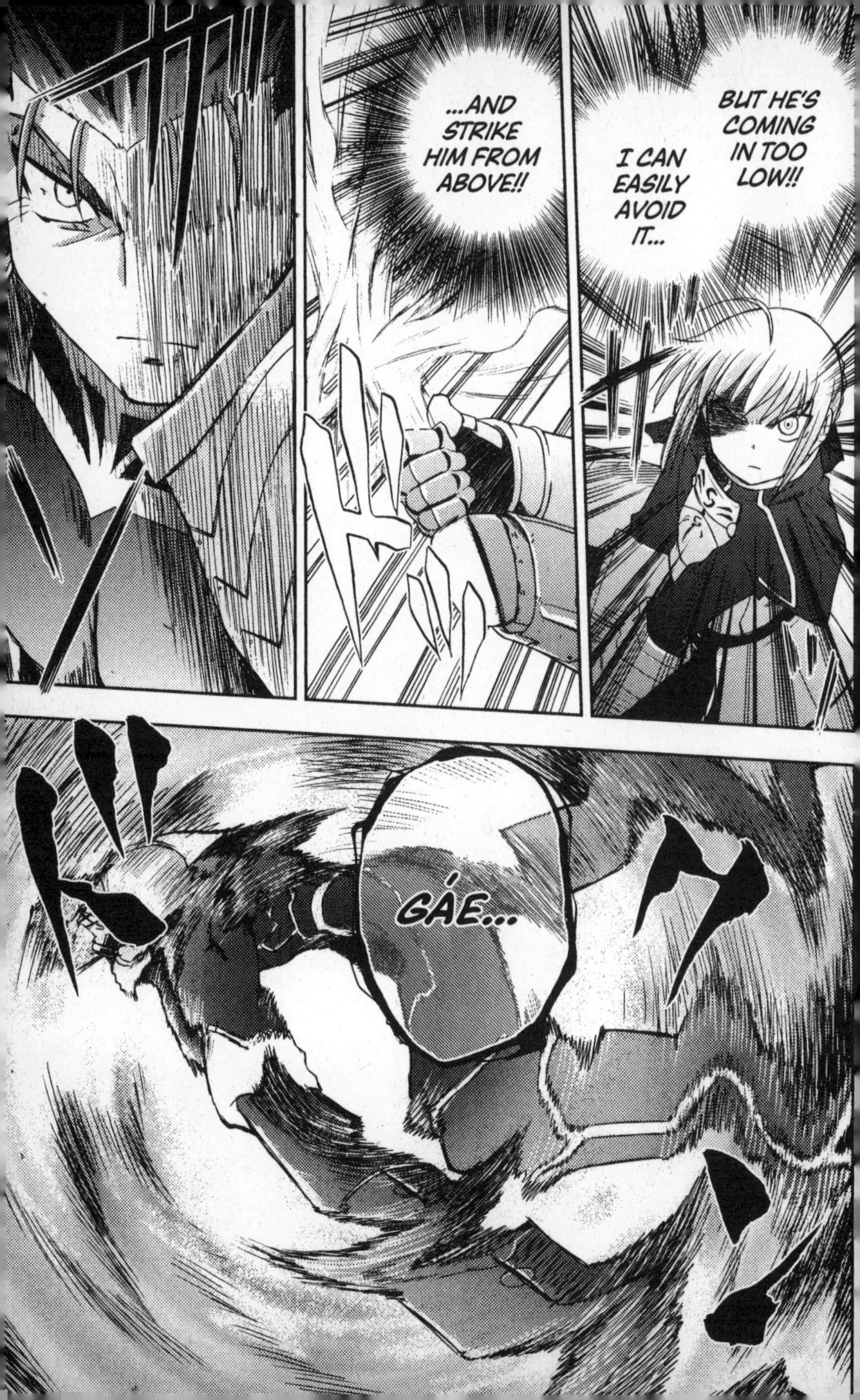
BUT HE'S COMING IN TOO LOW!!
I CAN EASILY AVOID IT...
...AND STRIKE HIM FROM ABOVE!!
GÁE...

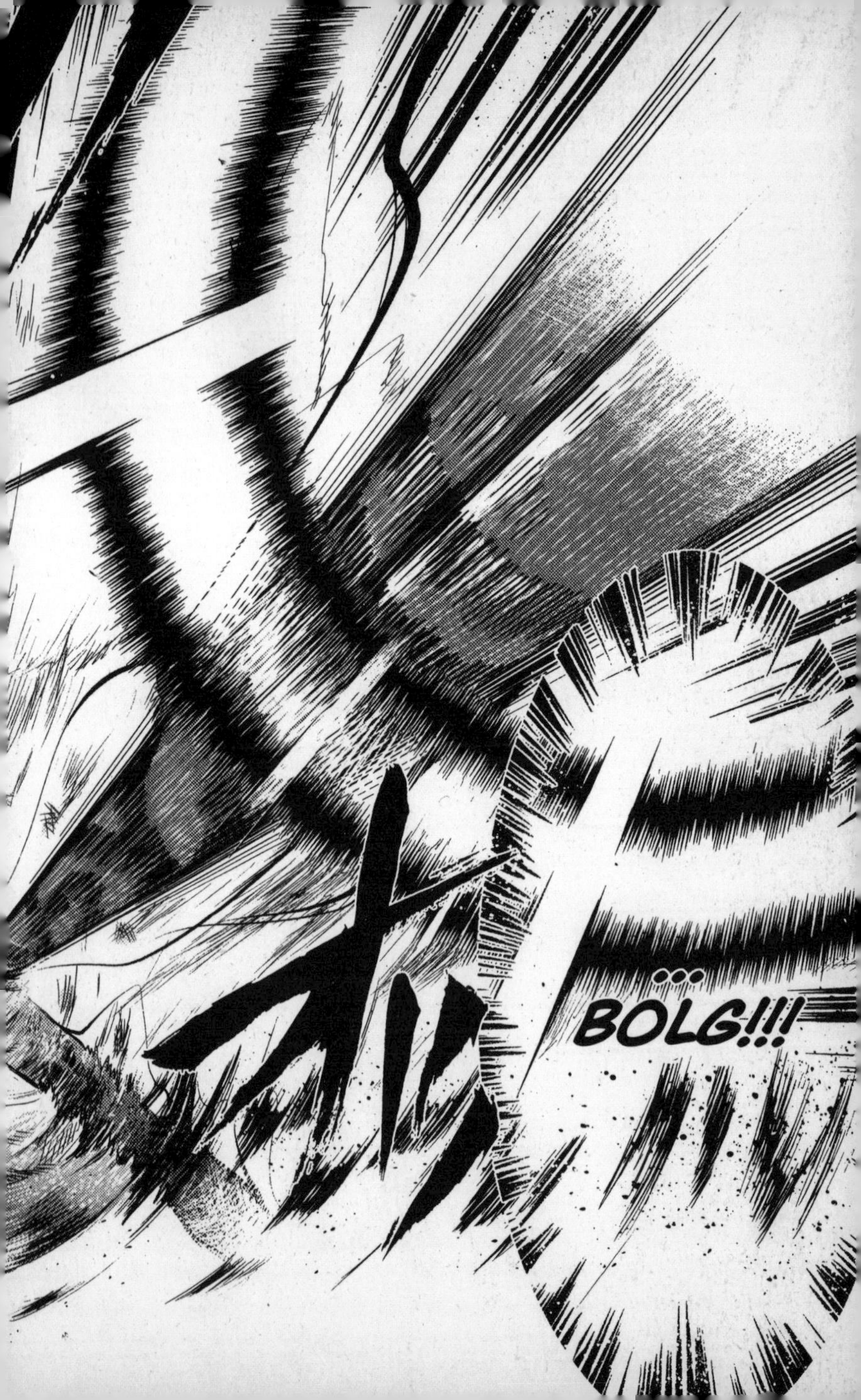
...BOLG!!!

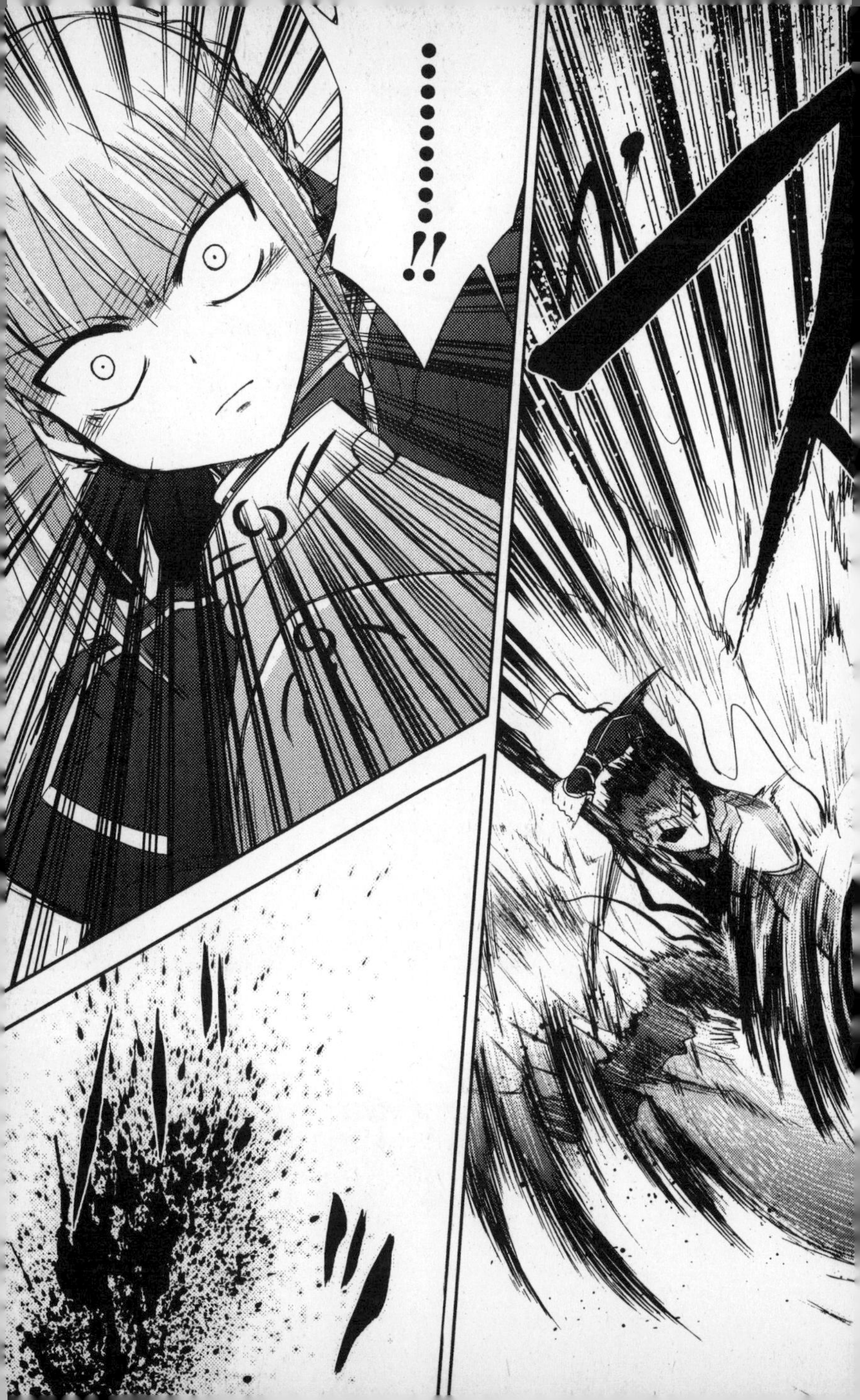
……!!

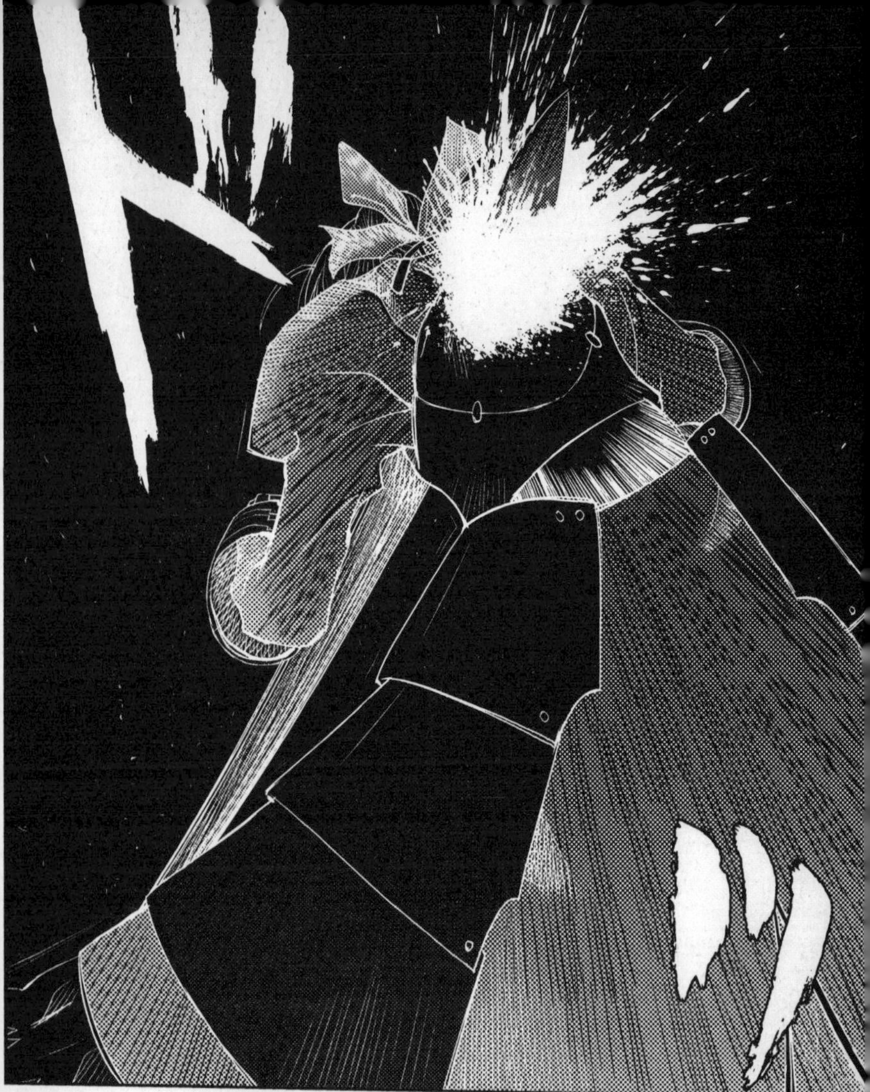
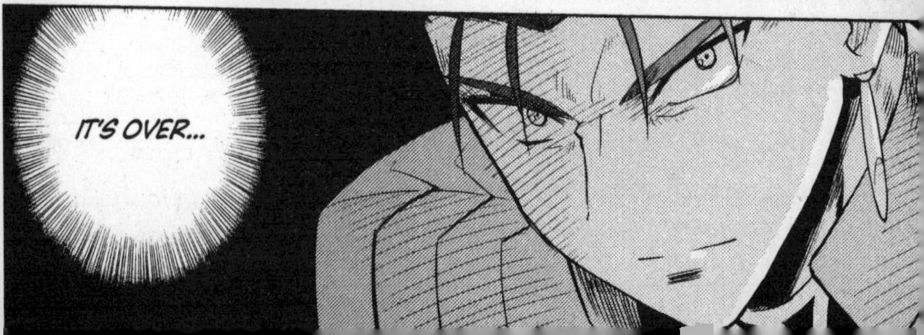
IT'S OVER...

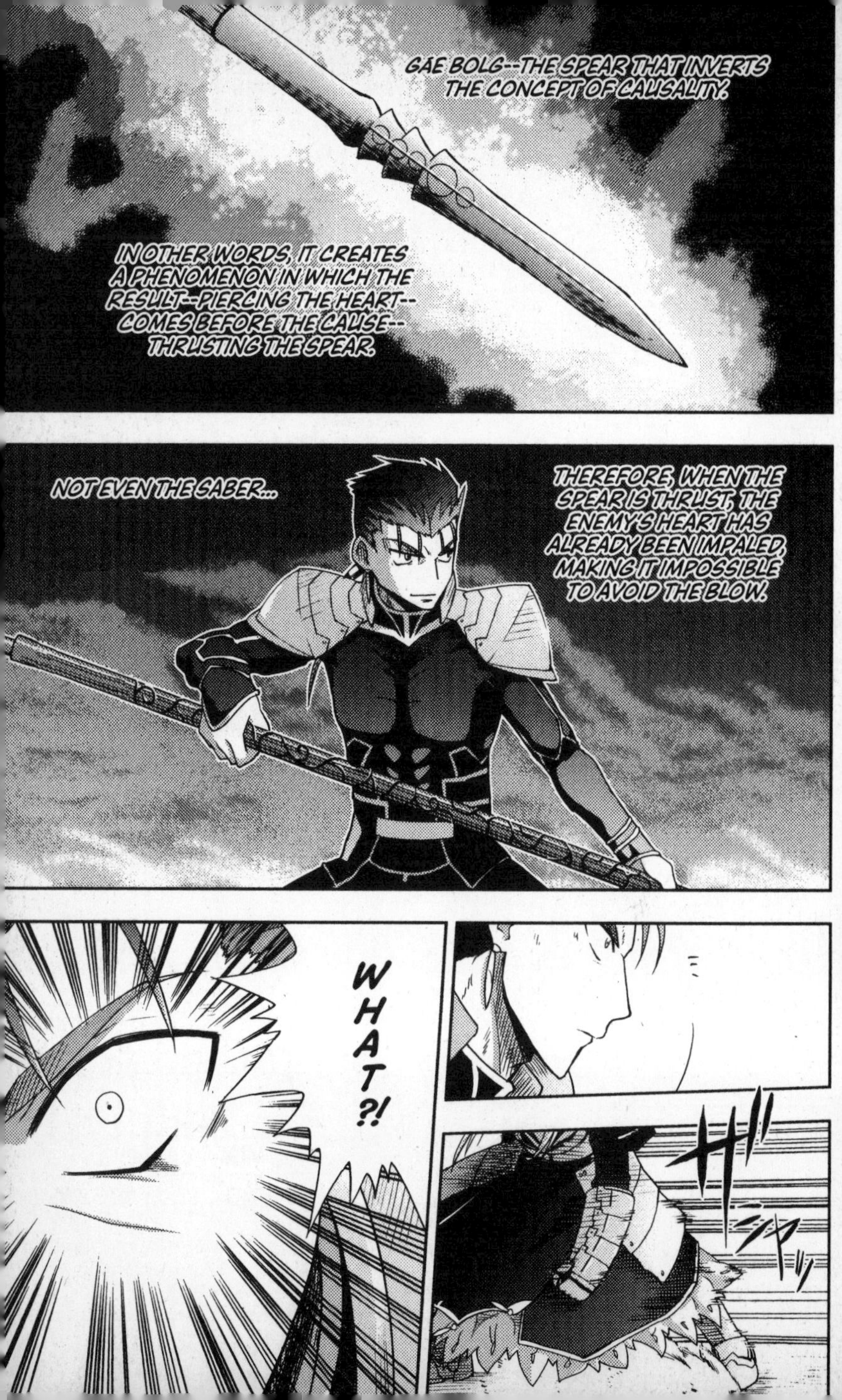
GÁE BOLG--THE SPEAR THAT INVERTS THE CONCEPT OF CAUSALITY.
IN OTHER WORDS, IT CREATES A PHENOMENON IN WHICH THE RESULT--PIERCING THE HEART--COMES BEFORE THE CAUSE--THRUSTING THE SPEAR.
THEREFORE, WHEN THE SPEAR IS THRUST, THE ENEMY'S HEART HAS ALREADY BEEN IMPALED, MAKING IT IMPOSSIBLE TO AVOID THE BLOW.
NOT EVEN THE SABER...
WHAT?!

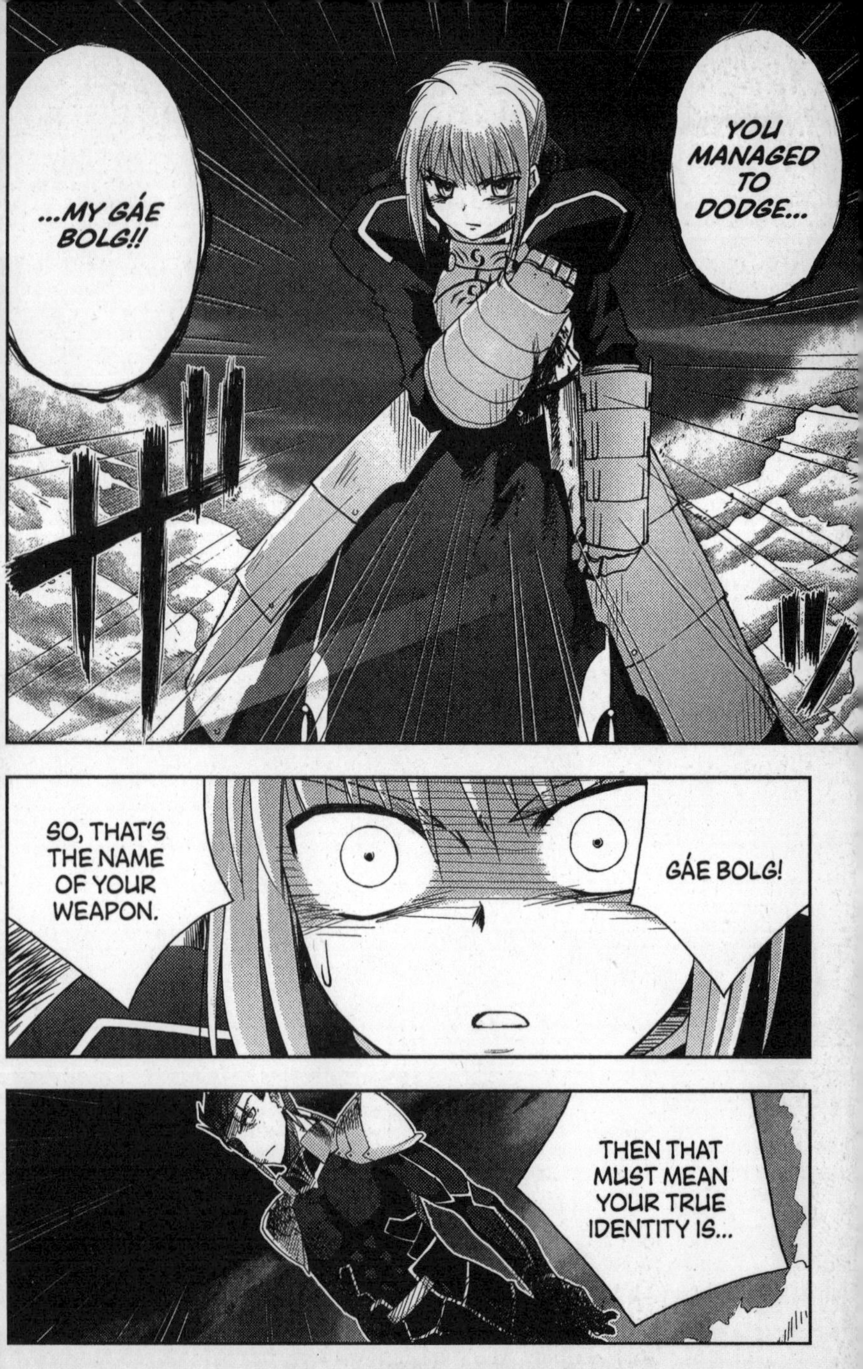
YOU MANAGED TO DODGE...
...MY GÁE BOLG!!
GÁE BOLG!
SO, THAT'S THE NAME OF YOUR WEAPON.
THEN THAT MUST MEAN YOUR TRUE IDENTITY IS...

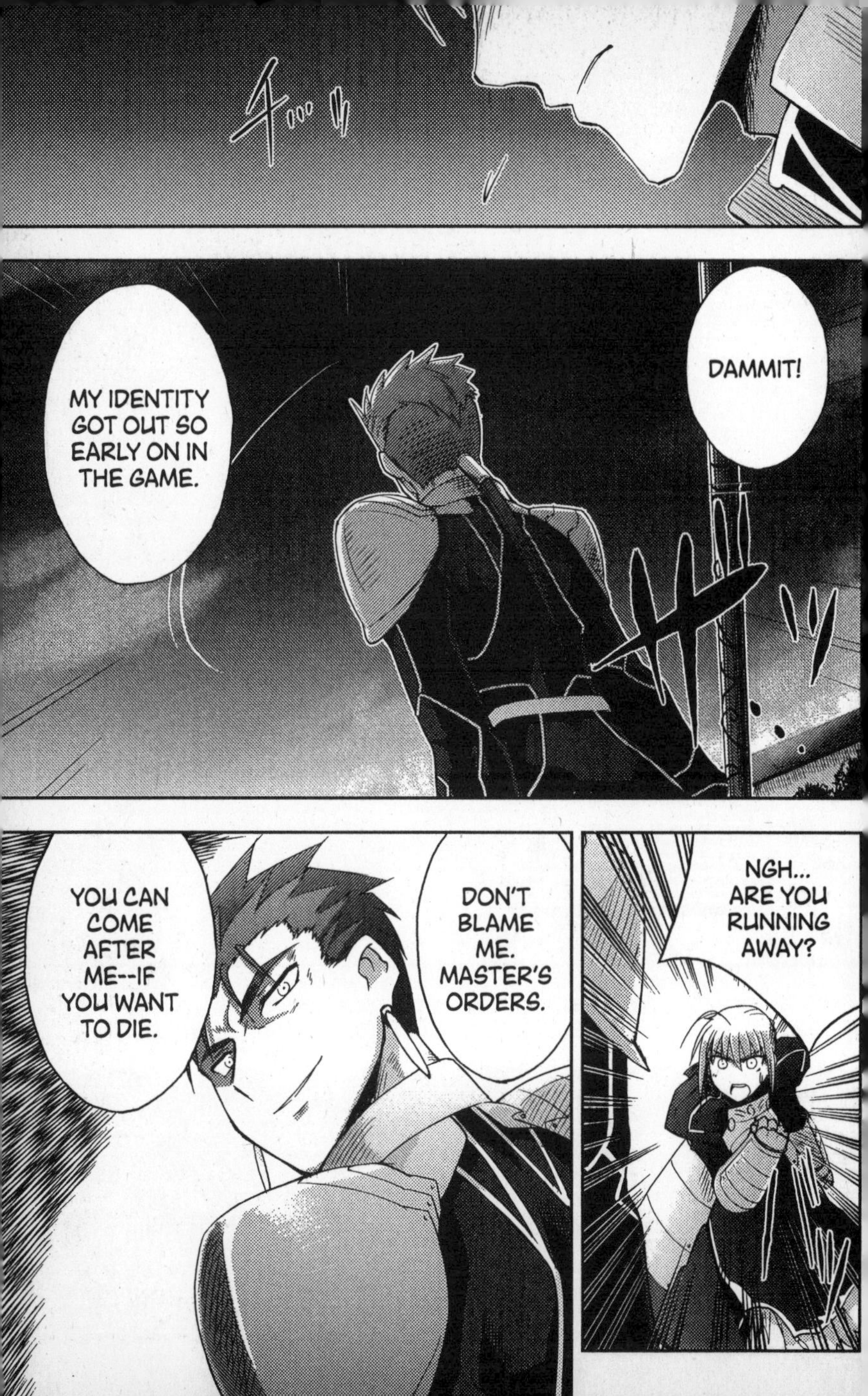
DAMMIT!
MY IDENTITY GOT OUT SO EARLY ON IN THE GAME.
NGH... ARE YOU RUNNING AWAY?
DON'T BLAME ME. MASTER'S ORDERS.
YOU CAN COME AFTER ME--IF YOU WANT TO DIE.

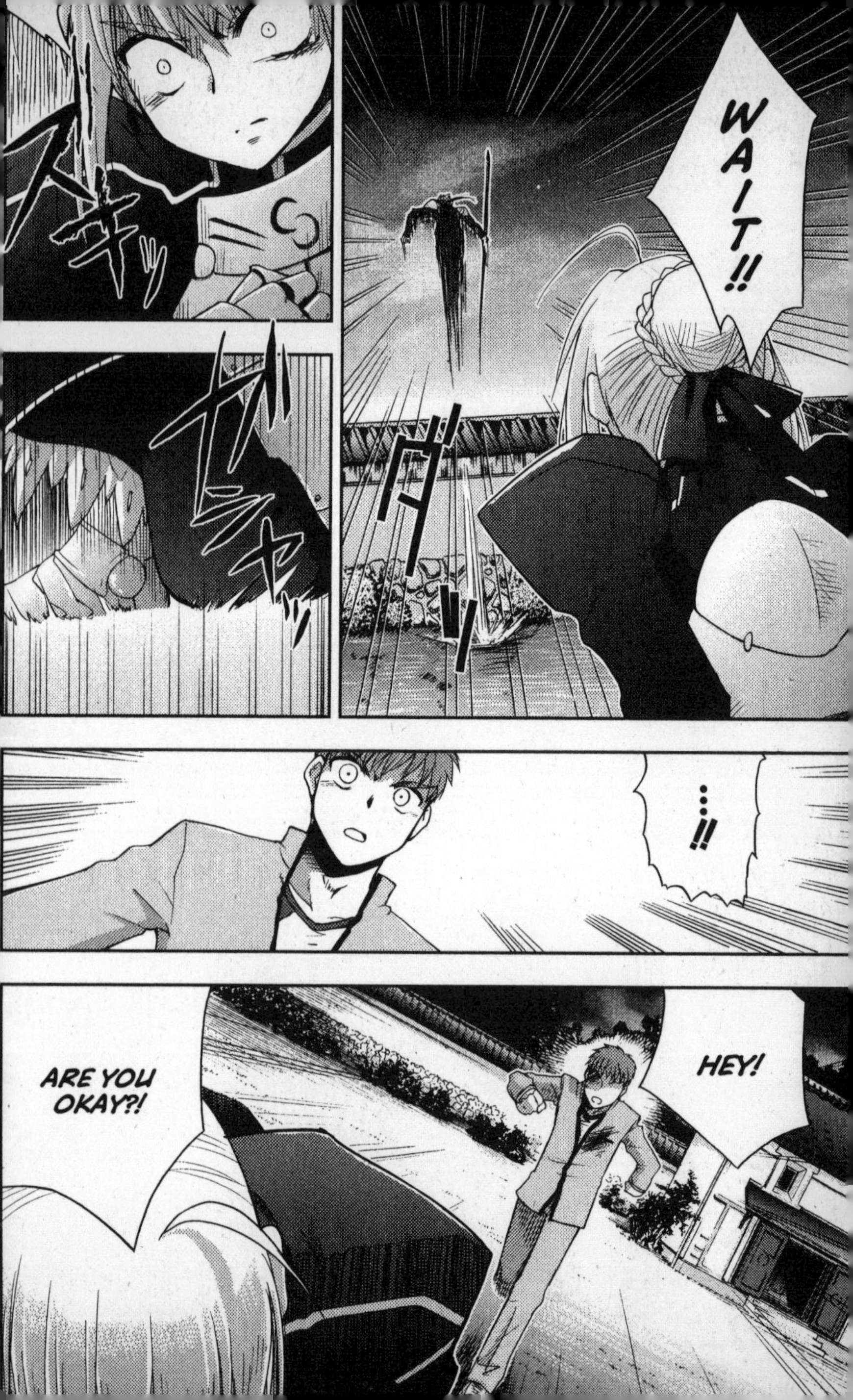
WAIT!!
...!!
HEY!
ARE YOU OKAY?!

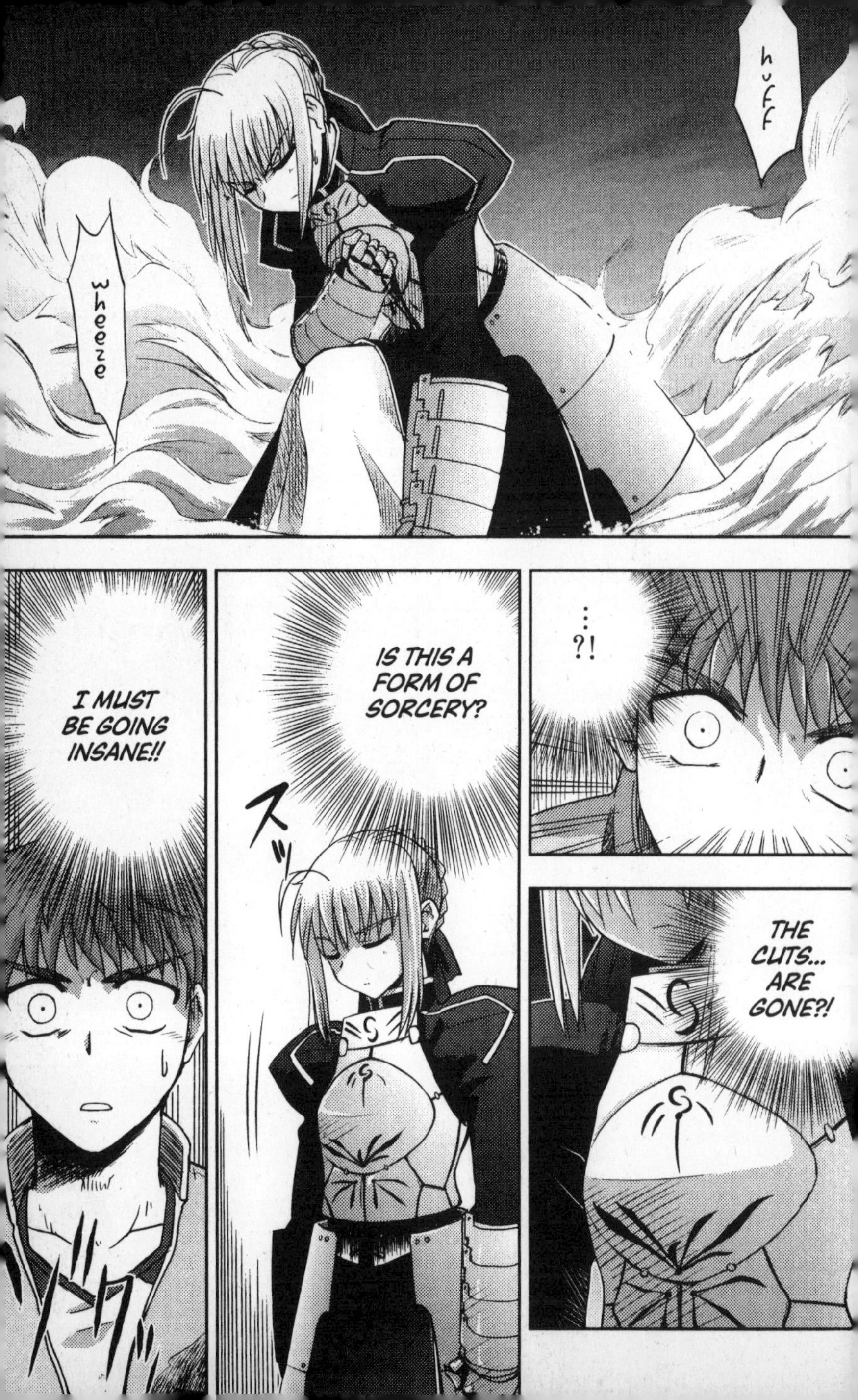
huff
wheeze
...?!
THE CUTS... ARE GONE?!
IS THIS A FORM OF SORCERY?
スッ
I MUST BE GOING INSANE!!

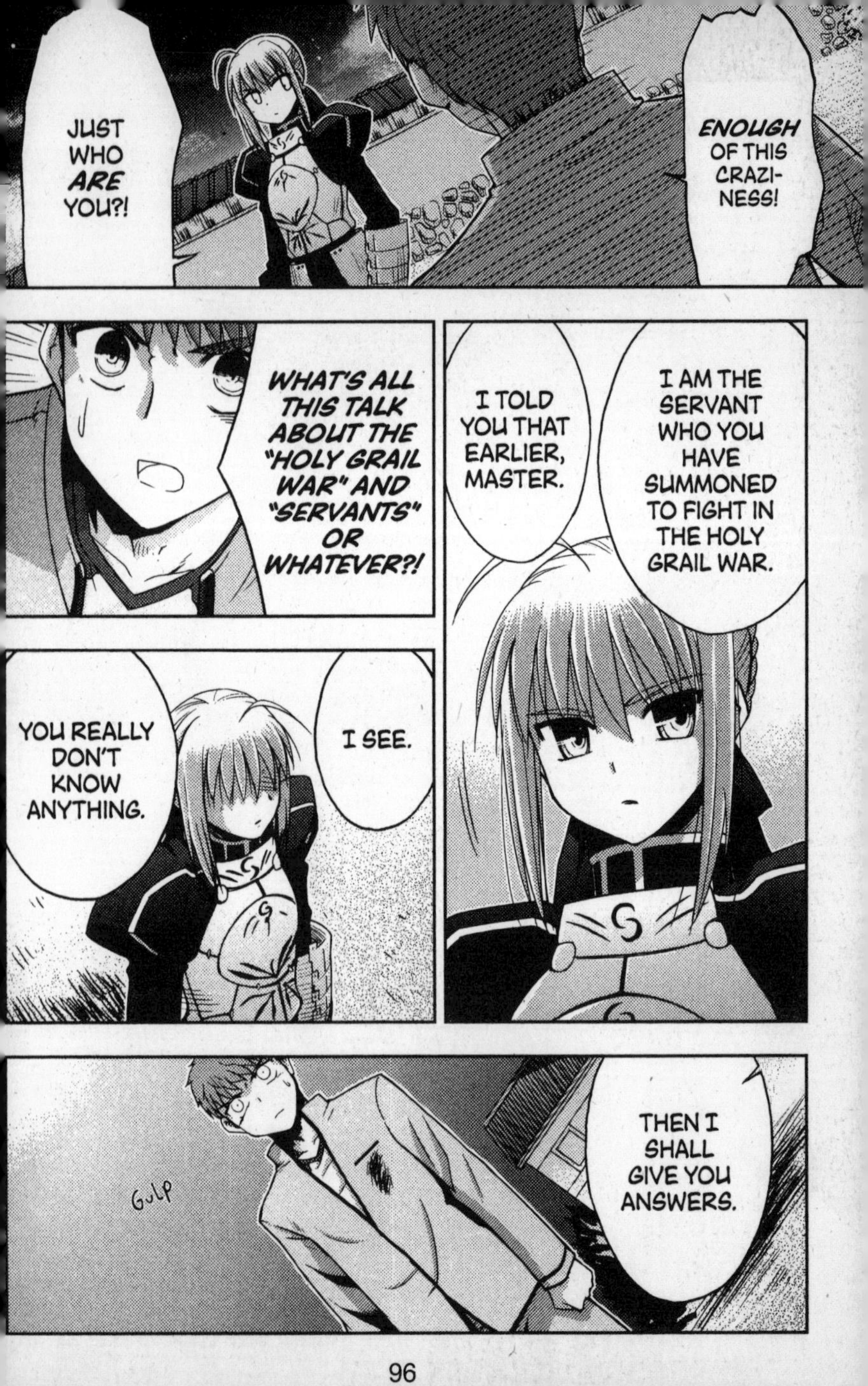
ENOUGH OF THIS CRAZINESS!
JUST WHO ARE YOU?!
I AM THE SERVANT WHO YOU HAVE SUMMONED TO FIGHT IN THE HOLY GRAIL WAR.
I TOLD YOU THAT EARLIER, MASTER.
WHAT'S ALL THIS TALK ABOUT THE "HOLY GRAIL WAR" AND "SERVANTS" OR WHATEVER?!
I SEE.
YOU REALLY DON'T KNOW ANYTHING.
THEN I SHALL GIVE YOU ANSWERS.
GULP

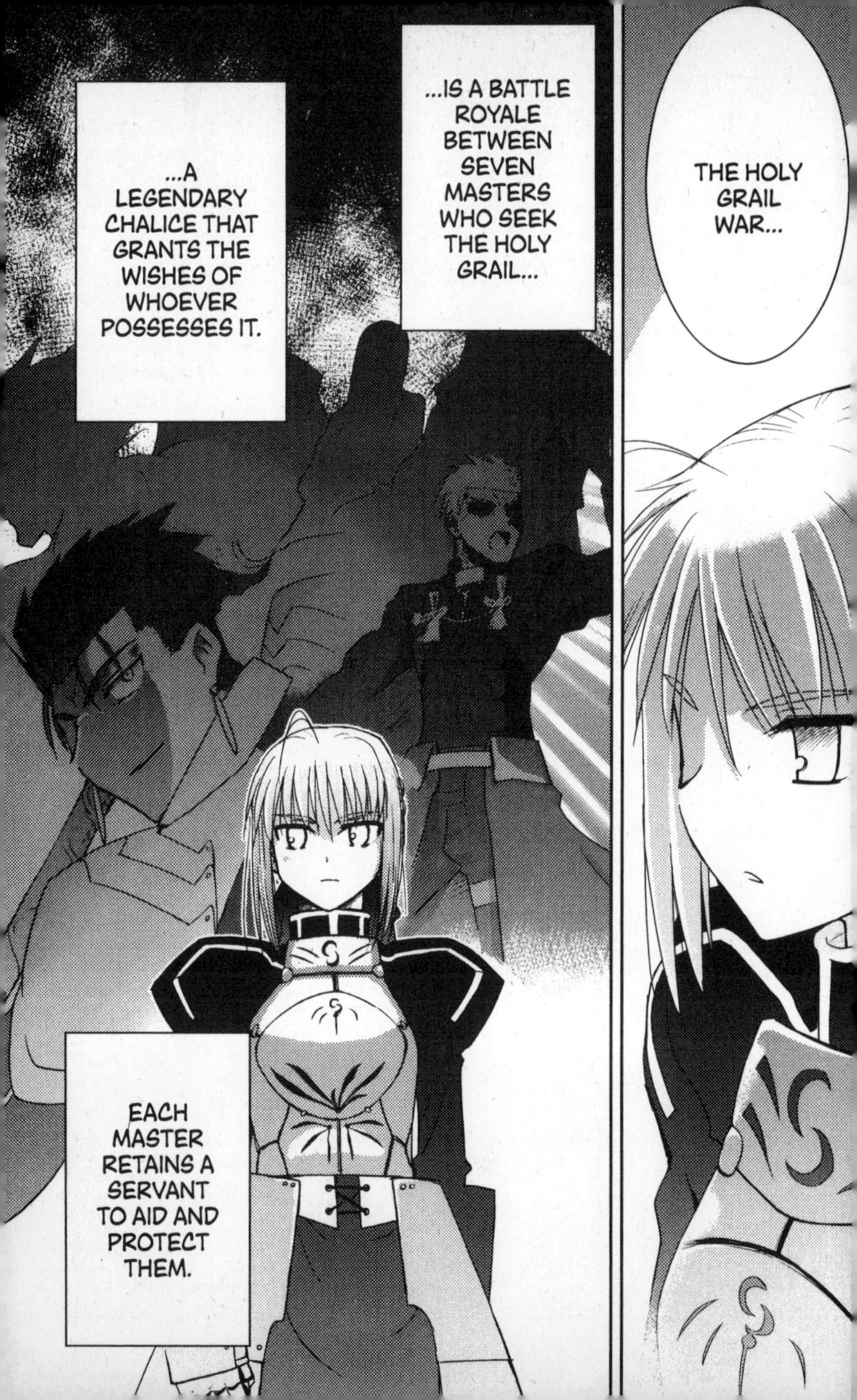
THE HOLY GRAIL WAR...
...IS A BATTLE ROYALE BETWEEN SEVEN MASTERS WHO SEEK THE HOLY GRAIL...
...A LEGENDARY CHALICE THAT GRANTS THE WISHES OF WHOEVER POSSESSES IT.
EACH MASTER RETAINS A SERVANT TO AID AND PROTECT THEM.

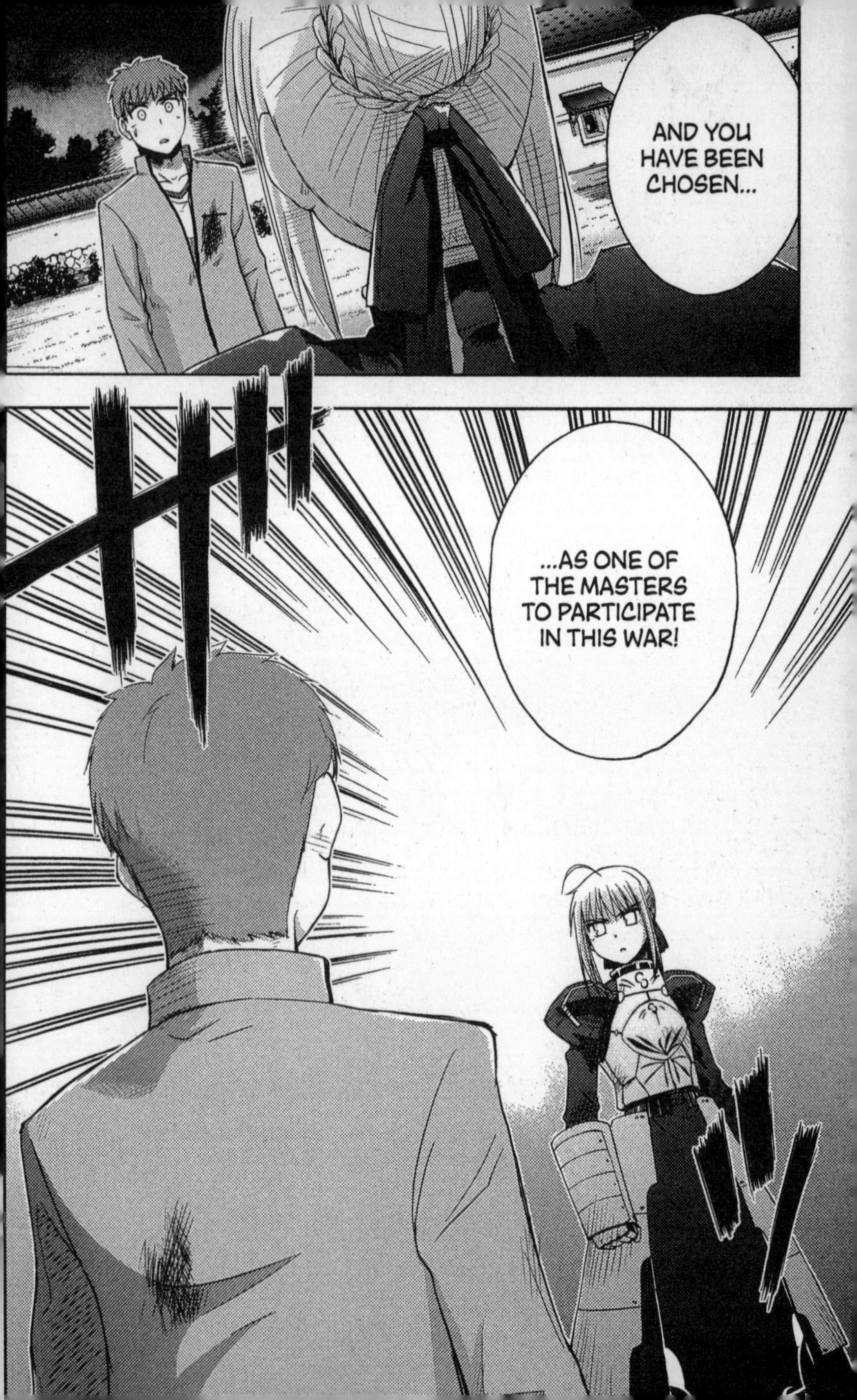
AND YOU HAVE BEEN CHOSEN...
...AS ONE OF THE MASTERS TO PARTICIPATE IN THIS WAR!

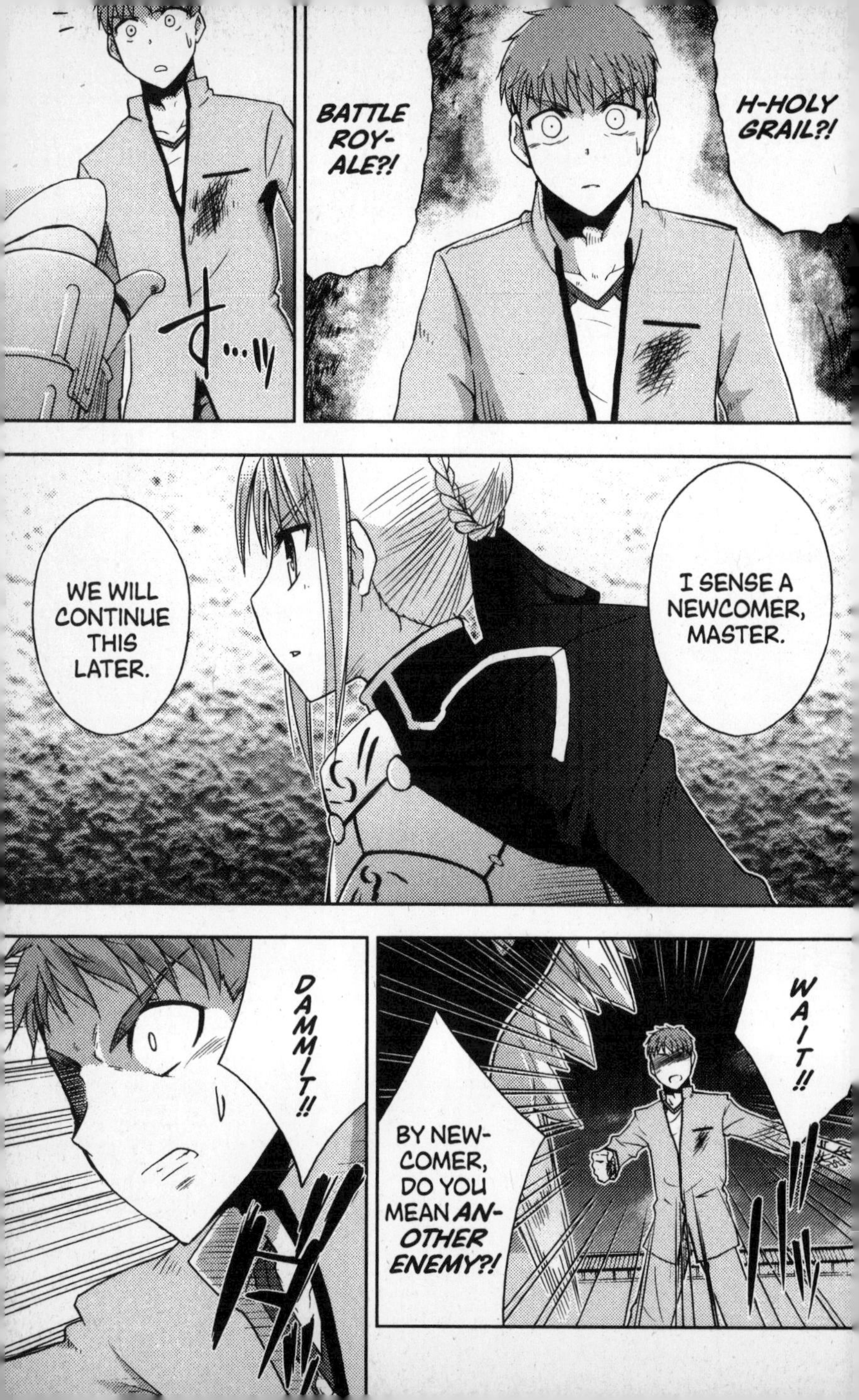
H-HOLY GRAIL?!
BATTLE ROY-ALE?!
す…ッ
I SENSE A NEWCOMER, MASTER.
WE WILL CONTINUE THIS LATER.
WAIT!!
BY NEW-COMER, DO YOU MEAN AN-OTHER ENEMY?!
DAMMIT!!

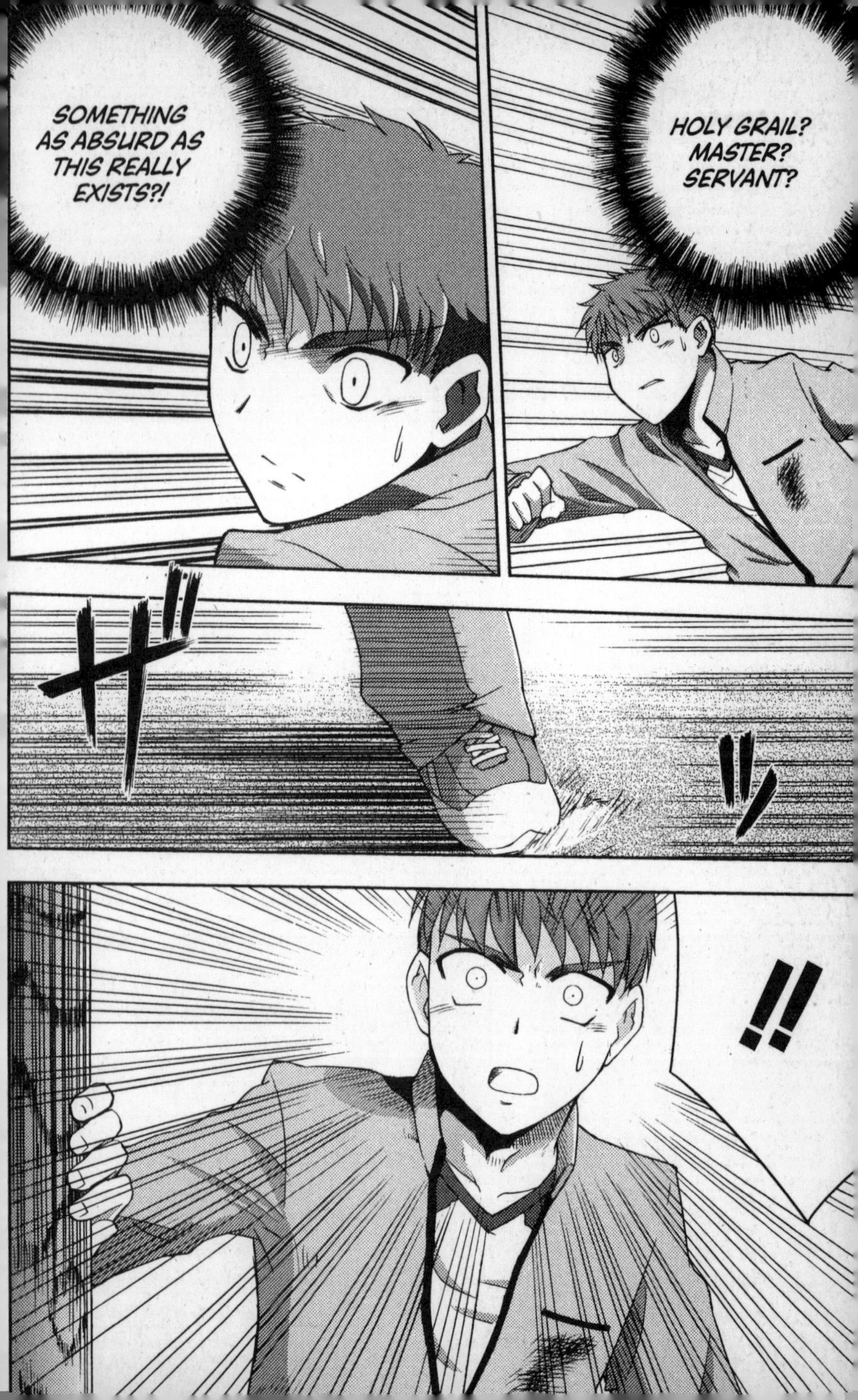
HOLY GRAIL? MASTER? SERVANT?
SOMETHING AS ABSURD AS THIS REALLY EXISTS?!
!!

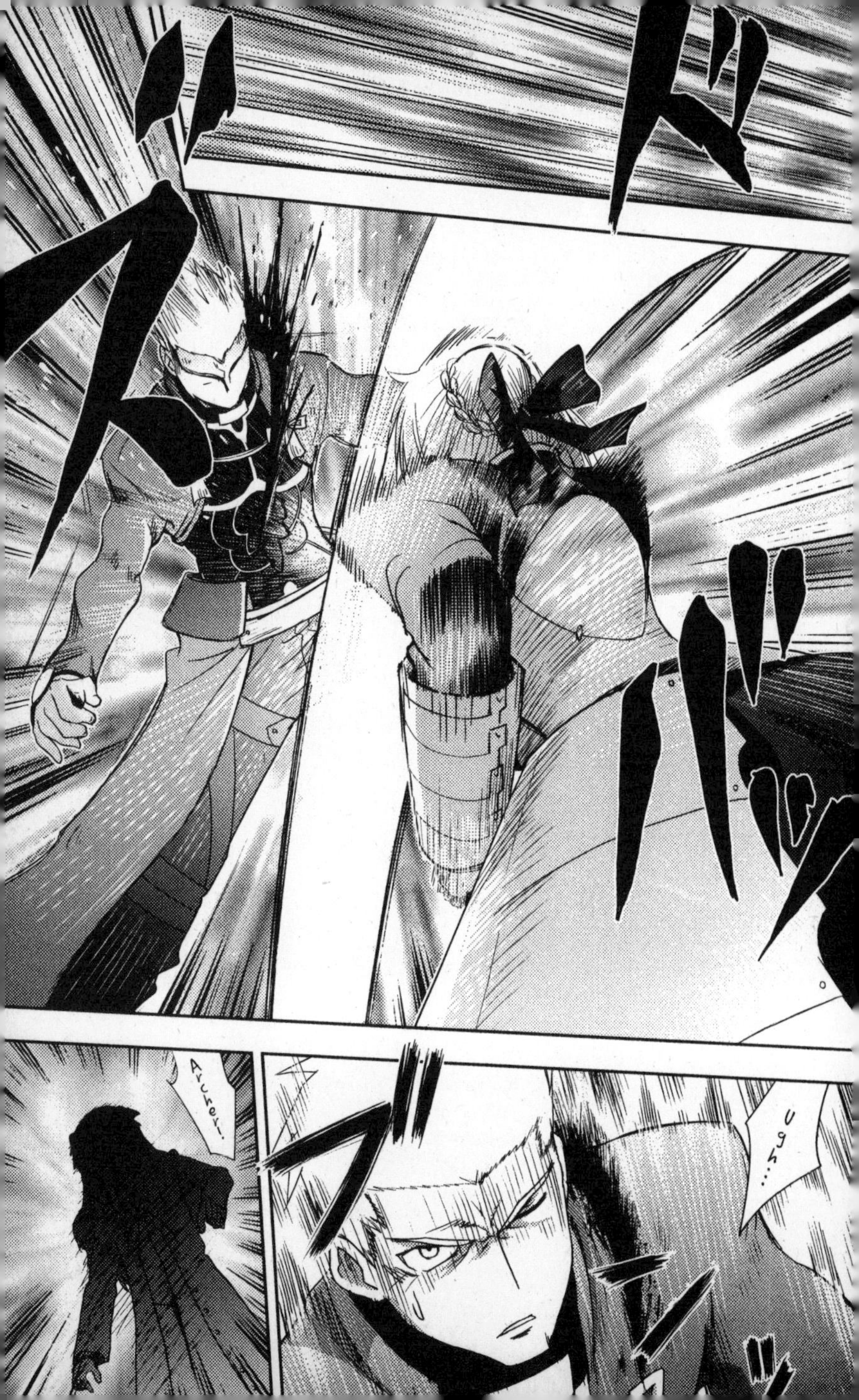
Ugh...
Archer!

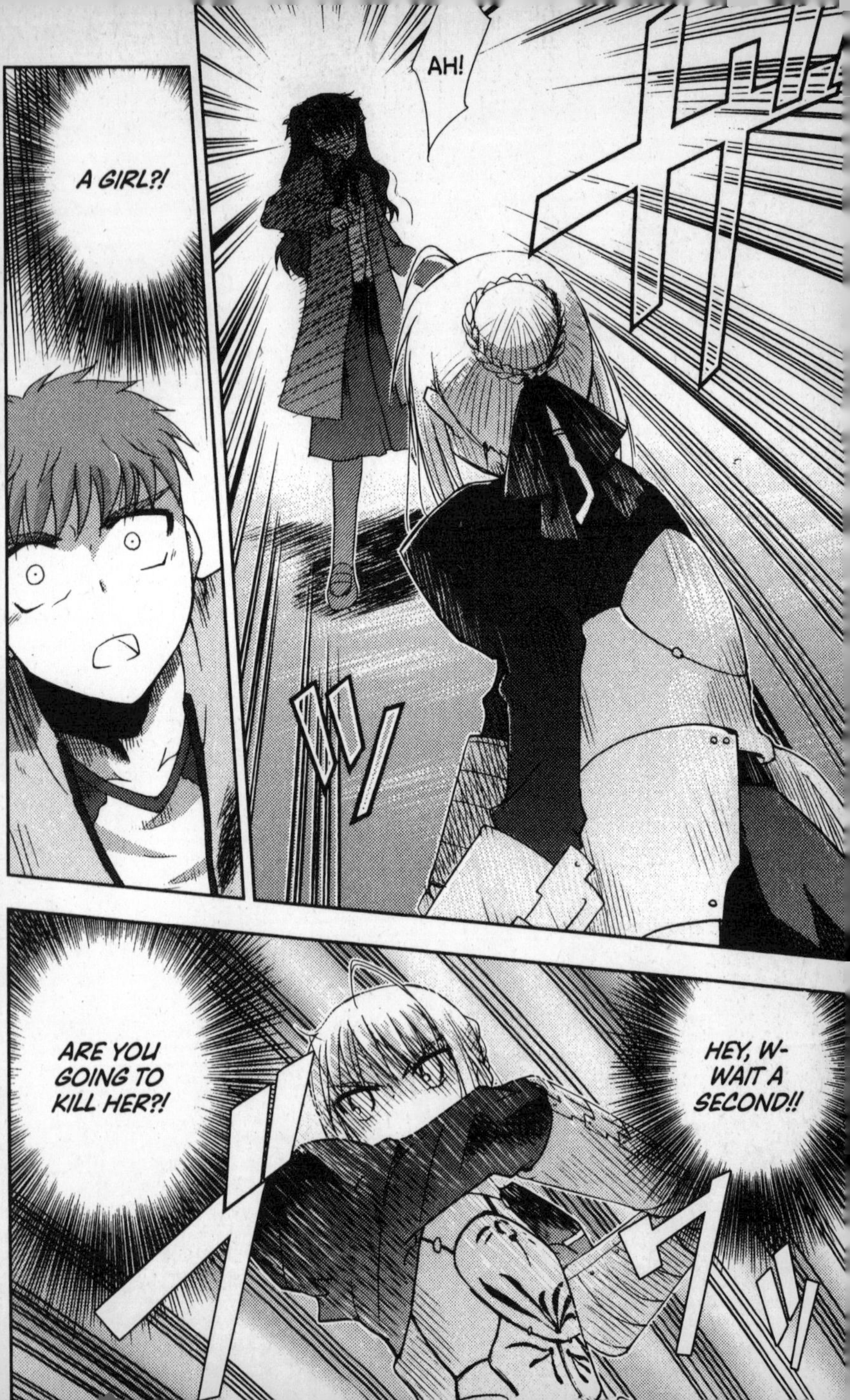
AH!
A GIRL?!
HEY, W- WAIT A SECOND!!
ARE YOU GOING TO KILL HER?!

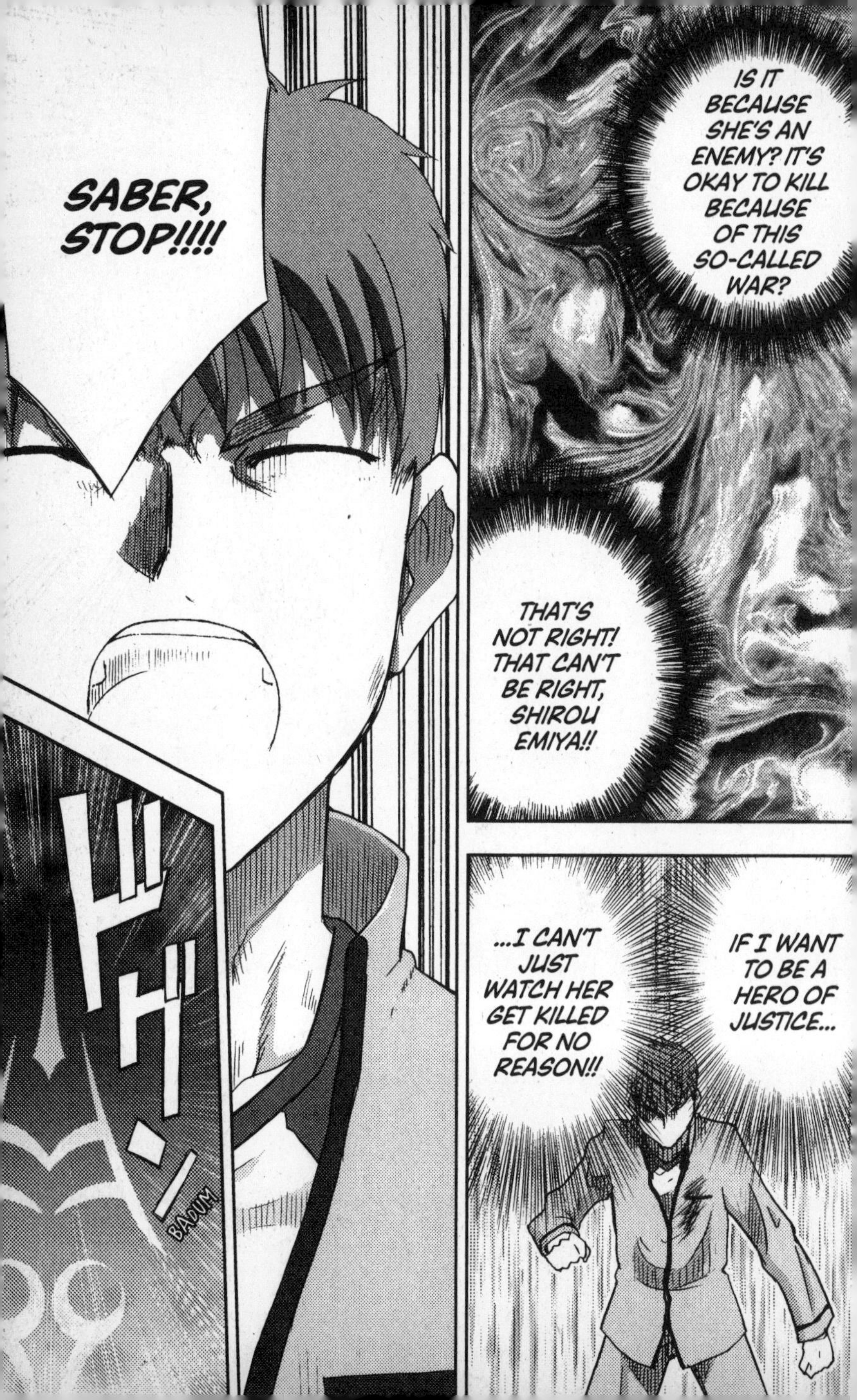
IS IT BECAUSE SHE'S AN ENEMY? IT'S OKAY TO KILL BECAUSE OF THIS SO-CALLED WAR?
THAT'S NOT RIGHT! THAT CAN'T BE RIGHT, SHIROU EMIYA!!
IF I WANT TO BE A HERO OF JUSTICE...
...I CAN'T JUST WATCH HER GET KILLED FOR NO REASON!!
SABER, STOP!!!!
BADUM

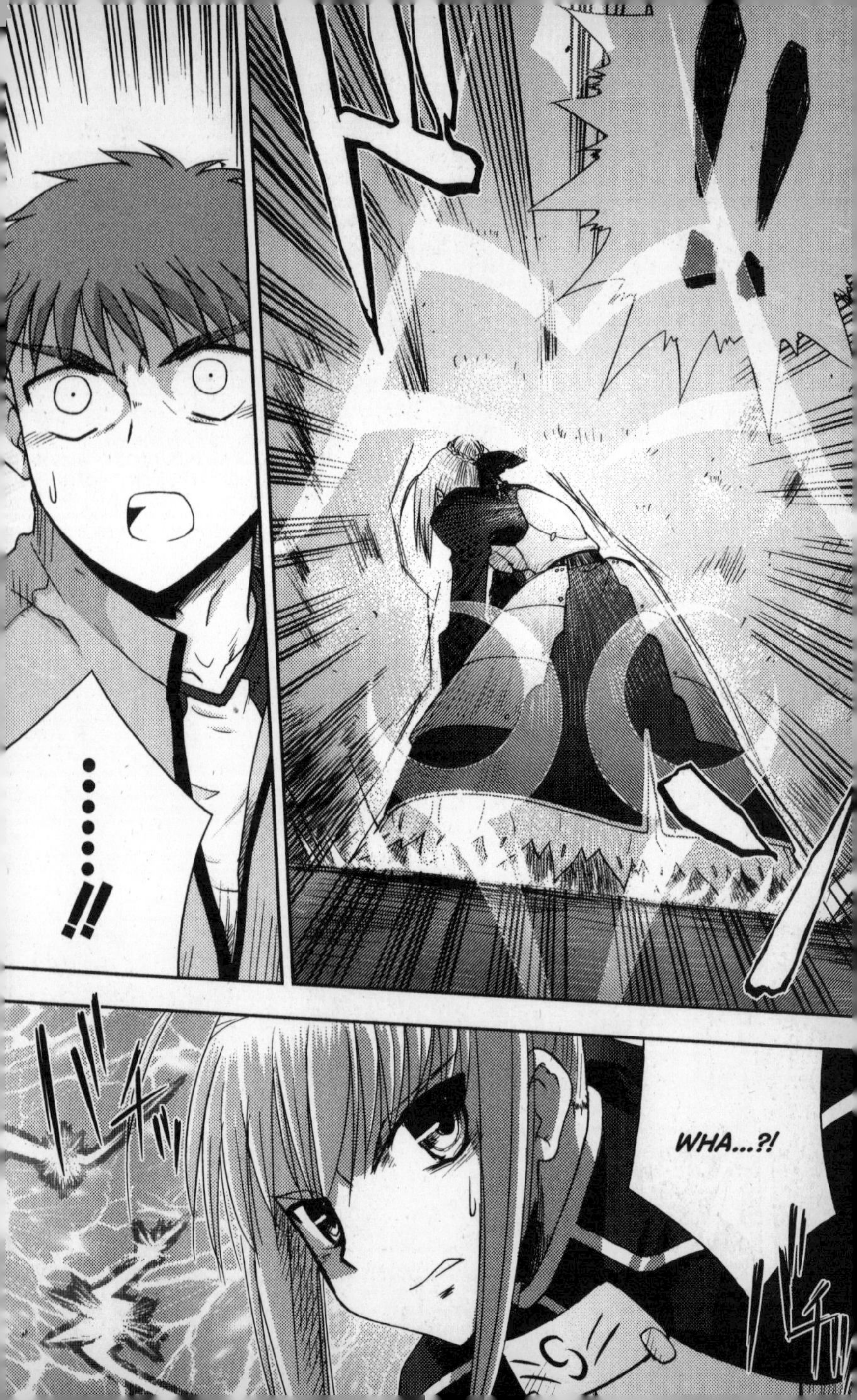
......!!
WHA...?!

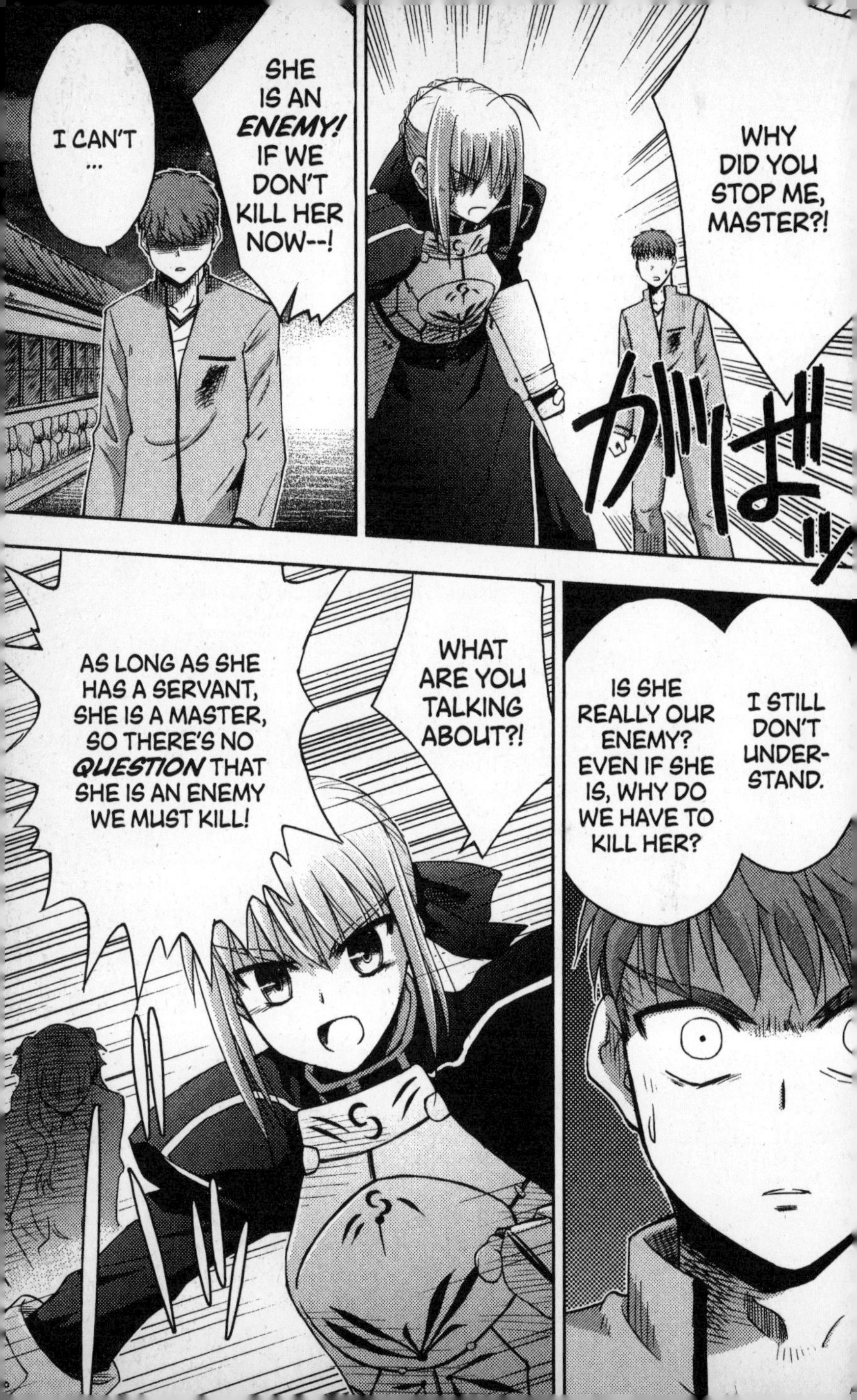
WHY DID YOU STOP ME, MASTER?!
がばッ
SHE IS AN *ENEMY!* IF WE DON'T KILL HER NOW--!
I CAN'T ...
I STILL DON'T UNDER-STAND.
IS SHE REALLY OUR ENEMY? EVEN IF SHE IS, WHY DO WE HAVE TO KILL HER?
WHAT ARE YOU TALKING ABOUT?!
AS LONG AS SHE HAS A SERVANT, SHE IS A MASTER, SO THERE'S NO *QUESTION* THAT SHE IS AN ENEMY WE MUST KILL!

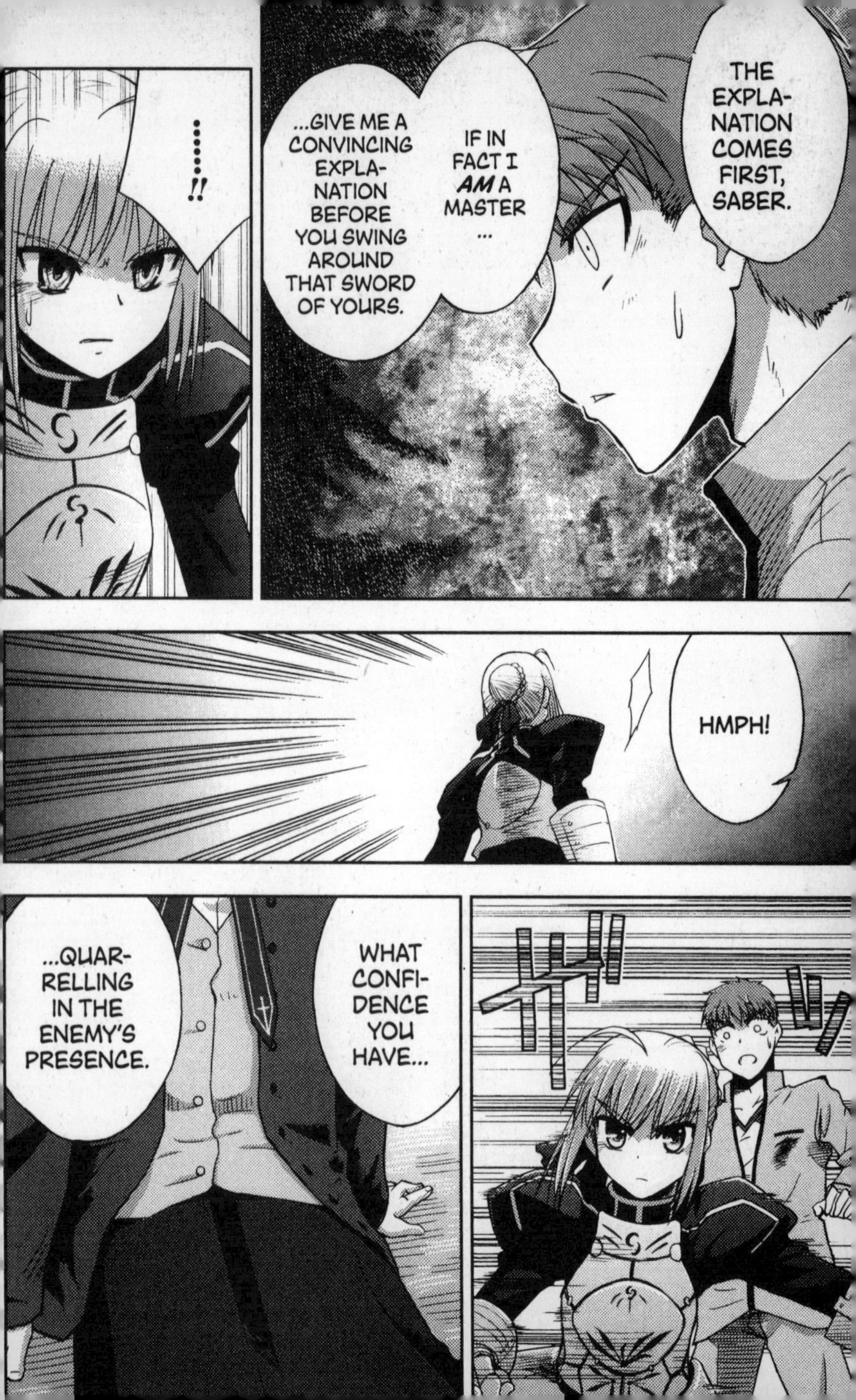
THE EXPLA-NATION COMES FIRST, SABER.
IF IN FACT I AM A MASTER ...
...GIVE ME A CONVINCING EXPLA-NATION BEFORE YOU SWING AROUND THAT SWORD OF YOURS.
......!!
HMPH!
WHAT CONFI-DENCE YOU HAVE...
...QUAR-RELLING IN THE ENEMY'S PRESENCE.

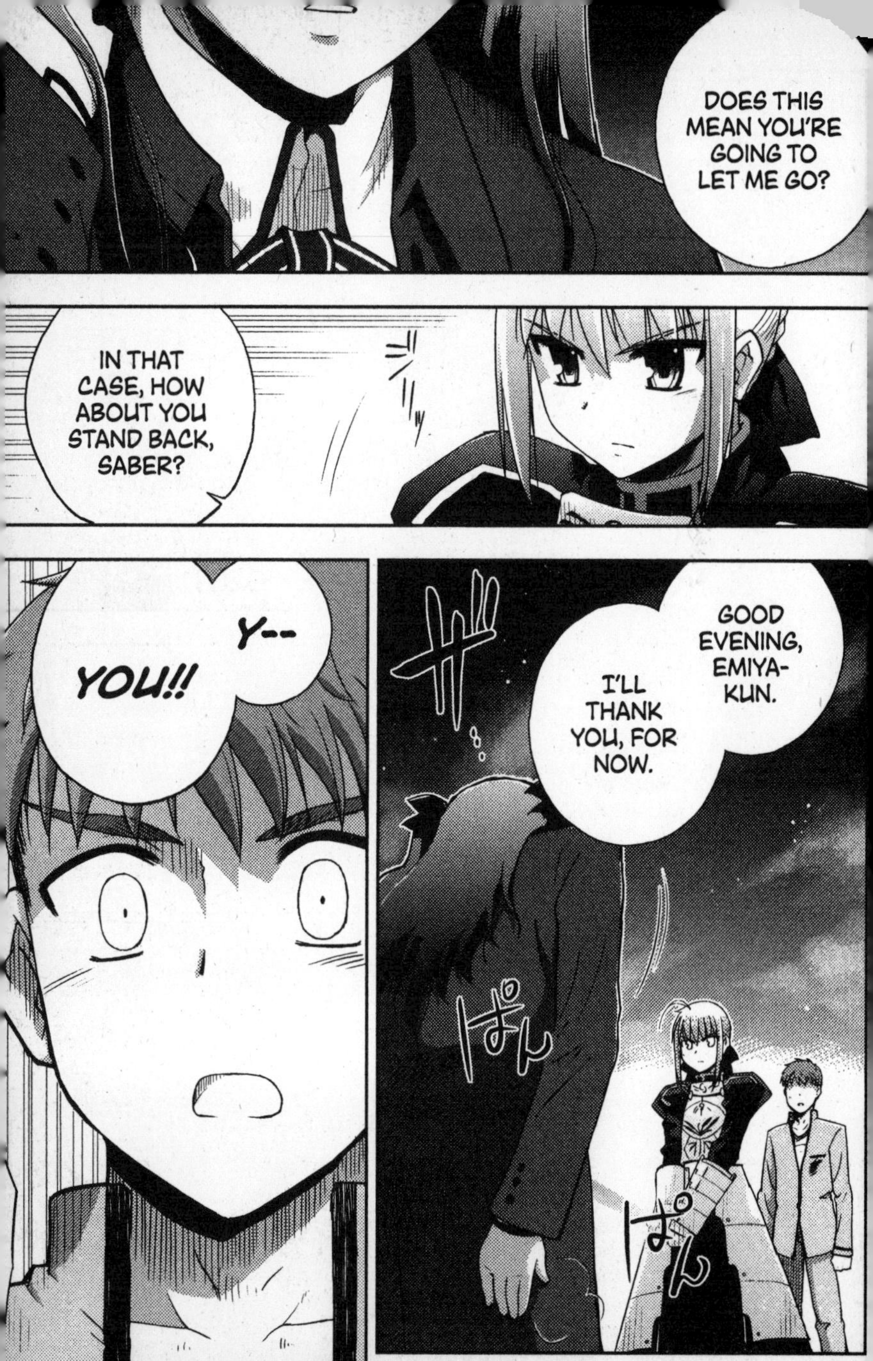
DOES THIS MEAN YOU'RE GOING TO LET ME GO?
IN THAT CASE, HOW ABOUT YOU STAND BACK, SABER?
GOOD EVENING, EMIYA-KUN.
I'LL THANK YOU, FOR NOW.
ぱん
ぱん
Y--
YOU!!

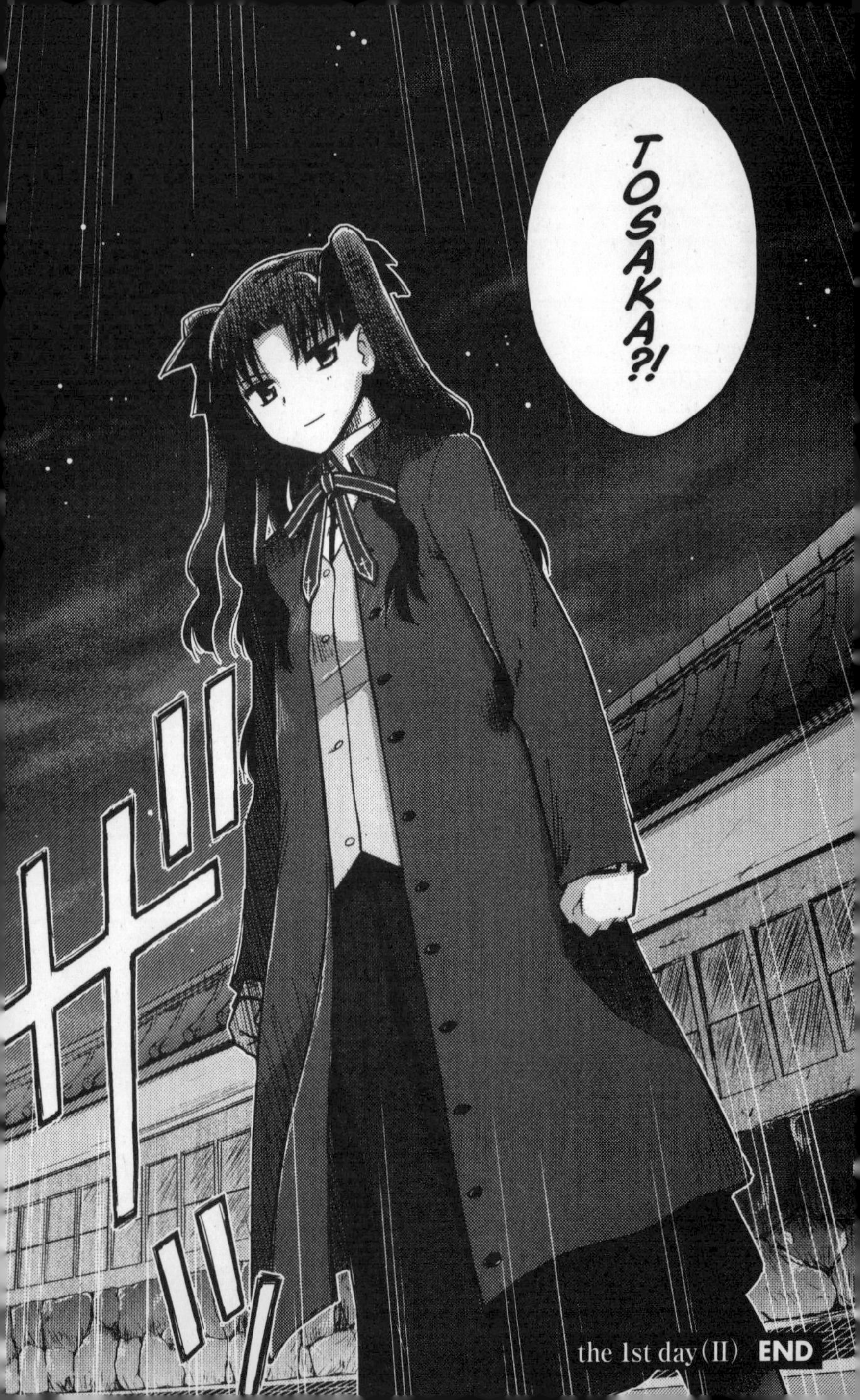
TOSAKA?!

the 1st day (II) **END**

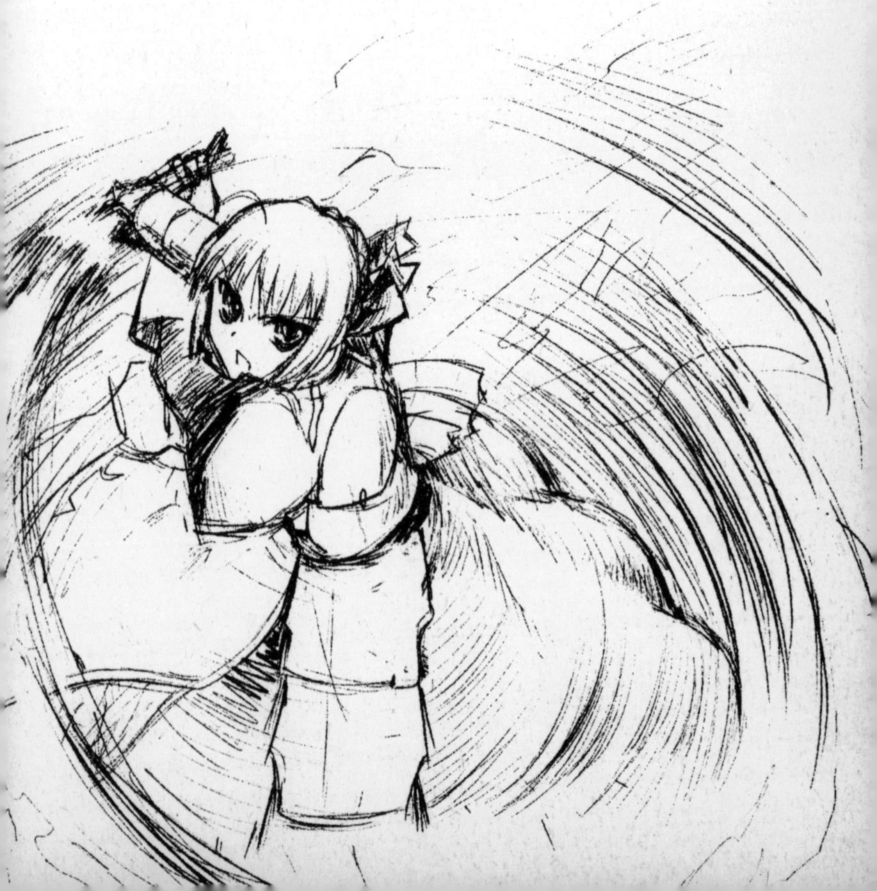

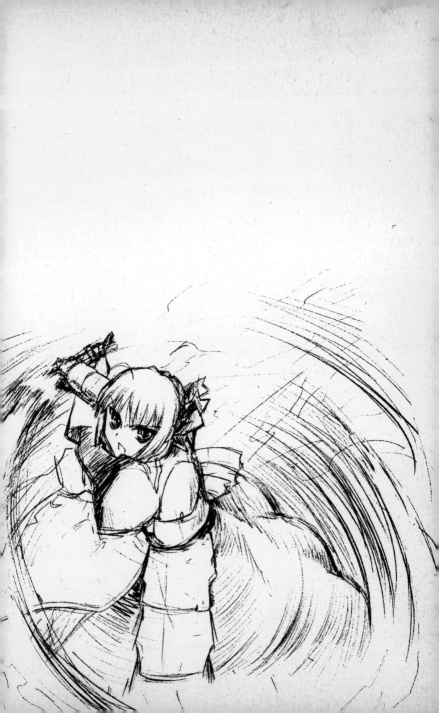

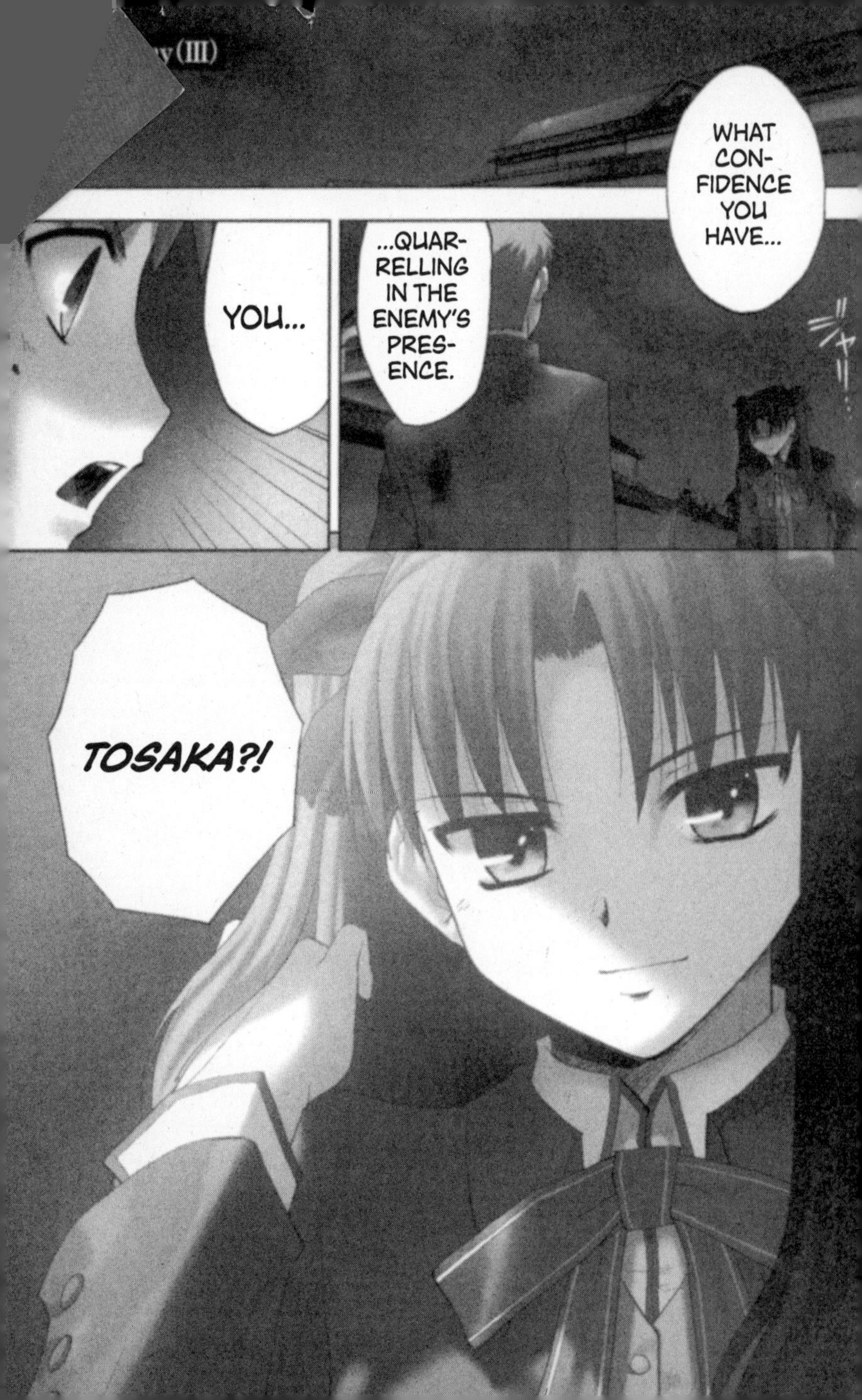
WHAT CON-FIDENCE YOU HAVE...
...QUAR-RELLING IN THE ENEMY'S PRES-ENCE.
YOU...
TOSAKA?!

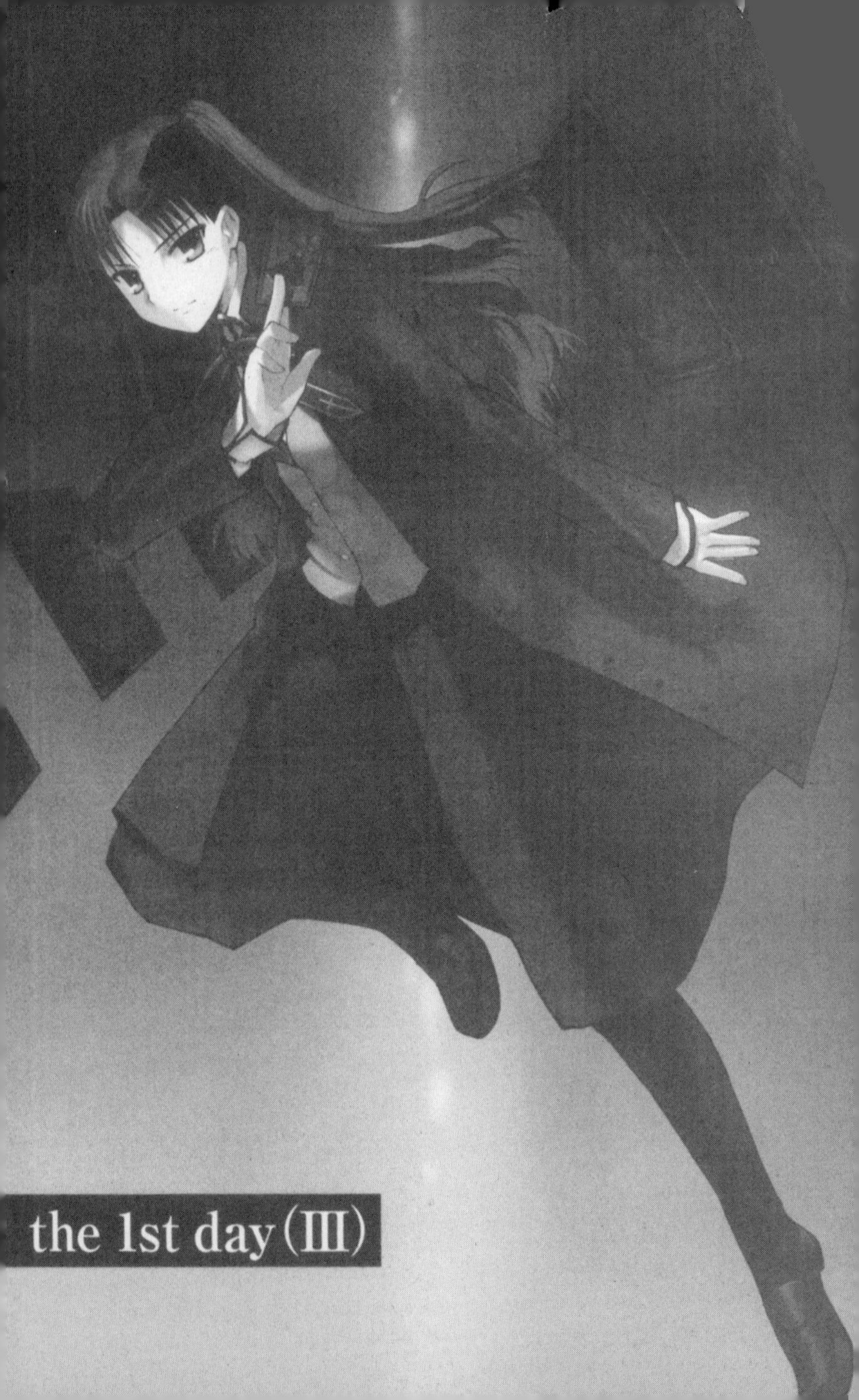

the 1st day (Ⅲ)

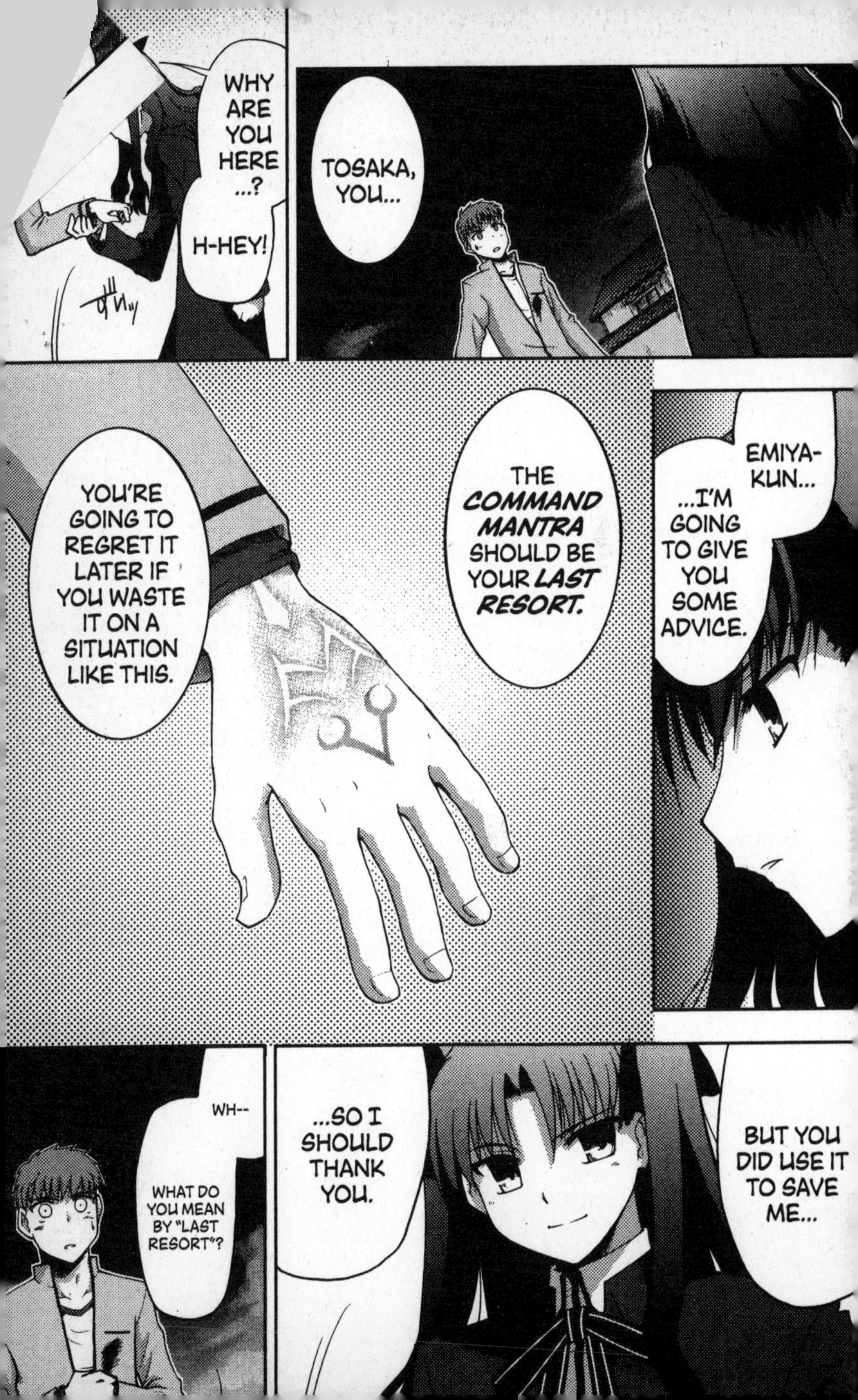

TOSAKA, YOU...
WHY ARE YOU HERE ...?
H-HEY!
EMIYA-KUN...
...I'M GOING TO GIVE YOU SOME ADVICE.
THE COMMAND MANTRA SHOULD BE YOUR LAST RESORT.
YOU'RE GOING TO REGRET IT LATER IF YOU WASTE IT ON A SITUATION LIKE THIS.
BUT YOU DID USE IT TO SAVE ME...
...SO I SHOULD THANK YOU.
WH--
WHAT DO YOU MEAN BY "LAST RESORT"?

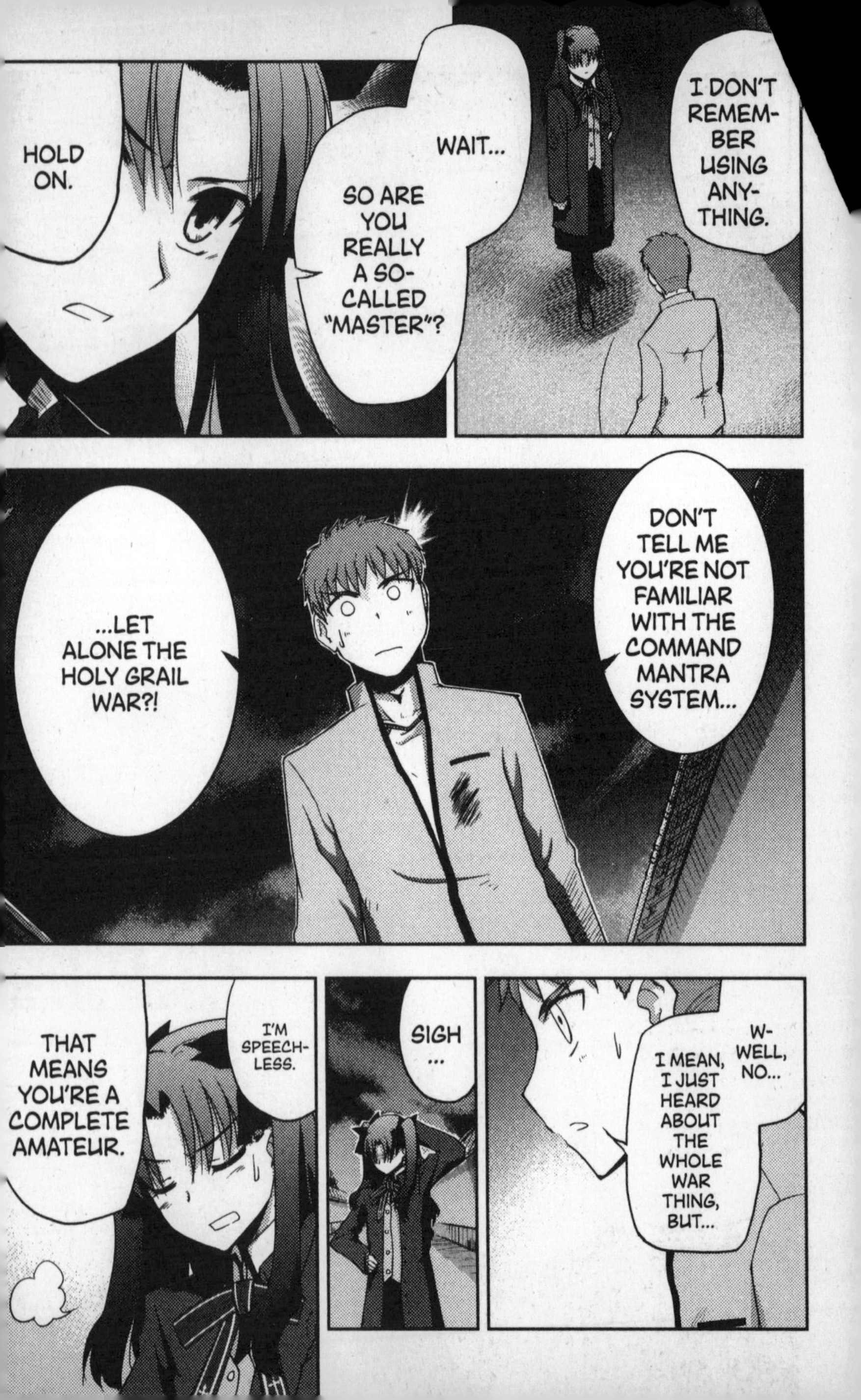
I DON'T REMEM-BER USING ANY-THING.
WAIT...
SO ARE YOU REALLY A SO-CALLED "MASTER"?
HOLD ON.
DON'T TELL ME YOU'RE NOT FAMILIAR WITH THE COMMAND MANTRA SYSTEM...
...LET ALONE THE HOLY GRAIL WAR?!
W-WELL, NO...
I MEAN, I JUST HEARD ABOUT THE WHOLE WAR THING, BUT...
SIGH ...
I'M SPEECH-LESS.
THAT MEANS YOU'RE A COMPLETE AMATEUR.

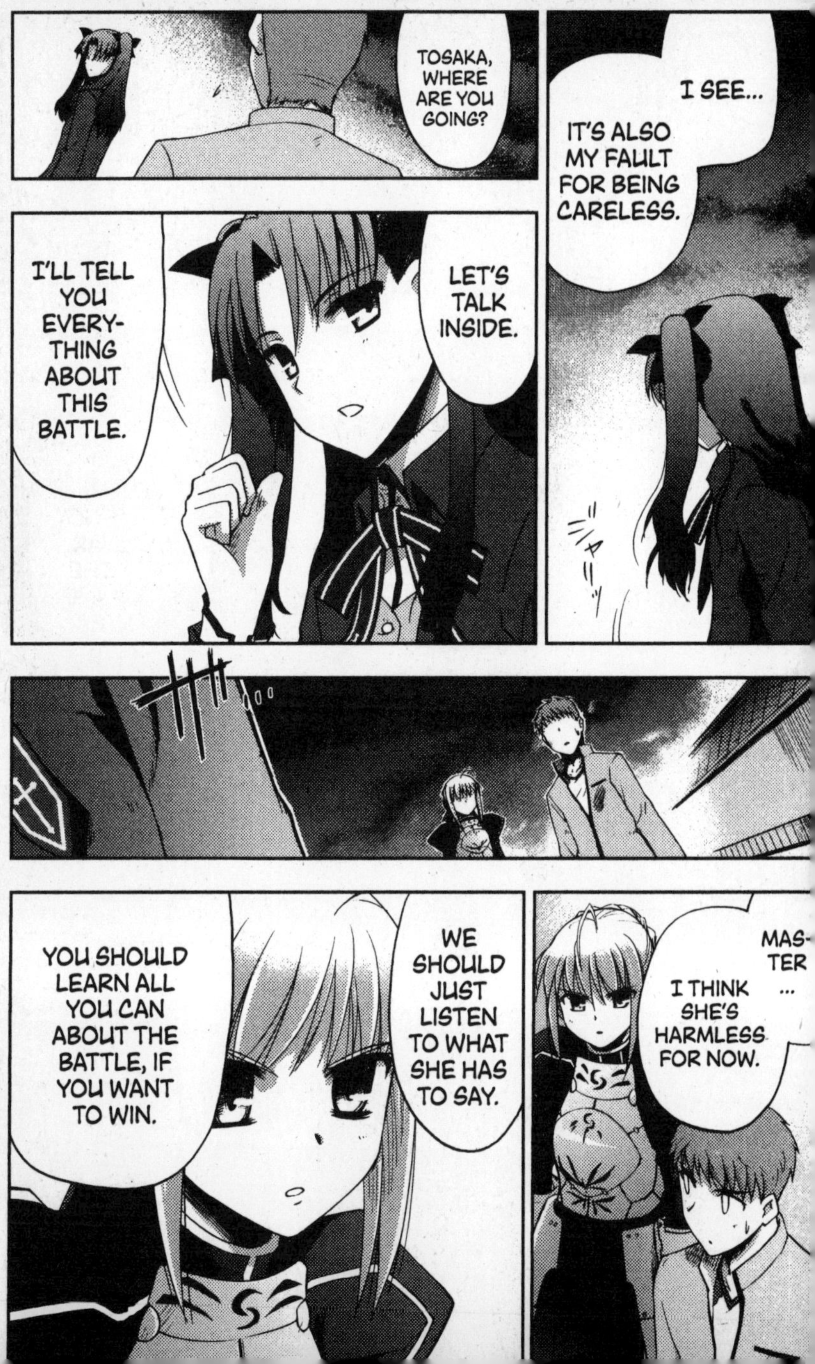
I SEE...
IT'S ALSO MY FAULT FOR BEING CARELESS.
TOSAKA, WHERE ARE YOU GOING?
LET'S TALK INSIDE.
I'LL TELL YOU EVERYTHING ABOUT THIS BATTLE.
MASTER...
I THINK SHE'S HARMLESS FOR NOW.
WE SHOULD JUST LISTEN TO WHAT SHE HAS TO SAY.
YOU SHOULD LEARN ALL YOU CAN ABOUT THE BATTLE, IF YOU WANT TO WIN.

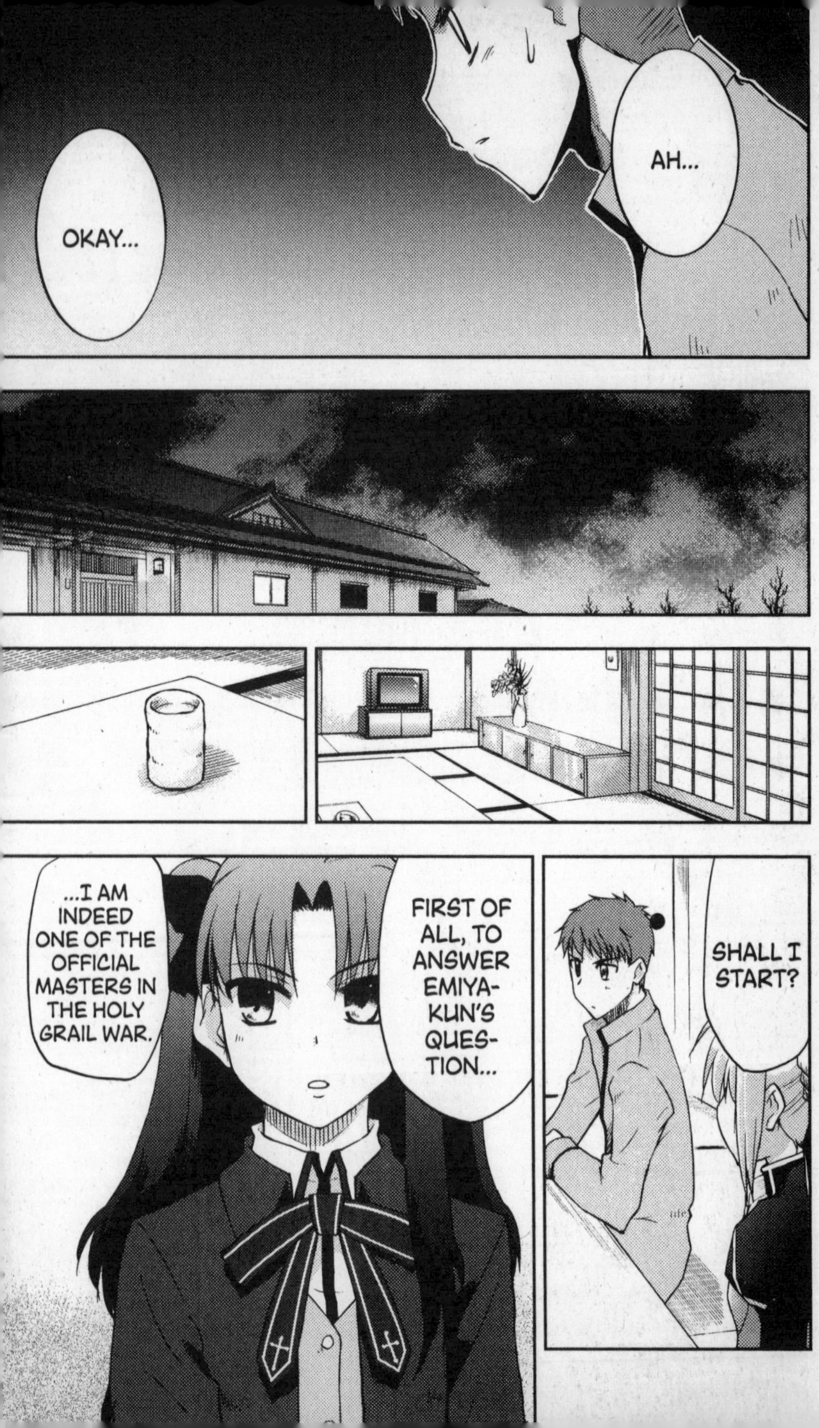
AH...
OKAY...
SHALL I START?
FIRST OF ALL, TO ANSWER EMIYA-KUN'S QUES-TION...
...I AM INDEED ONE OF THE OFFICIAL MASTERS IN THE HOLY GRAIL WAR.

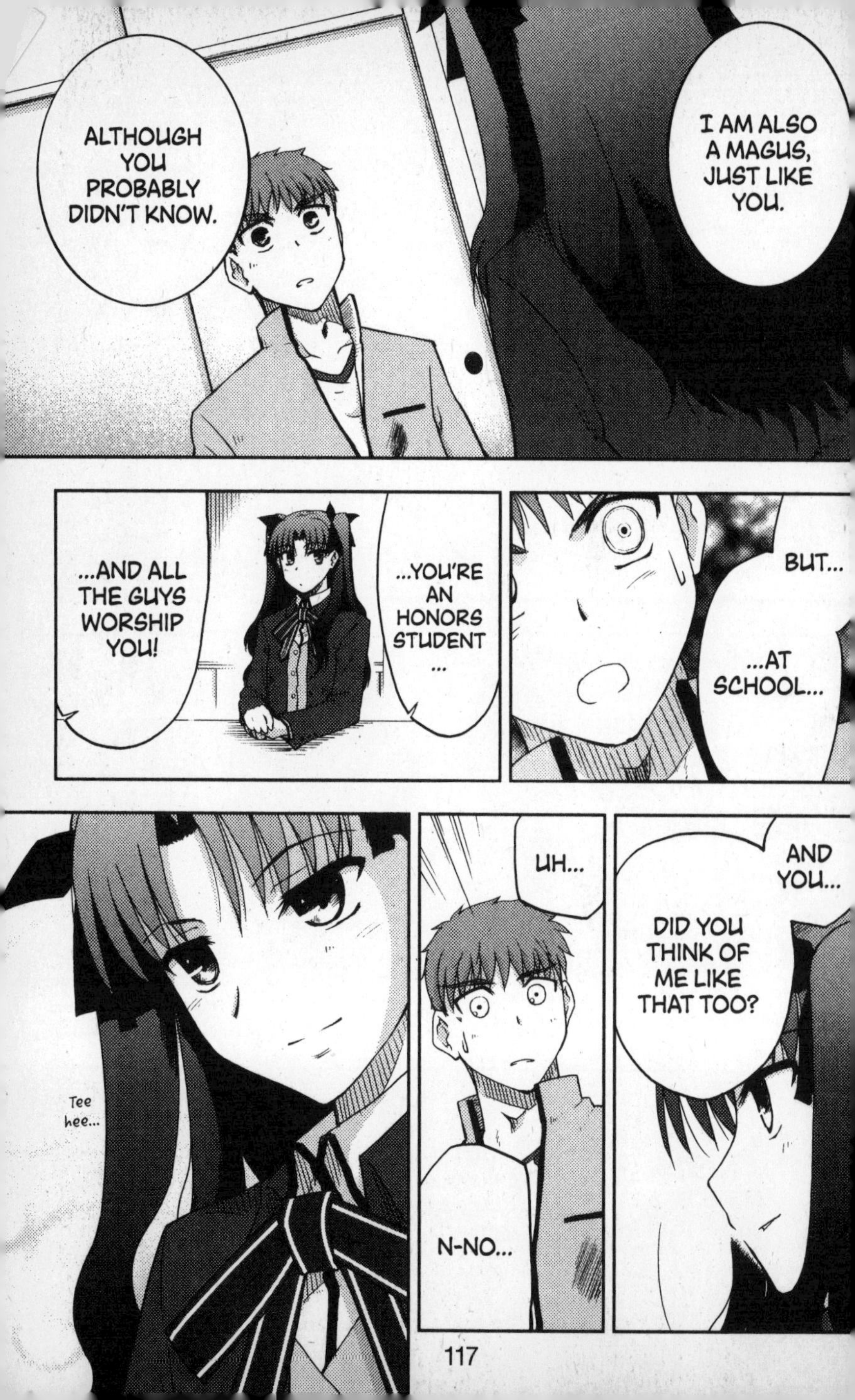
I AM ALSO A MAGUS, JUST LIKE YOU.
ALTHOUGH YOU PROBABLY DIDN'T KNOW.
BUT...
...AT SCHOOL...
...YOU'RE AN HONORS STUDENT...
...AND ALL THE GUYS WORSHIP YOU!
AND YOU...
DID YOU THINK OF ME LIKE THAT TOO?
UH...
N-NO...
Tee hee...

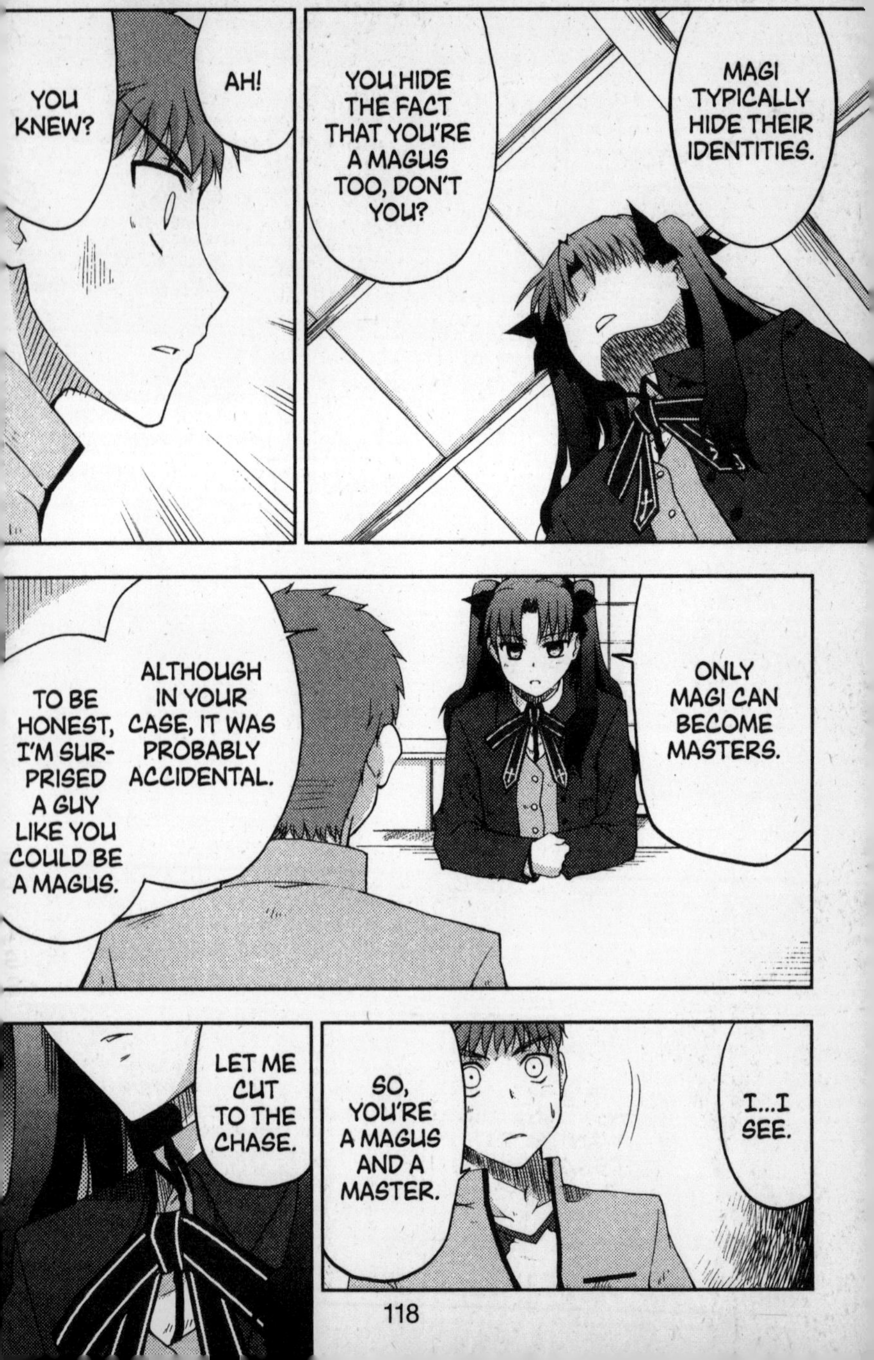
MAGI TYPICALLY HIDE THEIR IDENTITIES.
YOU HIDE THE FACT THAT YOU'RE A MAGUS TOO, DON'T YOU?
AH!
YOU KNEW?
ONLY MAGI CAN BECOME MASTERS.
ALTHOUGH IN YOUR CASE, IT WAS PROBABLY ACCIDENTAL.
TO BE HONEST, I'M SUR-PRISED A GUY LIKE YOU COULD BE A MAGUS.
I...I SEE.
SO, YOU'RE A MAGUS AND A MASTER.
LET ME CUT TO THE CHASE.

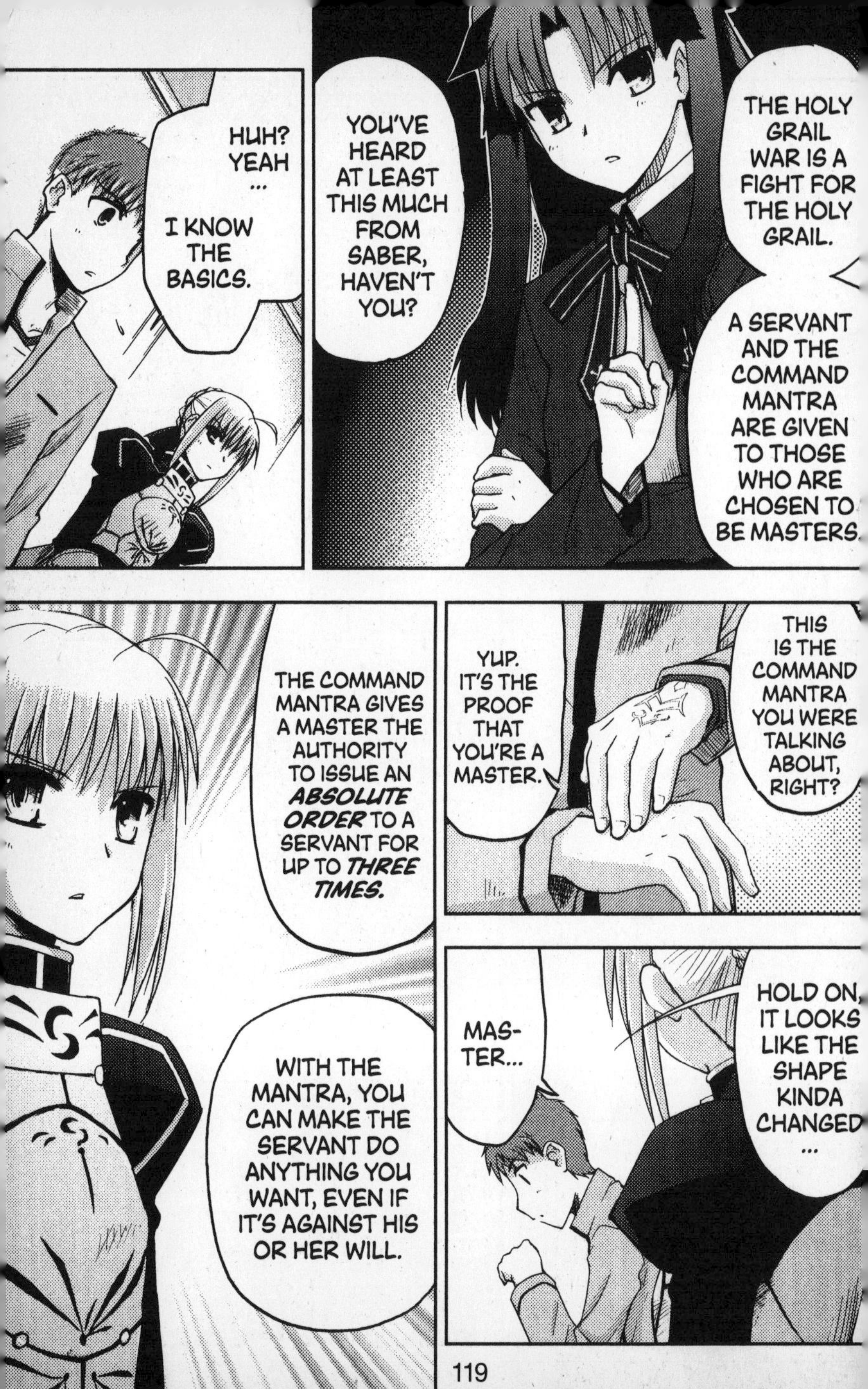
THE HOLY GRAIL WAR IS A FIGHT FOR THE HOLY GRAIL.
A SERVANT AND THE COMMAND MANTRA ARE GIVEN TO THOSE WHO ARE CHOSEN TO BE MASTERS.
YOU'VE HEARD AT LEAST THIS MUCH FROM SABER, HAVEN'T YOU?
HUH? YEAH ...
I KNOW THE BASICS.
THIS IS THE COMMAND MANTRA YOU WERE TALKING ABOUT, RIGHT?
YUP. IT'S THE PROOF THAT YOU'RE A MASTER.
HOLD ON, IT LOOKS LIKE THE SHAPE KINDA CHANGED ...
MAS-TER...
THE COMMAND MANTRA GIVES A MASTER THE AUTHORITY TO ISSUE AN ***ABSOLUTE ORDER*** TO A SERVANT FOR UP TO ***THREE TIMES.***
WITH THE MANTRA, YOU CAN MAKE THE SERVANT DO ANYTHING YOU WANT, EVEN IF IT'S AGAINST HIS OR HER WILL.

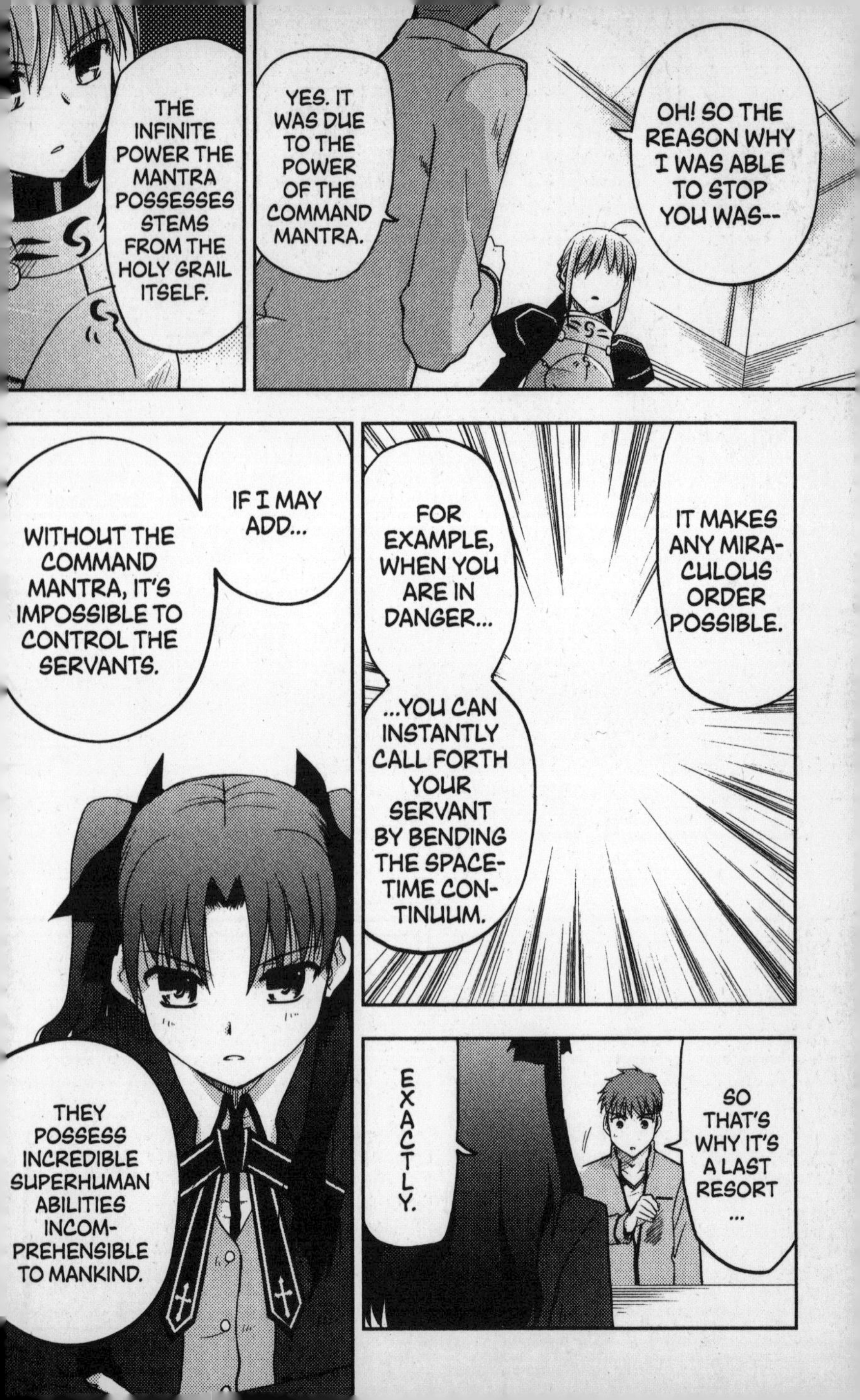
OH! SO THE REASON WHY I WAS ABLE TO STOP YOU WAS--
YES. IT WAS DUE TO THE POWER OF THE COMMAND MANTRA.
THE INFINITE POWER THE MANTRA POSSESSES STEMS FROM THE HOLY GRAIL ITSELF.
IT MAKES ANY MIRA-CULOUS ORDER POSSIBLE.
FOR EXAMPLE, WHEN YOU ARE IN DANGER...
...YOU CAN INSTANTLY CALL FORTH YOUR SERVANT BY BENDING THE SPACE-TIME CON-TINUUM.
SO THAT'S WHY IT'S A LAST RESORT...
EXACTLY.
IF I MAY ADD...
WITHOUT THE COMMAND MANTRA, IT'S IMPOSSIBLE TO CONTROL THE SERVANTS.
THEY POSSESS INCREDIBLE SUPERHUMAN ABILITIES INCOM-PREHENSIBLE TO MANKIND.

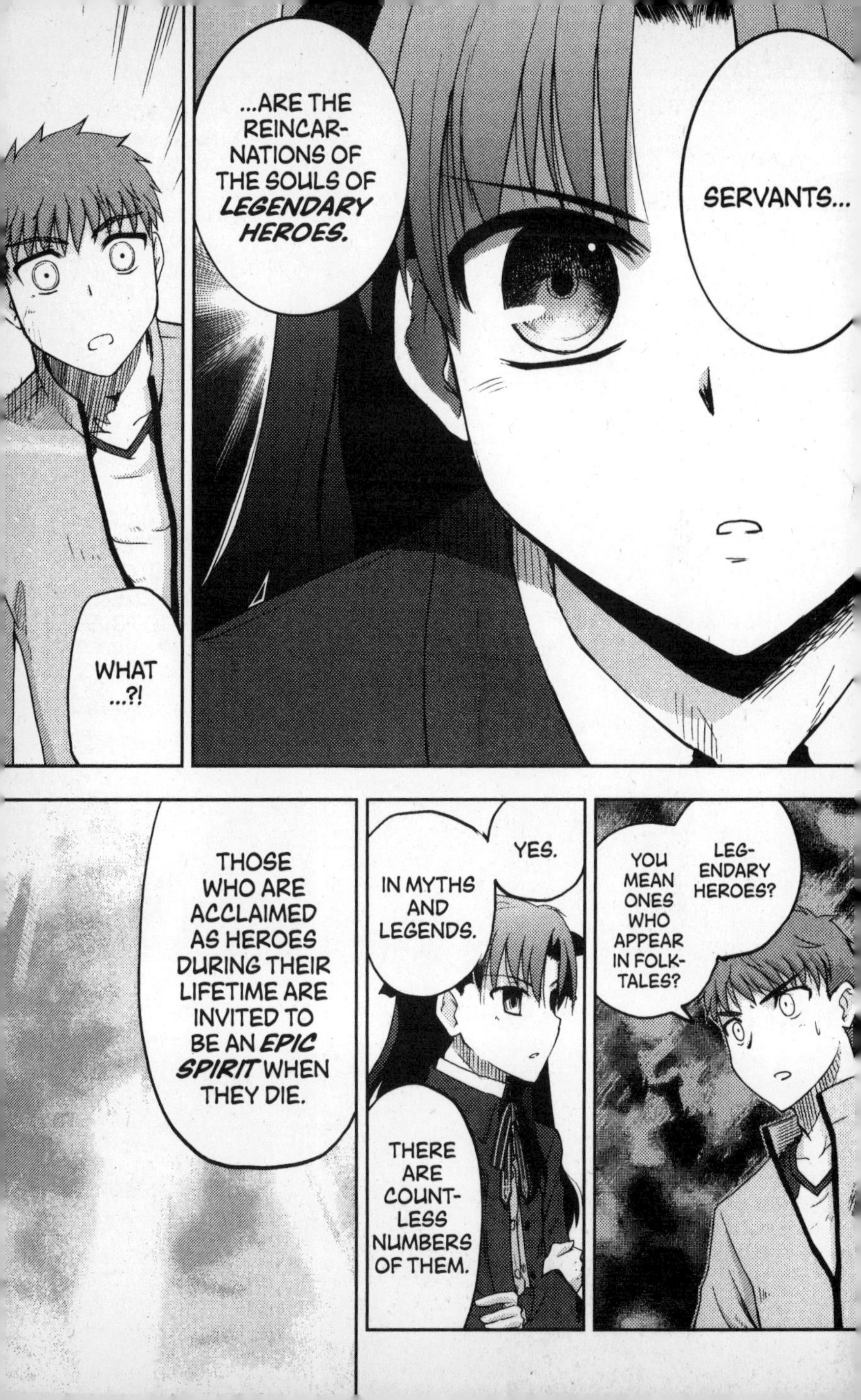
SERVANTS...
...ARE THE REINCARNATIONS OF THE SOULS OF LEGENDARY HEROES.
WHAT ...?!
LEGENDARY HEROES?
YOU MEAN ONES WHO APPEAR IN FOLKTALES?
YES.
IN MYTHS AND LEGENDS.
THERE ARE COUNTLESS NUMBERS OF THEM.
THOSE WHO ARE ACCLAIMED AS HEROES DURING THEIR LIFETIME ARE INVITED TO BE AN EPIC SPIRIT WHEN THEY DIE.

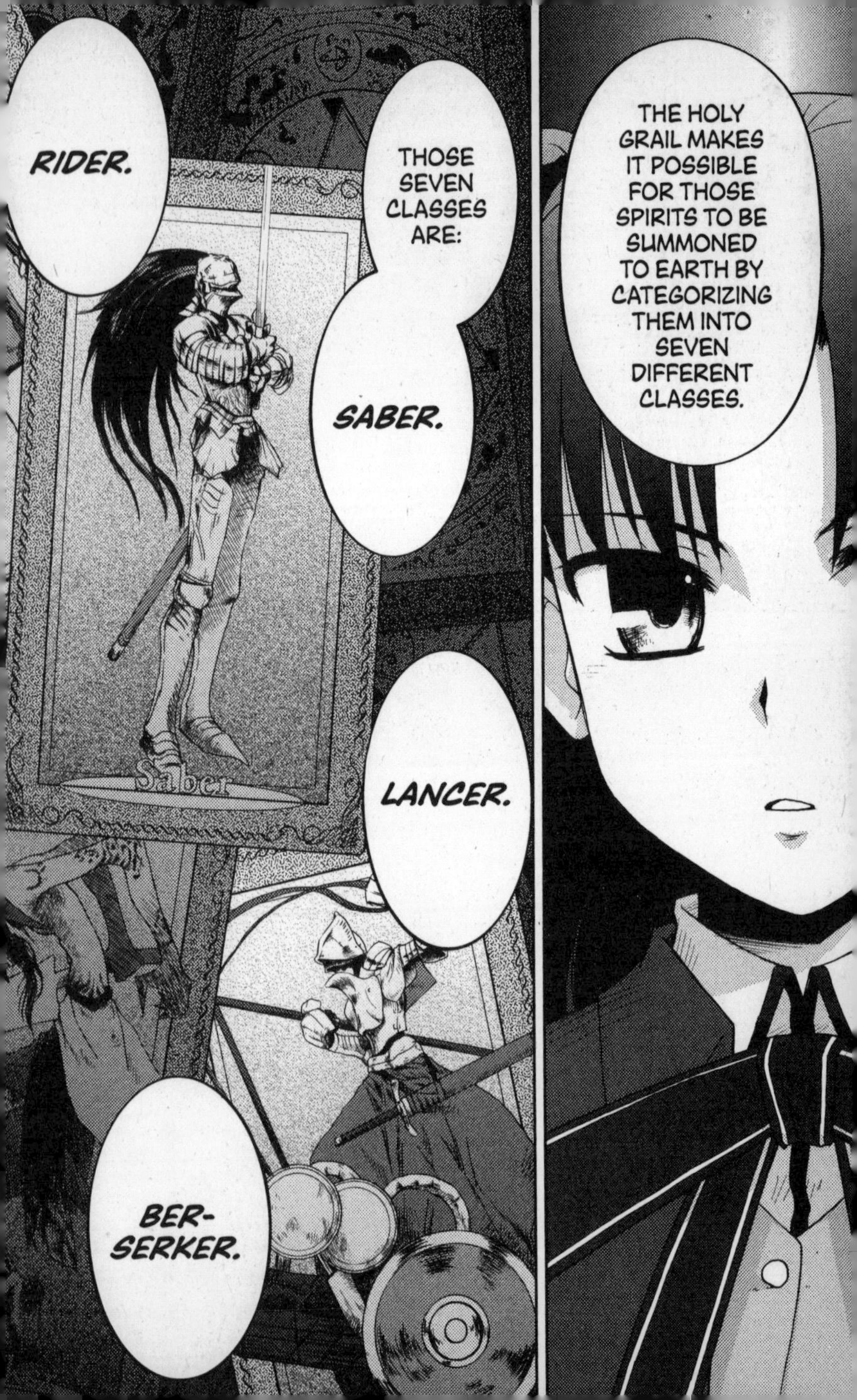
THE HOLY GRAIL MAKES IT POSSIBLE FOR THOSE SPIRITS TO BE SUMMONED TO EARTH BY CATEGORIZING THEM INTO SEVEN DIFFERENT CLASSES.
THOSE SEVEN CLASSES ARE:
SABER.
RIDER.
LANCER.
BER-SERKER.
Saber

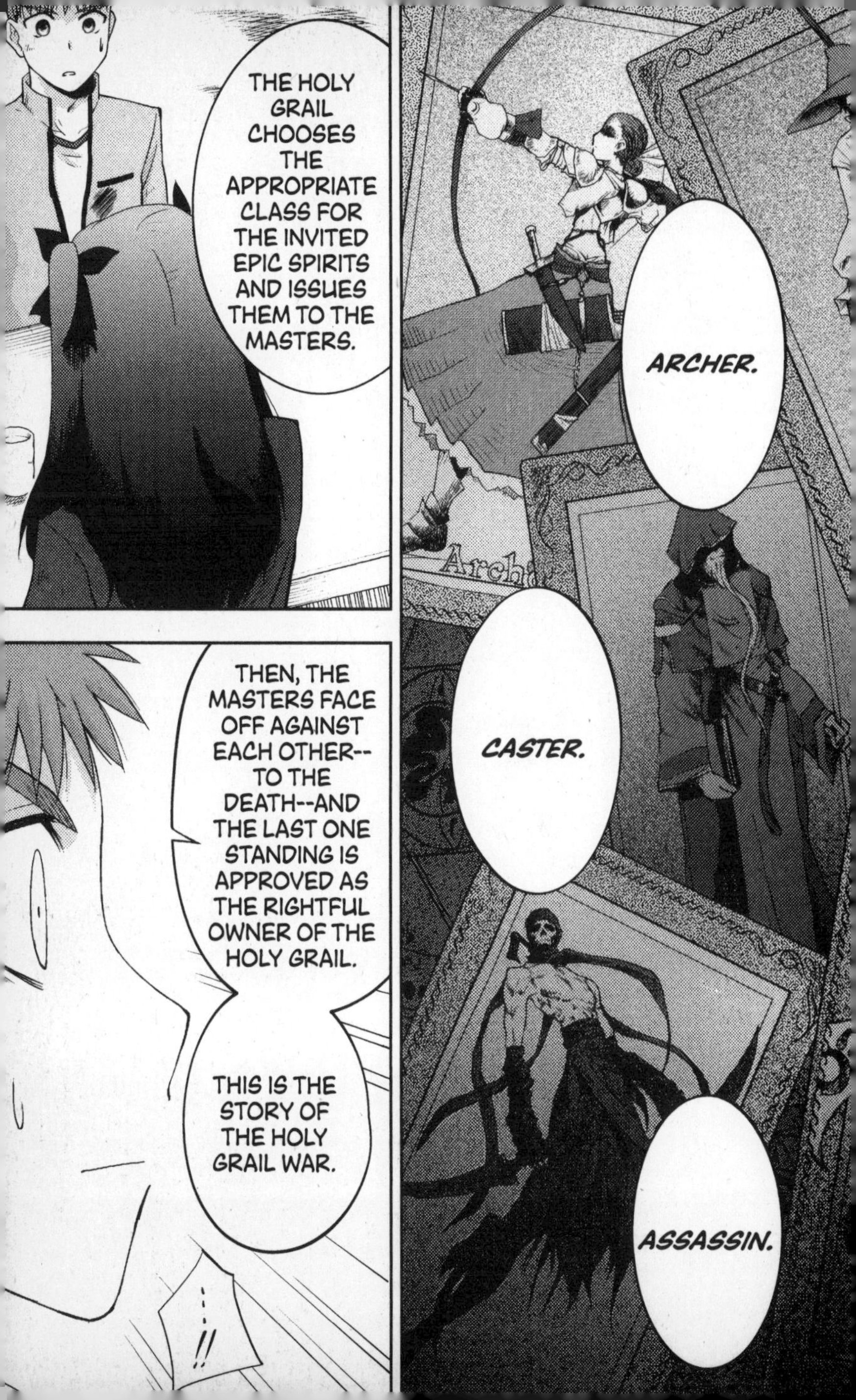
ARCHER.
CASTER.
ASSASSIN.
THE HOLY GRAIL CHOOSES THE APPROPRIATE CLASS FOR THE INVITED EPIC SPIRITS AND ISSUES THEM TO THE MASTERS.
THEN, THE MASTERS FACE OFF AGAINST EACH OTHER-- TO THE DEATH--AND THE LAST ONE STANDING IS APPROVED AS THE RIGHTFUL OWNER OF THE HOLY GRAIL.
THIS IS THE STORY OF THE HOLY GRAIL WAR.
...!!

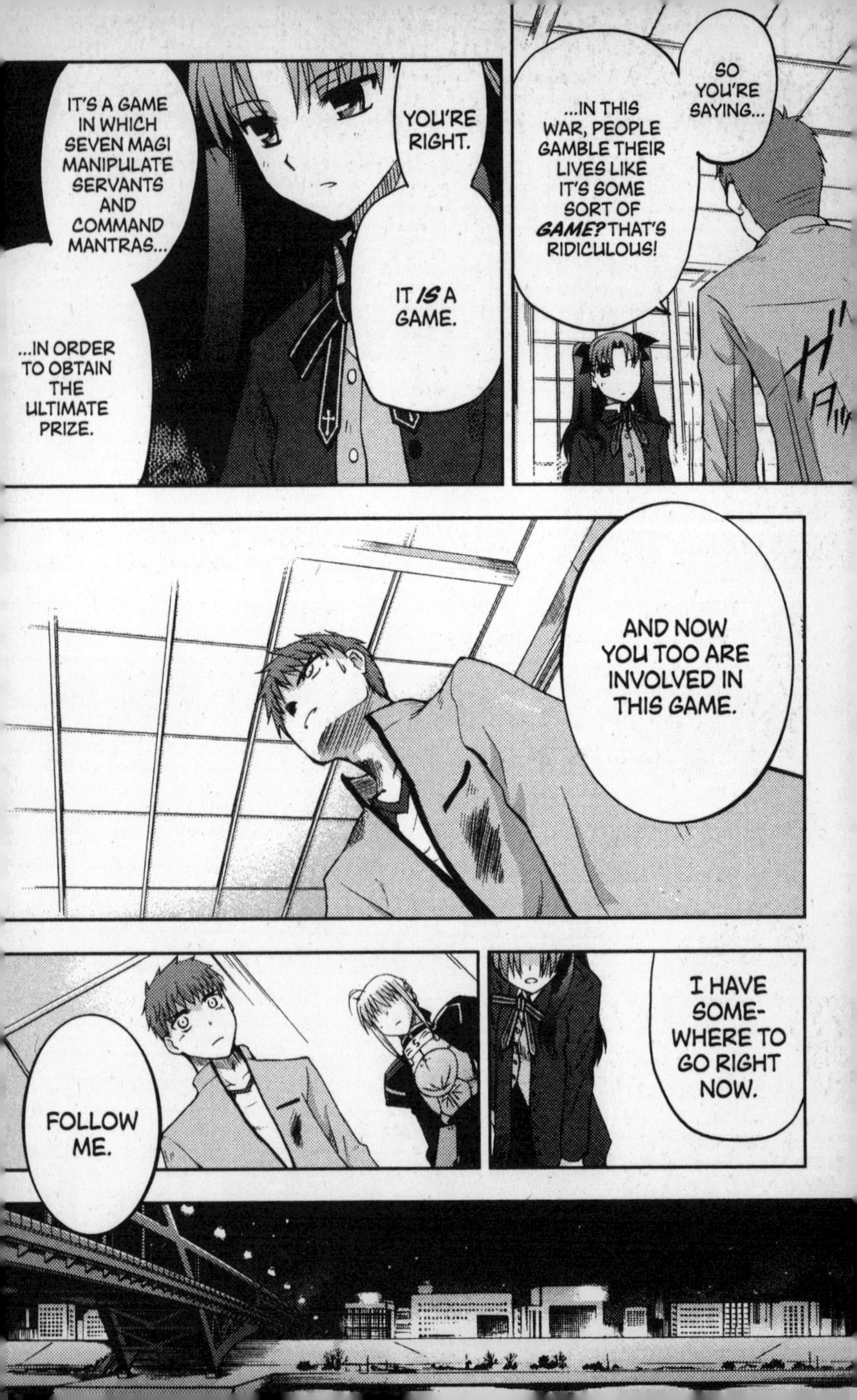
SO YOU'RE SAYING...
...IN THIS WAR, PEOPLE GAMBLE THEIR LIVES LIKE IT'S SOME SORT OF *GAME?* THAT'S RIDICULOUS!
YOU'RE RIGHT.
IT *IS* A GAME.
IT'S A GAME IN WHICH SEVEN MAGI MANIPULATE SERVANTS AND COMMAND MANTRAS...
...IN ORDER TO OBTAIN THE ULTIMATE PRIZE.
AND NOW YOU TOO ARE INVOLVED IN THIS GAME.
I HAVE SOME-WHERE TO GO RIGHT NOW.
FOLLOW ME.

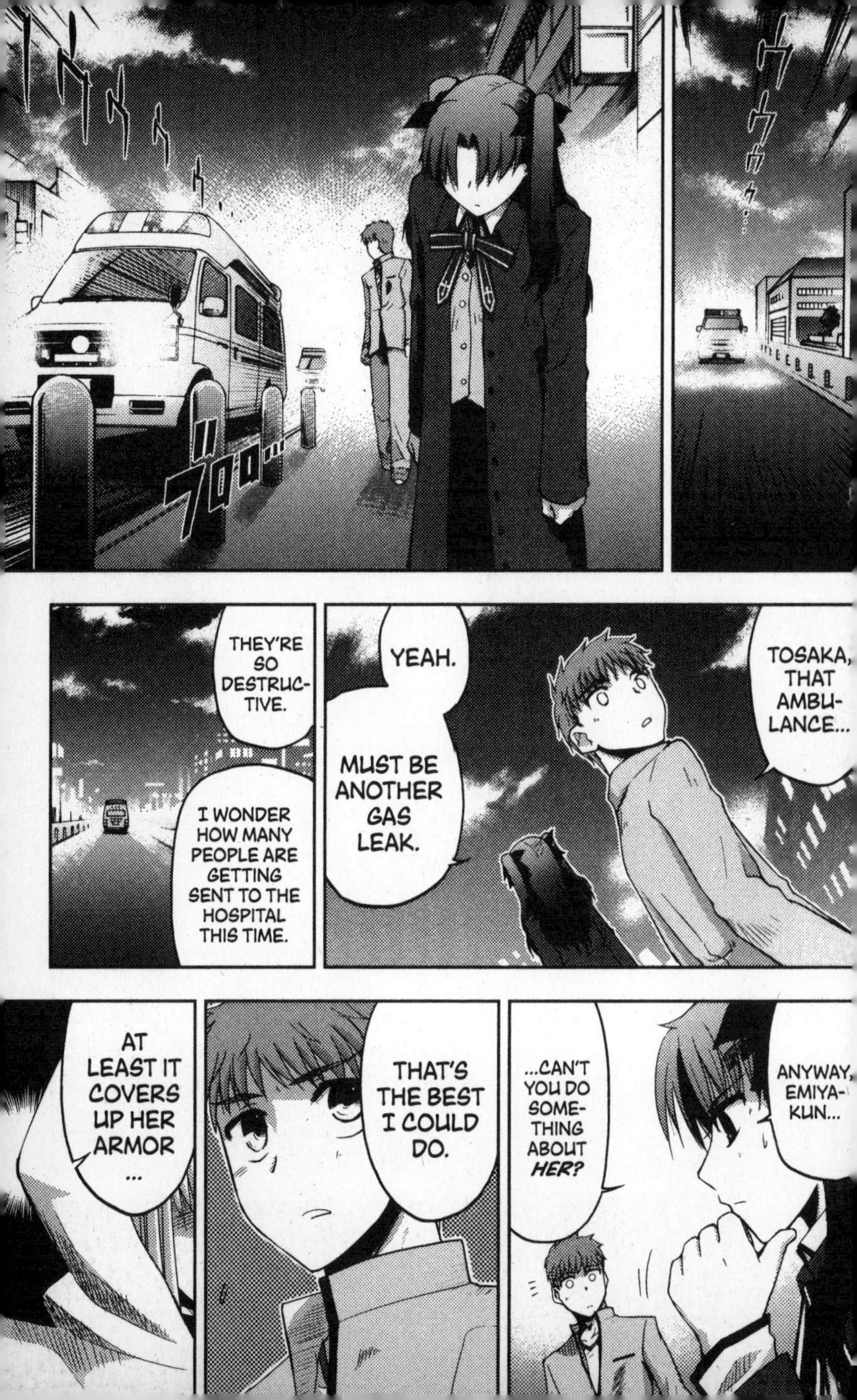
ウゥゥゥゥ…
ウゥゥゥゥ…
ブロロ…
TOSAKA, THAT AMBULANCE...
YEAH.
MUST BE ANOTHER GAS LEAK.
THEY'RE SO DESTRUCTIVE.
I WONDER HOW MANY PEOPLE ARE GETTING SENT TO THE HOSPITAL THIS TIME.
ANYWAY, EMIYA-KUN...
...CAN'T YOU DO SOMETHING ABOUT *HER?*
THAT'S THE BEST I COULD DO.
AT LEAST IT COVERS UP HER ARMOR...

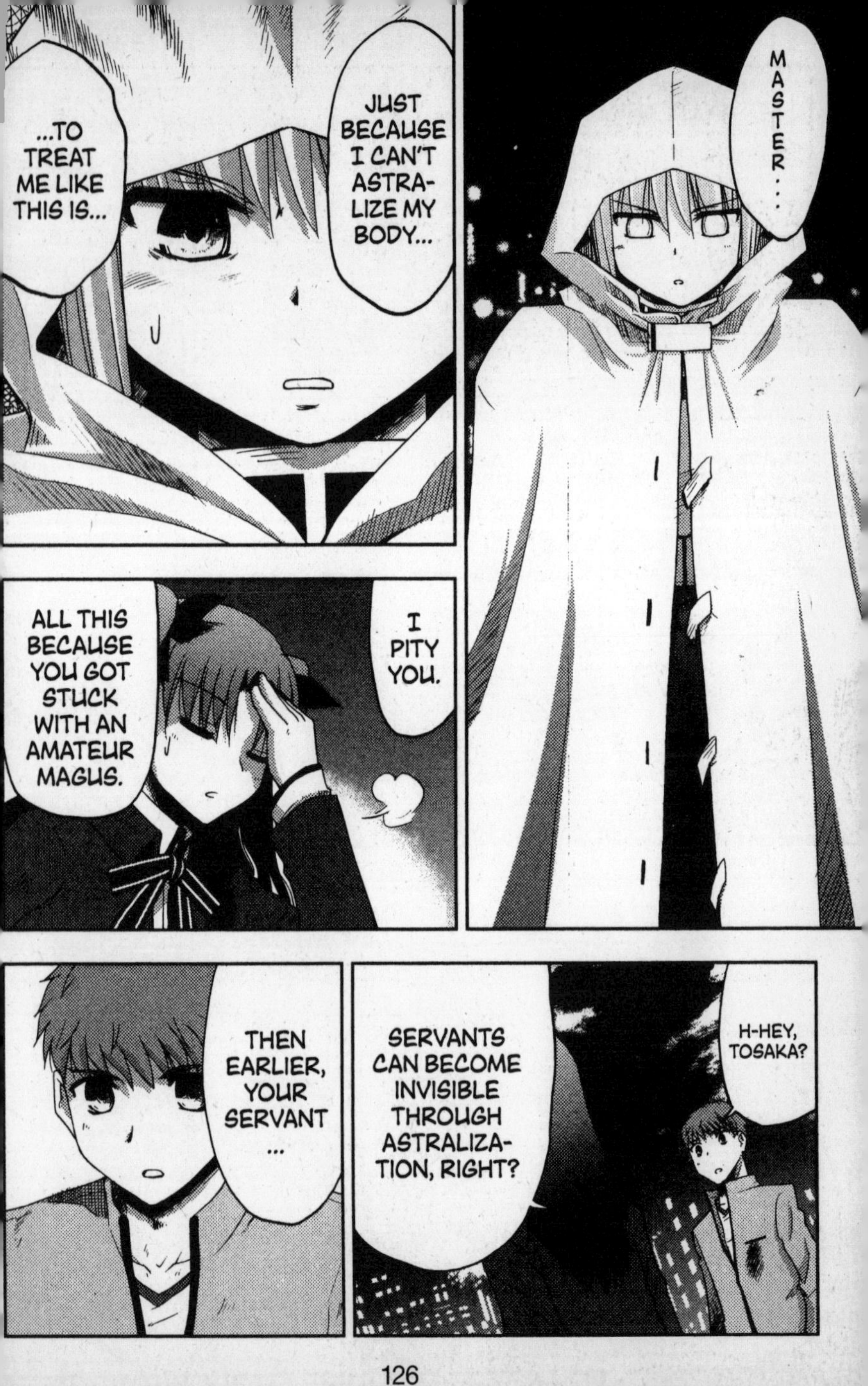
MASTER...
JUST BECAUSE I CAN'T ASTRA-LIZE MY BODY...
...TO TREAT ME LIKE THIS IS...
I PITY YOU.
ALL THIS BECAUSE YOU GOT STUCK WITH AN AMATEUR MAGUS.
H-HEY, TOSAKA?
SERVANTS CAN BECOME INVISIBLE THROUGH ASTRALIZA-TION, RIGHT?
THEN EARLIER, YOUR SERVANT ...

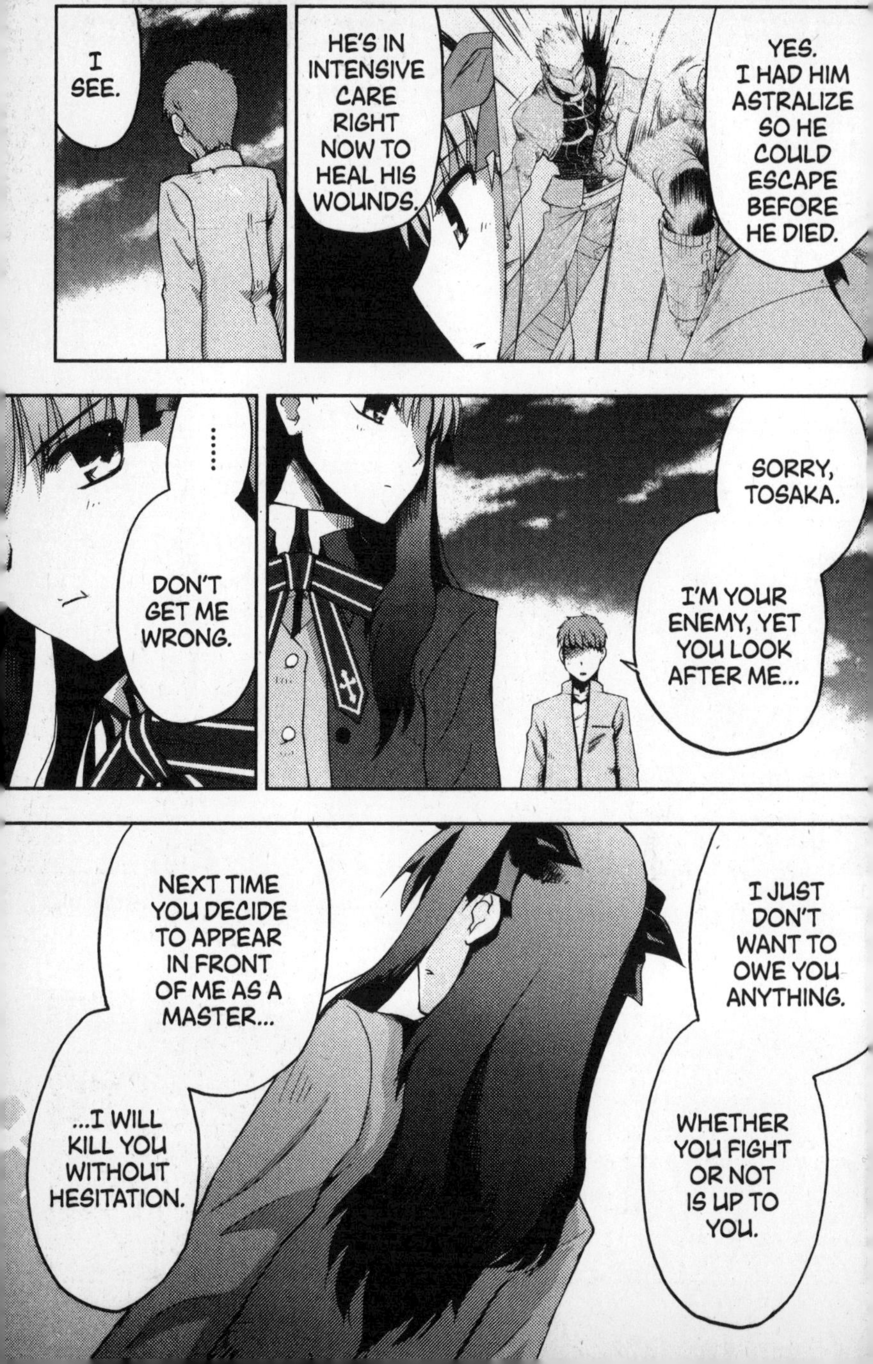
YES. I HAD HIM ASTRALIZE SO HE COULD ESCAPE BEFORE HE DIED.
HE'S IN INTENSIVE CARE RIGHT NOW TO HEAL HIS WOUNDS.
I SEE.
SORRY, TOSAKA.
I'M YOUR ENEMY, YET YOU LOOK AFTER ME...
......
DON'T GET ME WRONG.
I JUST DON'T WANT TO OWE YOU ANYTHING.
WHETHER YOU FIGHT OR NOT IS UP TO YOU.
NEXT TIME YOU DECIDE TO APPEAR IN FRONT OF ME AS A MASTER...
...I WILL KILL YOU WITHOUT HESITATION.

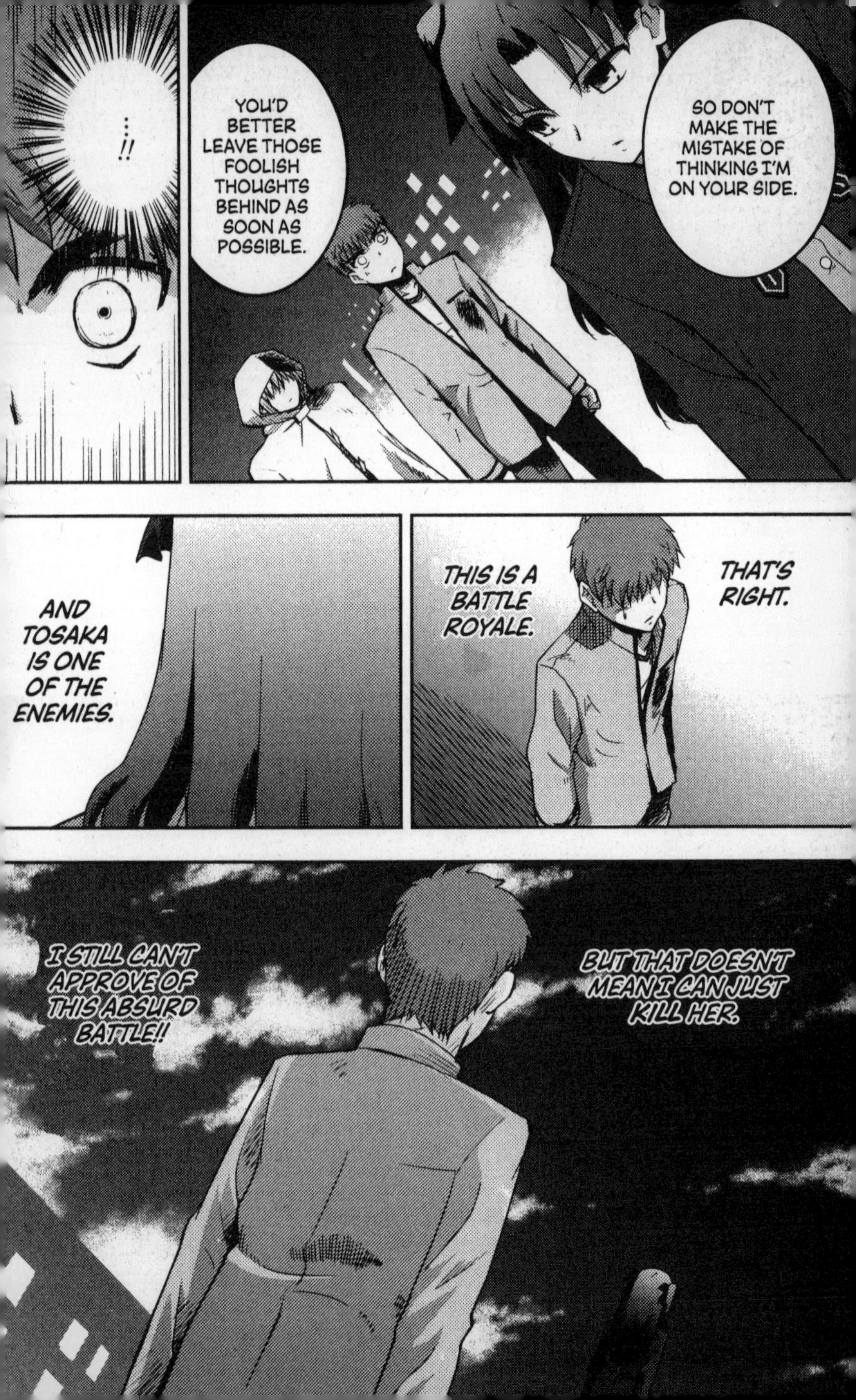
SO DON'T MAKE THE MISTAKE OF THINKING I'M ON YOUR SIDE.
YOU'D BETTER LEAVE THOSE FOOLISH THOUGHTS BEHIND AS SOON AS POSSIBLE.
...!!
THAT'S RIGHT.
THIS IS A BATTLE ROYALE.
AND TOSAKA IS ONE OF THE ENEMIES.
BUT THAT DOESN'T MEAN I CAN JUST KILL HER.
I STILL CAN'T APPROVE OF THIS ABSURD BATTLE!!

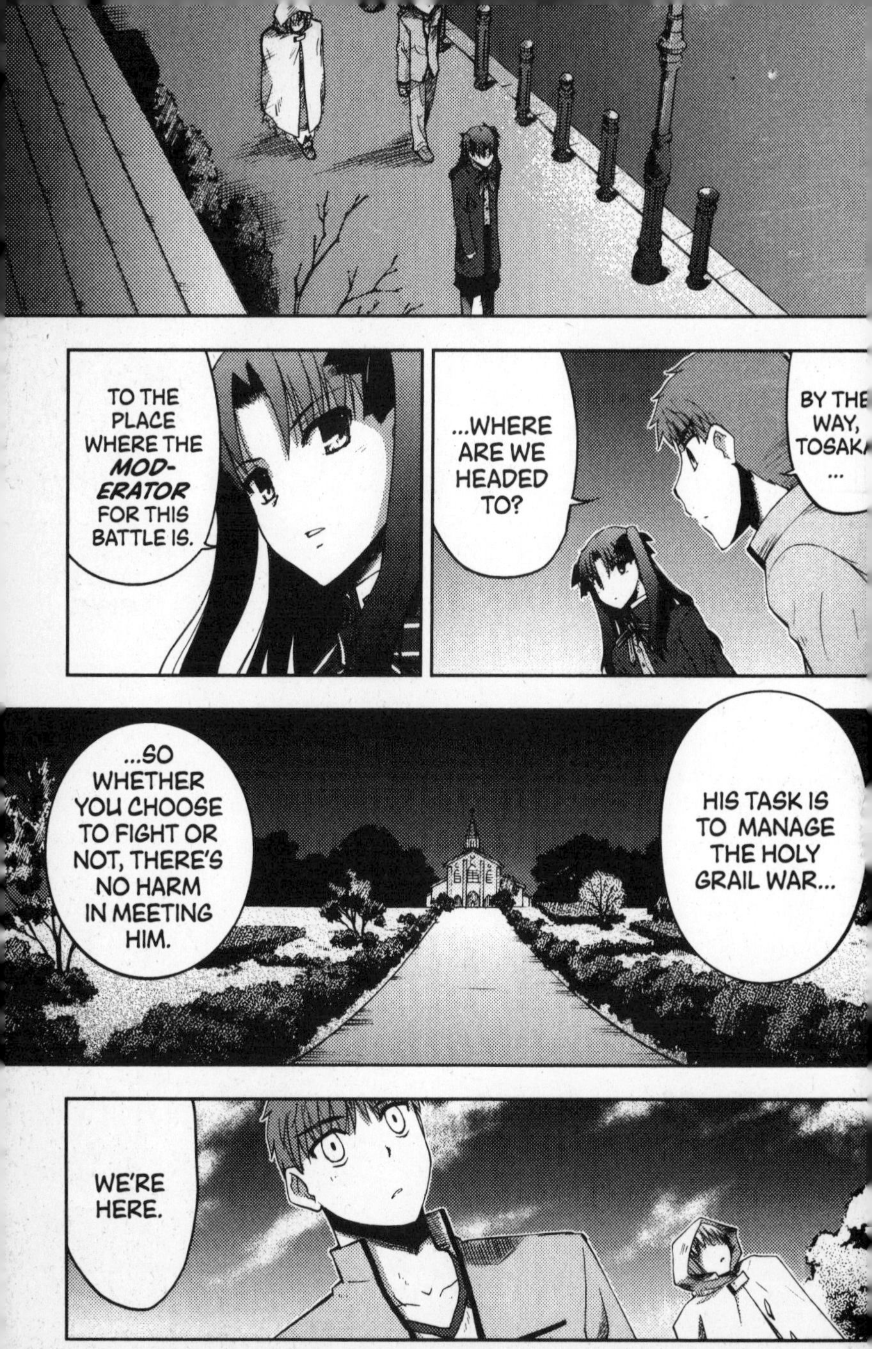
BY THE WAY, TOSAKA ...
...WHERE ARE WE HEADED TO?
TO THE PLACE WHERE THE *MODERATOR* FOR THIS BATTLE IS.
HIS TASK IS TO MANAGE THE HOLY GRAIL WAR...
...SO WHETHER YOU CHOOSE TO FIGHT OR NOT, THERE'S NO HARM IN MEETING HIM.
WE'RE HERE.

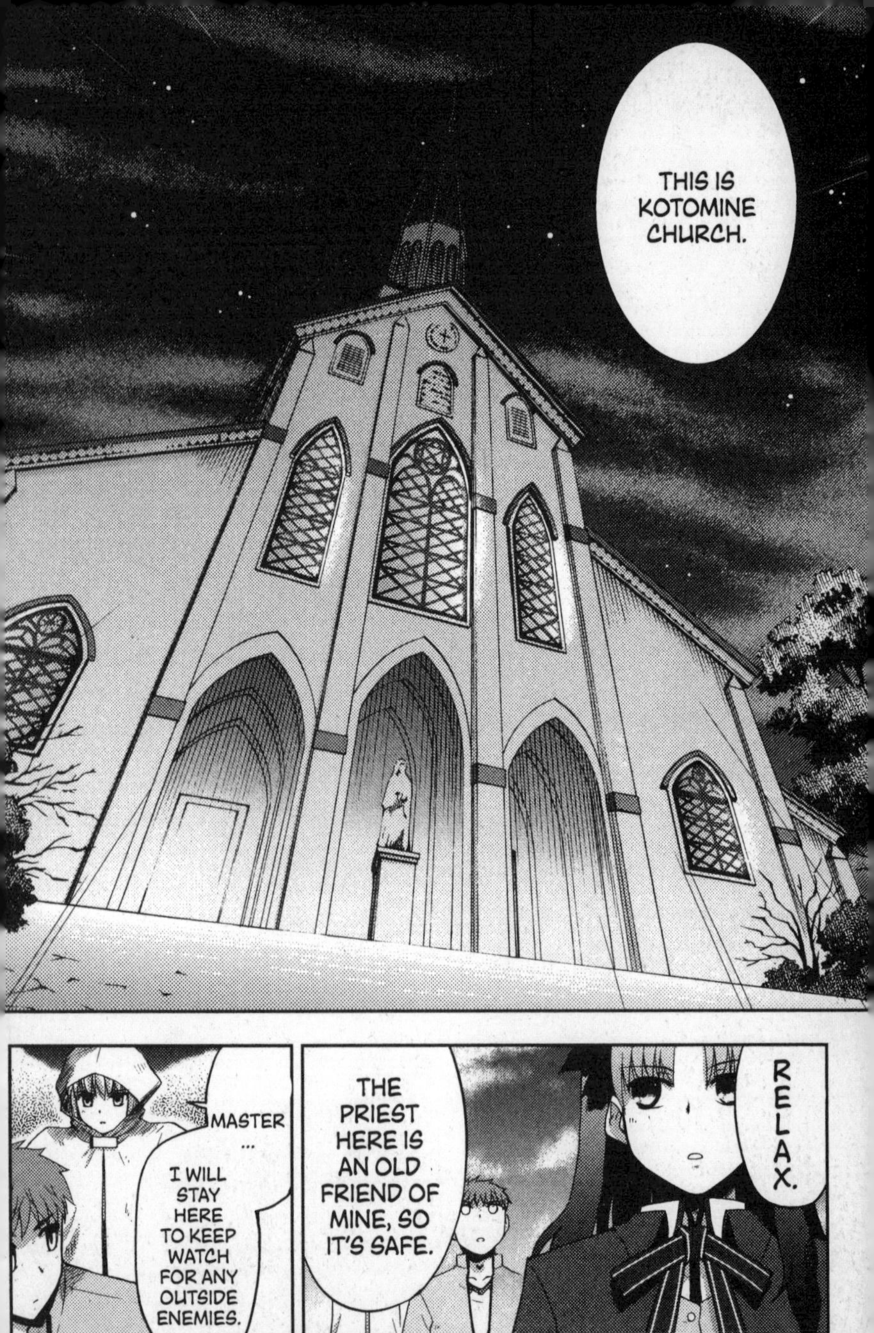
THIS IS KOTOMINE CHURCH.
RELAX.
THE PRIEST HERE IS AN OLD FRIEND OF MINE, SO IT'S SAFE.
MASTER ...
I WILL STAY HERE TO KEEP WATCH FOR ANY OUTSIDE ENEMIES.

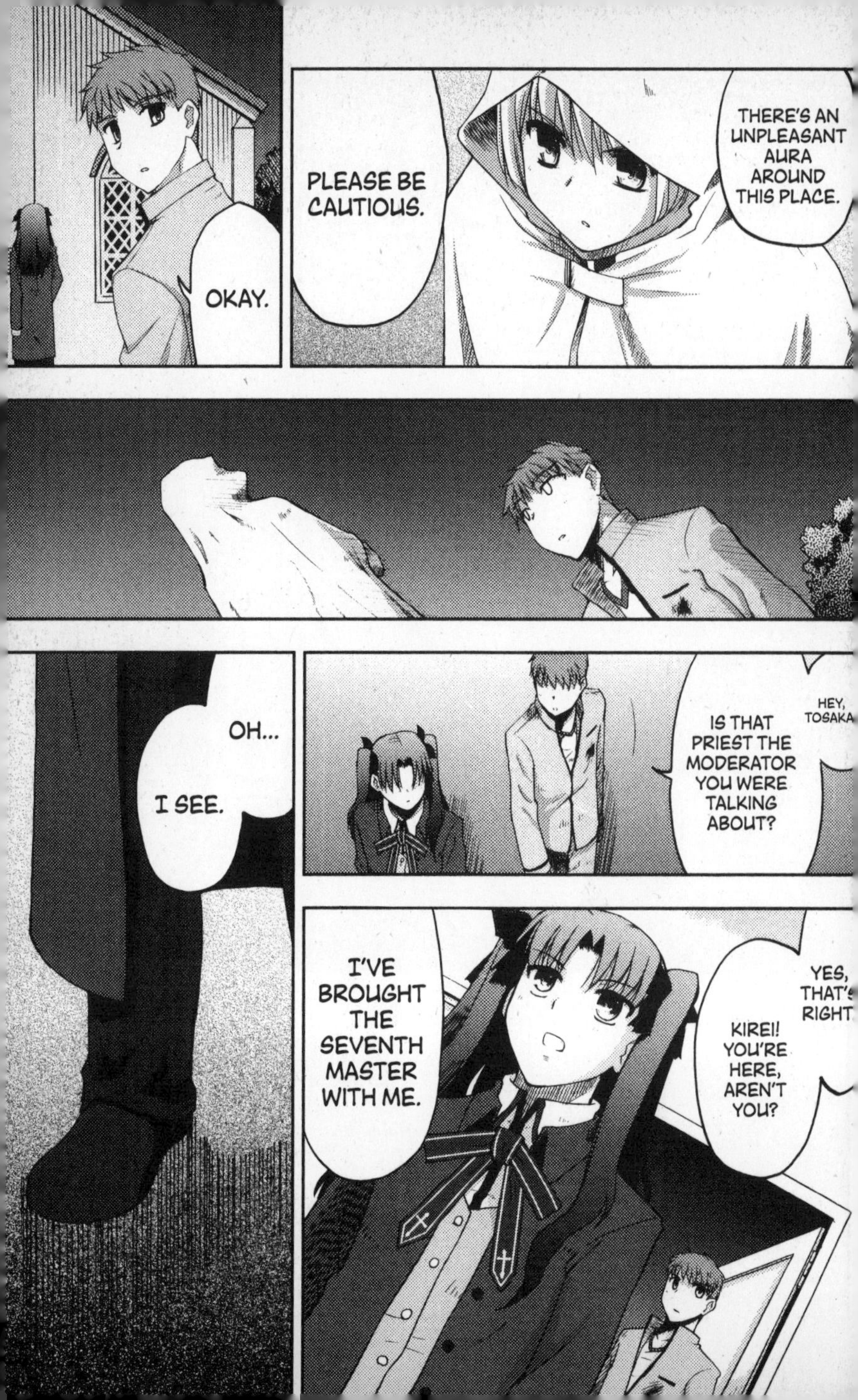
THERE'S AN UNPLEASANT AURA AROUND THIS PLACE.
PLEASE BE CAUTIOUS.
OKAY.
HEY, TOSAKA
IS THAT PRIEST THE MODERATOR YOU WERE TALKING ABOUT?
YES, THAT'S RIGHT
KIREI! YOU'RE HERE, AREN'T YOU?
I'VE BROUGHT THE SEVENTH MASTER WITH ME.
OH...
I SEE.

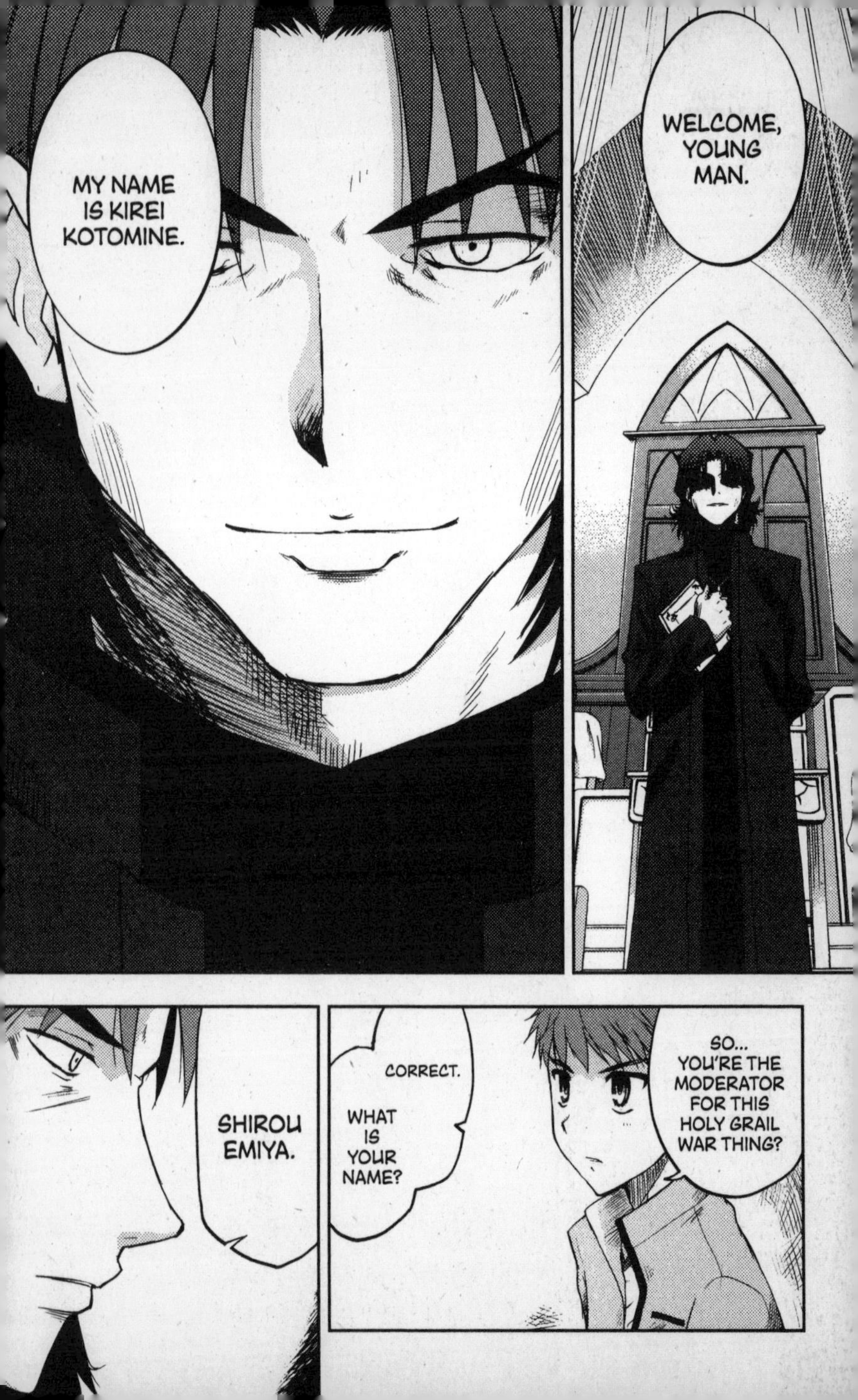
WELCOME, YOUNG MAN.
MY NAME IS KIREI KOTOMINE.
SO... YOU'RE THE MODERATOR FOR THIS HOLY GRAIL WAR THING?
CORRECT.
WHAT IS YOUR NAME?
SHIROU EMIYA.

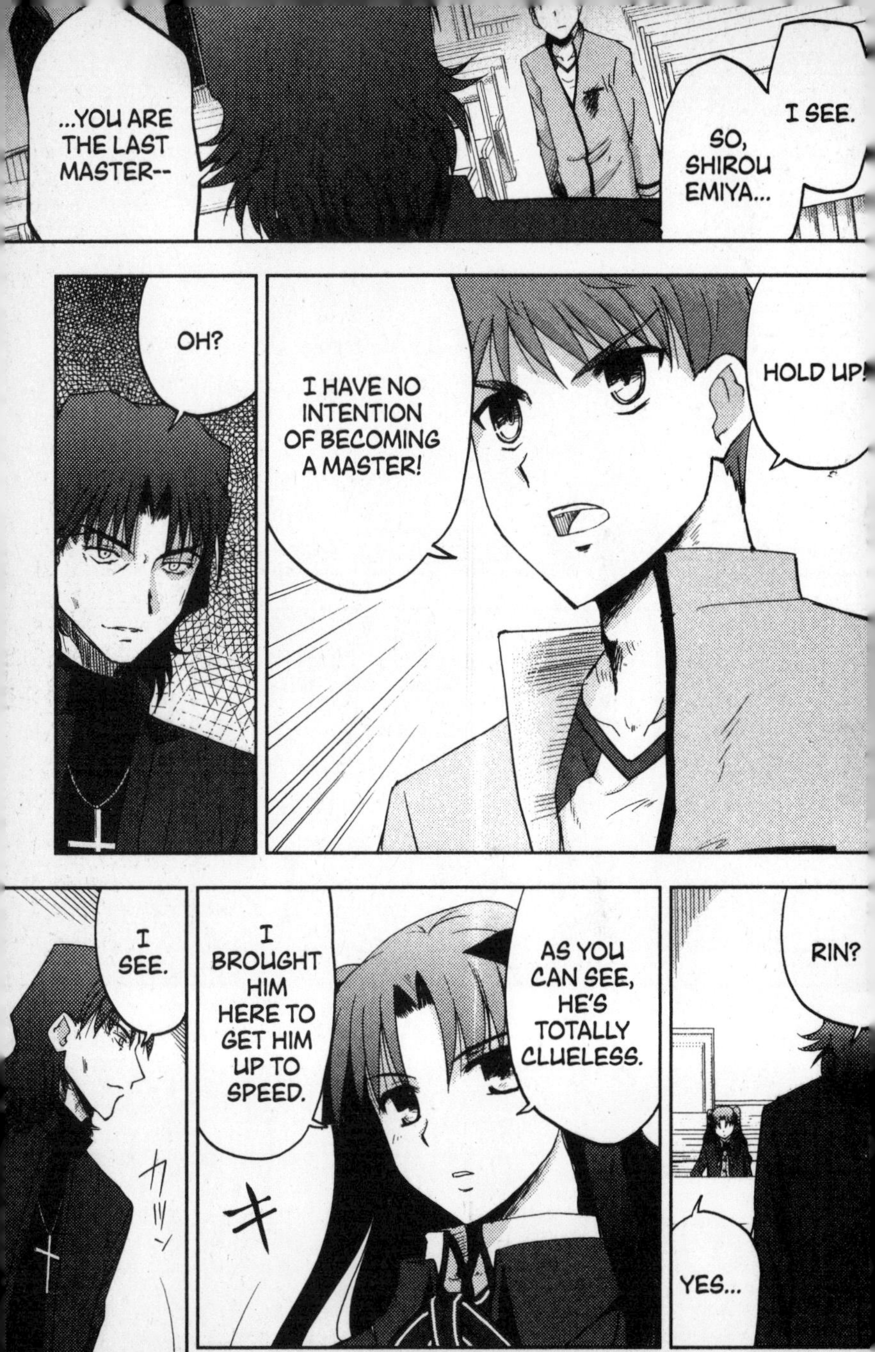
I SEE. SO, SHIROU EMIYA...
...YOU ARE THE LAST MASTER--
HOLD UP!
I HAVE NO INTENTION OF BECOMING A MASTER!
OH?
RIN?
YES...
AS YOU CAN SEE, HE'S TOTALLY CLUELESS.
I BROUGHT HIM HERE TO GET HIM UP TO SPEED.
I SEE.

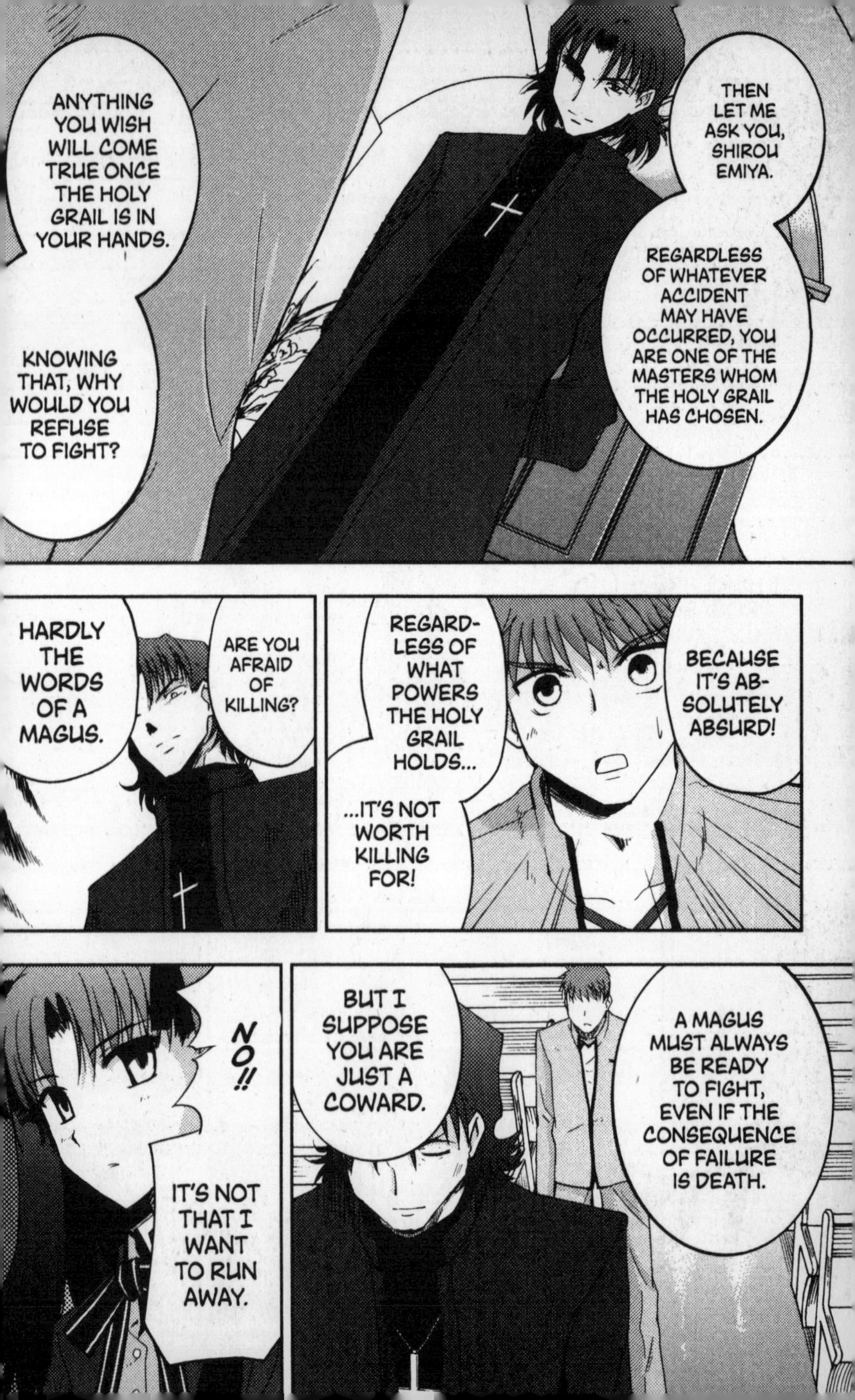
THEN LET ME ASK YOU, SHIROU EMIYA.
REGARDLESS OF WHATEVER ACCIDENT MAY HAVE OCCURRED, YOU ARE ONE OF THE MASTERS WHOM THE HOLY GRAIL HAS CHOSEN.
ANYTHING YOU WISH WILL COME TRUE ONCE THE HOLY GRAIL IS IN YOUR HANDS.
KNOWING THAT, WHY WOULD YOU REFUSE TO FIGHT?
BECAUSE IT'S ABSOLUTELY ABSURD!
REGARDLESS OF WHAT POWERS THE HOLY GRAIL HOLDS...
...IT'S NOT WORTH KILLING FOR!
ARE YOU AFRAID OF KILLING?
HARDLY THE WORDS OF A MAGUS.
A MAGUS MUST ALWAYS BE READY TO FIGHT, EVEN IF THE CONSEQUENCE OF FAILURE IS DEATH.
BUT I SUPPOSE YOU ARE JUST A COWARD.
NO!!
IT'S NOT THAT I WANT TO RUN AWAY.

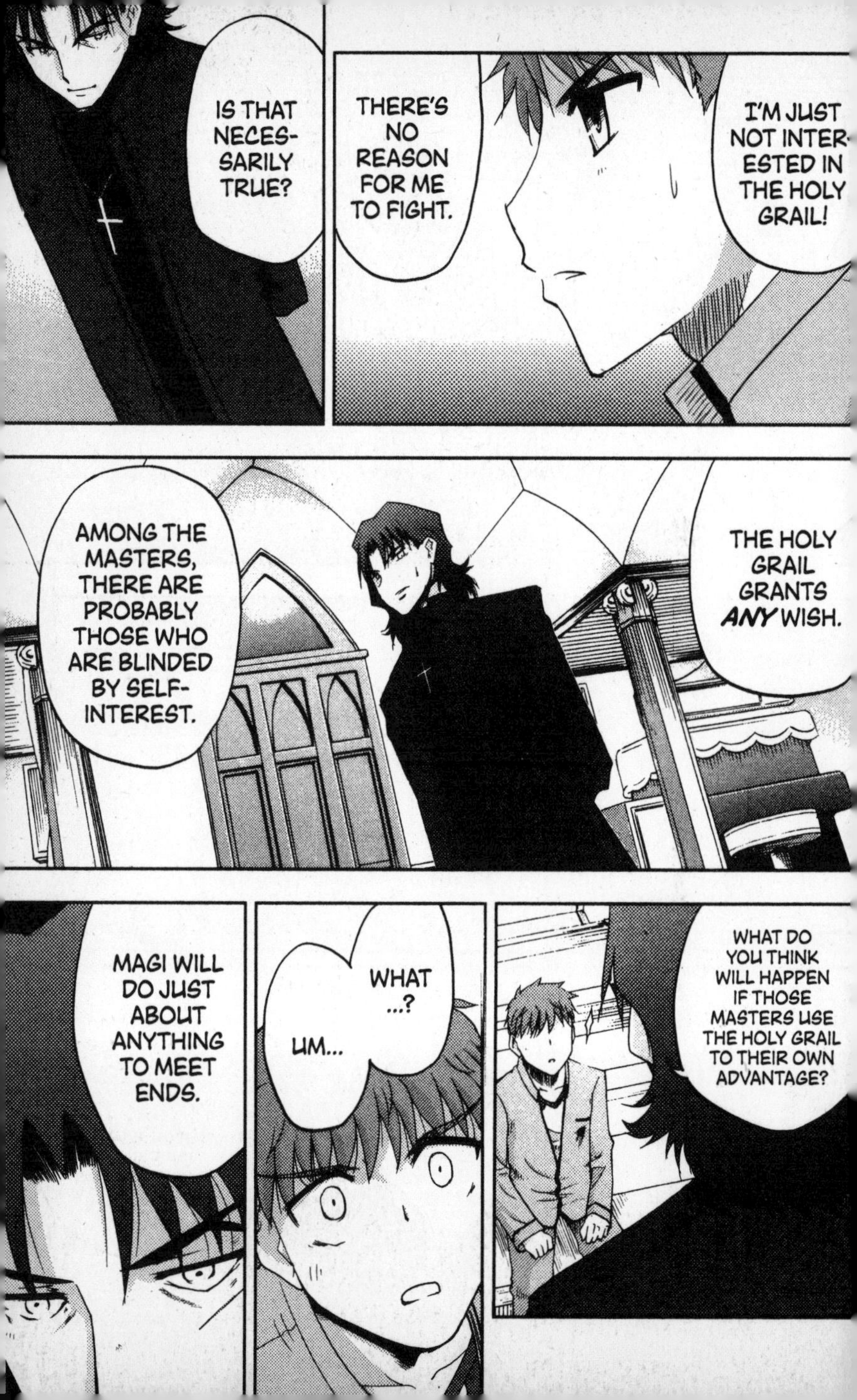
I'M JUST NOT INTERESTED IN THE HOLY GRAIL!
THERE'S NO REASON FOR ME TO FIGHT.
IS THAT NECESSARILY TRUE?
THE HOLY GRAIL GRANTS *ANY* WISH.
AMONG THE MASTERS, THERE ARE PROBABLY THOSE WHO ARE BLINDED BY SELF-INTEREST.
WHAT DO YOU THINK WILL HAPPEN IF THOSE MASTERS USE THE HOLY GRAIL TO THEIR OWN ADVANTAGE?
WHAT ...?
UM...
MAGI WILL DO JUST ABOUT ANYTHING TO MEET ENDS.

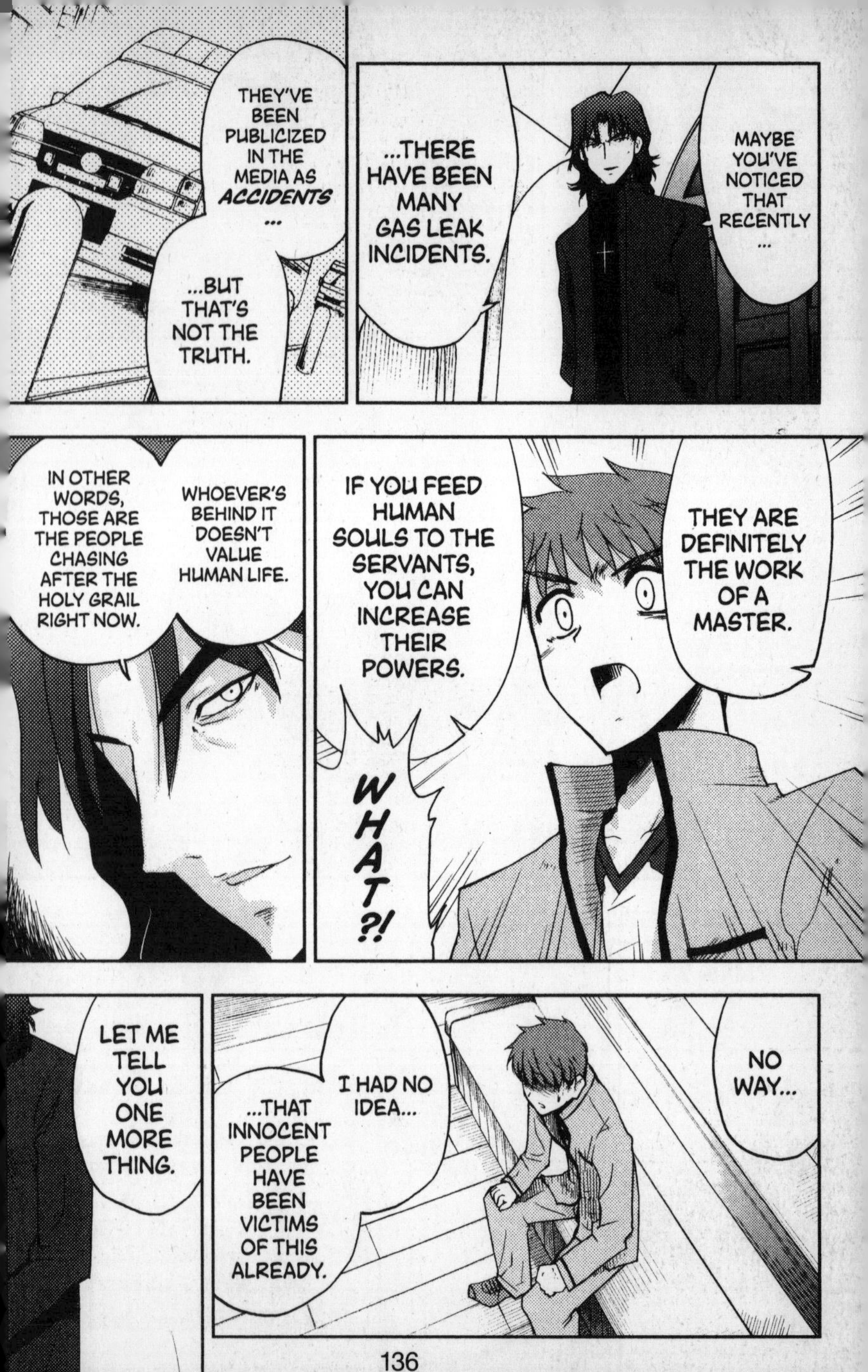

MAYBE YOU'VE NOTICED THAT RECENTLY...
...THERE HAVE BEEN MANY GAS LEAK INCIDENTS.
THEY'VE BEEN PUBLICIZED IN THE MEDIA AS *ACCIDENTS*...
...BUT THAT'S NOT THE TRUTH.
THEY ARE DEFINITELY THE WORK OF A MASTER.
IF YOU FEED HUMAN SOULS TO THE SERVANTS, YOU CAN INCREASE THEIR POWERS.
WHAT?!
WHOEVER'S BEHIND IT DOESN'T VALUE HUMAN LIFE.
IN OTHER WORDS, THOSE ARE THE PEOPLE CHASING AFTER THE HOLY GRAIL RIGHT NOW.
NO WAY...
I HAD NO IDEA...
...THAT INNOCENT PEOPLE HAVE BEEN VICTIMS OF THIS ALREADY.
LET ME TELL YOU ONE MORE THING.

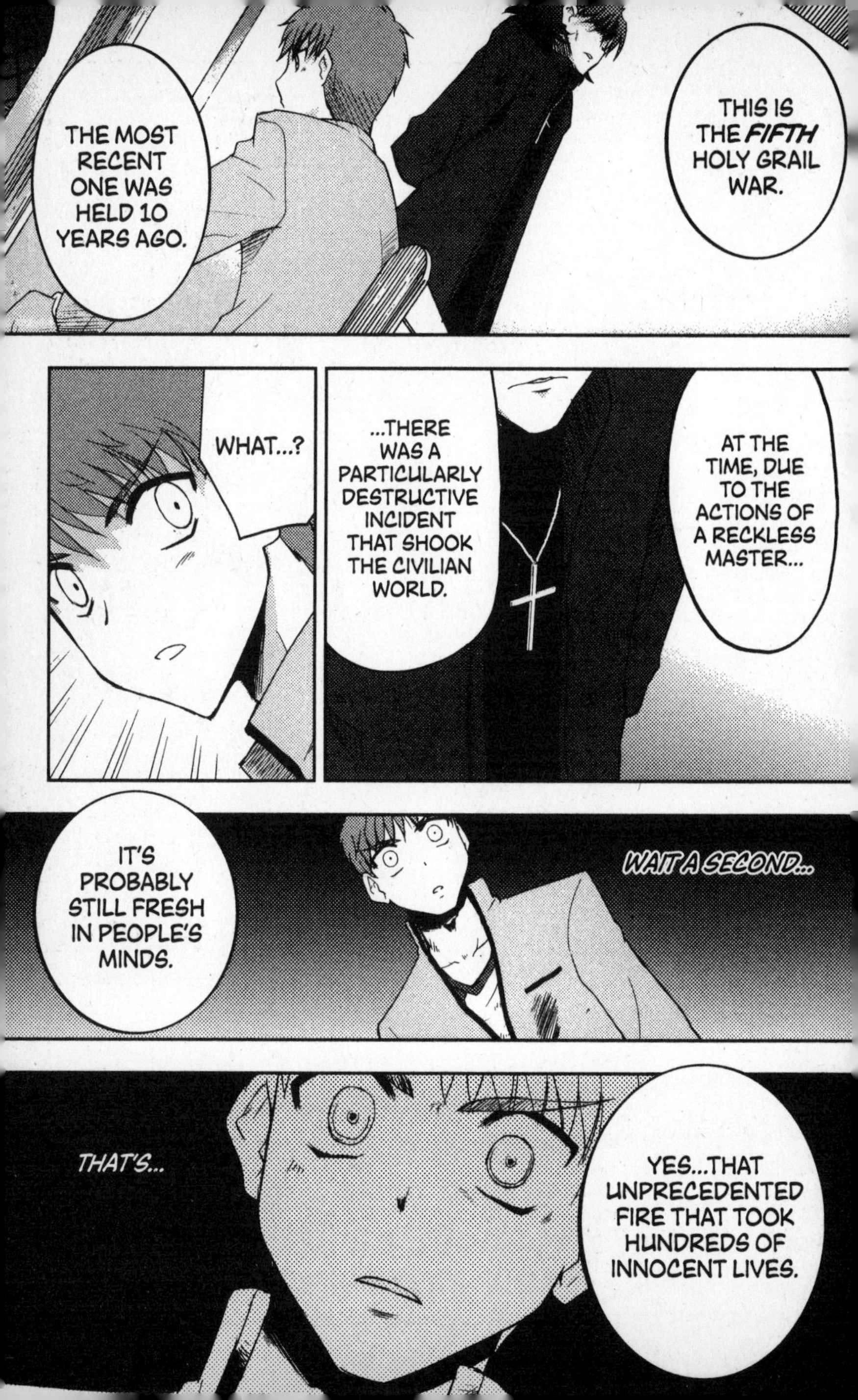
THIS IS THE *FIFTH* HOLY GRAIL WAR.
THE MOST RECENT ONE WAS HELD 10 YEARS AGO.
AT THE TIME, DUE TO THE ACTIONS OF A RECKLESS MASTER...
...THERE WAS A PARTICULARLY DESTRUCTIVE INCIDENT THAT SHOOK THE CIVILIAN WORLD.
WHAT...?
WAIT A SECOND...
IT'S PROBABLY STILL FRESH IN PEOPLE'S MINDS.
YES...THAT UNPRECEDENTED FIRE THAT TOOK HUNDREDS OF INNOCENT LIVES.
THAT'S...

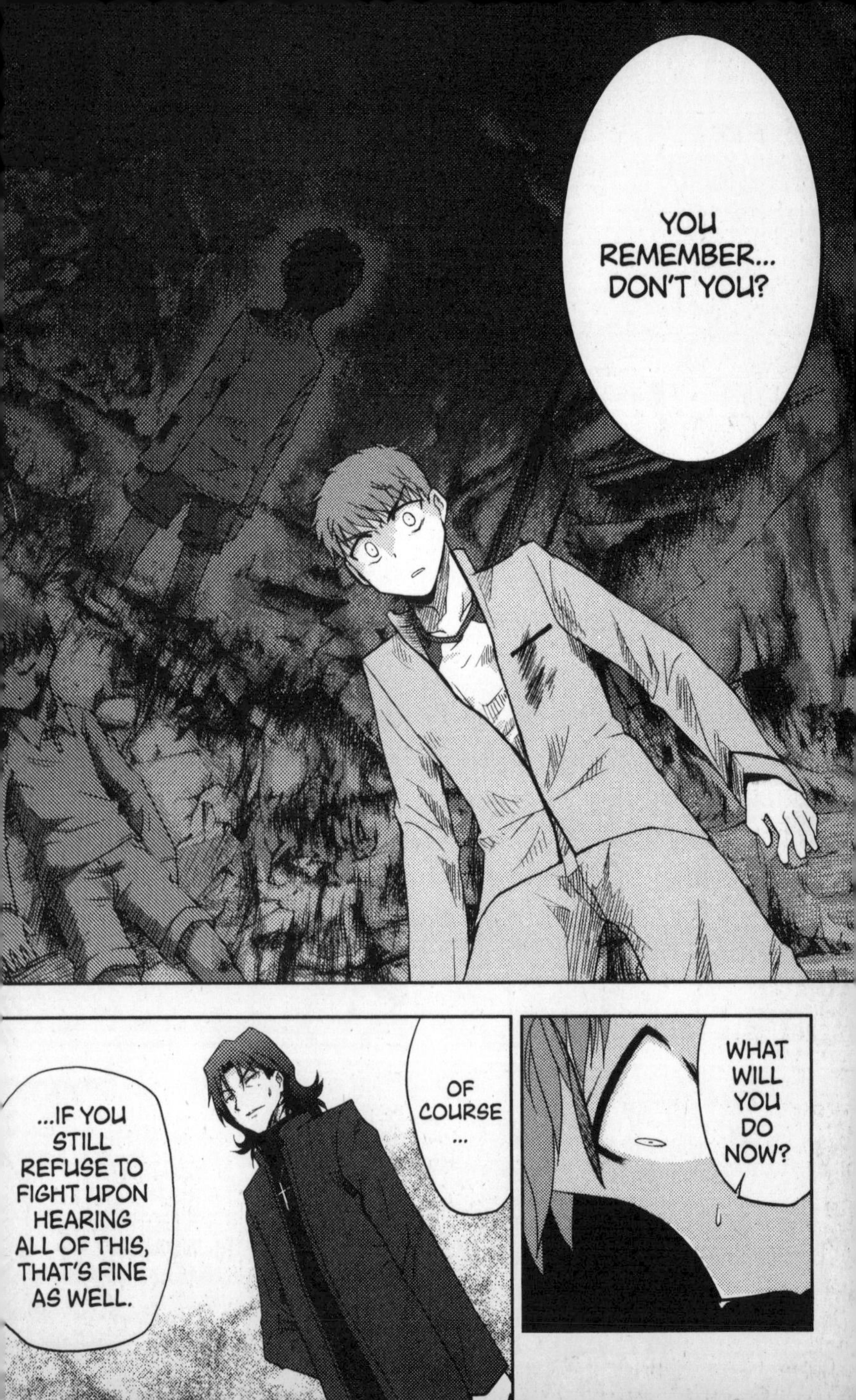
YOU REMEMBER... DON'T YOU?
WHAT WILL YOU DO NOW?
OF COURSE ...
...IF YOU STILL REFUSE TO FIGHT UPON HEARING ALL OF THIS, THAT'S FINE AS WELL.

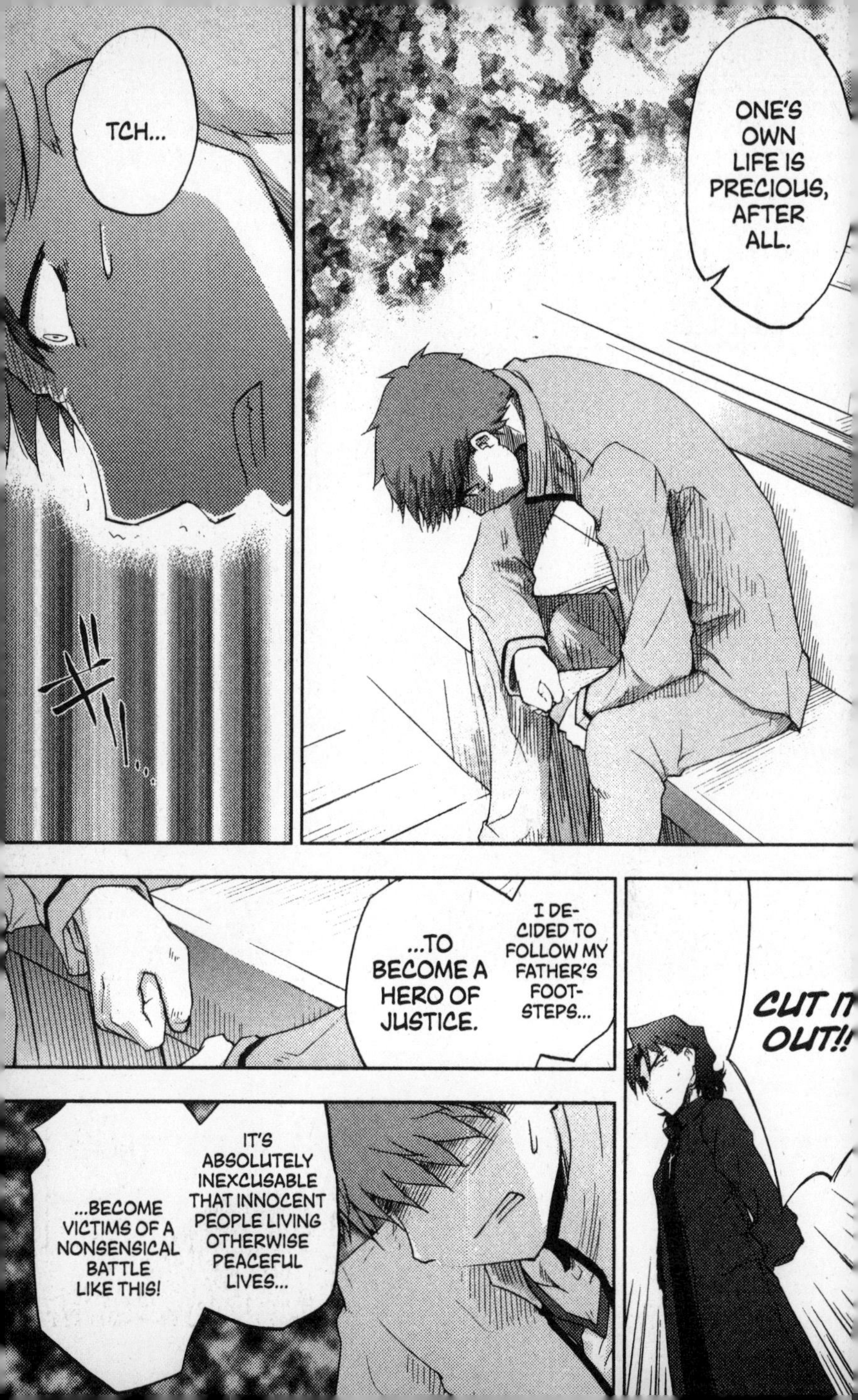
ONE'S OWN LIFE IS PRECIOUS, AFTER ALL.
TCH...
CUT IT OUT!!
I DE-CIDED TO FOLLOW MY FATHER'S FOOT-STEPS...
...TO BECOME A HERO OF JUSTICE.
IT'S ABSOLUTELY INEXCUSABLE THAT INNOCENT PEOPLE LIVING OTHERWISE PEACEFUL LIVES...
...BECOME VICTIMS OF A NONSENSICAL BATTLE LIKE THIS!

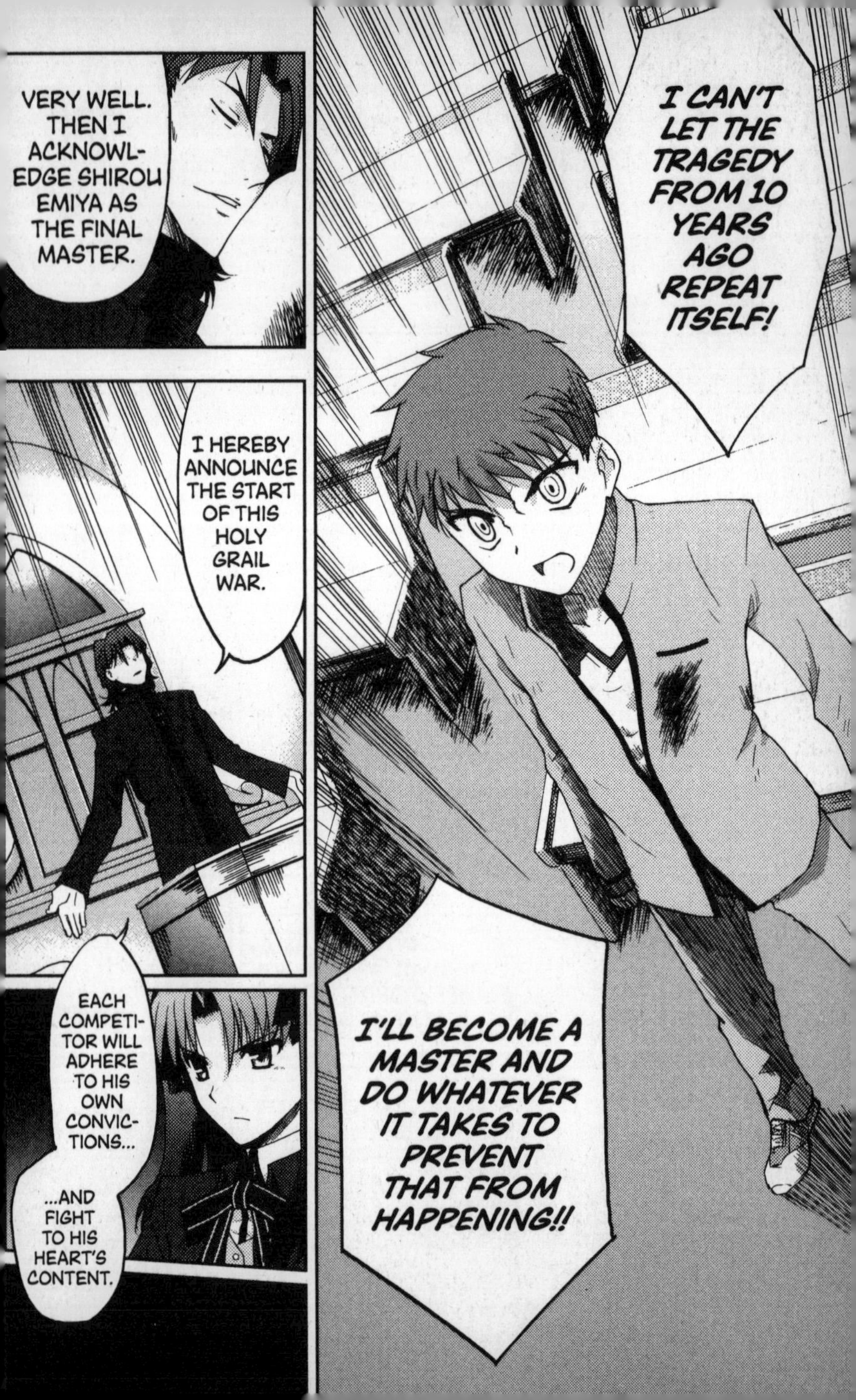
I CAN'T LET THE TRAGEDY FROM 10 YEARS AGO REPEAT ITSELF!
I'LL BECOME A MASTER AND DO WHATEVER IT TAKES TO PREVENT THAT FROM HAPPENING!!
VERY WELL. THEN I ACKNOWLEDGE SHIROU EMIYA AS THE FINAL MASTER.
I HEREBY ANNOUNCE THE START OF THIS HOLY GRAIL WAR.
EACH COMPETITOR WILL ADHERE TO HIS OWN CONVICTIONS...
...AND FIGHT TO HIS HEART'S CONTENT.

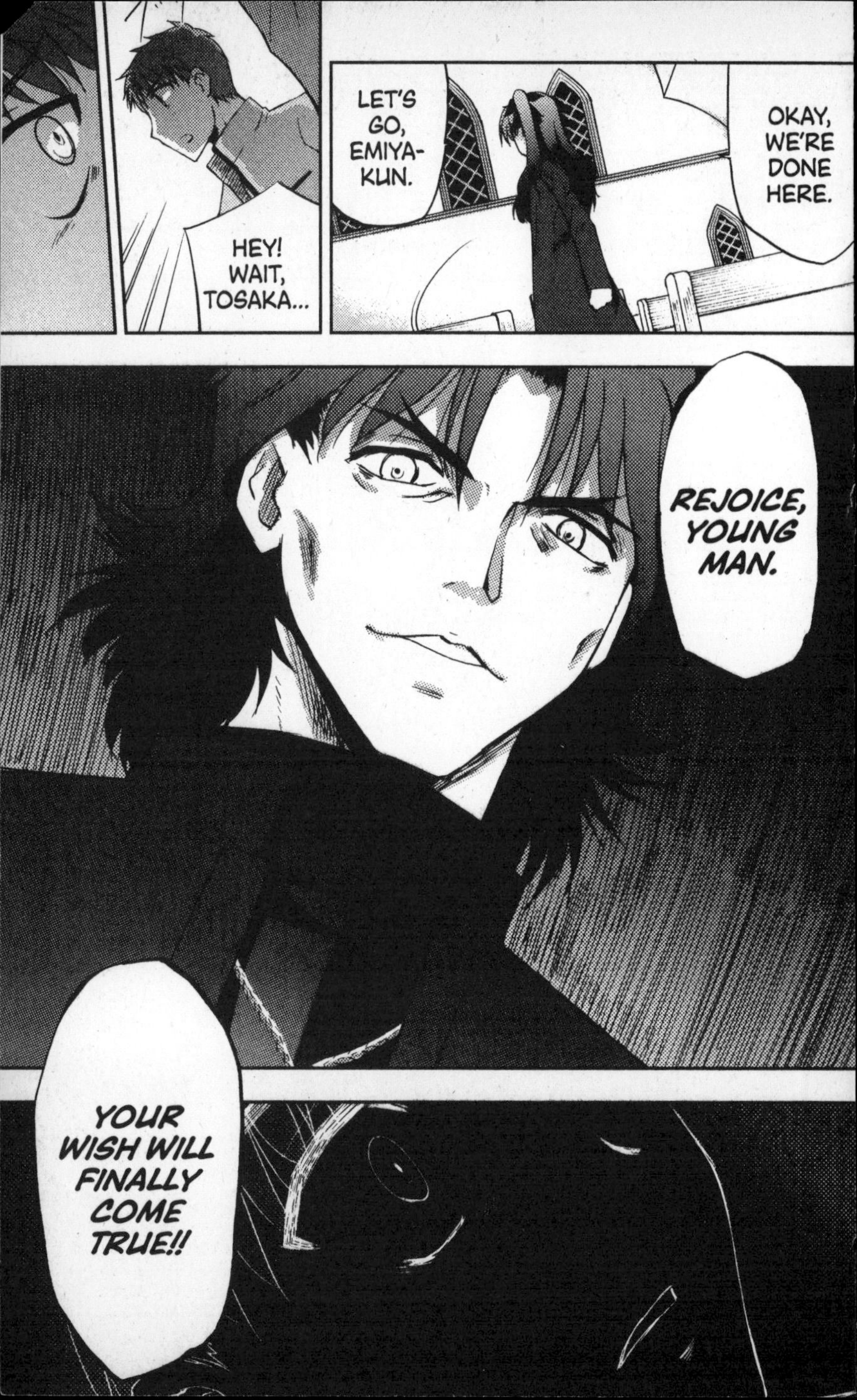
OKAY, WE'RE DONE HERE.
LET'S GO, EMIYA-KUN.
HEY! WAIT, TOSAKA...
REJOICE, YOUNG MAN.
YOUR WISH WILL FINALLY COME TRUE!!

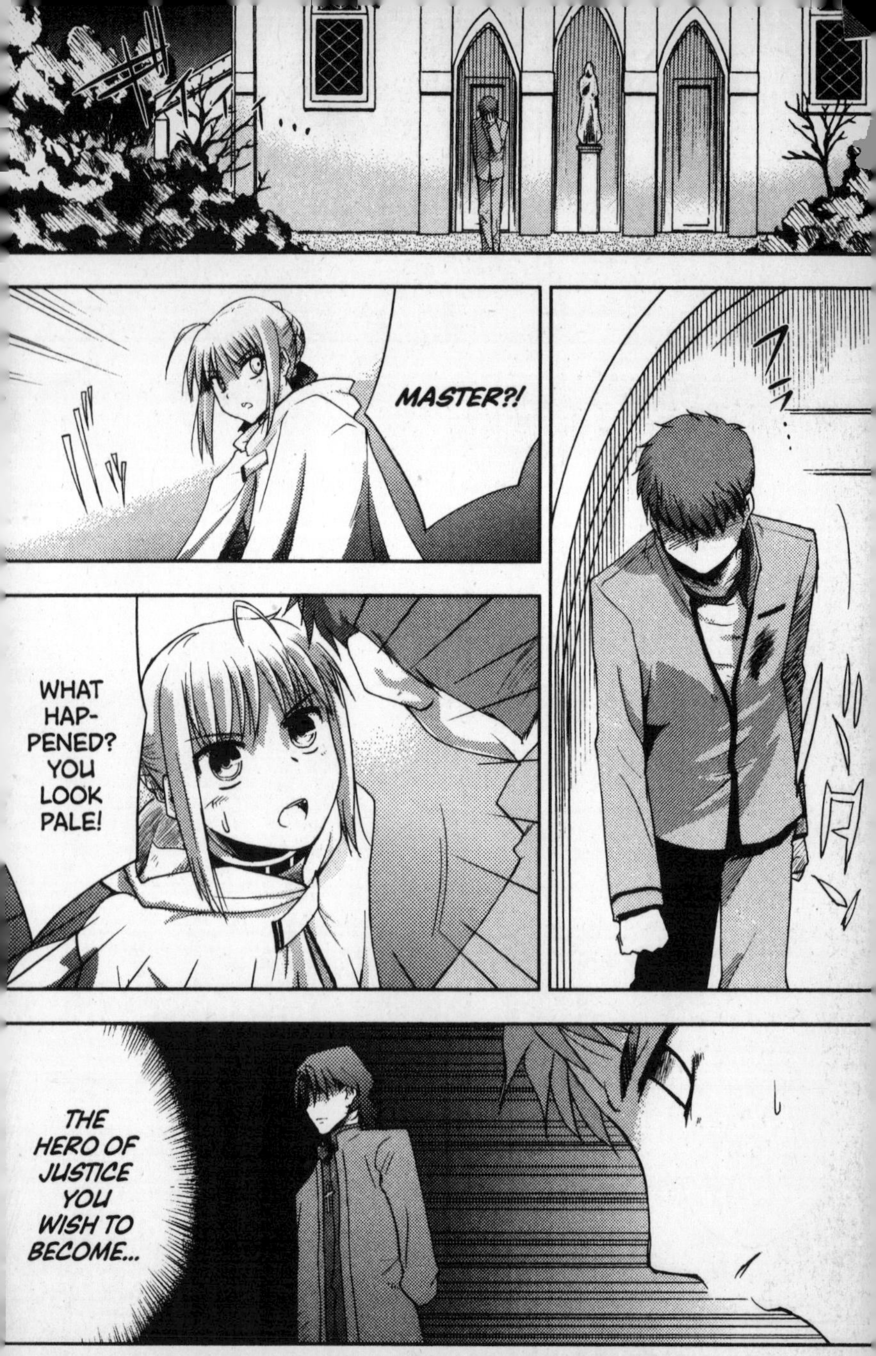
MASTER?!
WHAT HAPPENED? YOU LOOK PALE!
THE HERO OF JUSTICE YOU WISH TO BECOME...

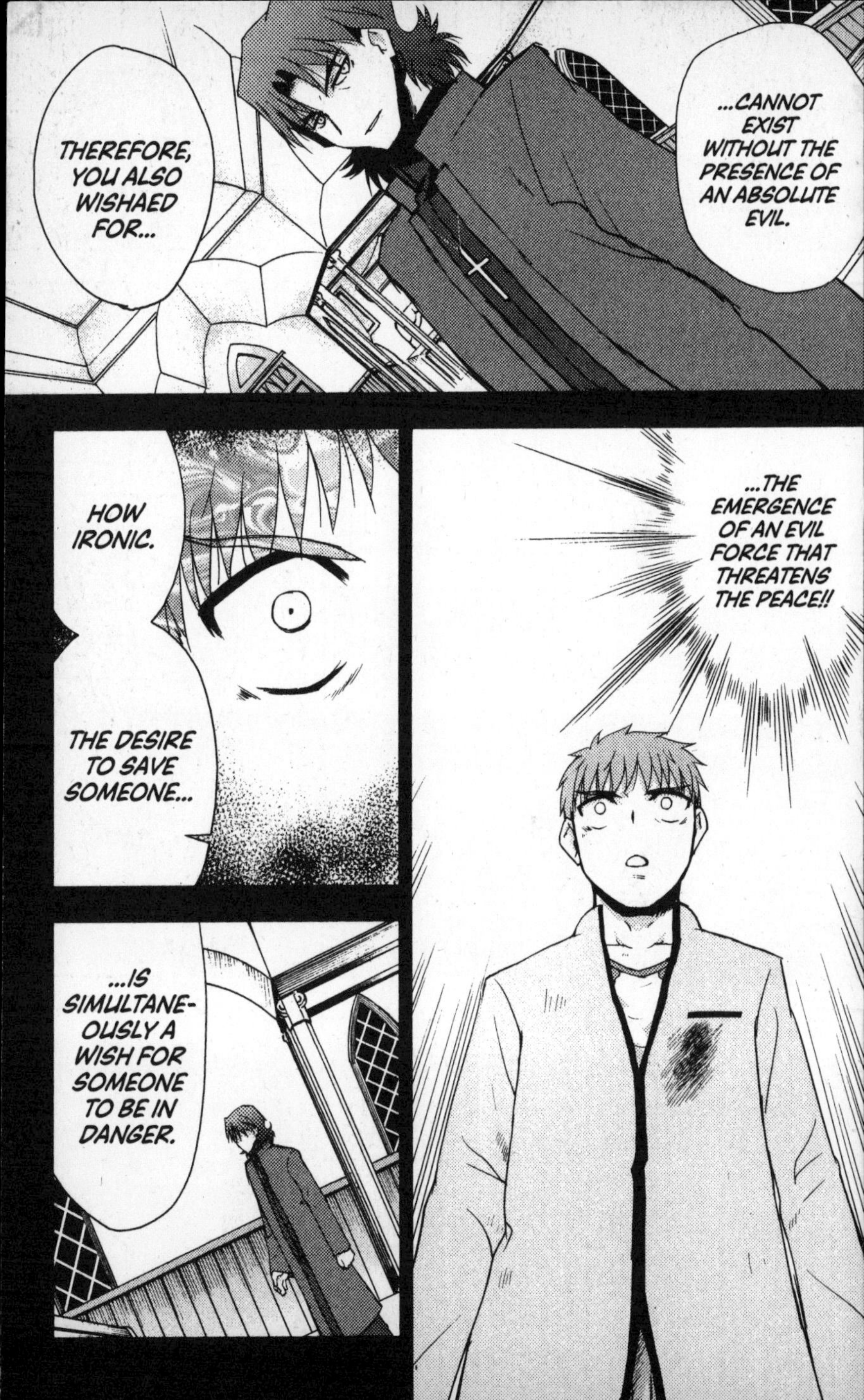
...CANNOT EXIST WITHOUT THE PRESENCE OF AN ABSOLUTE EVIL.
THEREFORE, YOU ALSO WISHAED FOR...
...THE EMERGENCE OF AN EVIL FORCE THAT THREATENS THE PEACE!!
HOW IRONIC.
THE DESIRE TO SAVE SOMEONE...
...IS SIMULTANE-OUSLY A WISH FOR SOMEONE TO BE IN DANGER.

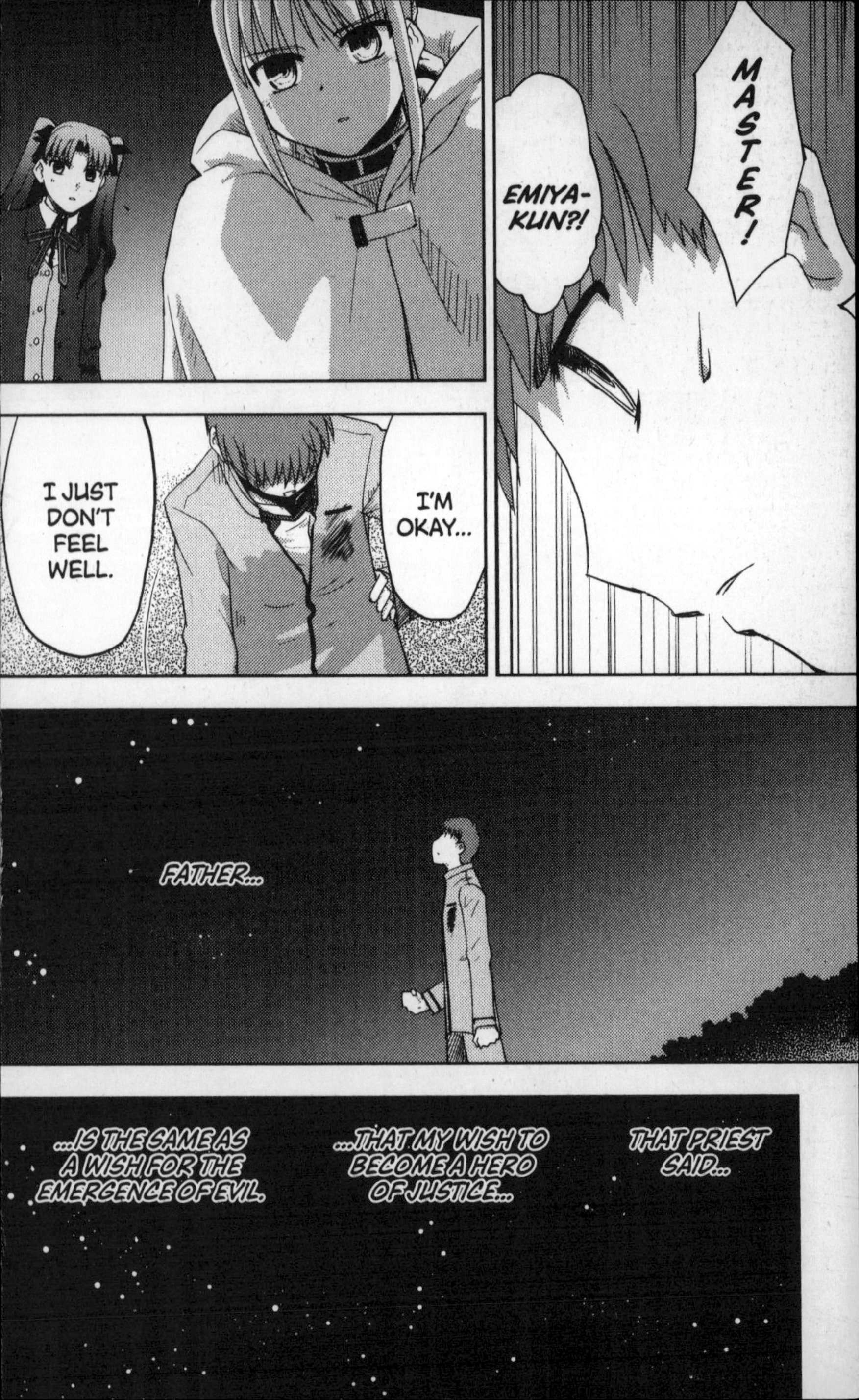
MASTER!
EMIYA-KUN?!
I'M OKAY...
I JUST DON'T FEEL WELL.
FATHER...
THAT PRIEST SAID...
...THAT MY WISH TO BECOME A HERO OF JUSTICE...
...IS THE SAME AS A WISH FOR THE EMERGENCE OF EVIL.

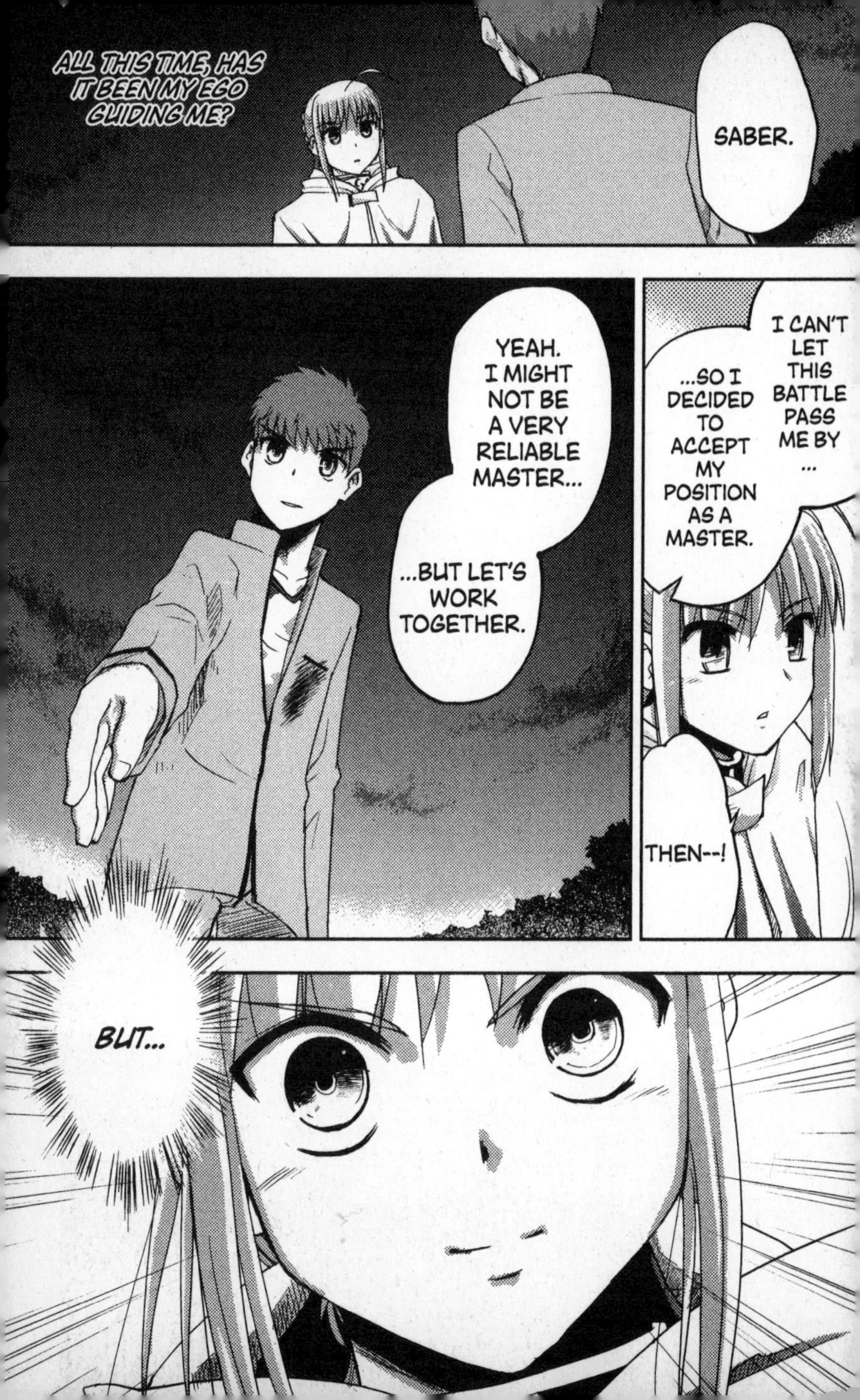
SABER.
ALL THIS TIME, HAS IT BEEN MY EGO GUIDING ME?
I CAN'T LET THIS BATTLE PASS ME BY ...
...SO I DECIDED TO ACCEPT MY POSITION AS A MASTER.
THEN--!
YEAH. I MIGHT NOT BE A VERY RELIABLE MASTER...
...BUT LET'S WORK TOGETHER.
BUT...

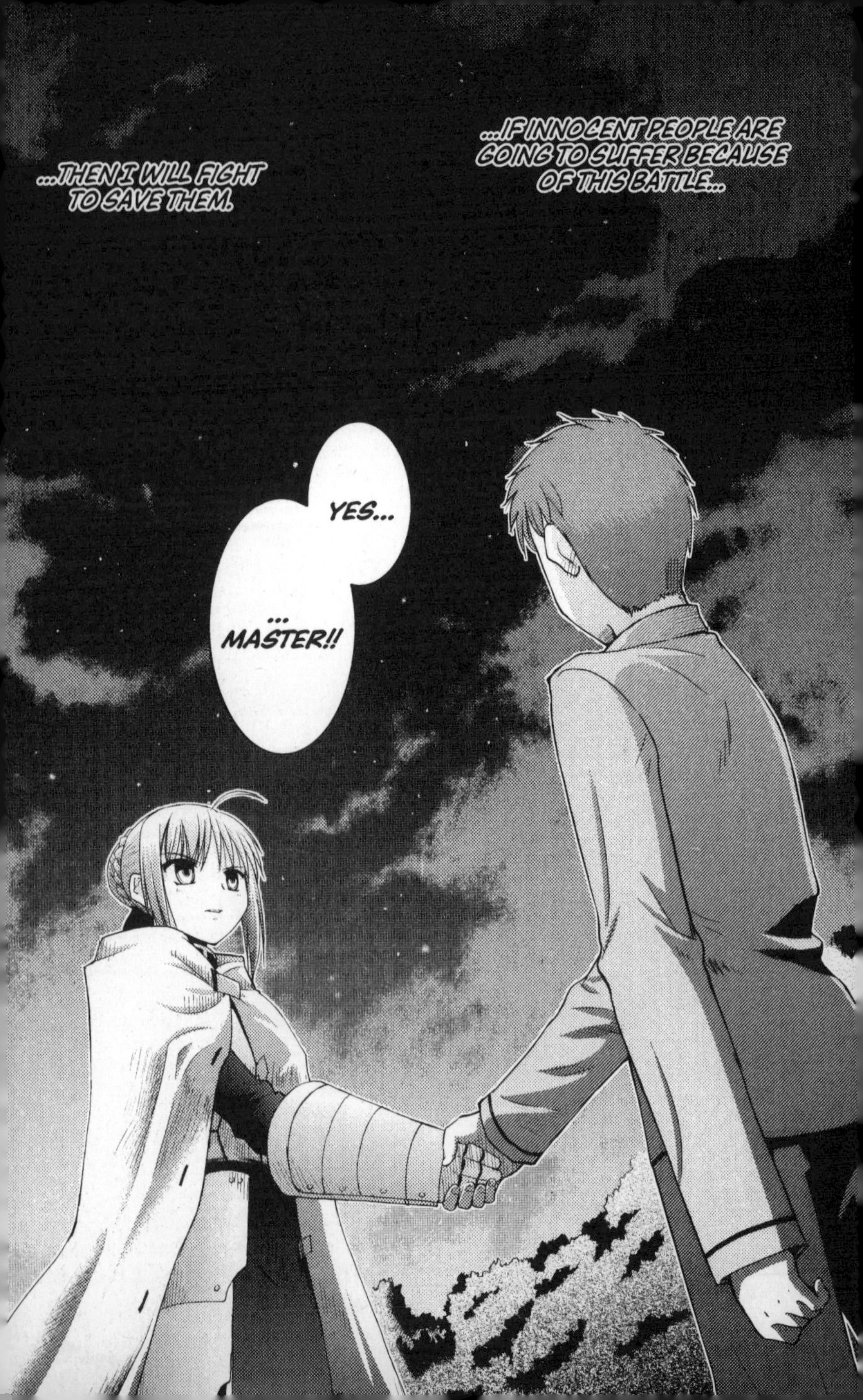
...IF INNOCENT PEOPLE ARE GOING TO SUFFER BECAUSE OF THIS BATTLE...
...THEN I WILL FIGHT TO SAVE THEM.
YES... ...MASTER!!

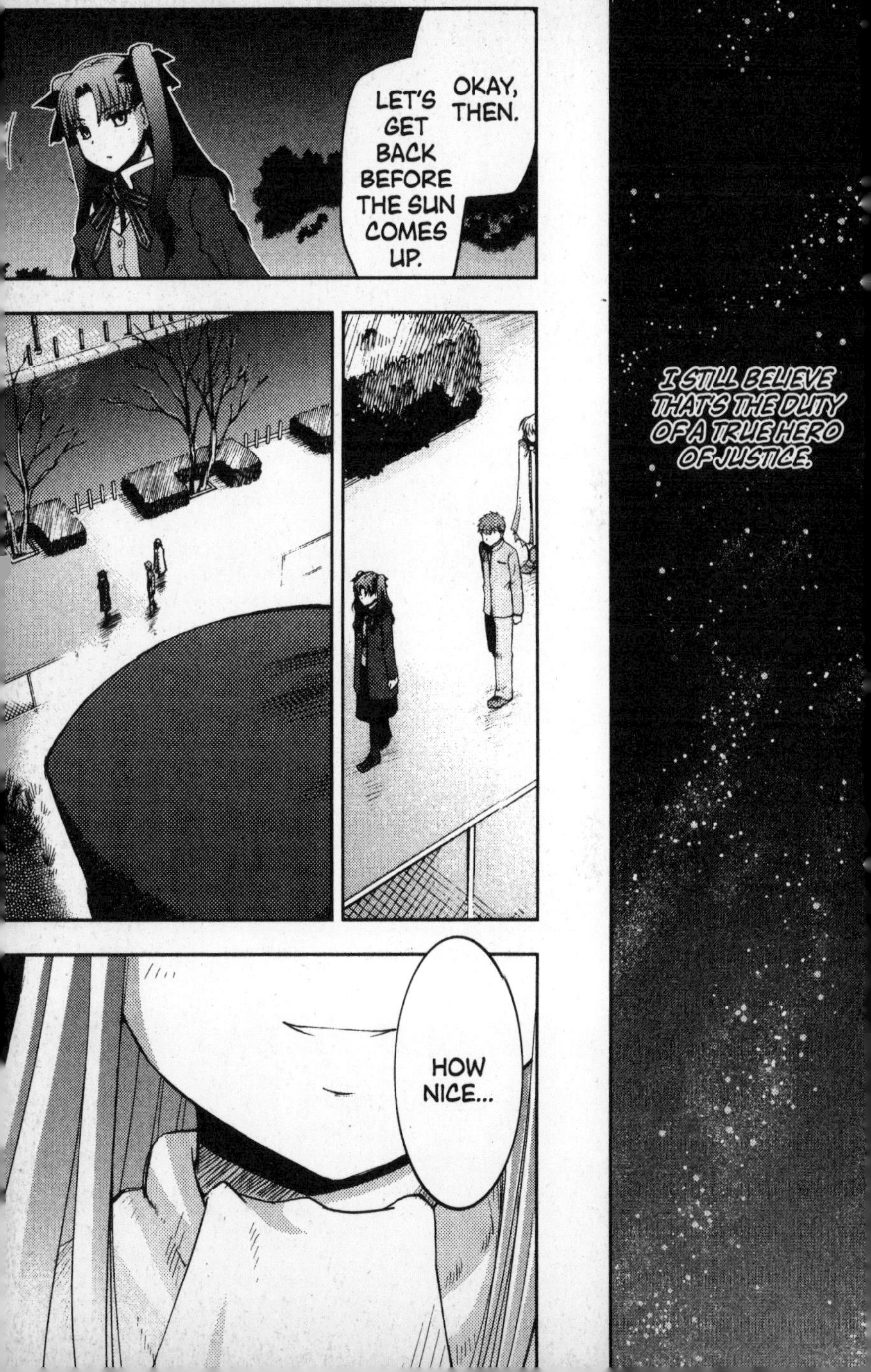
I STILL BELIEVE THAT'S THE DUTY OF A TRUE HERO OF JUSTICE.
OKAY, THEN.
LET'S GET BACK BEFORE THE SUN COMES UP.
HOW NICE...

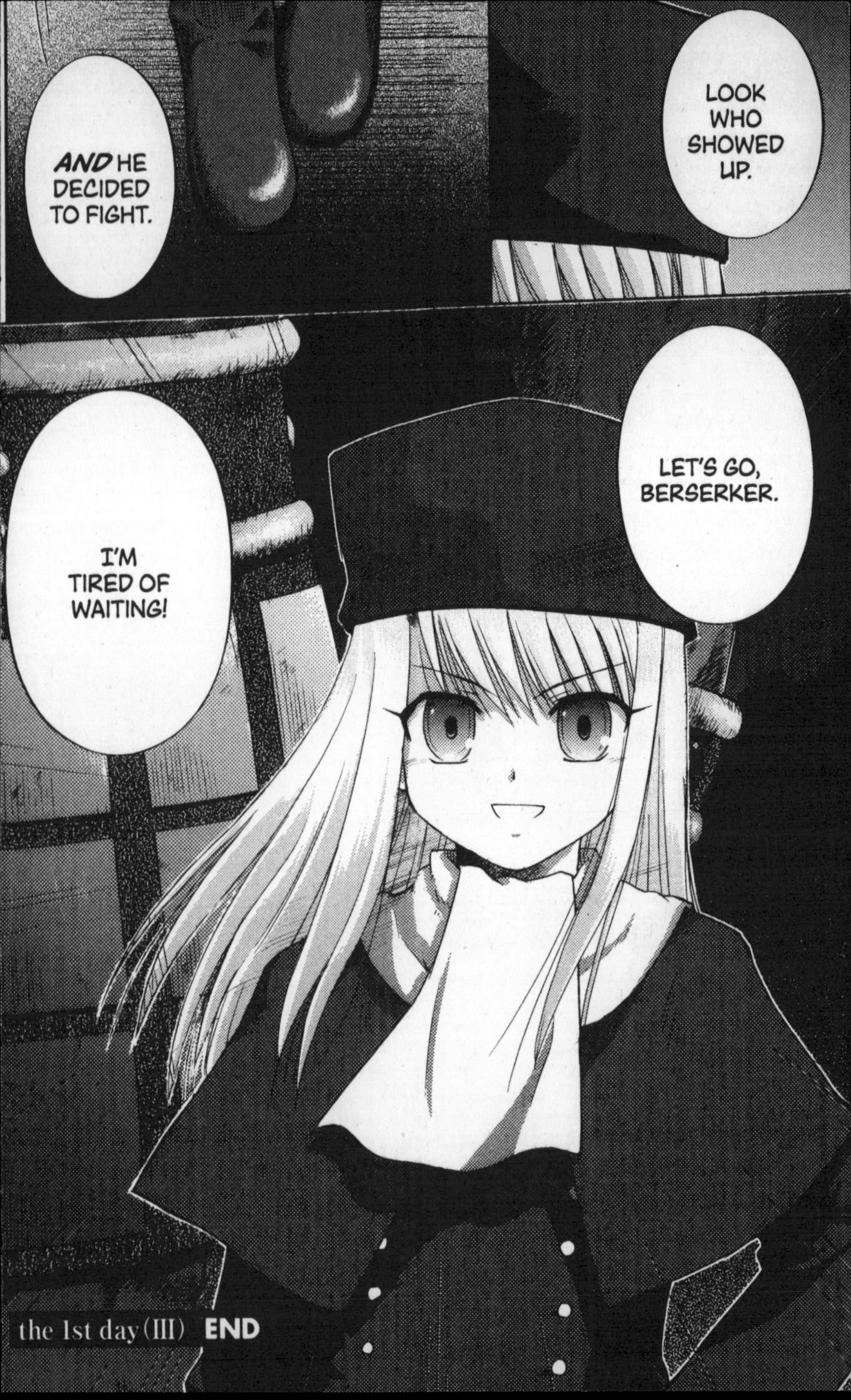
LOOK WHO SHOWED UP.
AND HE DECIDED TO FIGHT.
LET'S GO, BERSERKER.
I'M TIRED OF WAITING!
the 1st day (III) END

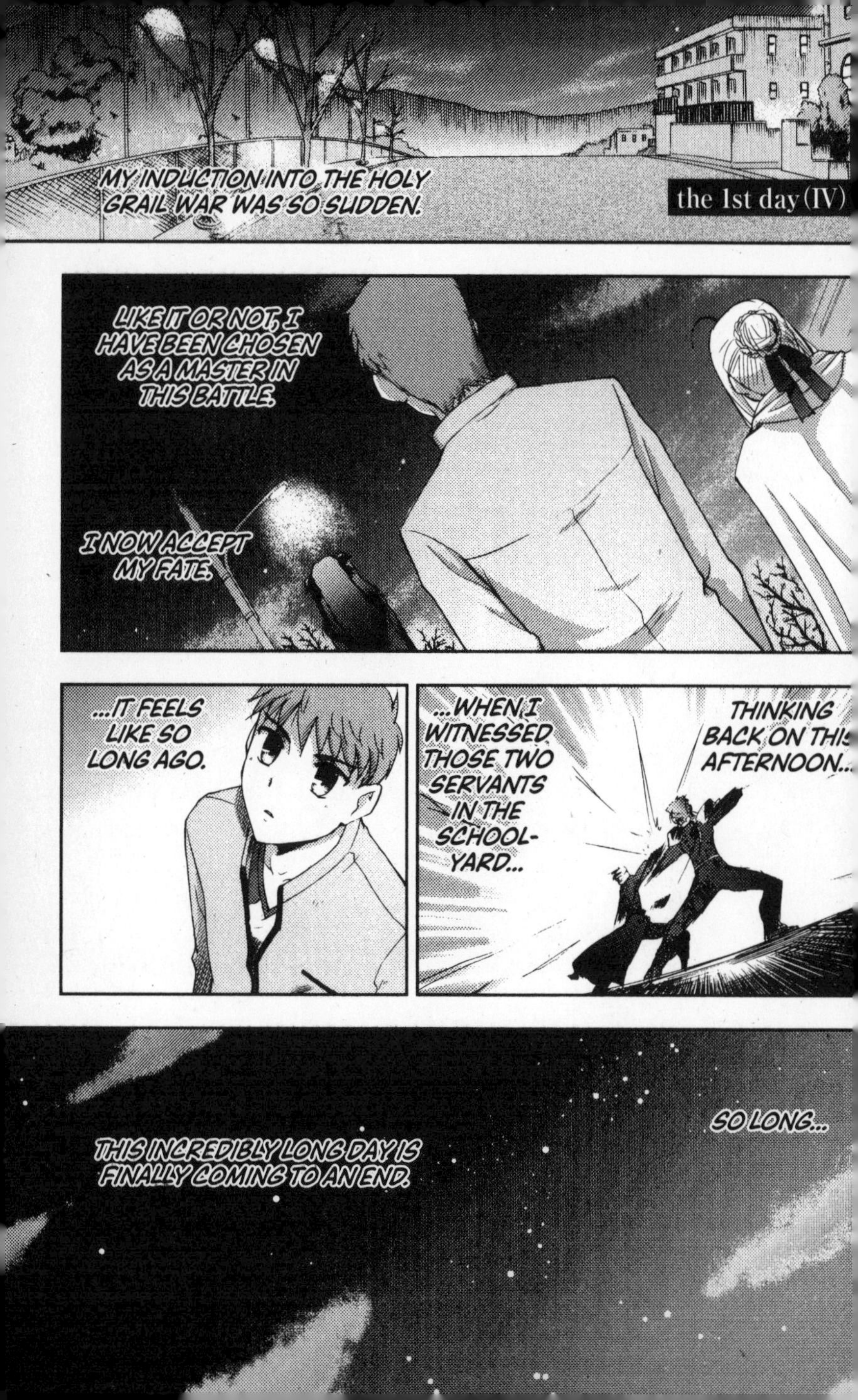
the 1st day (IV)
MY INDUCTION INTO THE HOLY GRAIL WAR WAS SO SUDDEN.
LIKE IT OR NOT, I HAVE BEEN CHOSEN AS A MASTER IN THIS BATTLE.
I NOW ACCEPT MY FATE.
THINKING BACK ON THIS AFTERNOON...
...WHEN I WITNESSED THOSE TWO SERVANTS IN THE SCHOOL-YARD...
...IT FEELS LIKE SO LONG AGO.
SO LONG...
THIS INCREDIBLY LONG DAY IS FINALLY COMING TO AN END.

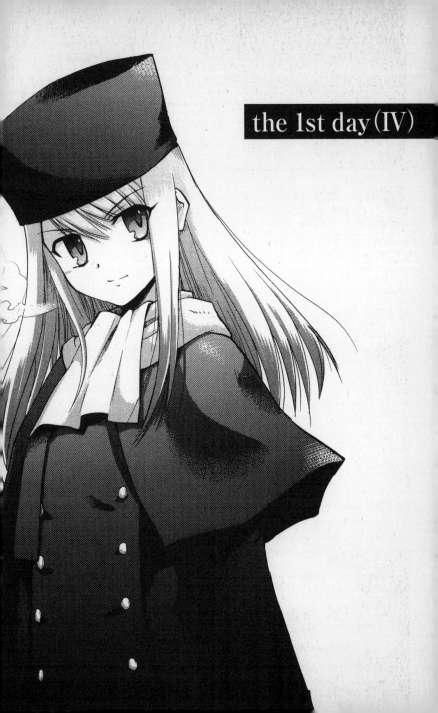

the 1st day (IV)

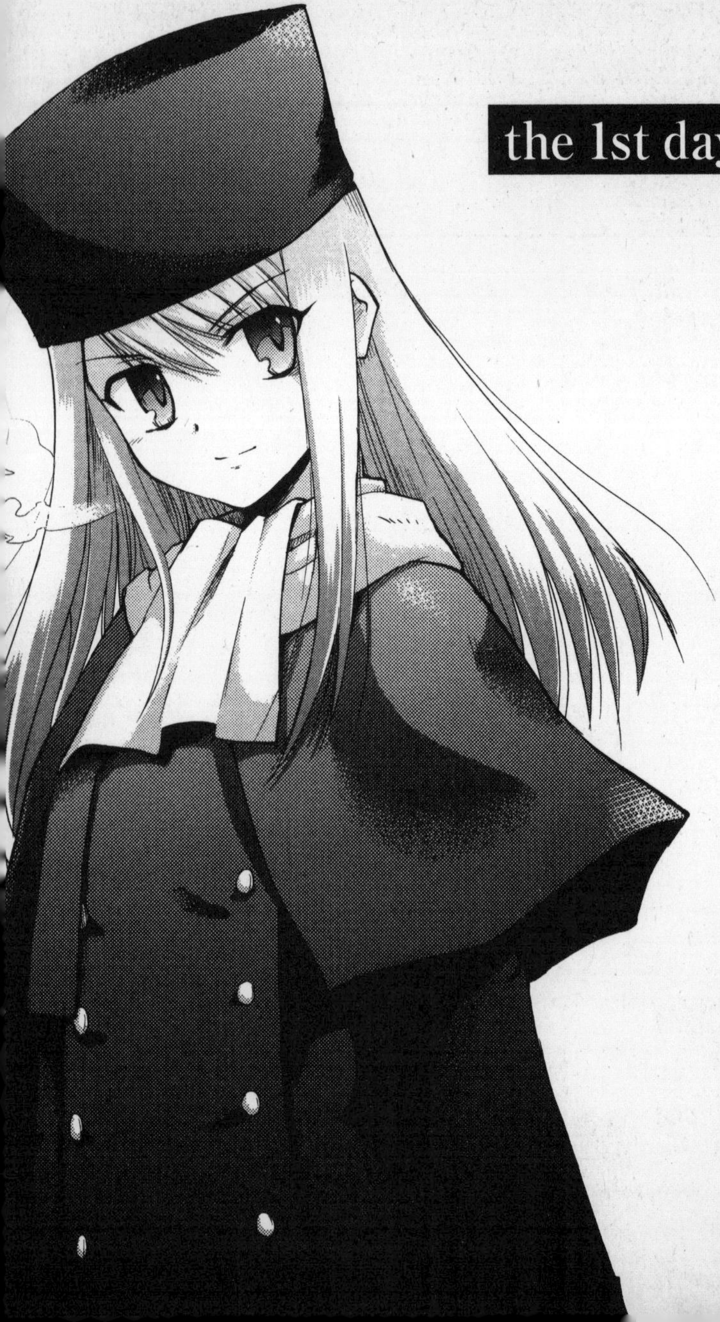

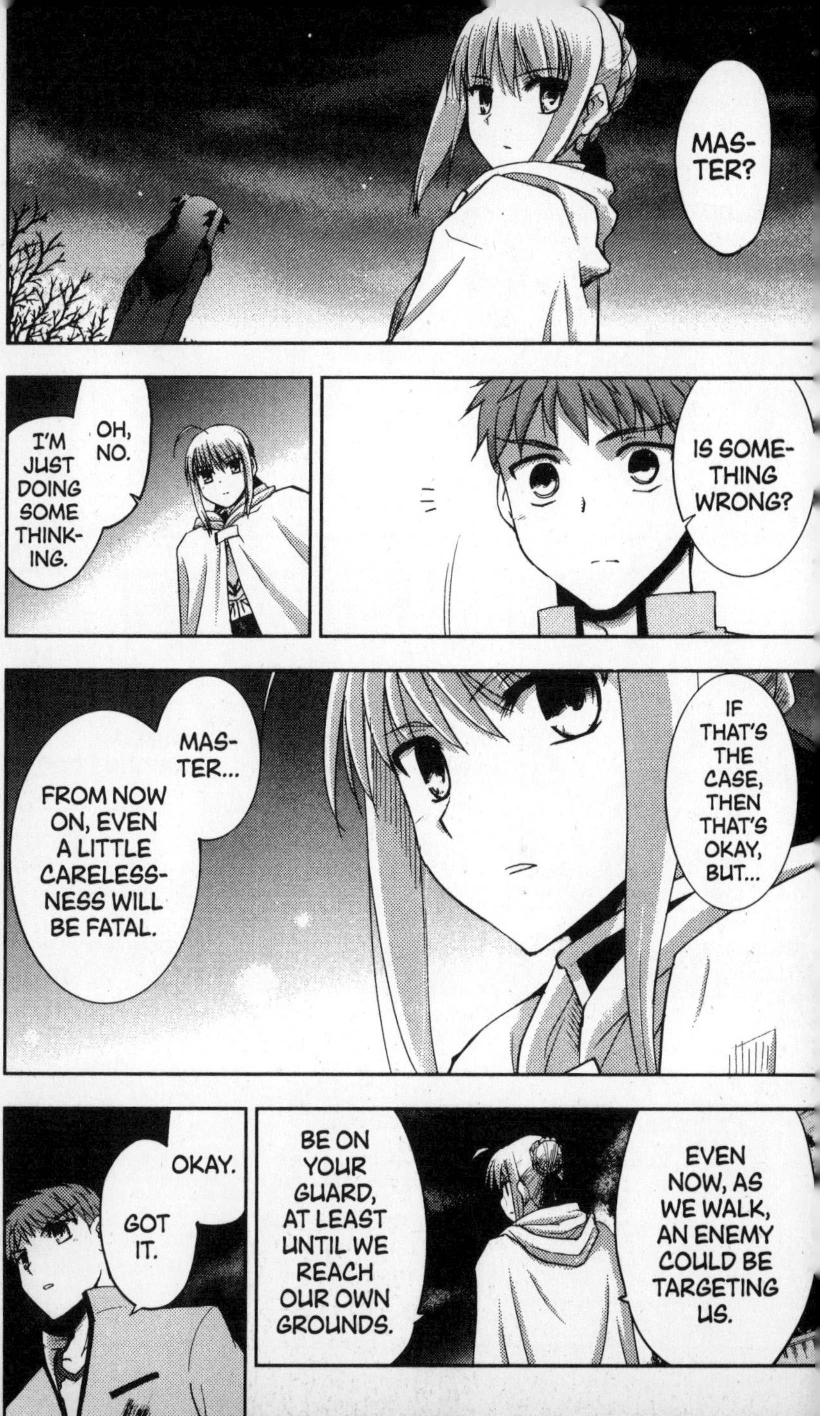
MASTER?
IS SOMETHING WRONG?
OH, NO.
I'M JUST DOING SOME THINKING.
IF THAT'S THE CASE, THEN THAT'S OKAY, BUT...
MASTER...
FROM NOW ON, EVEN A LITTLE CARELESSNESS WILL BE FATAL.
EVEN NOW, AS WE WALK, AN ENEMY COULD BE TARGETING US.
BE ON YOUR GUARD, AT LEAST UNTIL WE REACH OUR OWN GROUNDS.
OKAY.
GOT IT.

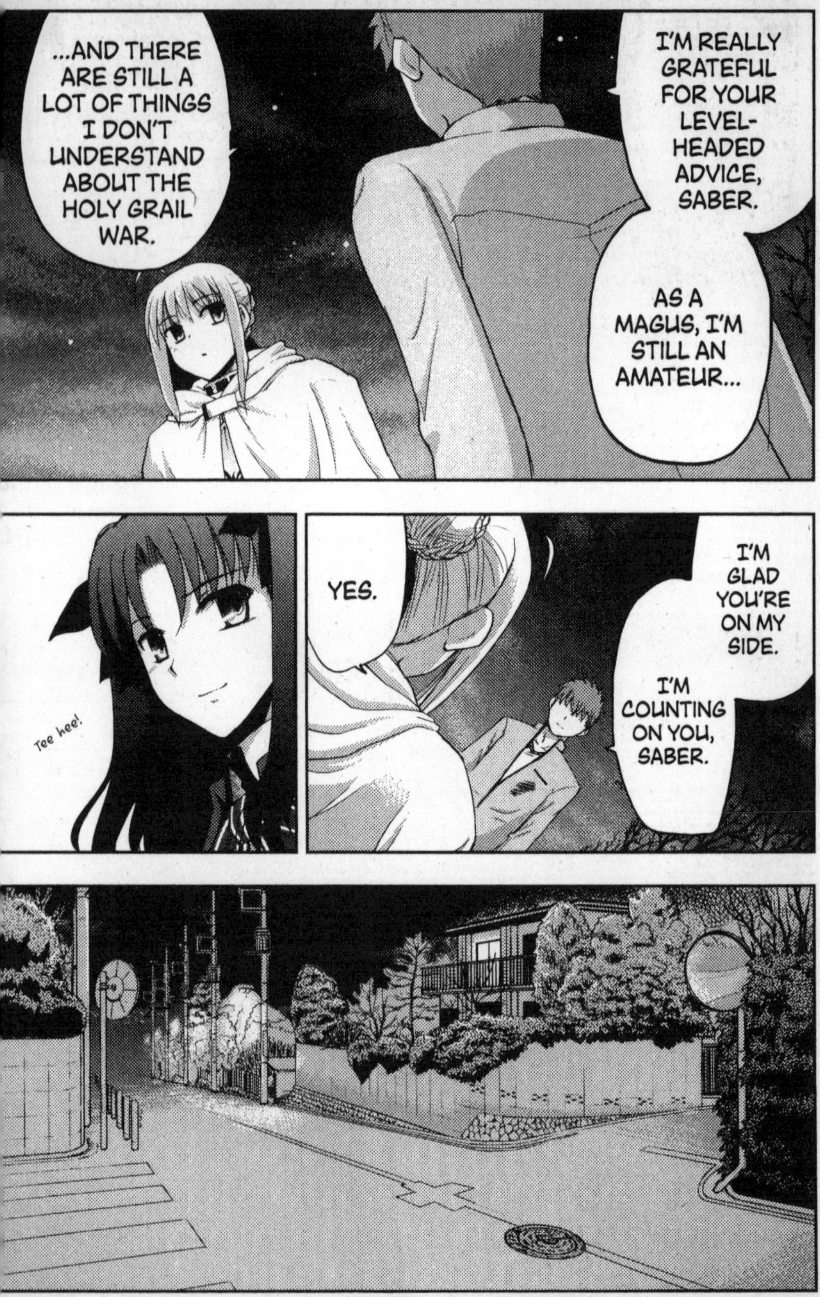
I'M REALLY GRATEFUL FOR YOUR LEVEL-HEADED ADVICE, SABER.
AS A MAGUS, I'M STILL AN AMATEUR...
...AND THERE ARE STILL A LOT OF THINGS I DON'T UNDERSTAND ABOUT THE HOLY GRAIL WAR.
I'M GLAD YOU'RE ON MY SIDE.
I'M COUNTING ON YOU, SABER.
YES.
Tee hee!

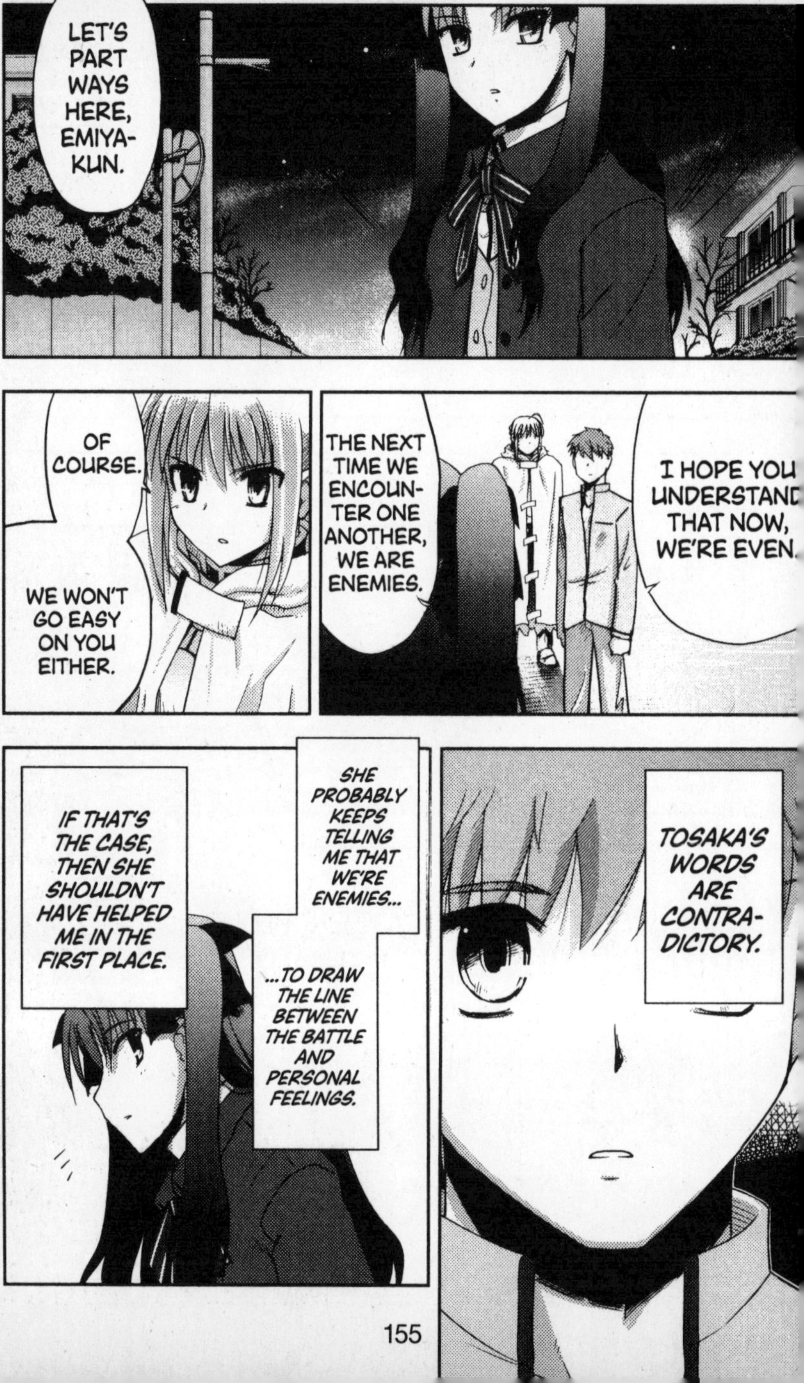
LET'S PART WAYS HERE, EMIYA-KUN.
I HOPE YOU UNDERSTAND THAT NOW, WE'RE EVEN.
THE NEXT TIME WE ENCOUN-TER ONE ANOTHER, WE ARE ENEMIES.
OF COURSE.
WE WON'T GO EASY ON YOU EITHER.
TOSAKA'S WORDS ARE CONTRA-DICTORY.
SHE PROBABLY KEEPS TELLING ME THAT WE'RE ENEMIES...
...TO DRAW THE LINE BETWEEN THE BATTLE AND PERSONAL FEELINGS.
IF THAT'S THE CASE, THEN SHE SHOULDN'T HAVE HELPED ME IN THE FIRST PLACE.

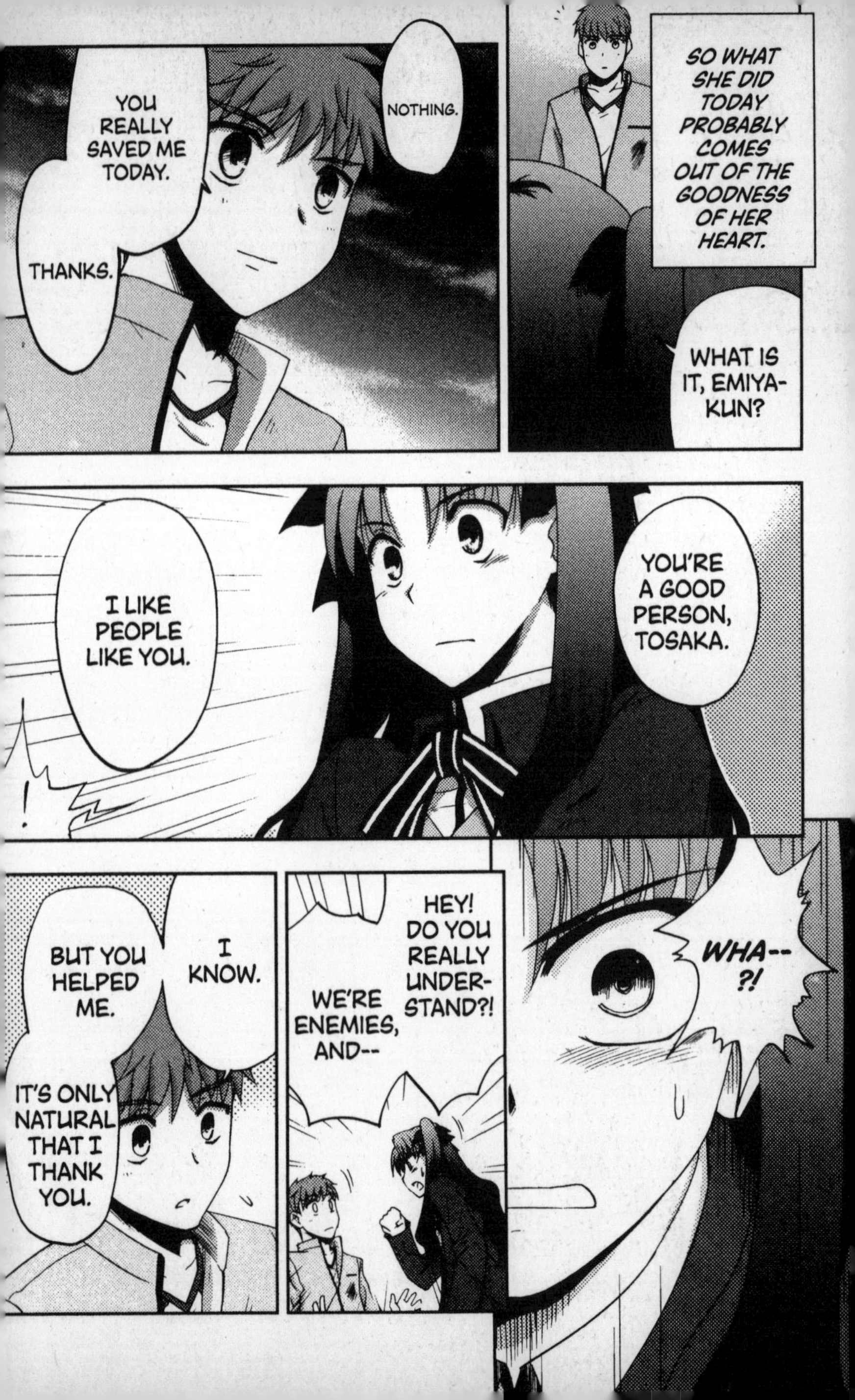
SO WHAT SHE DID TODAY PROBABLY COMES OUT OF THE GOODNESS OF HER HEART.
WHAT IS IT, EMIYA-KUN?
NOTHING.
YOU REALLY SAVED ME TODAY.
THANKS.
YOU'RE A GOOD PERSON, TOSAKA.
I LIKE PEOPLE LIKE YOU.
!
WHA--?!
HEY! DO YOU REALLY UNDER-STAND?!
WE'RE ENEMIES, AND--
I KNOW.
BUT YOU HELPED ME.
IT'S ONLY NATURAL THAT I THANK YOU.

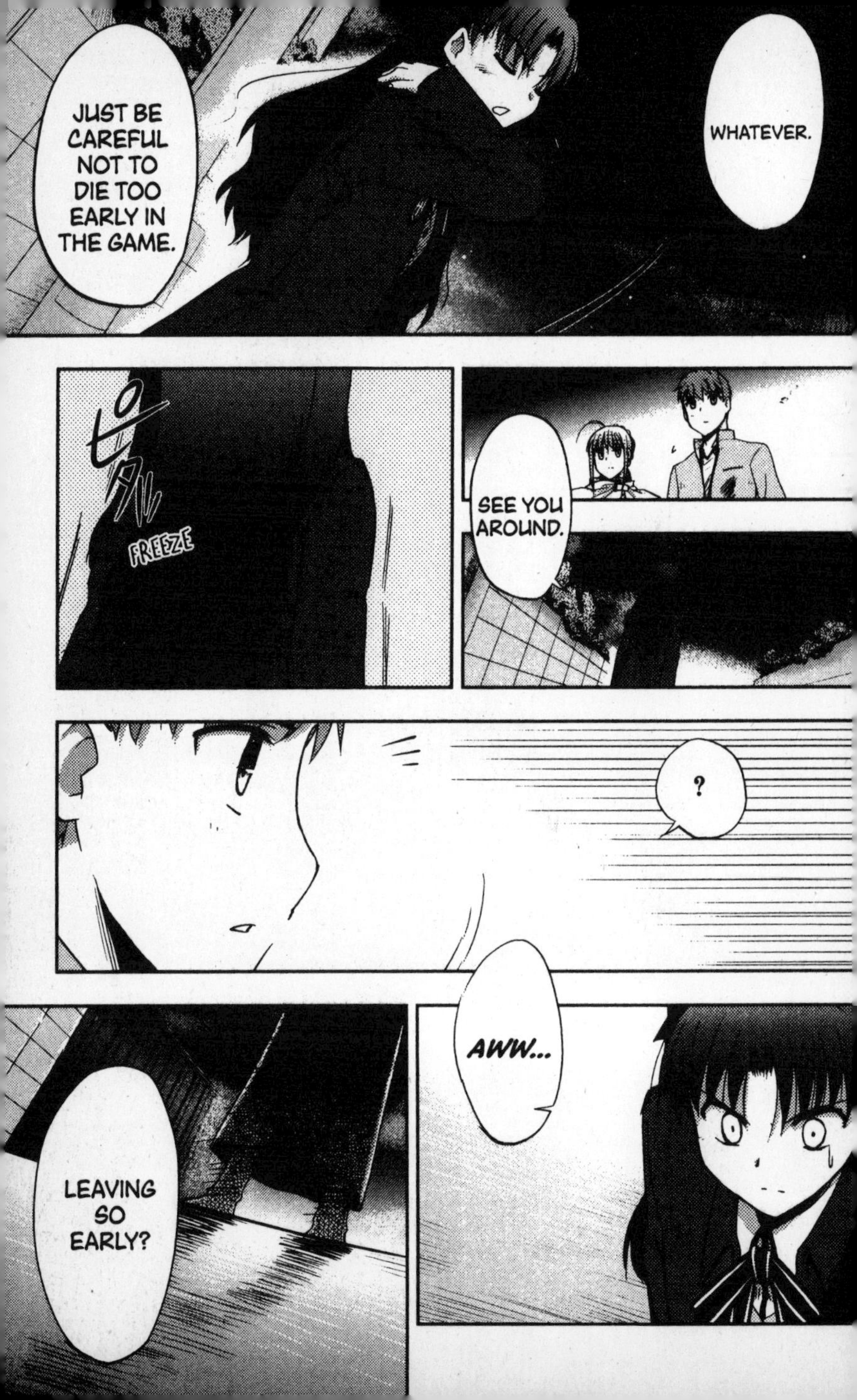
WHATEVER.
JUST BE CAREFUL NOT TO DIE TOO EARLY IN THE GAME.
SEE YOU AROUND.
FREEZE
?
AWW...
LEAVING SO EARLY?

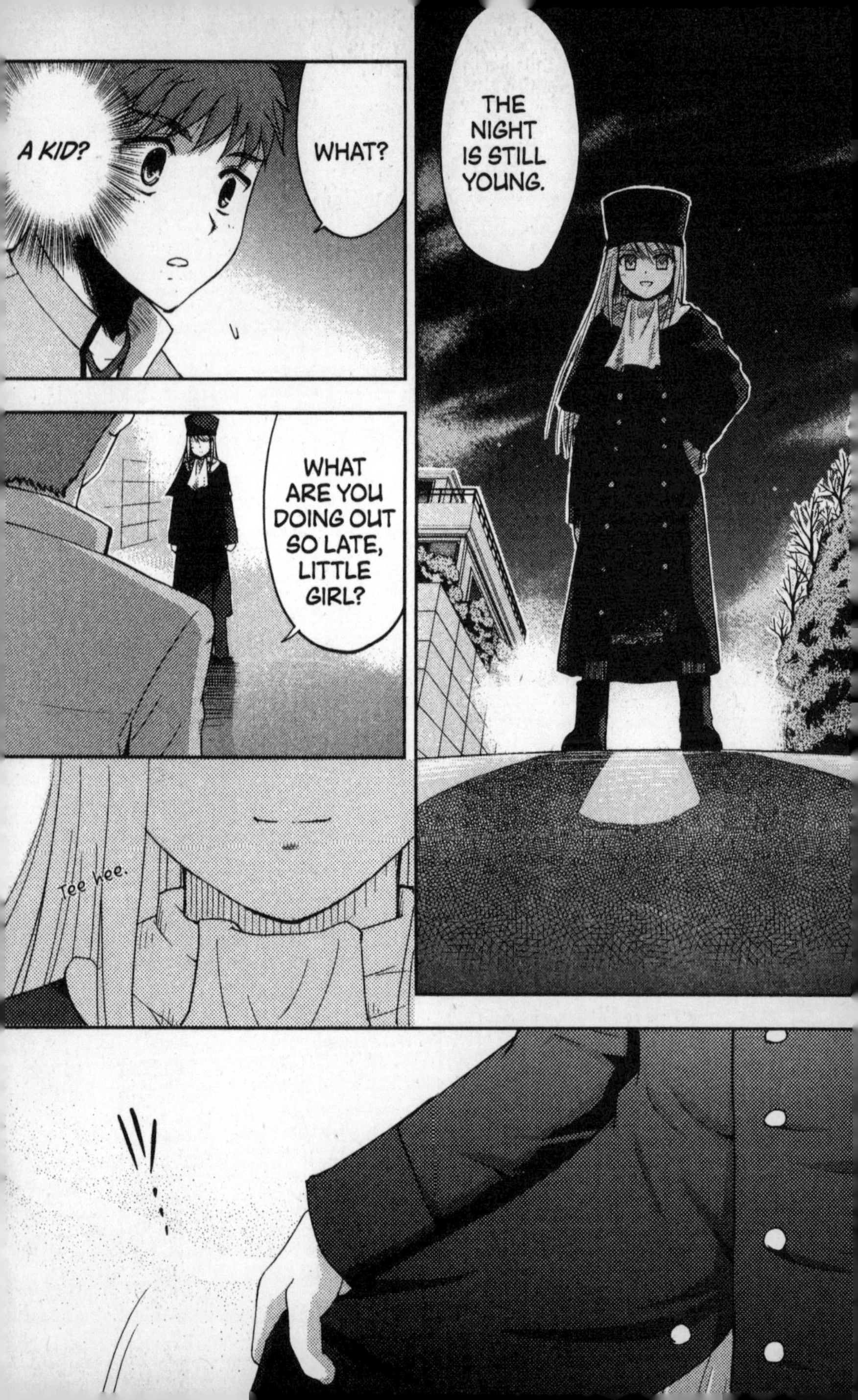
THE NIGHT IS STILL YOUNG.
WHAT?
A KID?
WHAT ARE YOU DOING OUT SO LATE, LITTLE GIRL?
Tee hee.

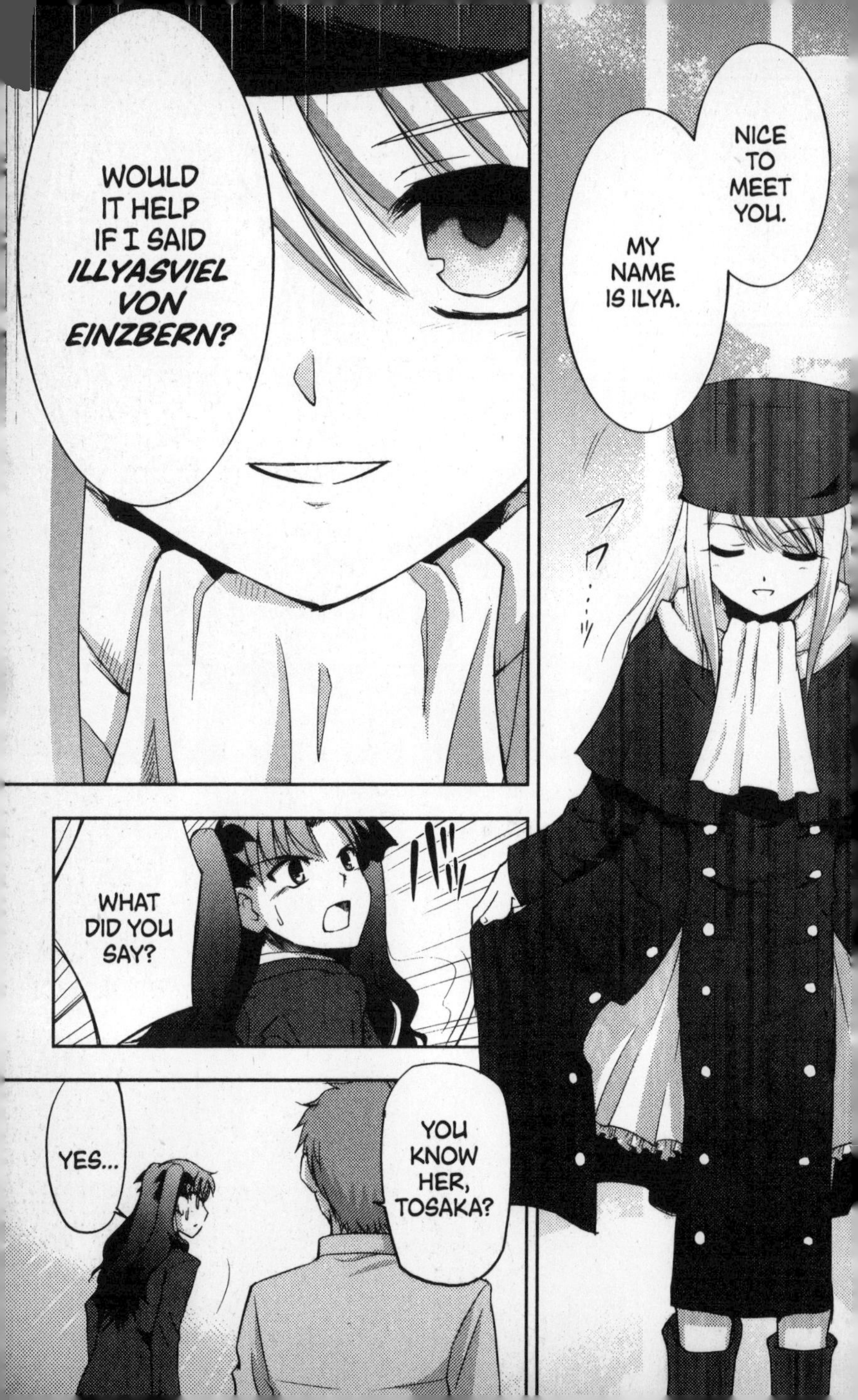
NICE TO MEET YOU.
MY NAME IS ILYA.
WOULD IT HELP IF I SAID *ILLYASVIEL VON EINZBERN?*
WHAT DID YOU SAY?
YOU KNOW HER, TOSAKA?
YES...

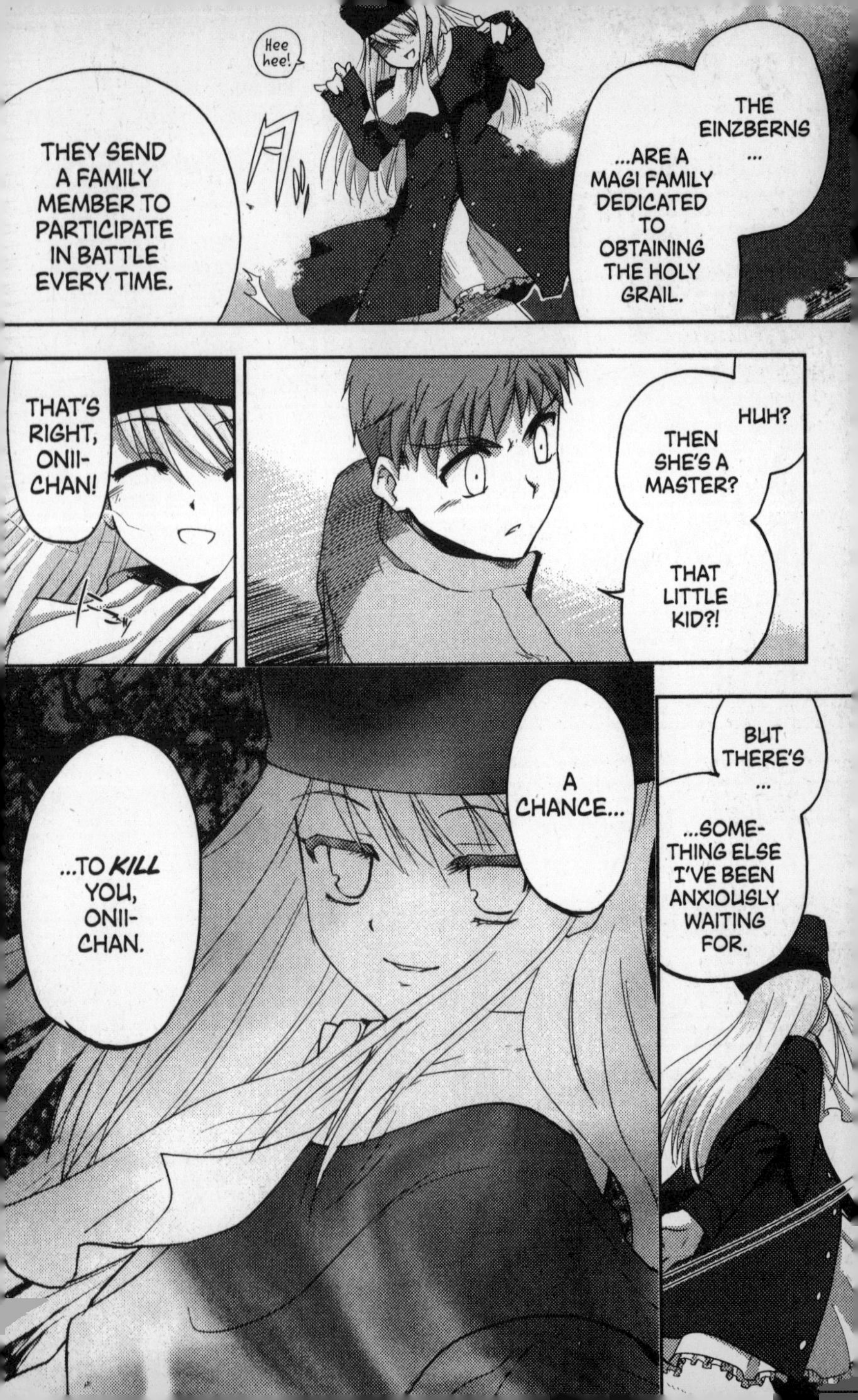
THE EINZBERNS ...
...ARE A MAGI FAMILY DEDICATED TO OBTAINING THE HOLY GRAIL.
Hee hee!
THEY SEND A FAMILY MEMBER TO PARTICIPATE IN BATTLE EVERY TIME.
HUH?
THEN SHE'S A MASTER?
THAT LITTLE KID?!
THAT'S RIGHT, ONII-CHAN!
BUT THERE'S ...
...SOME-THING ELSE I'VE BEEN ANXIOUSLY WAITING FOR.
A CHANCE...
...TO KILL YOU, ONII-CHAN.

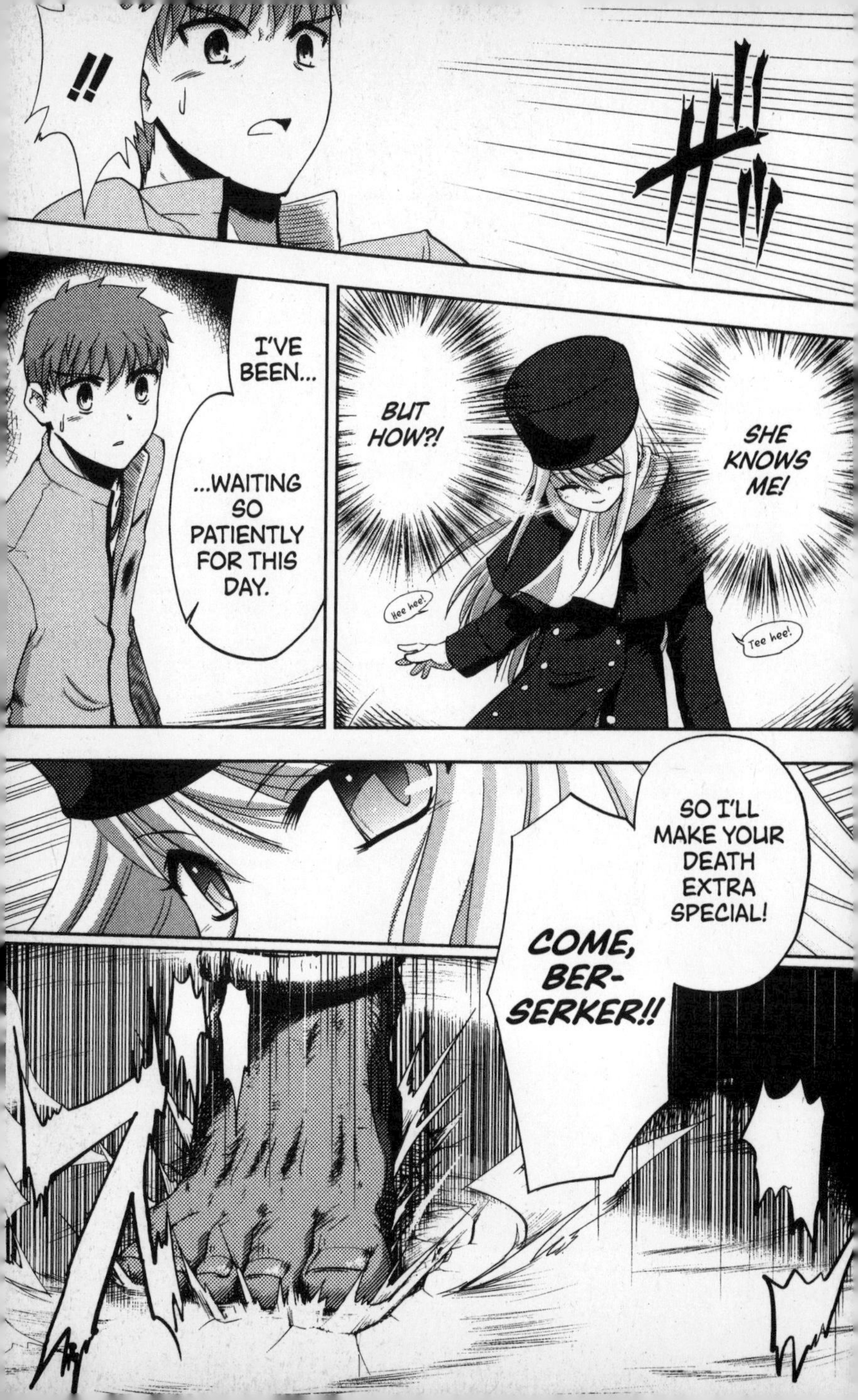

ザッ
!!
SHE KNOWS ME!
BUT HOW?!
Tee hee!
Hee hee!
I'VE BEEN...
...WAITING SO PATIENTLY FOR THIS DAY.
SO I'LL MAKE YOUR DEATH EXTRA SPECIAL!
COME, BER-SERKER!!

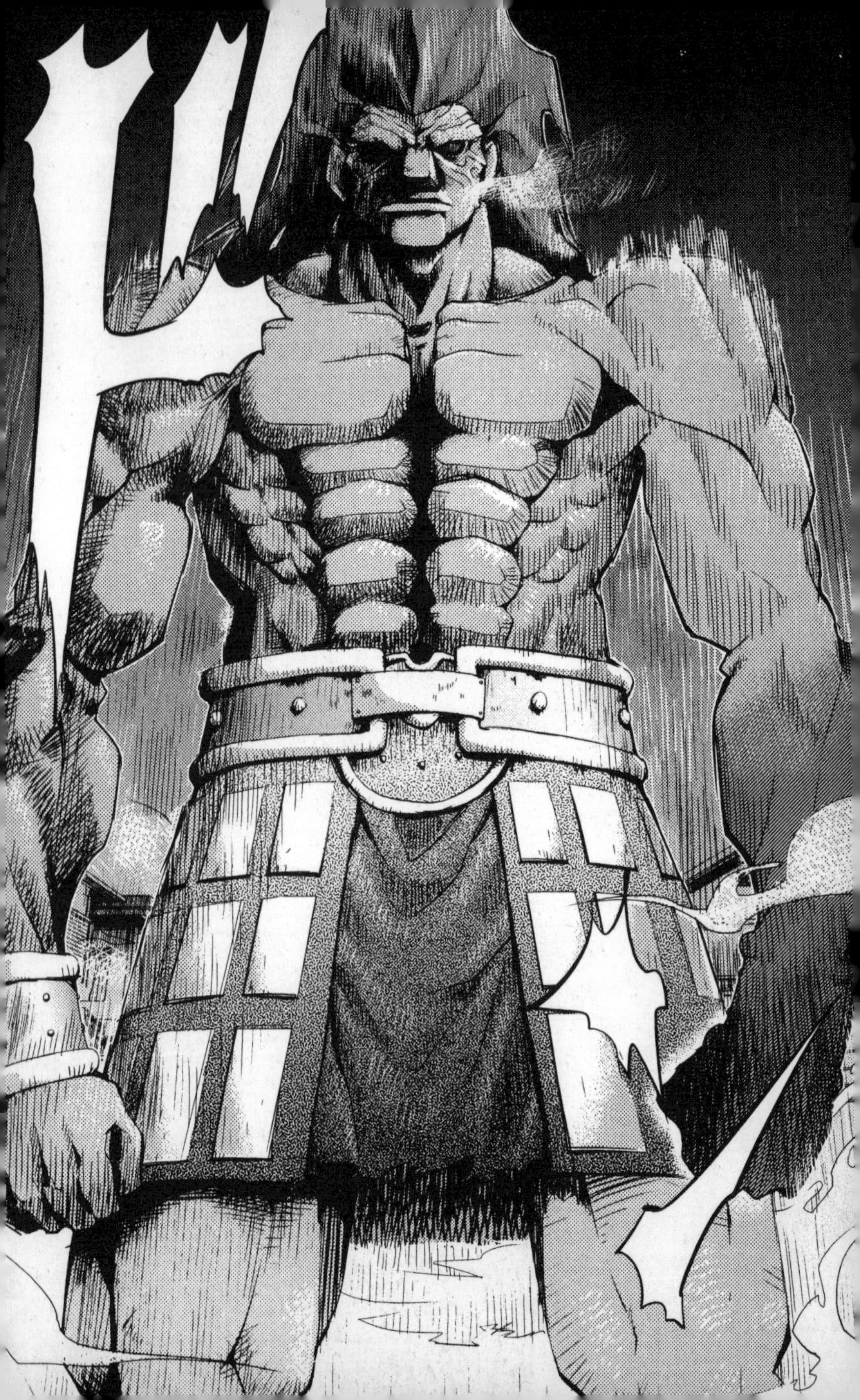

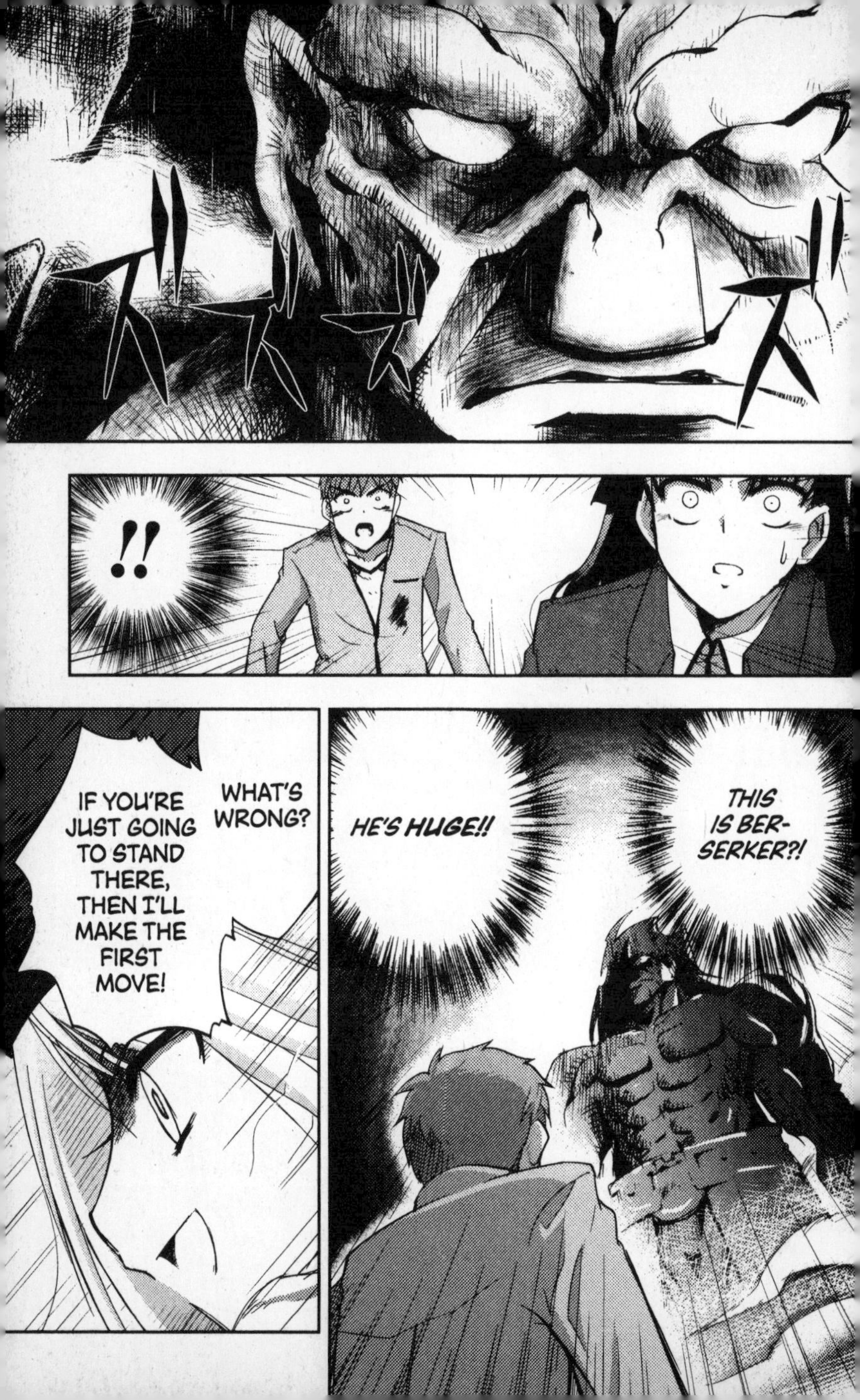
!!
THIS IS BER-SERKER?!
HE'S HUGE!!
WHAT'S WRONG?
IF YOU'RE JUST GOING TO STAND THERE, THEN I'LL MAKE THE FIRST MOVE!

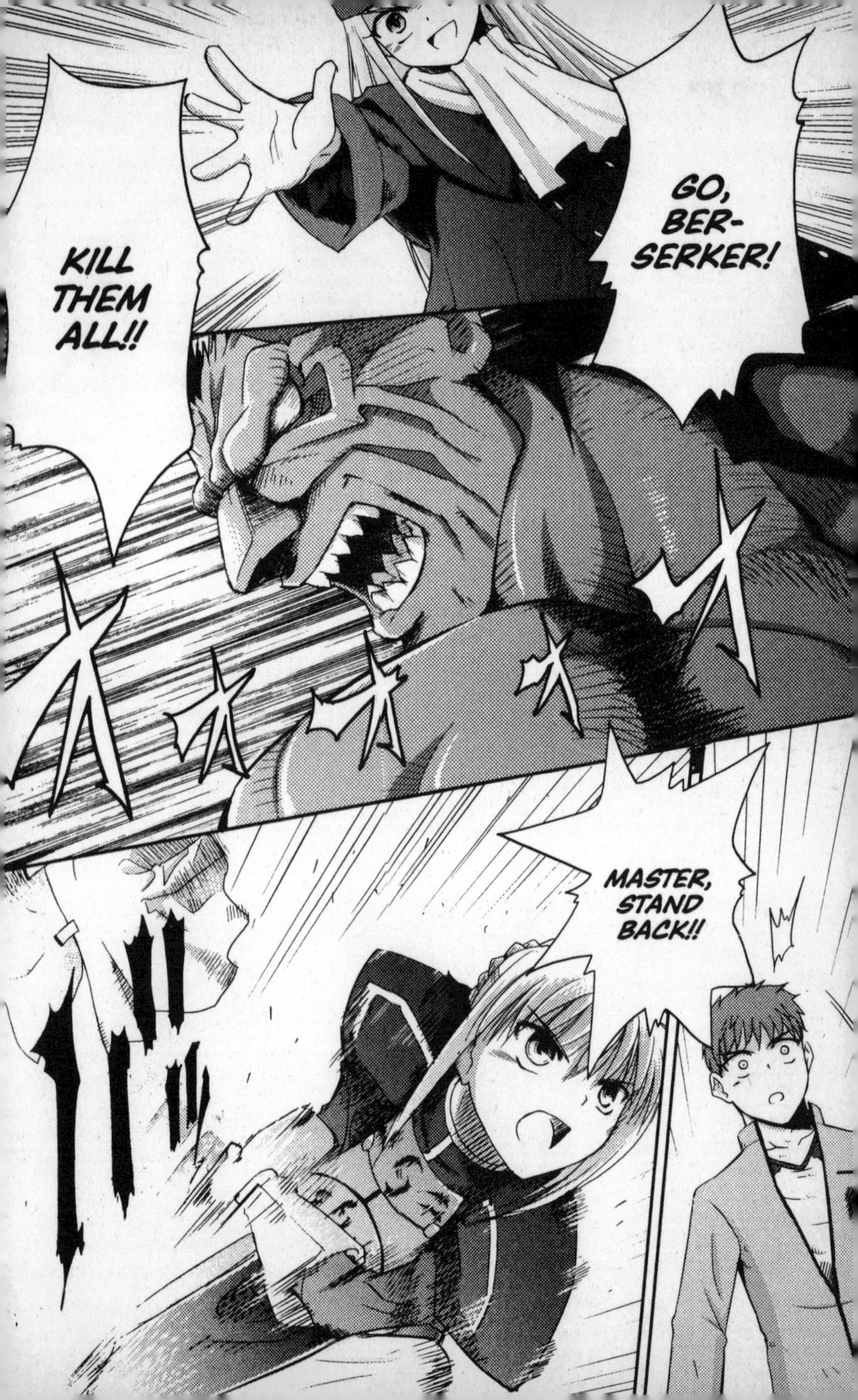
GO, BER-SERKER!
KILL THEM ALL!!
MASTER, STAND BACK!!

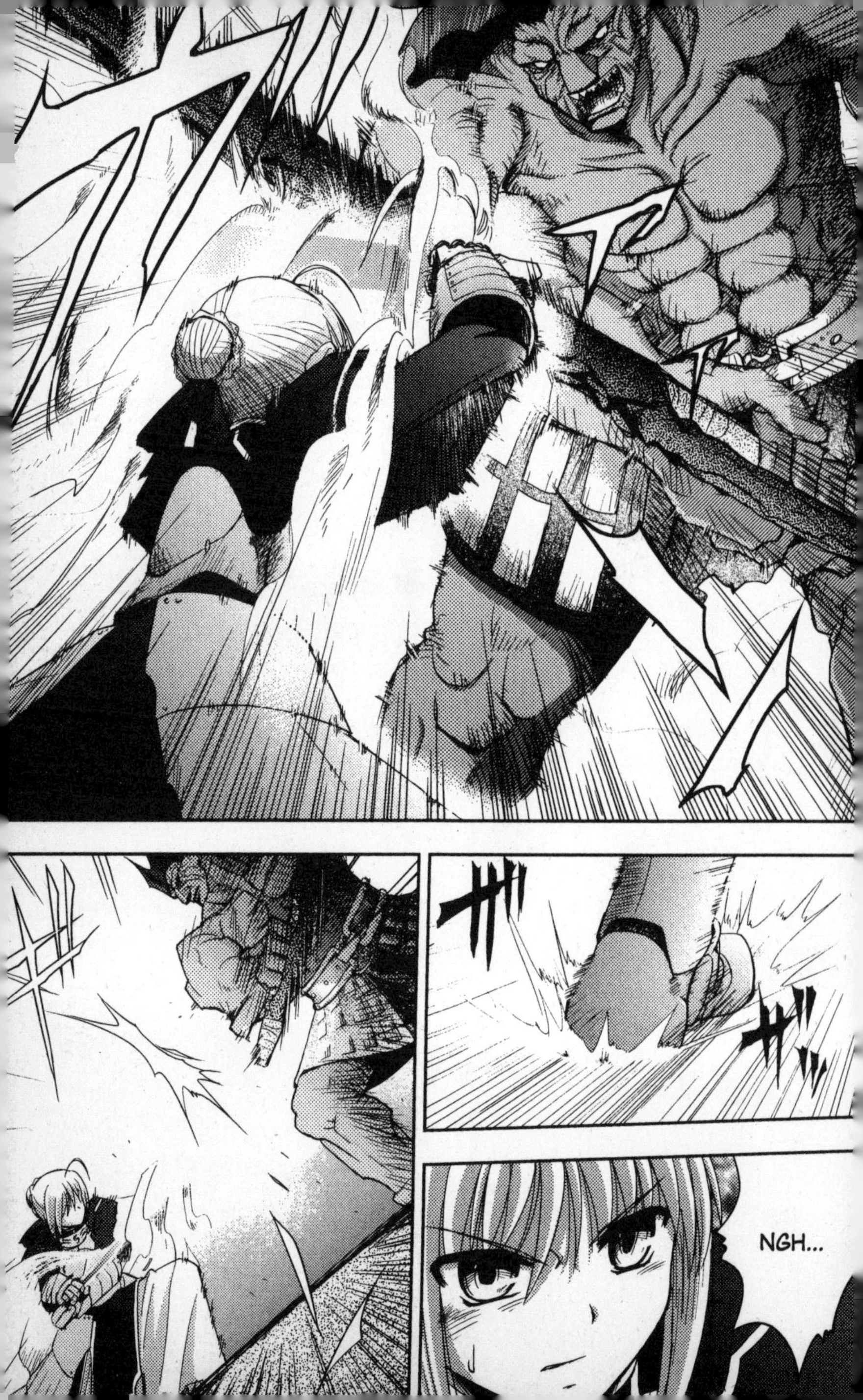
NGH...

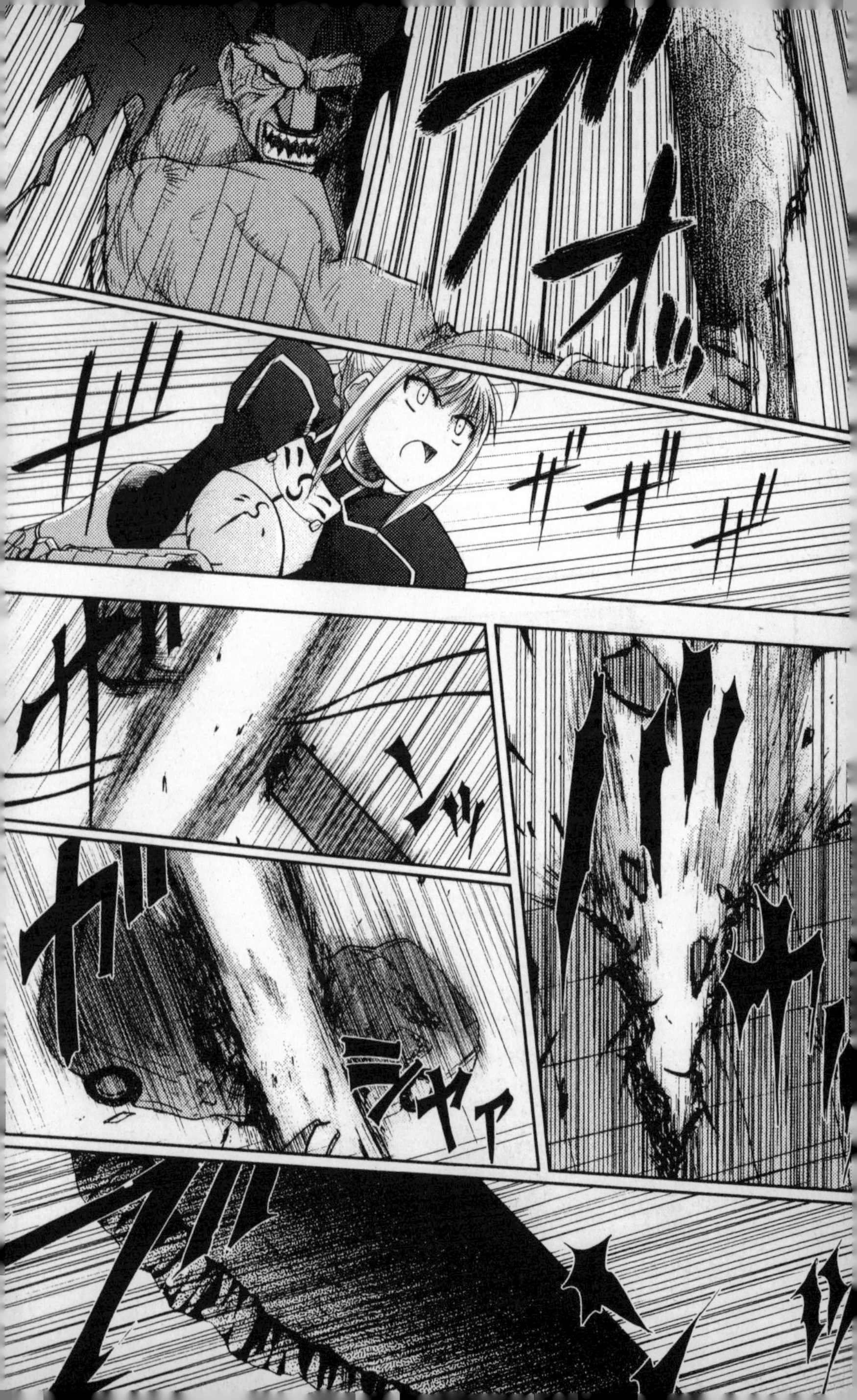
ザザ
ザザザ

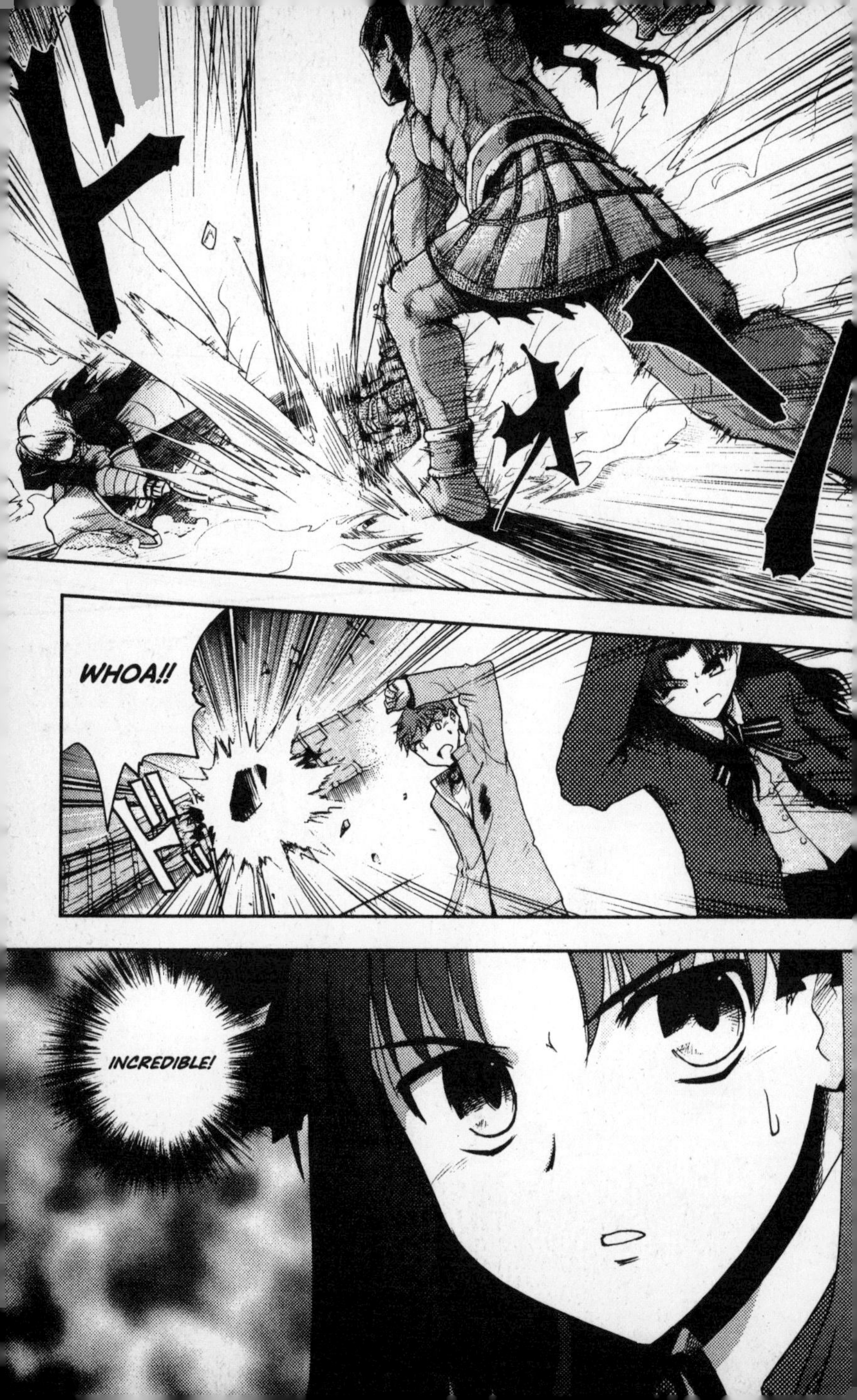
WHOA!!
INCREDIBLE!

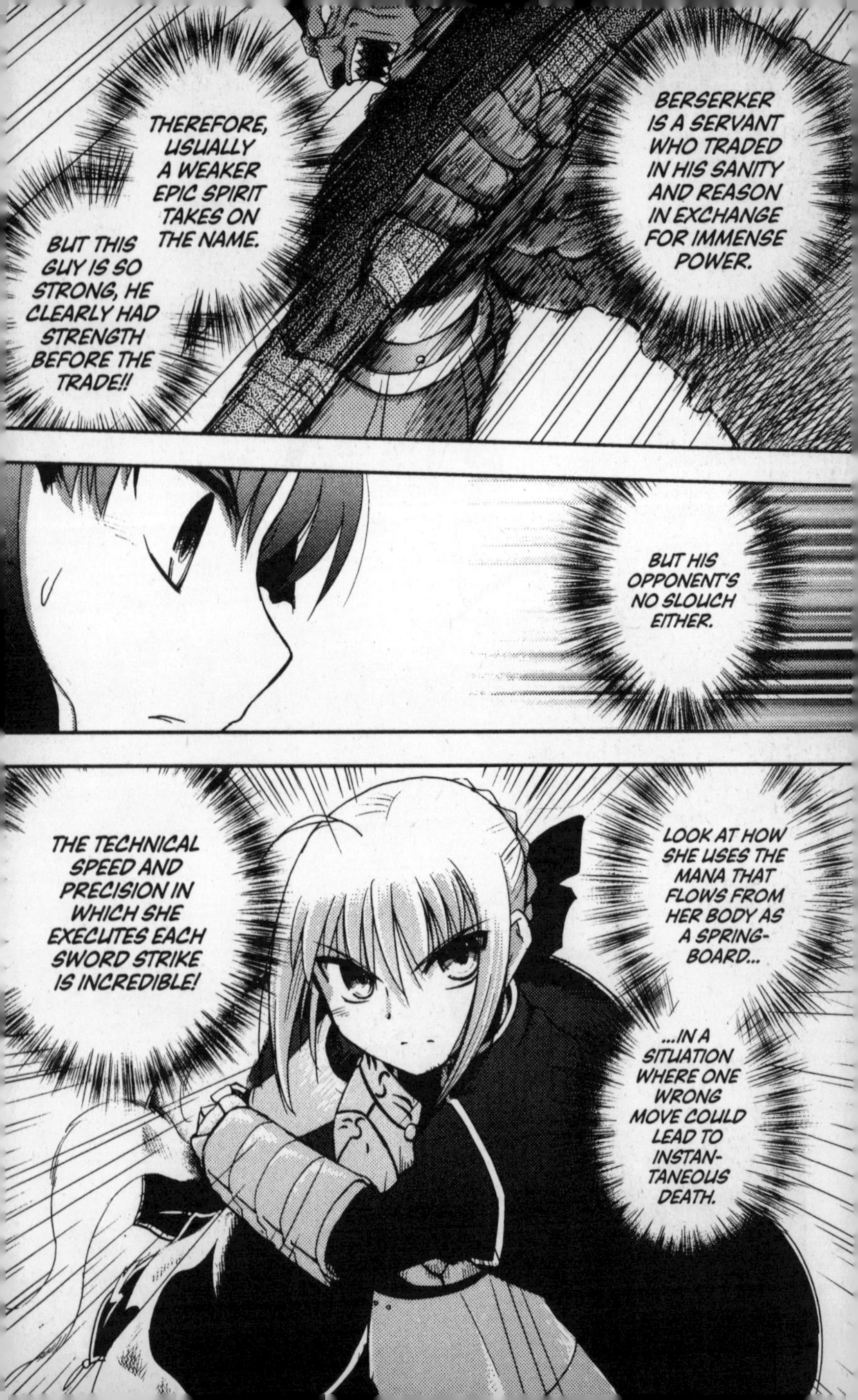
BERSERKER IS A SERVANT WHO TRADED IN HIS SANITY AND REASON IN EXCHANGE FOR IMMENSE POWER.
THEREFORE, USUALLY A WEAKER EPIC SPIRIT TAKES ON THE NAME.
BUT THIS GUY IS SO STRONG, HE CLEARLY HAD STRENGTH BEFORE THE TRADE!!
BUT HIS OPPONENT'S NO SLOUCH EITHER.
LOOK AT HOW SHE USES THE MANA THAT FLOWS FROM HER BODY AS A SPRING-BOARD...
...IN A SITUATION WHERE ONE WRONG MOVE COULD LEAD TO INSTAN-TANEOUS DEATH.
THE TECHNICAL SPEED AND PRECISION IN WHICH SHE EXECUTES EACH SWORD STRIKE IS INCREDIBLE!

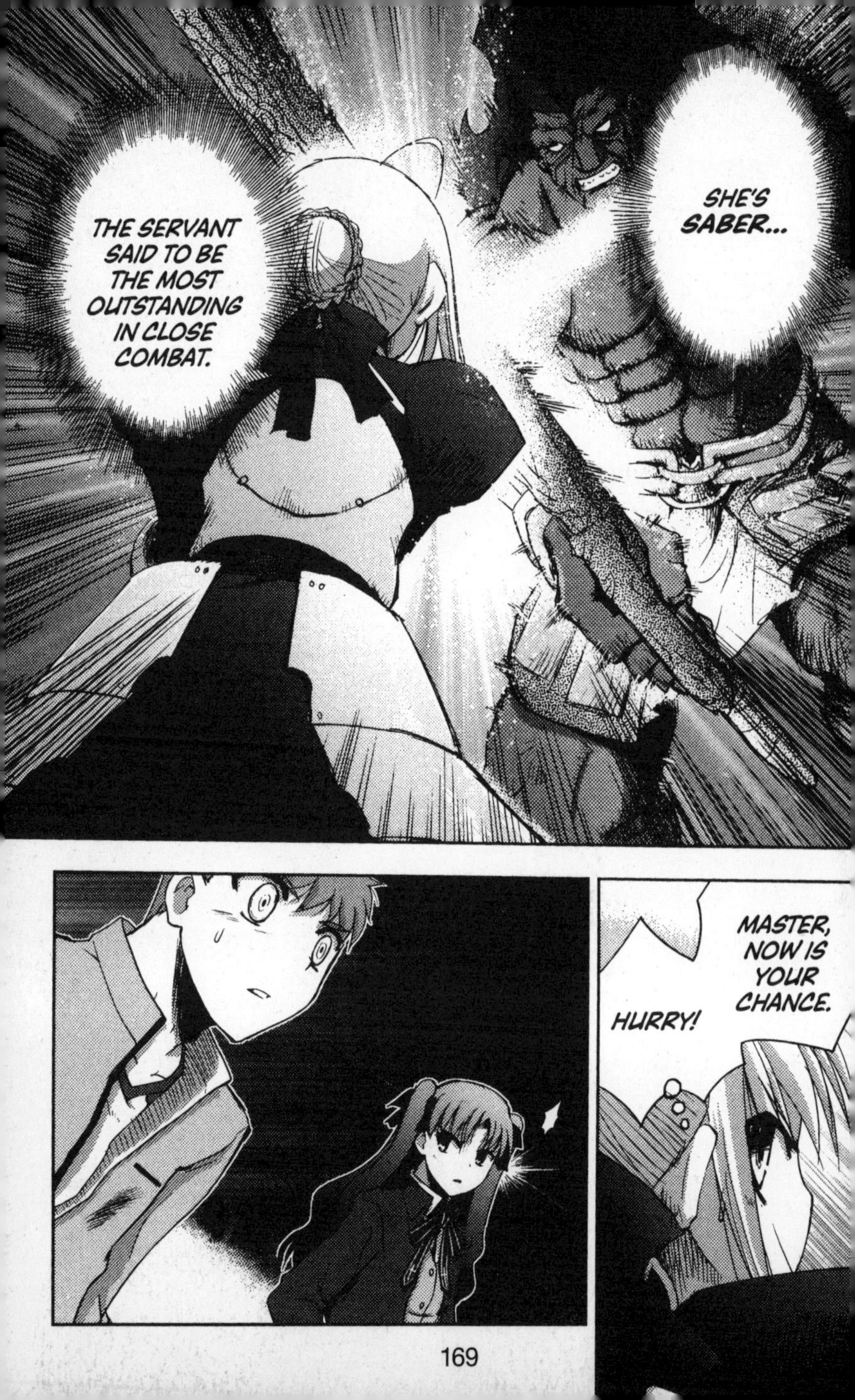
SHE'S SABER...
THE SERVANT SAID TO BE THE MOST OUTSTANDING IN CLOSE COMBAT.
MASTER, NOW IS YOUR CHANCE.
HURRY!

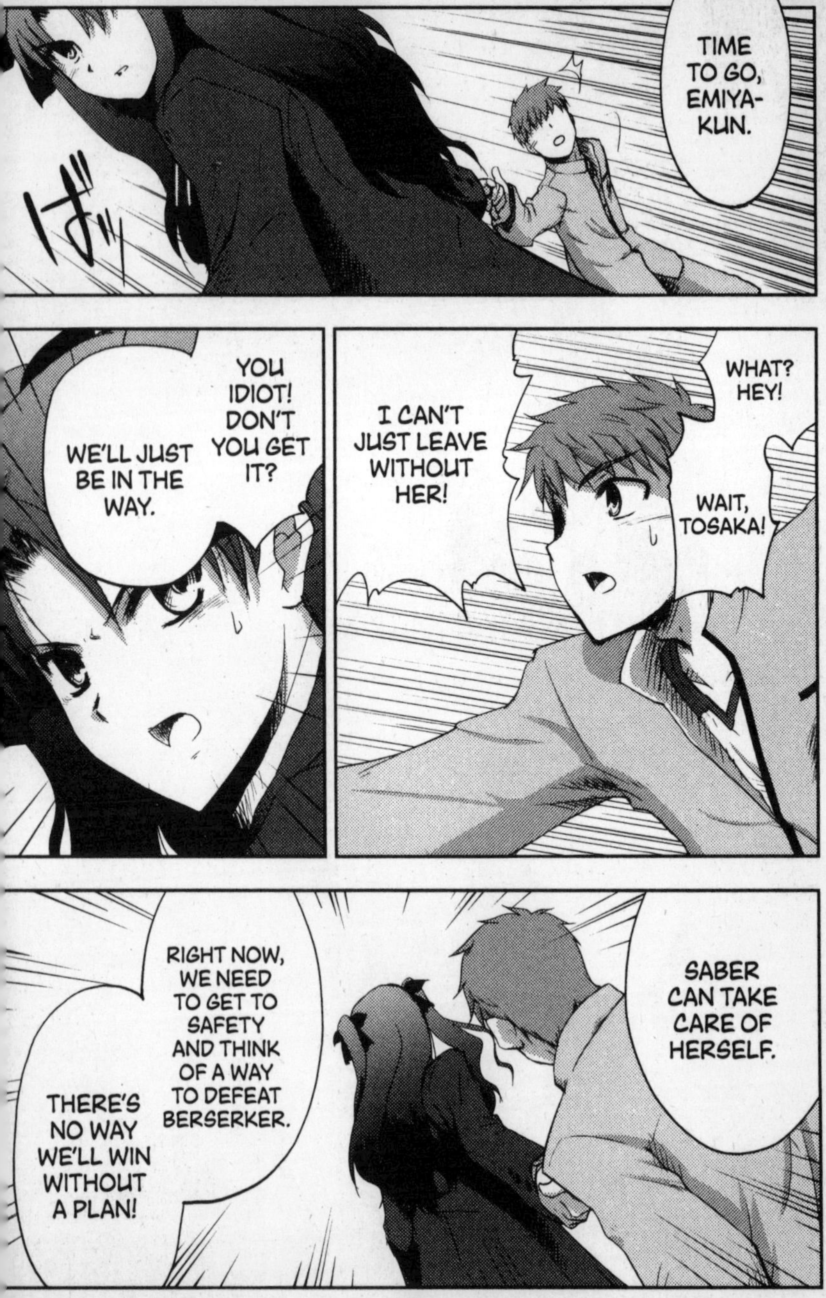
TIME TO GO, EMIYA-KUN.
ばッ
WHAT? HEY!
WAIT, TOSAKA!
I CAN'T JUST LEAVE WITHOUT HER!
YOU IDIOT! DON'T YOU GET IT?
WE'LL JUST BE IN THE WAY.
SABER CAN TAKE CARE OF HERSELF.
RIGHT NOW, WE NEED TO GET TO SAFETY AND THINK OF A WAY TO DEFEAT BERSERKER.
THERE'S NO WAY WE'LL WIN WITHOUT A PLAN!

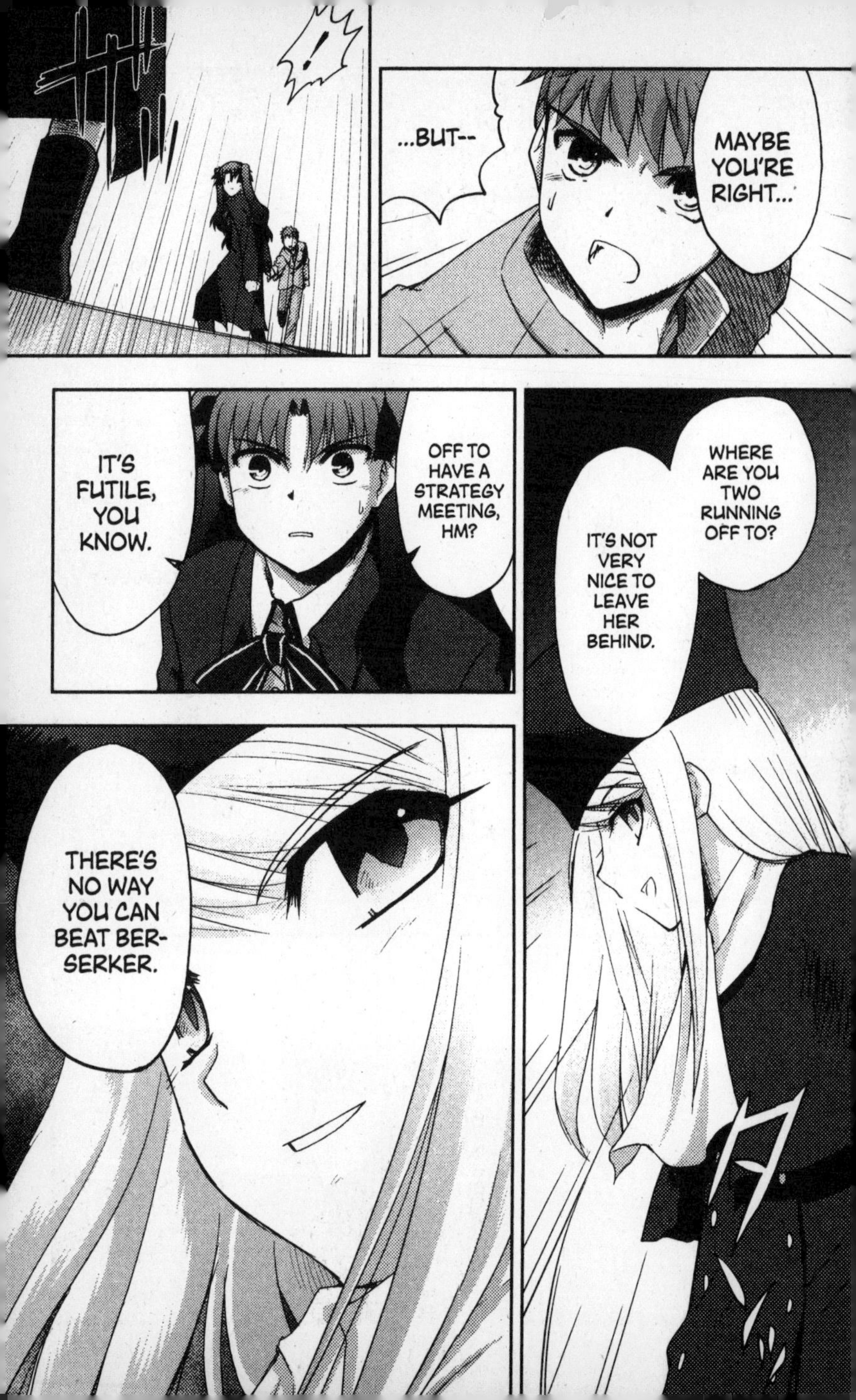
MAYBE YOU'RE RIGHT...
...BUT--
!
WHERE ARE YOU TWO RUNNING OFF TO?
IT'S NOT VERY NICE TO LEAVE HER BEHIND.
OFF TO HAVE A STRATEGY MEETING, HM?
IT'S FUTILE, YOU KNOW.
THERE'S NO WAY YOU CAN BEAT BER-SERKER.

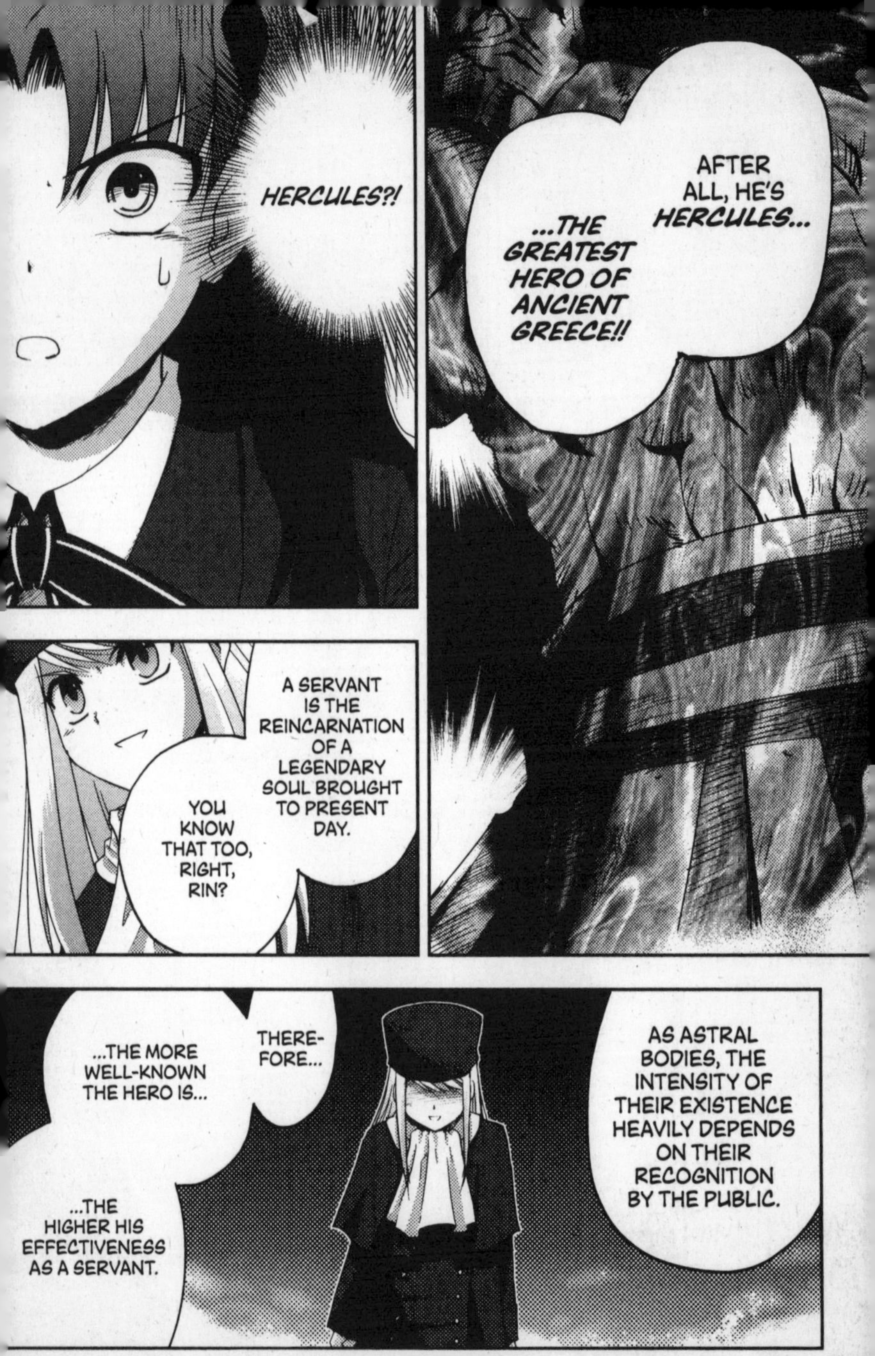
AFTER ALL, HE'S HERCULES...
...THE GREATEST HERO OF ANCIENT GREECE!!
HERCULES?!
A SERVANT IS THE REINCARNATION OF A LEGENDARY SOUL BROUGHT TO PRESENT DAY.
YOU KNOW THAT TOO, RIGHT, RIN?
AS ASTRAL BODIES, THE INTENSITY OF THEIR EXISTENCE HEAVILY DEPENDS ON THEIR RECOGNITION BY THE PUBLIC.
THERE-FORE...
...THE MORE WELL-KNOWN THE HERO IS...
...THE HIGHER HIS EFFECTIVENESS AS A SERVANT.

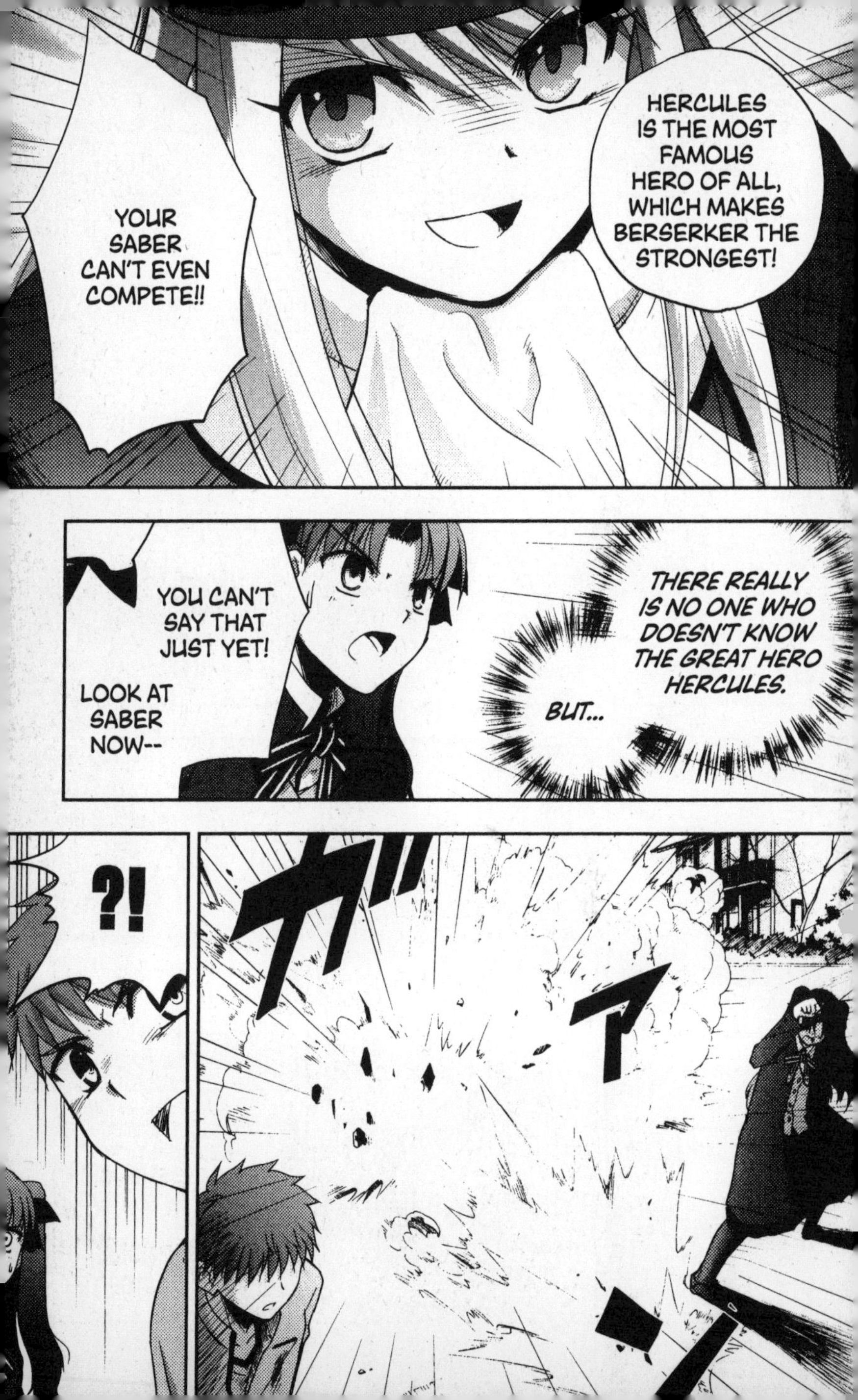
HERCULES IS THE MOST FAMOUS HERO OF ALL, WHICH MAKES BERSERKER THE STRONGEST!
YOUR SABER CAN'T EVEN COMPETE!!
THERE REALLY IS NO ONE WHO DOESN'T KNOW THE GREAT HERO HERCULES.
BUT...
YOU CAN'T SAY THAT JUST YET!
LOOK AT SABER NOW--
?!

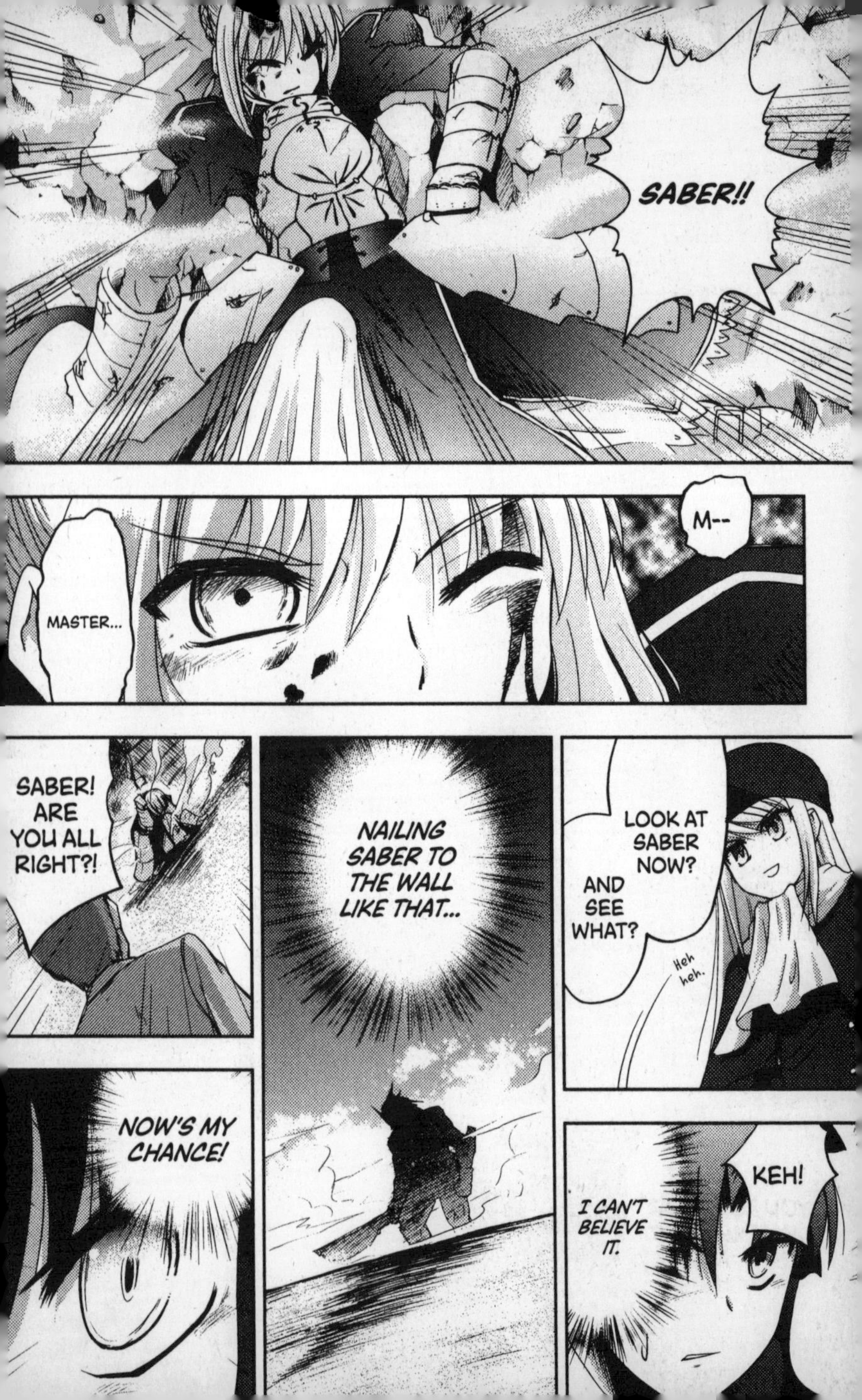
SABER!!
M--
MASTER...
LOOK AT SABER NOW?
AND SEE WHAT?
Heh heh.
KEH!
I CAN'T BELIEVE IT.
NAILING SABER TO THE WALL LIKE THAT...
SABER! ARE YOU ALL RIGHT?!
NOW'S MY CHANCE!

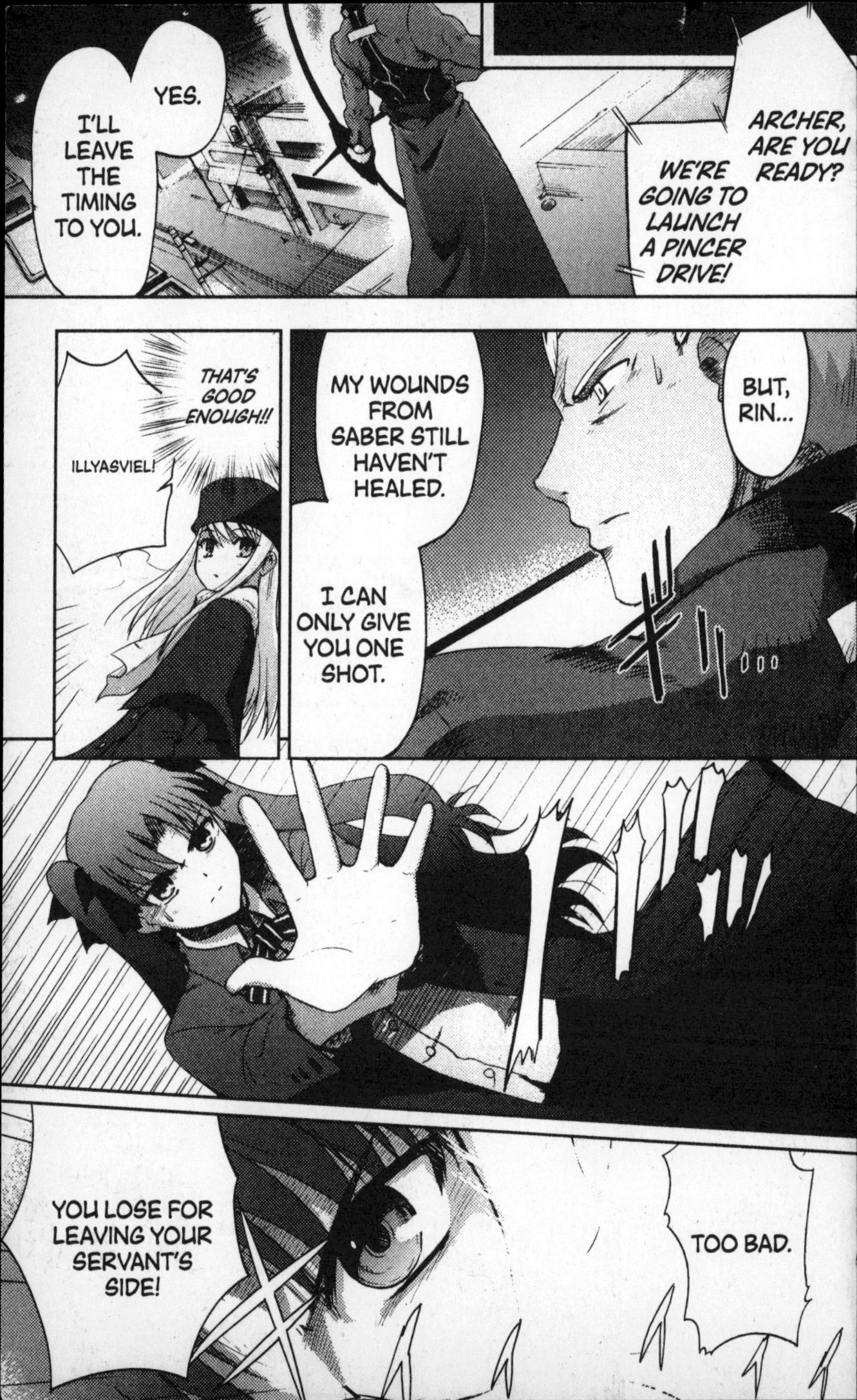
ARCHER, ARE YOU READY?
WE'RE GOING TO LAUNCH A PINCER DRIVE!
YES.
I'LL LEAVE THE TIMING TO YOU.
BUT, RIN...
MY WOUNDS FROM SABER STILL HAVEN'T HEALED.
I CAN ONLY GIVE YOU ONE SHOT.
THAT'S GOOD ENOUGH!!
ILLYASVIEL!
TOO BAD.
YOU LOSE FOR LEAVING YOUR SERVANT'S SIDE!

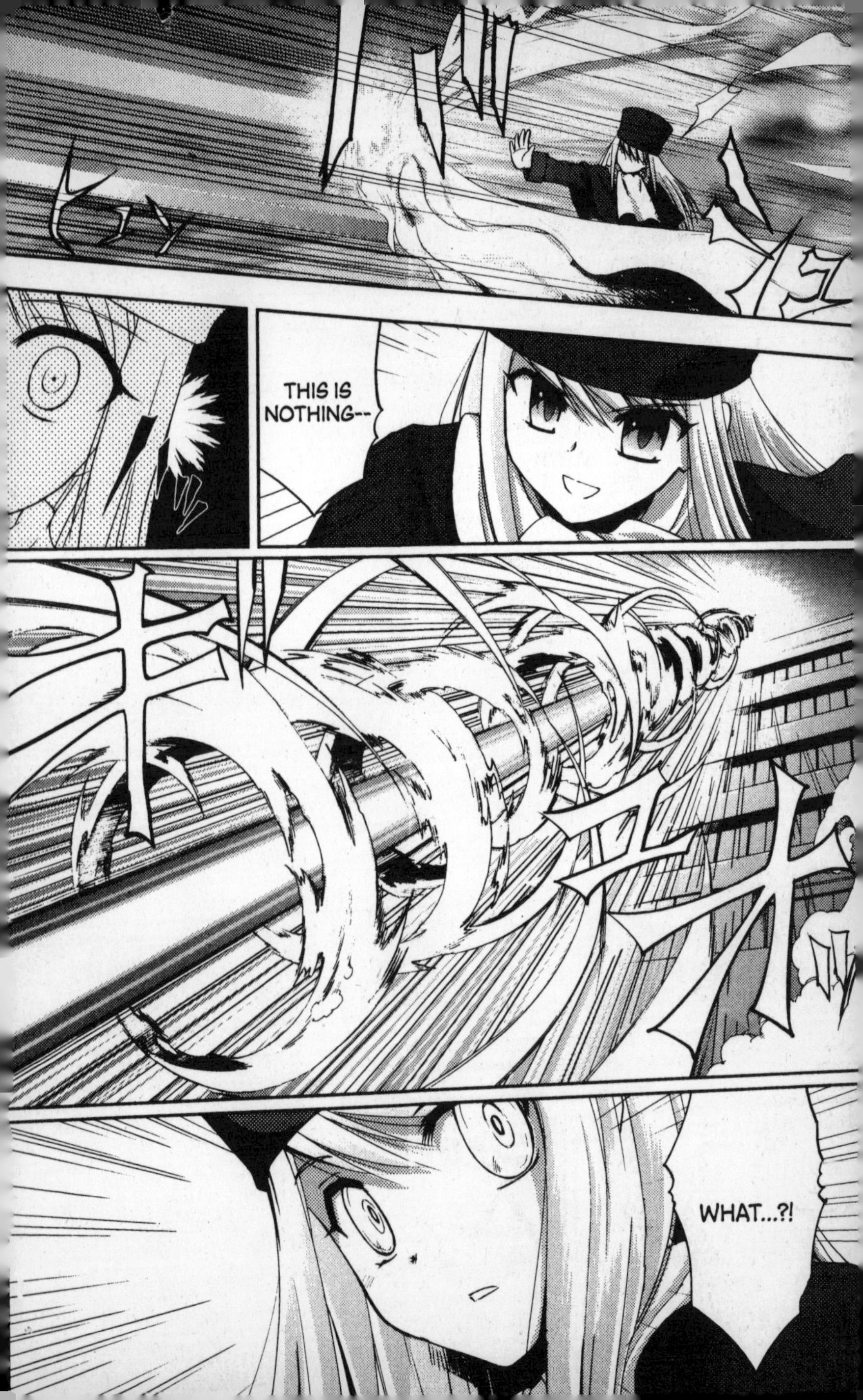
THIS IS NOTHING--
WHAT...?!

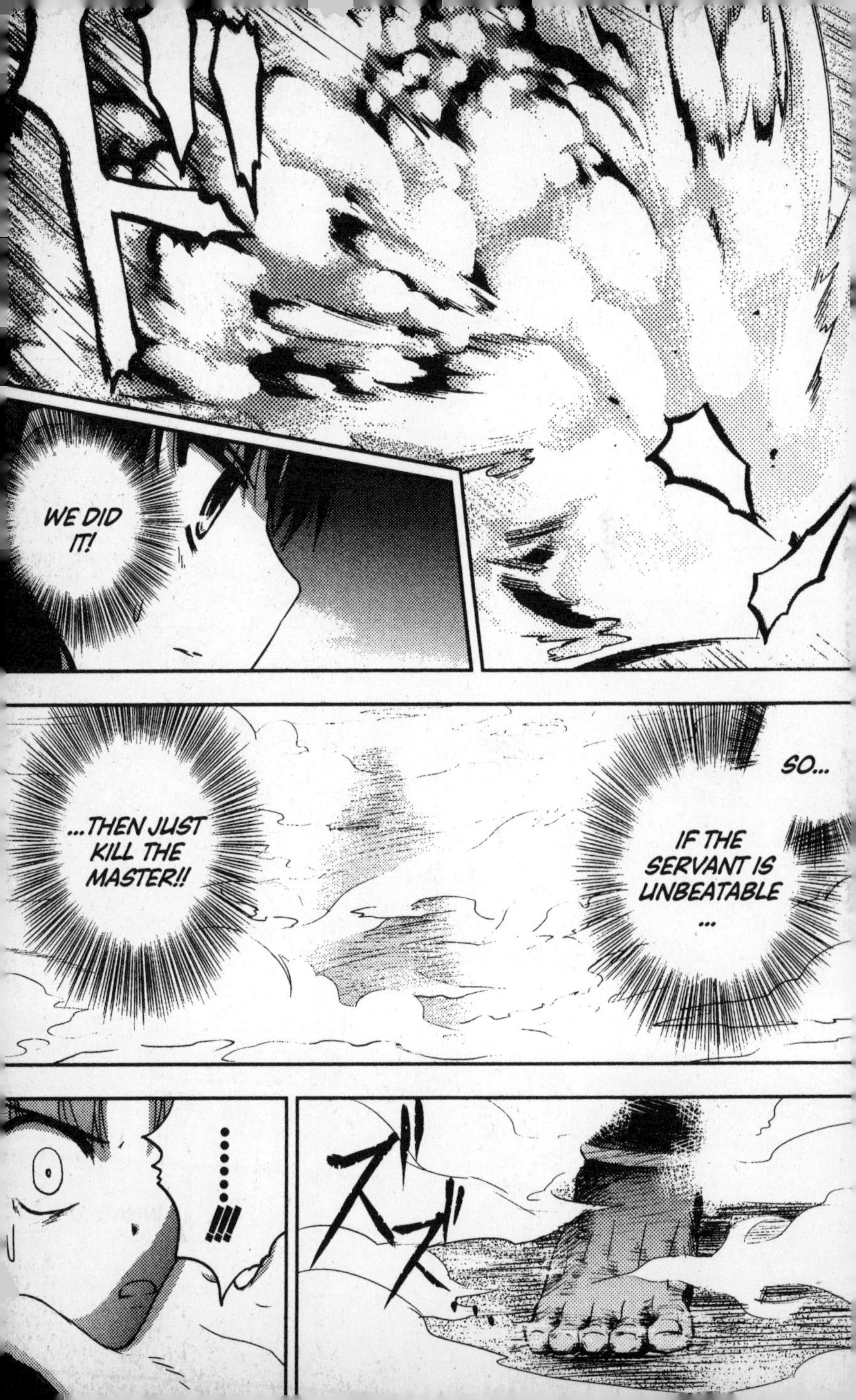
WE DID IT!
SO...
IF THE SERVANT IS UNBEATABLE ...
...THEN JUST KILL THE MASTER!!
......!!!

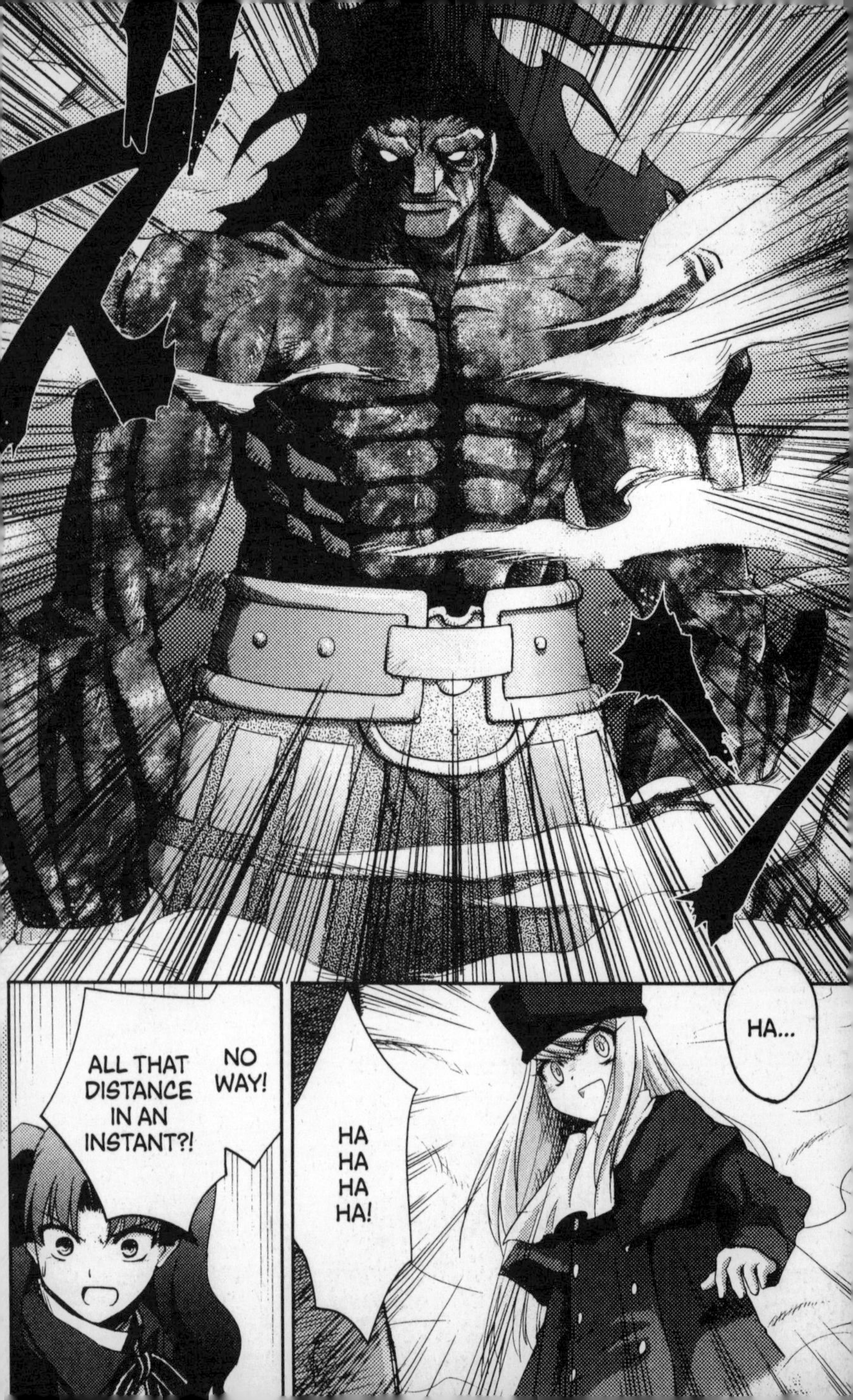
HA...
HA HA HA HA!
NO WAY!
ALL THAT DISTANCE IN AN INSTANT?!

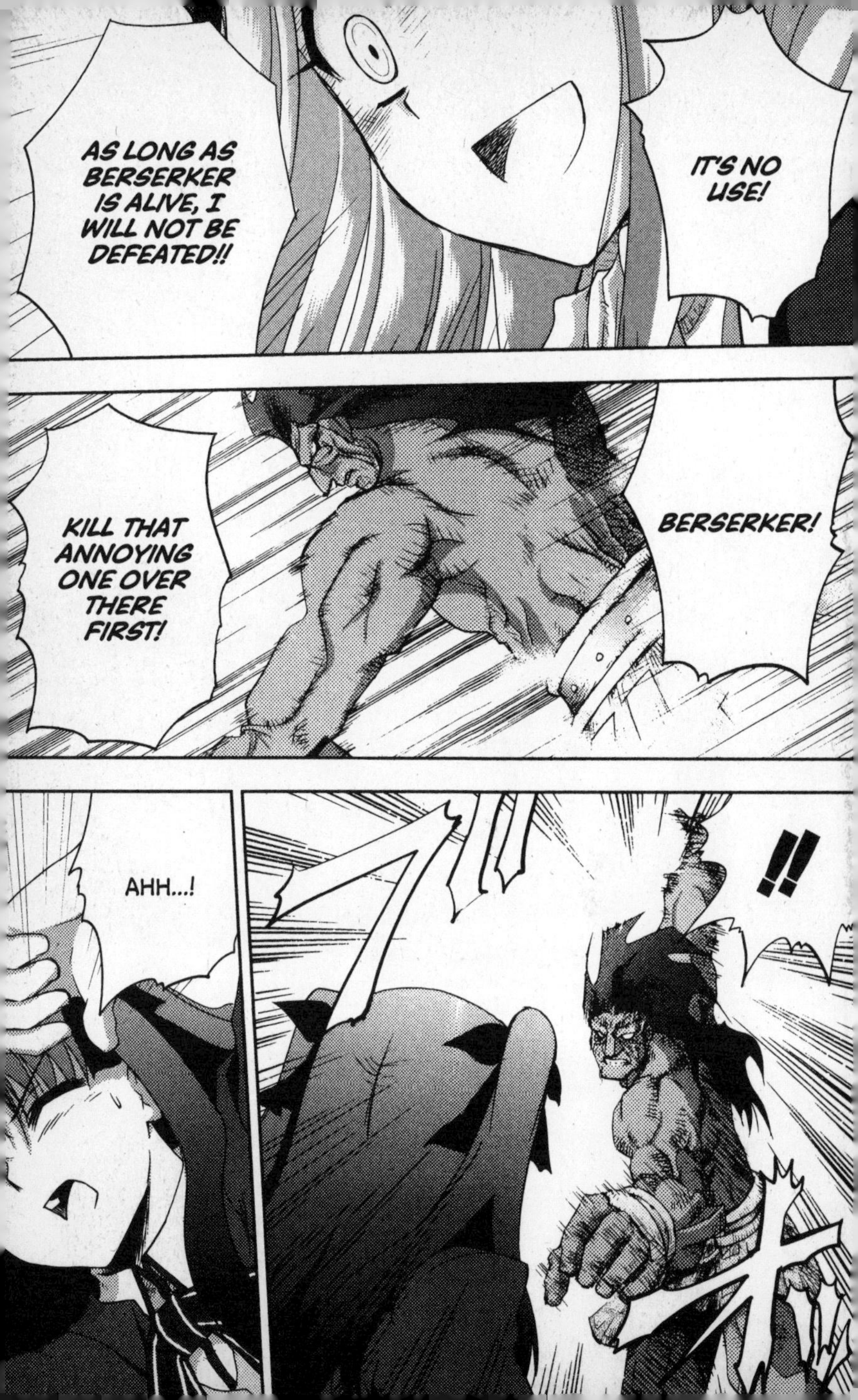
IT'S NO USE!
AS LONG AS BERSERKER IS ALIVE, I WILL NOT BE DEFEATED!!
BERSERKER!
KILL THAT ANNOYING ONE OVER THERE FIRST!
!!
AHH...!

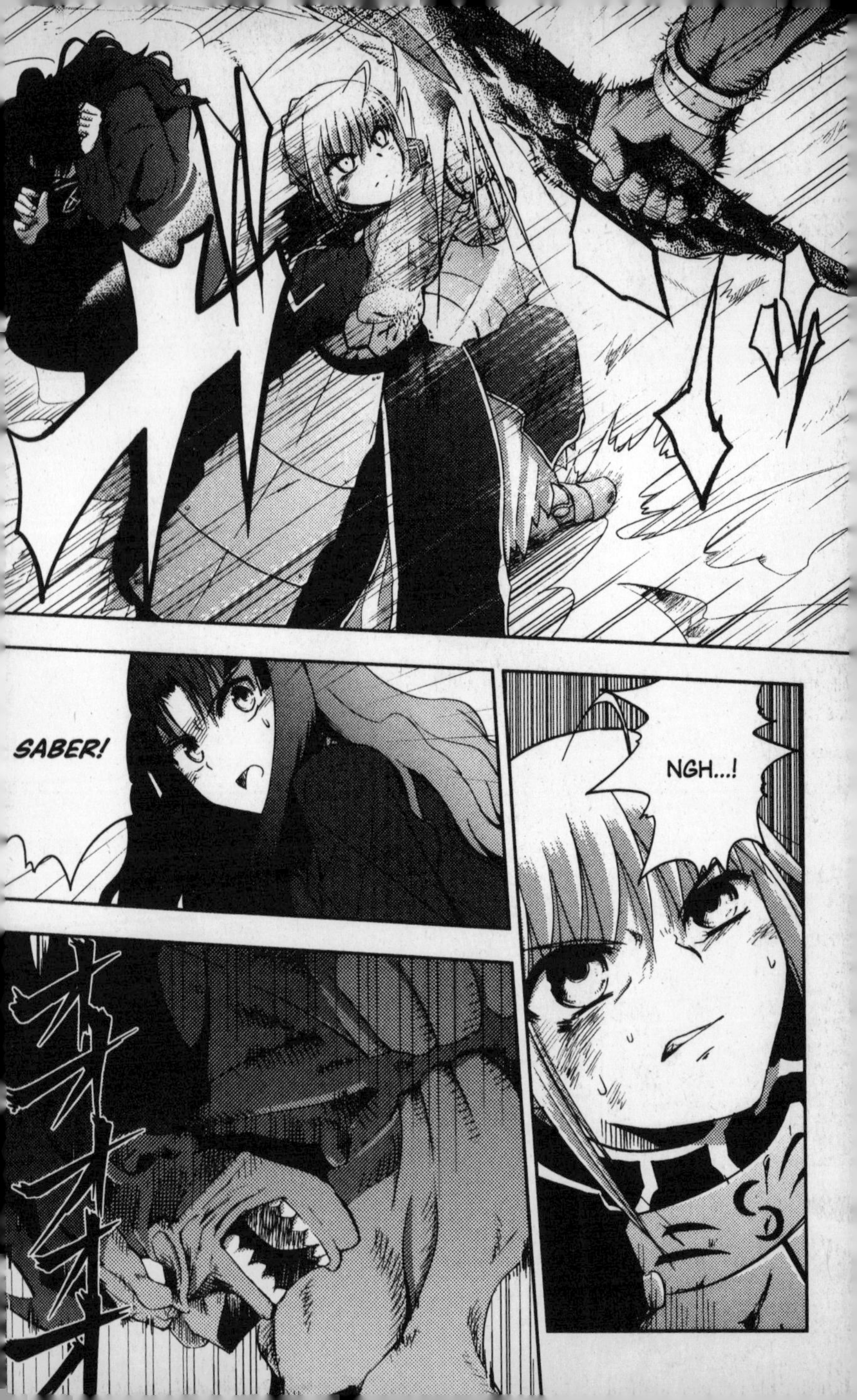
NGH...!
SABER!

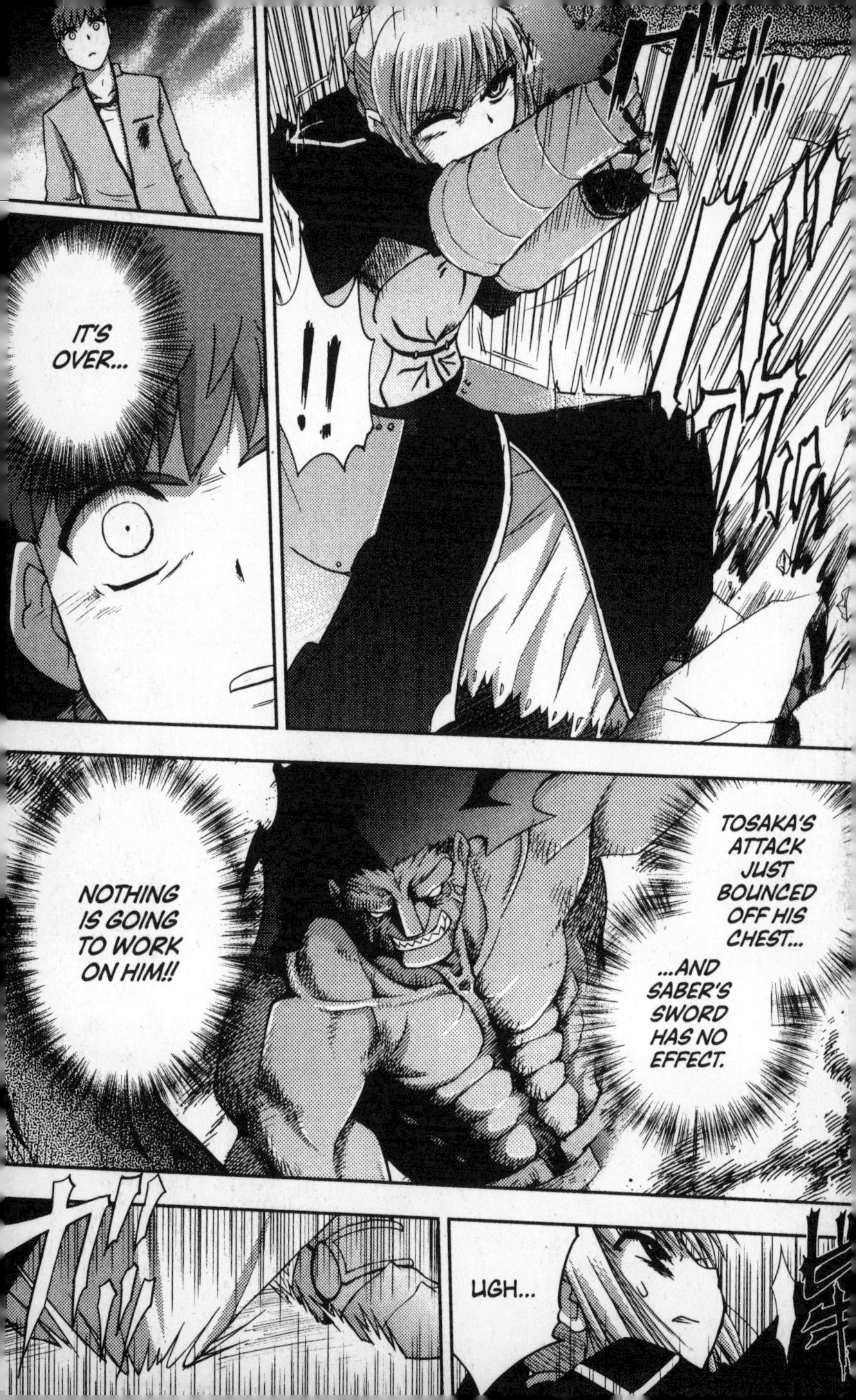
!!
IT'S OVER...
TOSAKA'S ATTACK JUST BOUNCED OFF HIS CHEST...
...AND SABER'S SWORD HAS NO EFFECT.
NOTHING IS GOING TO WORK ON HIM!!
UGH...

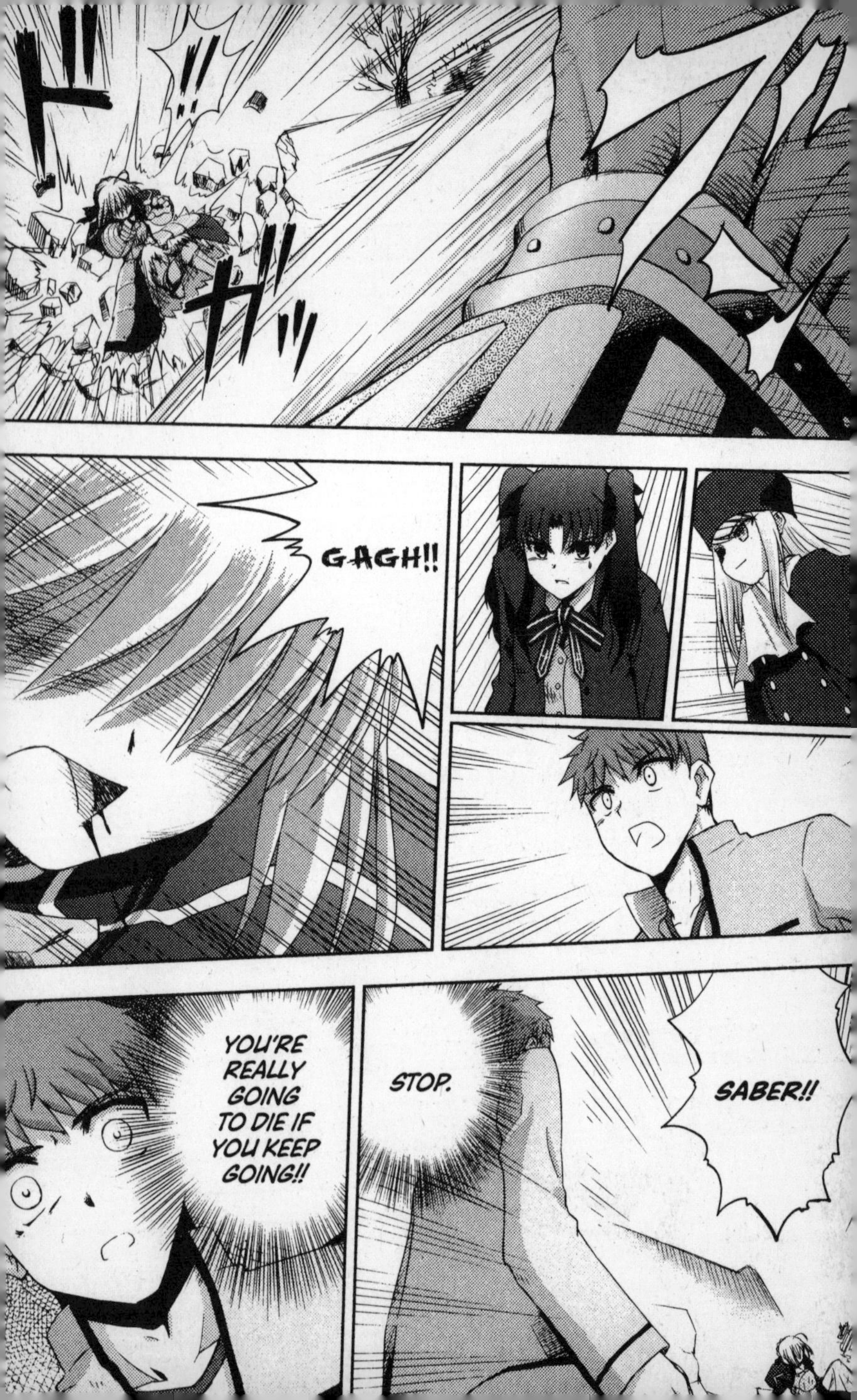
ド
ガッ
GAGH!!
SABER!!
STOP.
YOU'RE REALLY GOING TO DIE IF YOU KEEP GOING!!

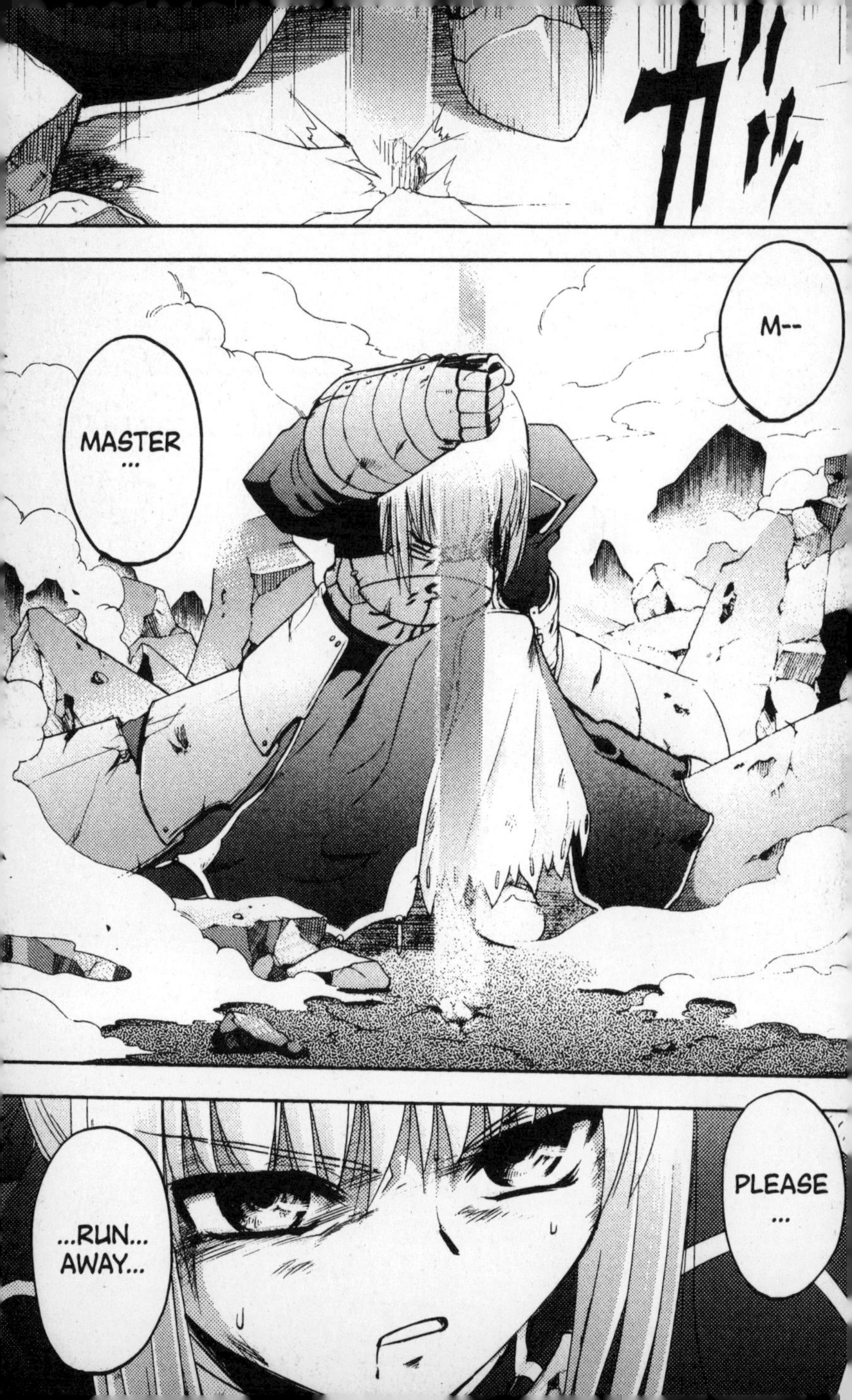
ガッ
M--
MASTER ...
PLEASE ...
...RUN... AWAY...

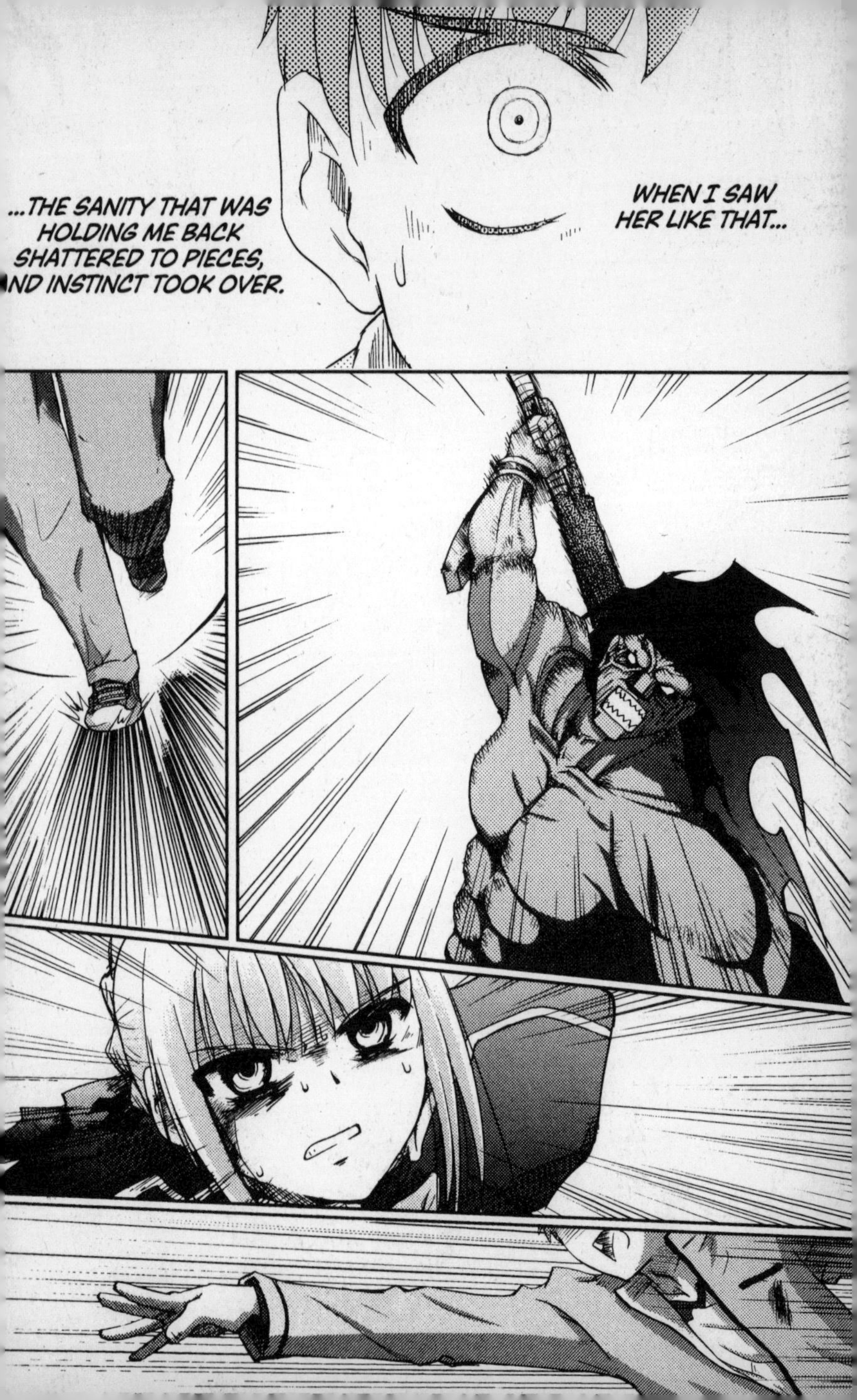
WHEN I SAW HER LIKE THAT...
...THE SANITY THAT WAS HOLDING ME BACK SHATTERED TO PIECES, AND INSTINCT TOOK OVER.

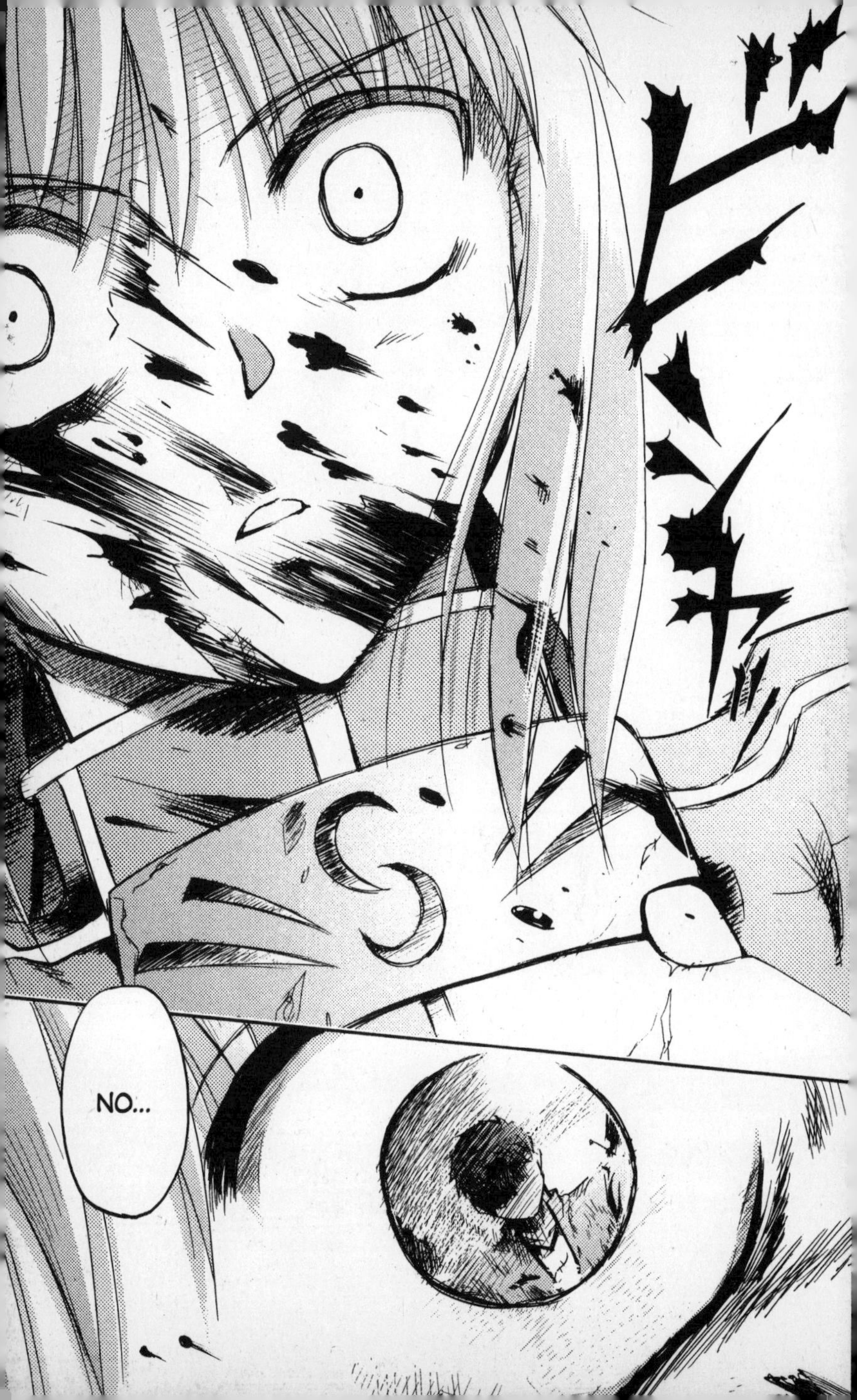
NO...

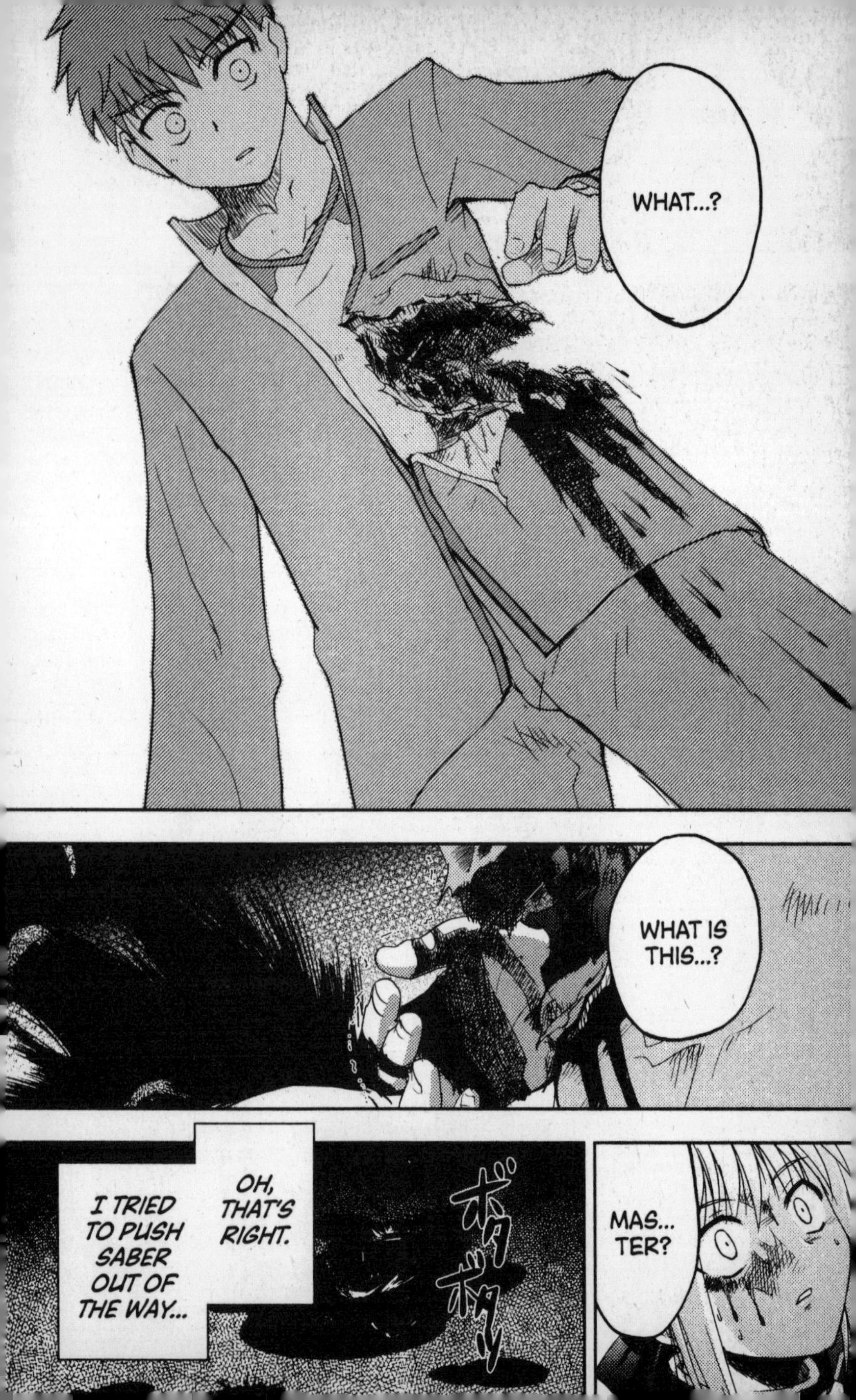
WHAT...?
WHAT IS THIS...?
MAS... TER?
OH, THAT'S RIGHT.
I TRIED TO PUSH SABER OUT OF THE WAY...
ボタ ボタ

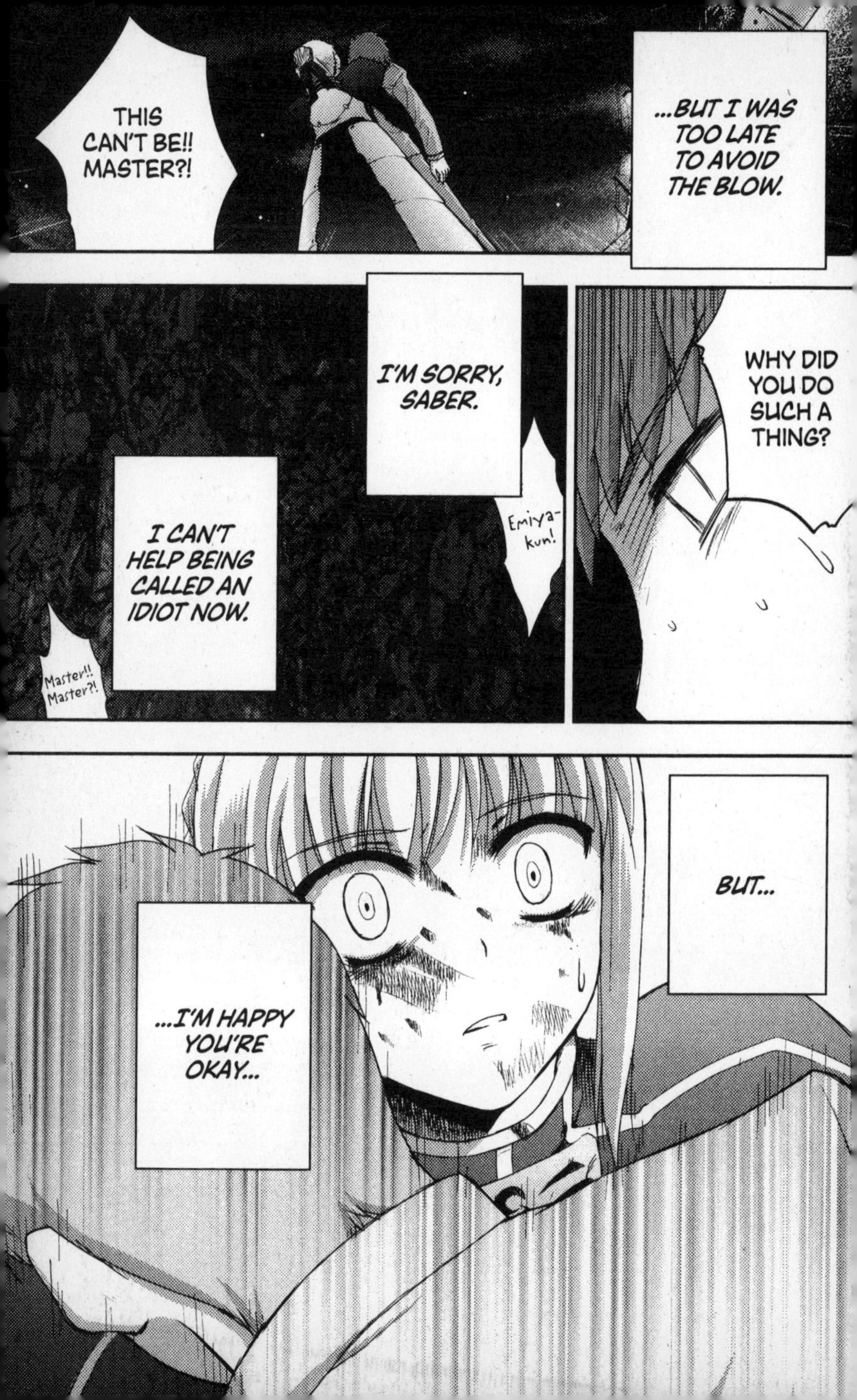
...BUT I WAS TOO LATE TO AVOID THE BLOW.
THIS CAN'T BE!! MASTER?!
WHY DID YOU DO SUCH A THING?
I'M SORRY, SABER.
Emiya-kun!
I CAN'T HELP BEING CALLED AN IDIOT NOW.
Master!! Master?!
BUT...
...I'M HAPPY YOU'RE OKAY...

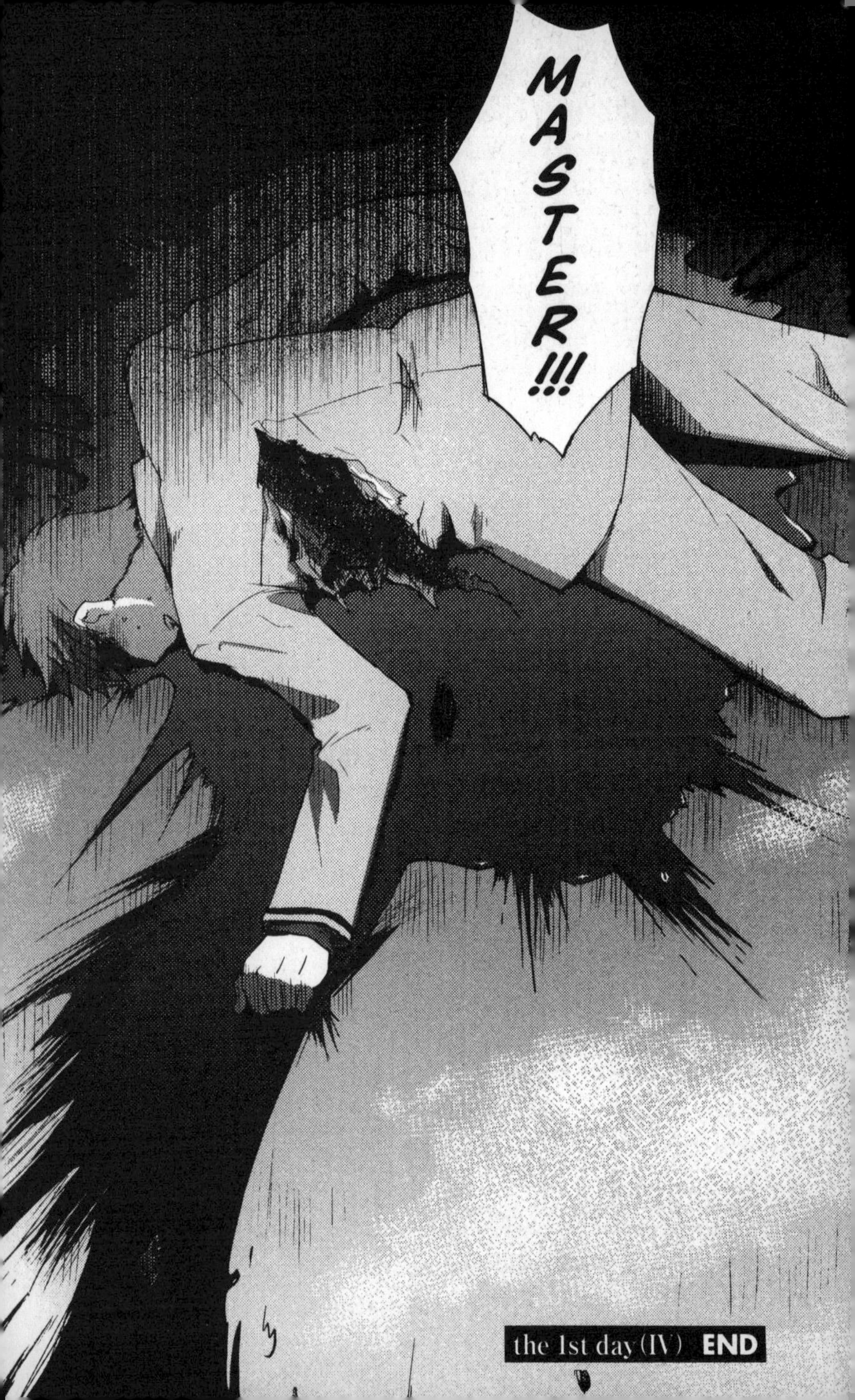
MASTER!!!
the 1st day (IV) END

fate/stay night

To Be Continued...

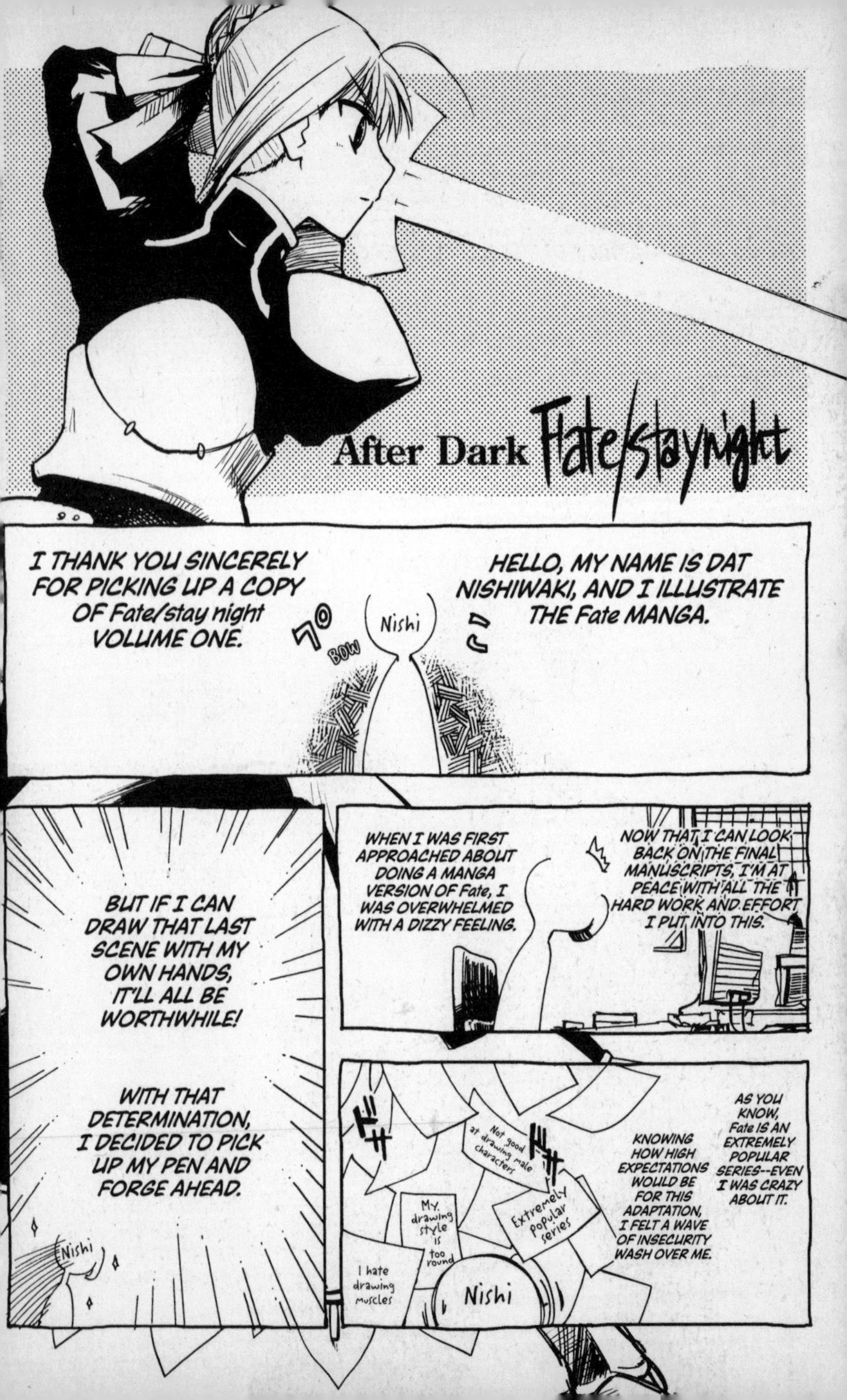
After Dark Fate/stay night
HELLO, MY NAME IS DAT NISHIWAKI, AND I ILLUSTRATE THE Fate MANGA.
Nishi
70° BOW
I THANK YOU SINCERELY FOR PICKING UP A COPY OF Fate/stay night VOLUME ONE.
NOW THAT I CAN LOOK BACK ON THE FINAL MANUSCRIPTS, I'M AT PEACE WITH ALL THE HARD WORK AND EFFORT I PUT INTO THIS.
WHEN I WAS FIRST APPROACHED ABOUT DOING A MANGA VERSION OF Fate, I WAS OVERWHELMED WITH A DIZZY FEELING.
AS YOU KNOW, Fate IS AN EXTREMELY POPULAR SERIES--EVEN I WAS CRAZY ABOUT IT.
KNOWING HOW HIGH EXPECTATIONS WOULD BE FOR THIS ADAPTATION, I FELT A WAVE OF INSECURITY WASH OVER ME.
Not good at drawing male characters
Extremely popular series
My drawing style is too round
I hate drawing muscles
Nishi
BUT IF I CAN DRAW THAT LAST SCENE WITH MY OWN HANDS, IT'LL ALL BE WORTHWHILE!
WITH THAT DETERMINATION, I DECIDED TO PICK UP MY PEN AND FORGE AHEAD.
Nishi

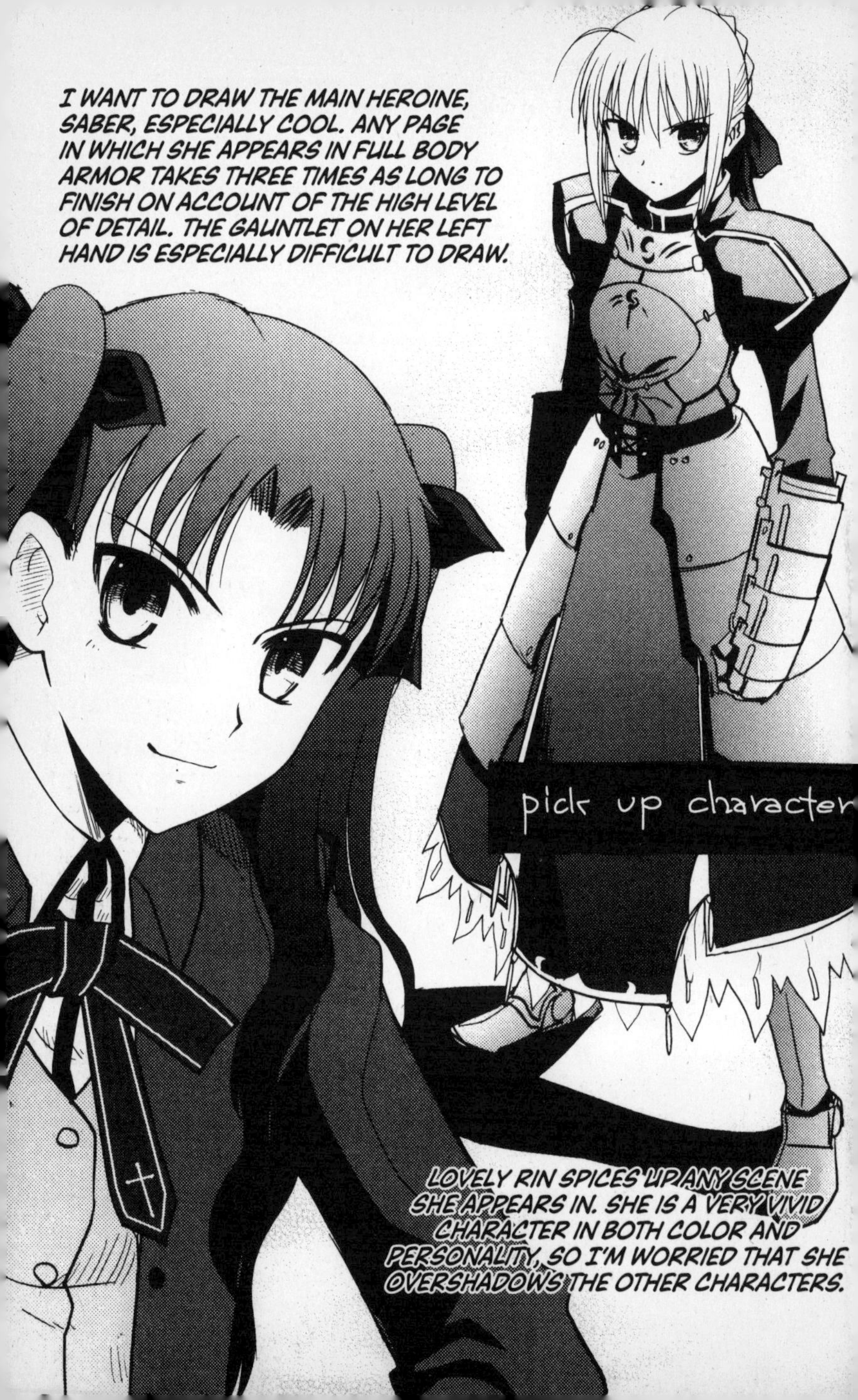
I WANT TO DRAW THE MAIN HEROINE, SABER, ESPECIALLY COOL. ANY PAGE IN WHICH SHE APPEARS IN FULL BODY ARMOR TAKES THREE TIMES AS LONG TO FINISH ON ACCOUNT OF THE HIGH LEVEL OF DETAIL. THE GAUNTLET ON HER LEFT HAND IS ESPECIALLY DIFFICULT TO DRAW.
pick up character
LOVELY RIN SPICES UP ANY SCENE SHE APPEARS IN. SHE IS A VERY VIVID CHARACTER IN BOTH COLOR AND PERSONALITY, SO I'M WORRIED THAT SHE OVERSHADOWS THE OTHER CHARACTERS.

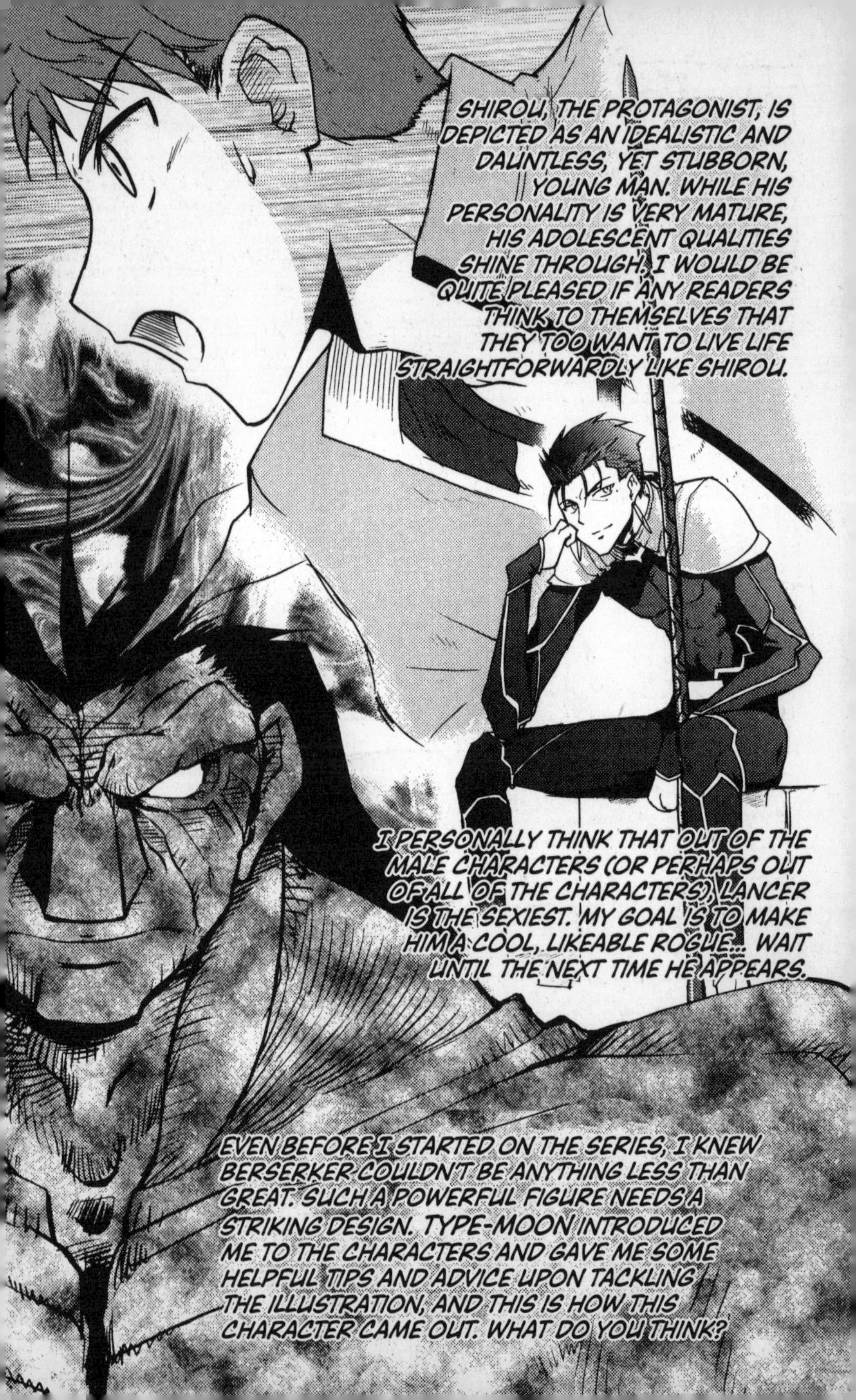
SHIROU, THE PROTAGONIST, IS DEPICTED AS AN IDEALISTIC AND DAUNTLESS, YET STUBBORN, YOUNG MAN. WHILE HIS PERSONALITY IS VERY MATURE, HIS ADOLESCENT QUALITIES SHINE THROUGH. I WOULD BE QUITE PLEASED IF ANY READERS THINK TO THEMSELVES THAT THEY TOO WANT TO LIVE LIFE STRAIGHTFORWARDLY LIKE SHIROU.
I PERSONALLY THINK THAT OUT OF THE MALE CHARACTERS (OR PERHAPS OUT OF ALL OF THE CHARACTERS), LANCER IS THE SEXIEST. MY GOAL IS TO MAKE HIM A COOL, LIKEABLE ROGUE... WAIT UNTIL THE NEXT TIME HE APPEARS.
EVEN BEFORE I STARTED ON THE SERIES, I KNEW BERSERKER COULDN'T BE ANYTHING LESS THAN GREAT. SUCH A POWERFUL FIGURE NEEDS A STRIKING DESIGN. TYPE-MOON INTRODUCED ME TO THE CHARACTERS AND GAVE ME SOME HELPFUL TIPS AND ADVICE UPON TACKLING THE ILLUSTRATION, AND THIS IS HOW THIS CHARACTER CAME OUT. WHAT DO YOU THINK?

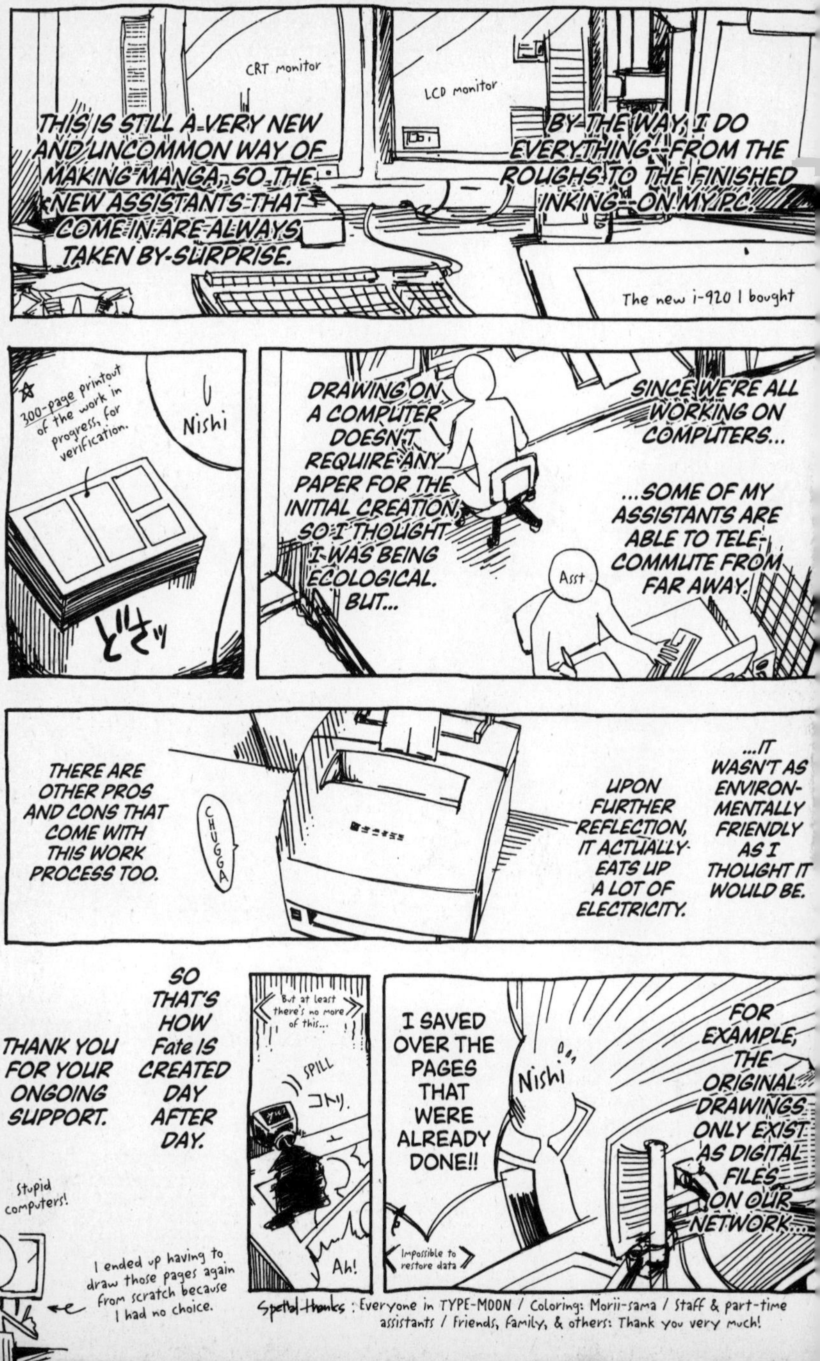
BY THE WAY, I DO EVERYTHING--FROM THE ROUGHS TO THE FINISHED INKING--ON MY PC.
The new i-920 I bought
LCD monitor
CRT monitor
THIS IS STILL A VERY NEW AND UNCOMMON WAY OF MAKING MANGA, SO THE NEW ASSISTANTS THAT COME IN ARE ALWAYS TAKEN BY SURPRISE.
SINCE WE'RE ALL WORKING ON COMPUTERS...
...SOME OF MY ASSISTANTS ARE ABLE TO TELE-COMMUTE FROM FAR AWAY.
Asst
DRAWING ON A COMPUTER DOESN'T REQUIRE ANY PAPER FOR THE INITIAL CREATION, SO I THOUGHT I WAS BEING ECOLOGICAL. BUT...
Nishi
☆ 300-page printout of the work in progress, for verification.
どさッ
...IT WASN'T AS ENVIRONMENTALLY FRIENDLY AS I THOUGHT IT WOULD BE.
UPON FURTHER REFLECTION, IT ACTUALLY EATS UP A LOT OF ELECTRICITY.
CHUGGA
THERE ARE OTHER PROS AND CONS THAT COME WITH THIS WORK PROCESS TOO.
FOR EXAMPLE, THE ORIGINAL DRAWINGS ONLY EXIST AS DIGITAL FILES ON OUR NETWORK...
Nishi
I SAVED OVER THE PAGES THAT WERE ALREADY DONE!!
Impossible to restore data
But at least there's no more of this...
SPILL
コトリ.
Ah!
SO THAT'S HOW Fate IS CREATED DAY AFTER DAY.
THANK YOU FOR YOUR ONGOING SUPPORT.
Stupid computers!
I ended up having to draw those pages again from scratch because I had no choice.

Special thanks: Everyone in TYPE-MOON / Coloring: Morii-sama / Staff & part-time assistants / Friends, family, & others: Thank you very much!

Next Time In...

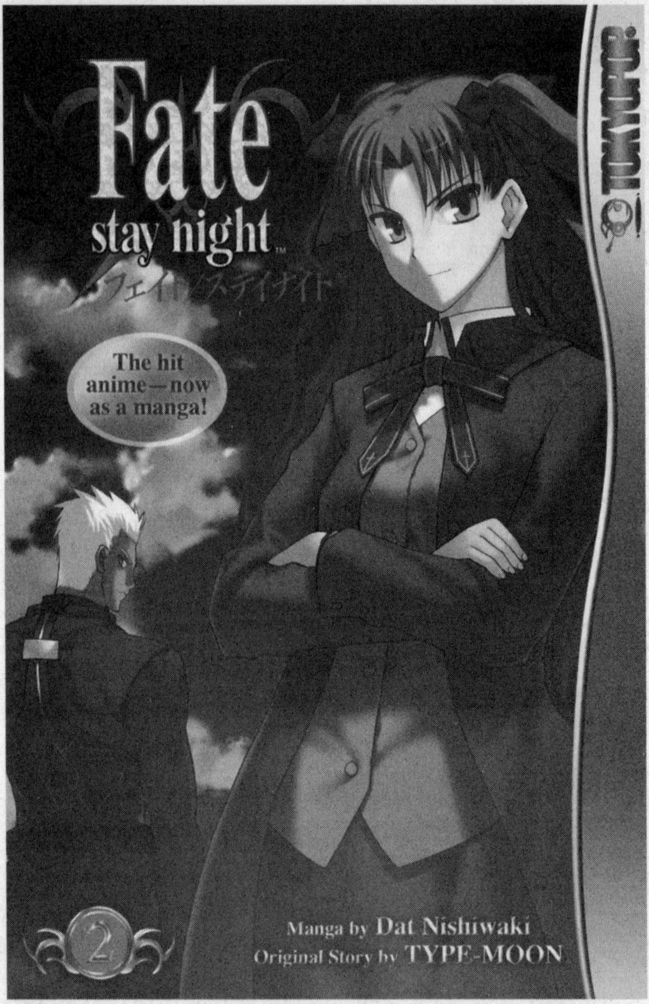
Fate
stay night™
The hit anime—now as a manga!
2
Manga by Dat Nishiwaki
Original Story by TYPE-MOON
TOKYOPOP

Emiya may have been dealt a deathblow from the Berserker, but it's not "game over" just yet! But as his participation in the Holy Grail War has been announced, Emiya must hurry and learn more about what he got himself into if he's to have any chance of fighting against the other Masters and their legendary Servants. Which Master-Servant team will strike next? Find out in volume 2 of *Fate/stay night!*

STOP!

This is the back of the book.
You wouldn't want to spoil a great ending!

This book is printed "manga-style," in the authentic Japanese right-to-left format. Since none of the artwork has been flipped or altered, readers get to experience the story just as the creator intended. You've been asking for it, so TOKYOPOP® delivered: authentic, hot-off-the-press, and far more fun!

DIRECTIONS

If this is your first time reading manga-style, here's a quick guide to help you understand how it works.

It's easy... just start in the top right panel and follow the numbers. Have fun, and look for more 100% authentic manga from TOKYOPOP®!